Econometric Analysis of Panel Data

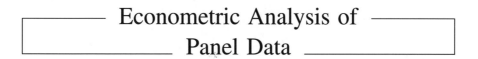

Econometric Analysis of Panel Data

Second edition

Badi H. Baltagi

JOHN WILEY & SONS, LTD
Chichester • New York • Weinheim • Brisbane • Singapore • Toronto

Baffins Lane, Chichester,
West Sussex PO19 1UD, England

National 01243 779777
International (+44) 1243 779777

e-mail (for orders and customer service enquiries): cs-books@wiley.co.uk

Visit our Home Page on http://www.wiley.co.uk

Other Wiley Editorial Offices

John Wiley & Sons, Inc., 605 Third Avenue,
New York, NY 10158-0012, USA

Wiley-VCH Verlag GmbH, Pappelallee 3,
D-69469 Weinheim, Germany

John Wiley & Sons Australia Ltd, 33 Park Road, Milton,
Queensland 4064, Australia

John Wiley & Sons (Asia) Pte Ltd, 2 Clementi Loop #02-01,
Jin Xing Distripark, Singapore 129809

John Wiley & Sons (Canada) Ltd, 22 Worcester Road,
Rexdale, Ontario M9W 1L1, Canada

Library of Congress Cataloging-in-Publication Data

Baltagi, Badi H. (Badi Hani)
Econometric analysis of panel data/Badi H. Baltagi.—2nd ed.
p. cm.
Includes bibliographical references and index.
ISBN 0-471-49937-4
1. Econometrics. 2. Panel analysis. I. Title.

HB139.B35 2001
330′.01′5195—dc21 2001033419

British Library Cataloguing in Publication Data

A catalogue record for this book is available from the British Library

ISBN 0-471-49937-4

Typeset in 10/12pt Times by Laser Words, Chennai, India
Printed and bound in Great Britain by Biddles Ltd, Guildford and King's Lynn
This book is printed on acid-free paper responsibly manufactured from sustainable forestry, in which at least two trees are planted for each one used for paper production.

Contents

Preface

This book is intended for a graduate econometrics course on panel data. The prerequisites include a good background in mathematical statistics and econometrics at the level of Kmenta (1986) and Greene (2000). Matrix presentations are necessary for this topic.

Some of the major features of this book are that it provides an *up-to-date* coverage of panel data techniques, especially for serial correlation, heteroskedasticity, seemingly unrelated regressions, simultaneous equations, dynamic models, incomplete panels, limited dependent variables and nonstationary panels. I have tried to keep things *simple*, illustrating the basic ideas using the *same notation* for a diverse literature with heterogeneous notation. Many of the estimation and testing techniques are illustrated with *data sets* which are available for classroom use on the Wiley web site. The book also cites and summarizes several empirical studies using panel data techniques, so that the reader can relate the econometric methods with the economic applications. The book proceeds from single equation methods to simultaneous equation methods as in any standard econometrics text, so it should prove friendly to graduate students.

The book gives the basic coverage without being encyclopedic. There is an extensive amount of research in this area and not all topics are covered. The *Journal of Economic Literature* (JEL) has 2780 citations using the words "panel data" between 1980 and 2000. The first conference on panel data was held in Paris more than 20 years ago and this resulted in two volumes of the *Annales de l'INSEE* edited by Mazodier (1978). Since then, there have been nine international conferences on panel data, the last one at the University of Geneva, June 2000.

In undertaking this revision, I benefited from teaching short panel data courses at the University of Arizona; Dörtmund University; Université Pathéon-Assas Paris II; Institute for Economic Research – Halle (IWH), Germany; Centro Interuniversitario di Econometria (CIDE) – Bertinoro, Italy; Institute for Advanced Studies, Vienna; and European Central Bank, Frankfurt. The second edition uses more recent empirical examples from the panel data literature to motivate the book. Data sets as well as the programs to implement the estimation and testing procedures described in the book are provided on the Wiley web site. Additional exercises are added to each chapter and solutions to selected exercises are also provided on the Wiley web site. More specifically, Chapter 1 now includes web site addresses for panel data sources. Chapters 2 and 3 have more recent empirical studies and worked examples. Chapters 4 to 9 have been updated and in some cases shortened. All proofs given in Appendices in the first edition have been deleted. For example, Chapter 8 surveys new developments in GMM estimation of dynamic panel data models. Chapter 9 now includes a new section on the unbalanced nested error component model. Chapter 10 now has a brief introduction of spatial panels. Chapter 11 deals with limited dependent variable panel data models, while Chapter 12 is a completely new chapter based on the recent explosion of research on nonstationary panels.

I would like to thank my co-authors for allowing me to draw freely on our joint work. In particular, I would like to thank Jim Griffin for keeping me immersed in applied economic work and Qi Li for the enormous energy he brought to our collaboration. Many colleagues who had direct and indirect influence on the contents of this book include Luc Anselin, George Battese, Alok Bhargava, Richard Blundell, Trevor Breusch, Young-Jae Chang, Bill Griffiths, Cheng Hsiao, Chihwa Kao, Max King, Walter Krämer, Kajal Lahiri, Dan Levin, Dong Li, G.S. Maddala, Roberto Mariano, László Mátyás, Peter Phillips, Peter Schmidt, Patrick Sevestre, Robin Sickles, Seuck Heun Song, Marno Verbeek, Tom Wansbeek and Arnold Zellner. Thanks also go to Steve Hardman, Sarah Booth and Catherine Braund at Wiley for their efficient and professional editorial help, Sarah Lewis for copyediting and proofreading, Teri Bush who typed numerous revisions of this book and my wife Phyllis whose encouragement and support gave me the required energy to complete this book. Responsibilities for errors and omissions are my own.

1 Introduction

1.1 PANEL DATA: SOME EXAMPLES

In this book, the term "panel data" refers to the pooling of observations on a cross-section of households, countries, firms, etc. over several time periods. This can be achieved by surveying a number of households or individuals and following them over time. Two well-known examples of US panel data are the Panel Study of Income Dynamics (PSID) collected by the Institute for Social Research at the University of Michigan (www.isr.umich.edu/src/psid/index.html), and the National Longitudinal Surveys of Labor Market Experience (NLS) from the Center for Human Resource Research at Ohio State University and the Census Bureau (www.bls.gov/nlshome.htm). These panels were designed to study the nature and causes of poverty in the United States. In addition, these panels were supposed to monitor and explain changes in economic well-being and to study the effects of economic and social programs. Therefore, data collection concentrated on employment, earnings and incomes, travel to work and mobility, and on housing and food consumption.

The PSID began in 1968 with 4802 families, including an oversampling of poor households. Annual interviews were conducted and socioeconomic characteristics of each of the families and of the roughly 31 000 individuals who have been in these or derivative families were recorded (see Becketti et al., 1988). The list of variables collected is over 5000. These include income, poverty status, public assistance in the form of food or housing, other financial matters (e.g. taxes, inter-household transfers), family structure and demographic measures, labor market work, housework time, housing, geographic mobility, socioeconomic background and health. Other supplemental topics include housing and neighborhood characteristics, achievement motivation, estimating risk tolerance, child care, child support and child development, job training and job acquisition, retirement plans, health, kinship, wealth, education, military combat experience, risk tolerance, immigration history and time use.

The NLS, on the other hand, follows five distinct segments of the labor force:

(1) Older men: civilian men who were between the ages of 45 and 49 in 1966.
(2) Young men: civilian men who were between the ages of 14 and 24 in 1966.
(3) Mature women: civilian women who were between the ages of 30 and 44 in 1967.
(4) Young women: civilian women who were between the ages of 14 and 21 in 1968. All four surveys included an oversampling of blacks.
(5) Youths: men and women aged 14–24 in 1979 with oversampling of blacks, hispanics, poor whites and military. This sample is called NLSY 79. In 1986, NLSY 79 was expanded to include children born to women in that cohort. This is called NLSY 79 children. In 1997, the NLS also included a cohort of young people aged 12–16 as of the end of 1996. This new cohort is known as NLSY 97.

The original NLS samples include 5020 older men, 5225 young men, 5083 mature women, 5159 young women and 12 686 youths, respectively. The list of variables collected runs into the thousands with emphasis on the supply side of the labor market. These include information on schooling and career transitions, marriage and fertility, training investments, child care usage and drug and alcohol use. A large number of studies have used the NLS and PSID data sets. Labor journals in particular have numerous applications of these panels. Klevmarken (1989) cites a bibliography of 600 published articles and monographs that used the PSID data set. These cover a wide range of topics including labor supply, earnings, family economic status, effects of transfer income programs, family composition changes, residential mobility, food consumption and housing. Another panel of importance to labor economists is the Longitudinal Retirement History Study which surveyed 11 153 men and nonmarried women aged 58–63 in 1969. Demographics, employment histories, debt, assets, income, attitudes towards work and retirement, health and living expenses were among the variables collected. Borus (1982) and Ashenfelter and Solon (1982) are early references on panel data sets of interest to economists. These include the Social Security Administration's Continuous Work History Sample, the Labor Department's Continuous Wage and Benefit History and its Continuous Longitudinal Manpower Survey, project TALENT, the NLS of the high school class of 1972, the Annual Housing Survey, the Continuous Disability-History Sample and several negative income tax experiments conducted in New Jersey and Pennsylvania, Seattle and Denver, Iowa and North Carolina and Gary, Indiana. Panels can also be constructed from the Current Population Survey (CPS), the monthly national household survey by the Census Bureau that generates the unemployment rate and other labor force statistics. Compared with the NLS and PSID data, the CPS contains fewer variables, spans a shorter period and does not follow movers. However, it covers a much larger sample and is representative of all demographic groups.

The Institute for Social Research at the University of Michigan also collects the Health and Retirement Study (HRS) (www.umich.edu/~hrswww/). This consists of two separate studies. The original HRS cohort born 1931–41 and first interviewed in 1992 (at 51–61 years of age), and the AHEAD cohort born before 1923 and first interviewed in 1993 (ages 70 and above). Spouses were included regardless of age. The studies were merged in the 1998 wave and combined with new respondents born 1924–30 and 1942–47, to become a complete panel for people over the age of 50, with over 21 000 participants. The variables collected include income, employment, wealth, health conditions, health status, health insurance coverage, intergenerational transfers, family structure and a set of expectations expressed as probability scales.

Although the US panels started in the 1960s, it was only in the 1980s that the European panels began setting up. In 1989, a special section of the *European Economic Review* published papers using the German Social Economic Panel (see Hujer and Schneider, 1989), the Swedish study of household market and nonmarket activities (see Björklund, 1989), and the Intomart Dutch panel of households (see Alessie, Kapteyn and Melenberg, 1989). The first wave of the German Socio-Economic Panel (GSOEP) was collected by the DIW (German Institute for Economic Research, Berlin) in 1984 and included 5921 West German households (www.diw.de/soep). This included a disproportionate number of foreign heads of households (1393) in order to allow separate analyses of Germany's five largest groups of foreign nationals. All persons above the age of 16 in the household were surveyed. This included 12 245 respondents. Standard demographic variables as well as wages, income, benefit payments, level of satisfaction with various aspects of life, hopes and fears, political involvement, etc. are collected. In 1990, 4453 adult respondents in 2179 households from East Germany were included in the GSOEP due to German unification. The attrition rate has been relatively low in GSOEP. Wagner, Burkhauser and Behringer (1993) report that through eight waves of the GSOEP, 54.9% of the original panel respondents have records without missing years. An inventory of national studies using panel data is given at http://www.isr.umich.edu/src/psid/panelstudies.html. These include the Belgian Socioeconomic Panel (www.ufsia.ac.be/~csb/eng/septab.htm) which includes a representative sample of 6471 Belgian households in 1985, 3800 in 1988 and 3800 in 1992 (including a new sample of 900 households). The Canadian Survey of Labor Income Dynamics (SLID) collected in 1993 by Statistics Canada (www.statcan.ca) which includes a sample of approximately 15 000 households or 31 000 individuals. The French Household Panel (1985–90) which included 715 households at the baseline and increased to 2092 in the second wave (www.ceps.lu/paco/pacofrpa.htm). The Hungarian Household Panel (1992–96) with a reference population of 2059 households collected by the Social Research Informatics Center (TARKI) (www.tarki.hu). The British Household Panel Survey (BHPS) which is an annual survey of private households in Britain first collected in 1991 by the Institute for Social and Economic Research at the University of Essex (www.irc.essex.ac.uk/bhps). This is a national representative sample of 5000 households containing demographic and household characteristics, household organization, labor market, health, education, housing, consumption, income, social and political values. The Japanese Panel Survey on Consumers (JPSC) collected in 1994 by the Institute for Household Economy (www.kakeiken.or.jp). This is a national representative sample of 1500 women aged 24 and 34 years in 1993. In 1997, 500 women were added with ages between 24 and 27. Information gathered includes family composition, labor market behavior, income, consumption, savings, assets, liabilities, housing, consumer durables, household management, time use and satisfaction. The Dutch Socio-Economic Panel (ISEP) collected over the period 1984–97 by Statistics Netherlands. The Russian Longitudinal Monitoring Survey (RLMS) collected in 1992 by the Carolina Population Center at the University of North Carolina (www.cpc.unc.edu/projects/rlms/home.html). The RLMS is a household-based survey designed to measure the effects of Russian reforms on economic well-being. The Swiss Household Panel (SHP) whose first wave in 1999 interviewed 5074 households comprising 7799 individuals (www.unine.ch/psm). The Luxembourg Panel Socio-Economique "Liewen zu Lëtzebuerg" (PSELL) (1985–94) is based on a representative sample of 2012 households and 6110 individuals. In 1994, the PSELL expanded to 2978 households and 8232 individuals.

The European Community Household Panel (ECHP) is centrally designed and coordinated by the Statistical Office of the European Communities (EuroStat), see Peracchi (2001). The first wave was conducted in 1994 and included all current members of the EU except Austria, Finland and Sweden. The project was launched to obtain comparable information across member countries on income, work and employment, poverty and social exclusion, housing, health, and many other diverse social indicators indicating living conditions of private households and persons. The EHCP was linked from the beginning to existing national panels (e.g. Belgium and Holland) or ran parallel to existing panels with similar content, namely GSOEP, PSELL and the BHPS. In 1997, the ECHP was merged into the GSOEP, PSELL and BHPS. The last three panels, as well as a number of waves of the PSID, are included in the panel comparability (PACO) database, see www.ceps.lu/paco/pacochar.htm.

Virtually every graduate text in econometrics contains a chapter or a major section on the econometrics of panel data. Classic readings on this subject include Hsiao's (1986) Econometric Society monograph along with Chamberlain's (1984) chapter in the *Handbook of Econometrics*. Maddala (1993) edited two volumes collecting some of the classic articles on the subject. Other books on the subject include Dielman (1989), Dormont (1989), Hartog, Ridder and Theeuwes (1990), a handbook on the econometrics of panel data which in its second edition contained 33 chapters edited by Mátyás and Sevestre (1996). A book in honor of G.S. Maddala edited by Hsiao et al. (1999). A book in honor of Pietro Balestra edited by Krishnakumar and Ronchetti (2000). Survey papers include Maddala (1987a, b), Baltagi and Raj (1992), Hsiao (2001), Banerjee (1999) and Baltagi and Kao (2000) and the recent *Handbook of Econometrics* chapter by Arellano and Honoré (2000). Special issues of journals on panel data include two volumes of the *Annales de l'INSEE* edited by Mazodier (1978), a special issue of *Empirical Economics* edited by Raj and Baltagi (1992), a special issue of *Structural Change and Economic Dynamics* edited by Mátyás (1992), two special issues of the *Journal of Econometrics*, the first edited by Carraro, Peracchi and Weber (1993) and the second edited by Baltagi (1995a), two volumes of the *Annales D'Economie et de Statistique* edited by Sevestre (1999), a special issue of the *Oxford Bulletin of Economics and Statistics* edited by Banerjee (1999), two special issues (Volume 19, Numbers 3 and 4) of *Econometric Reviews* edited by Maasoumi and Heshmati (2000), and a special issue of *Advances in Econometrics* edited by Baltagi, Fomby and Hill (2000).

The objective of this book is to provide a simple introduction to some of the basic issues of panel data analysis. It is intended for economists and social scientists with the usual background in statistics and econometrics. While restricting the focus of the book to basic topics may not do justice to this rapidly growing literature, it is nevertheless unavoidable in view of the space limitations of the book. Topics not covered in this book include duration models and hazard functions (see Kiefer, 1988; Heckman and Singer, 1985; Lancaster, 1991), semiparametric and nonparametric methods using panel data (see Manski, 1987; Lee, 1987; Li and Stengos, 1994, 1995, 1996; Ullah and Roy, 1998) and experimental design issues (see DeStavola, 1986; Aigner and Balestra, 1988; Nijman and Verbeek, 1990, 1992b; Nijman, Verbeek and van Soest, 1991). Also, the frontier production function literature using panel data (see Pitt and Lee, 1981; Schmidt and Sickles, 1984; Battese and Coelli, 1988; Cornwell, Schmidt and Sickles, 1990; Kumbhakar, 1991, 1992; Koop and Steel, 2001), and the literature on time-varying parameters, random coefficients and Bayesian models which is contained in the extensive work of Swamy (1971), Swamy and Tavlas (2001), Dielman (1989) and Hsiao, Appelbe and Dineen (1993).

1.2 WHY SHOULD WE USE PANEL DATA? THEIR BENEFITS AND LIMITATIONS

Hsiao (1985, 1986), Klevmarken (1989) and Solon (1989) list several benefits from using panel data. These include the following:

(1) Controlling for *individual heterogeneity*. Panel data suggest that individuals, firms, states or countries are heterogeneous. Time-series and cross-section studies not controlling for this heterogeneity run the risk of obtaining biased results, e.g. see Moulton (1986, 1987). Let us demonstrate this with an empirical example. Baltagi and Levin (1992) consider cigarette demand across 46 American states for the years 1963–88. Consumption is modeled as a function of lagged consumption, price and income. These variables vary with states and time. However, there are a lot of other variables that may be state-invariant or time-invariant that may affect consumption. Let us call these Z_i and W_t, respectively. Examples of Z_i are religion and education. For the religion variable, one may not be able to get the percentage of the population that is, say, Mormon in each state for every year, nor does one expect that to change much across time. The same holds true for the percentage of the population completing high school or a college degree. Examples of W_t include advertising on TV and radio. This advertising is nationwide and does not vary across states. In addition, some of these variables

are difficult to measure or hard to obtain so that not all the Z_i or W_t variables are available for inclusion in the consumption equation. Omission of these variables leads to bias in the resulting estimates. Panel data are able to control for these state- and time-invariant variables whereas a time-series study or a cross-section study cannot. In fact, from the data one observes that Utah has less than half the average per capita consumption of cigarettes in the USA. This is because it is mostly a Mormon state, a religion that prohibits smoking. Controlling for Utah in a cross-section regression may be done with a dummy variable which has the effect of removing that state's observation from the regression. This would not be the case for panel data as we will shortly discover. In fact, with panel data, one might first difference the data to get rid of all Z_i type variables and hence effectively control for all state-specific characteristics. This holds whether the Z_i are observable or not. Alternatively, the dummy variable for Utah controls for every state-specific effect that is distinctive of Utah without omitting the observations for Utah.

Another example is given by Hajivassiliou (1987) who studies the external debt repayments problem using a panel of 79 developing countries observed over the period 1970–82. These countries differ in terms of their colonial history, financial institutions, religious affiliations and political regimes. All of these country-specific variables affect the attitudes that these countries have with regards to borrowing and defaulting and the way they are treated by the lenders. Not accounting for this country heterogeneity causes serious misspecification.

(2) Panel data give *more informative data, more variability, less collinearity among the variables, more degrees of freedom and more efficiency*. Time-series studies are plagued with multicollinearity; for example, in the case of demand for cigarettes above, there is high collinearity between price and income in the aggregate time series for the USA. This is less likely with a panel across American states since the cross-section dimension adds a lot of variability, adding more informative data on price and income. In fact, the variation in the data can be decomposed into variation between states of different sizes and characteristics, and variation within states. The former variation is usually bigger. With additional, more informative data one can produce more reliable parameter estimates. Of course, the same relationship has to hold for each state, i.e. the data have to be poolable. This is a testable assumption and one that we will tackle in due course.

(3) Panel data are better able to study the *dynamics of adjustment*. Cross-sectional distributions that look relatively stable hide a multitude of changes. Spells of unemployment, job turnover, residential and income mobility are better studied with panels. Panel data are also well suited to study the duration of economic states like unemployment and poverty, and if these panels are long enough, they can shed light on the speed of adjustments to economic policy changes. For example, in measuring unemployment, cross-sectional data can estimate what proportion of the population is unemployed at a point in time. Repeated cross-sections can show how this proportion changes over time. Only panel data can estimate what proportion of those who are unemployed in one period remain

unemployed in another period. Ashenfelter and Solon (1982) emphasize that important policy questions like determining whether families' experiences of poverty, unemployment and welfare dependence are transitory or chronic necessitate the use of panels. Panels are also necessary for the estimation of intertemporal relations, life-cycle and intergenerational models. In fact, panels can relate the individual's experiences and behavior at one point in time to other experiences and behavior at another point in time. For example, Ashenfelter (1978) studied the effects of federal training programs on future earnings of program participants. This was done using a comparison group of nonparticipants. Ashenfelter (1978) analyzed the earnings records of both groups before and after the training program and concluded that training did increase participants' earnings.

(4) Panel data are better able to *identify and measure effects that are simply not detectable in pure cross-section or pure time-series data*. Ben-Porath (1973) gives an example. Suppose that we have a cross-section of women with a 50% average yearly labor force participation rate. This might be due to (a) each woman having a 50% chance of being in the labor force, in any given year, or (b) 50% of the women working all the time and 50% not at all. Case (a) has high turnover, while case (b) has no turnover. Only panel data could discriminate between these cases. Another example is the determination of whether union membership increases or decreases wages. This can be better answered as we observe a worker moving from union to nonunion jobs or vice versa. Holding the individual's characteristics constant, we will be better equipped to determine whether union membership affects wage and by how much (see Freeman, 1984). This analysis extends to the estimation of other types of wage differentials holding individuals' characteristics constant; see Duncan and Holmlund (1983) for the estimation of wage premiums paid in dangerous or unpleasant jobs using panel data.

(5) Panel data models allow us to *construct and test more complicated behavioral models than purely cross-section or time-series data*. For example, technical efficiency is better studied and modeled with panels (see Baltagi and Griffin, 1988b; Cornwell, Schmidt and Sickles, 1990; Kumbhakar, 1991, 1992; Baltagi, Griffin and Rich, 1995; Koop and Steel, 2001). Also, fewer restrictions can be imposed in panels on a distributed lag model than in a purely time-series study (see Hsiao, 1986).

(6) Panel data are usually gathered on micro units, like individuals, firms and households. Many variables can be more accurately measured at the micro level, and *biases resulting from aggregation over firms or individuals are eliminated* (see Blundell, 1988; Klevmarken, 1989). For more specific advantages and disadvantages of estimating life-cycle models using micro panel data, see Blundell and Meghir (1990).

Limitations of panel data include:

(1) *Design and data collection problems*. For an extensive discussion of problems that arise in designing panel surveys as well as data collection and data management issues see Kasprzyk et al. (1989). These include problems of coverage (incomplete account of the population of interest), nonresponse (due to lack of cooperation of the respondent or because of interviewer error), recall (respondent

not remembering correctly), frequency of interviewing, interview spacing, reference period, the use of bounding and time-in-sample bias (see Bailar, 1989).[1]

(2) *Distortions of measurement errors*. Measurement errors may arise because of faulty responses due to unclear questions, memory errors, deliberate distortion of responses (e.g. prestige bias), inappropriate informants, misrecording of responses and interviewer effects (see Kalton, Kasprzyk and McMillen, 1989). Herriot and Spiers (1975), for example, match CPS and Internal Revenue Service data on earnings of the same individuals and show that there are discrepancies of at least 15% between the two sources of earnings for almost 30% of the matched sample. The validation study by Duncan and Hill (1985) on the PSID also illustrates the significance of the measurement error problem. They compare the responses of the employees of a large firm with the records of the employer. Duncan and Hill (1985) find small response biases except for work hours which are overestimated. The ratio of measurement error variance to the true variance is found to be 15% for annual earnings, 37% for annual work hours and 184% for average hourly earnings. These figures are for a one-year recall, i.e. 1983 for 1982, and are more than doubled with two years' recall. Brown and Light (1992) investigate the inconsistency in job tenure responses in the PSID and NLS. Cross-section data users have little choice but to believe the reported values of tenure (unless they have external information) while users of panel data can check for inconsistencies of tenure responses with elapsed time between interviews. For example, a respondent may claim to have three years of tenure in one interview and a year later claim six years. This should alert the user of this panel to the presence of measurement error. Brown and Light (1992) show that failure to use internally consistent tenure sequences can lead to misleading conclusions about the slope of wage–tenure profiles.

(3) *Selectivity problems*. These include:

(a) *Self-selectivity*. People choose not to work because the reservation wage is higher than the offered wage. In this case we observe the characteristics of these individuals but not their wage. Since only their wage is missing, the sample is censored. However, if we do not observe all data on these people this would be a truncated sample. An example of truncation is the New Jersey negative income tax experiment. We are only interested in poverty, and people with income larger than 1.5 times the poverty level are dropped from the sample. Inference from this truncated sample introduces bias that is not helped by more data, because of the truncation (see Hausman and Wise, 1979).

(b) *Nonresponse*. This can occur at the initial wave of the panel due to refusal to participate, nobody at home, untraced sample unit, and other reasons. Item (or partial) nonresponse occurs when one or more questions are left unanswered or are found not to provide a useful response. Complete nonresponse occurs when no information is available from the sampled household. Besides the efficiency loss due to missing data, this nonresponse can cause serious identification problems for the population parameters. Horowitz and Manski (1998) show that the seriousness of the problem is directly proportional to the amount of nonresponse. Nonresponse rates in the first wave of the European panels vary across countries from 10% in Greece and Italy where participation is compulsory, to 52% in Germany and 60% in Luxembourg. The overall nonresponse rate is 28%, see Peracchi (2001). The comparable nonresponse rate for the first wave of the PSID is 24%, for the BHPS (26%), for the GSOEP (38%) and for PSELL (35%).

(c) *Attrition.* While nonresponse occurs also in cross-section studies, it is a more serious problem in panels because subsequent waves of the panel are still subject to nonresponse. Respondents may die, or move, or find that the cost of responding is high. See Björklund (1989) and Ridder (1990, 1992) on the consequences of attrition. The degree of attrition varies depending on the panel studied; see Kalton, Kasprzyk and McMillen (1989) for several examples. In general, the overall rates of attrition increase from one wave to the next, but the rate of increase declines over time. Becketti et al. (1988) study the representativeness of the PSID after 14 years since it started. The authors find that only 40% of those originally in the sample in 1968 remained in the sample in 1981. However, they do find that as far as the dynamics of entry and exit are concerned, the PSID is still representative. Attrition rates between the first and second wave vary from 6% in Italy to 24% in the UK. The average attrition rate is about 10%. The comparable rates of attrition from the first to the second wave are 12% in the BHPS, 12.4% for the West German sample and 8.9% for the East German sample in the GSOEP and 15% for PSELL, see Peracchi (2001). In order to counter the effects of attrition, rotating panels are sometimes used, where a fixed percentage of the respondents are replaced in every wave to replenish the sample. More on rotating and pseudo-panels in Chapter 10.

(4) *Short time-series dimension.* Typical panels involve annual data covering a short span of time for each individual. This means that asymptotic arguments rely crucially on the number of individuals tending to infinity. Increasing the time span of the panel is not without cost either. In fact, this increases the chances of attrition and increases the computational difficulty for limited dependent variable panel data models (see Chapter 11).

NOTE

1. Bounding is used to prevent the shifting of events from outside the recall period into the recall period. Time-in-sample bias is observed when a significantly different level for a characteristic occurs in the first interview than in later interviews, when one would expect the same level.

2 The One-way Error Component Regression Model

2.1 INTRODUCTION

A panel data regression differs from a regular time-series or cross-section regression in that it has a double subscript on its variables, i.e.

$$y_{it} = \alpha + X'_{it}\beta + u_{it} \quad i = 1, \ldots, N; \; t = 1, \ldots, T \tag{2.1}$$

with i denoting households, individuals, firms, countries, etc. and t denoting time. The i subscript, therefore, denotes the cross-section dimension whereas t denotes the time-series dimension. α is a scalar, β is $K \times 1$ and X_{it} is the itth observation on K explanatory variables. Most of the panel data applications utilize a one-way error component model for the disturbances, with

$$u_{it} = \mu_i + \nu_{it} \tag{2.2}$$

where μ_i denotes the *unobservable* individual specific effect and ν_{it} denotes the remainder disturbance. For example, in an earnings equation in labor economics, y_{it} will measure earnings of the head of the household, whereas X_{it} may contain a set of variables like experience, education, union membership, sex, race, etc. Note that μ_i is time-invariant and accounts for any individual-specific effect that is not included in the regression. In this case we could think of it as the individual's unobserved ability. The remainder disturbance ν_{it} varies with individuals and time and can be thought of as the usual disturbance in the regression. Alternatively, for a production function utilizing data on firms across time, y_{it} will measure output and X_{it} will measure inputs. The unobservable firm-specific effects will be captured by the μ_i and we can think of these as the unobservable entrepreneurial or managerial skills of the firm's executives. Early applications of error components in economics include Kuh (1959) on investment, Mundlak (1961) and Hoch (1962) on production functions and Balestra and Nerlove (1966) on demand for natural gas. In vector form (2.1) can be written as

$$y = \alpha\iota_{NT} + X\beta + u = Z\delta + u \tag{2.3}$$

where y is $NT \times 1$, X is $NT \times K$, $Z = [\iota_{NT}, X]$, $\delta' = (\alpha', \beta')$ and ι_{NT} is a vector of ones of dimension NT. Also, (2.2) can be written as

$$u = Z_\mu \mu + \nu \tag{2.4}$$

where $u' = (u_{11}, \ldots, u_{1T}, u_{21}, \ldots, u_{2T}, \ldots, u_{N1}, \ldots, u_{NT})$ with the observations stacked such that the slower index is over individuals and the faster index is over time. $Z_\mu = I_N \otimes \iota_T$ where I_N is an identity matrix of dimension N, ι_T is a vector of ones of dimension T and $\otimes$ denotes Kronecker product. Z_μ is a selector matrix of ones and zeros, or simply the matrix of individual dummies that one may include in the regression to estimate the μ_i if they are assumed to be fixed parameters. $\mu' = (\mu_1, \ldots, \mu_N)$ and $\nu' = (\nu_{11}, \ldots, \nu_{1T}, \ldots, \nu_{N1}, \ldots, \nu_{NT})$. Note that $Z_\mu Z_\mu' = I_N \otimes J_T$ where J_T is a matrix of ones of dimension T and $P = Z_\mu(Z_\mu' Z_\mu)^{-1} Z_\mu'$, the projection matrix on Z_μ, reduces to $I_N \otimes \bar{J}_T$ where $\bar{J}_T = J_T/T$. P is a matrix which averages the observation across time for each individual and $Q = I_{NT} - P$ is a matrix which obtains the deviations from individual means. For example, Pu has a typical element $\bar{u}_{i.} = \sum_{t=1}^T u_{it}/T$ repeated T times for each individual and Qu has a typical element $(u_{it} - \bar{u}_{i.})$. P and Q are (i) symmetric idempotent matrices, i.e. $P' = P$ and $P^2 = P$. This means that $\text{rank}(P) = \text{tr}(P) = N$ and $\text{rank}(Q) = \text{tr}(Q) = N(T-1)$. This uses the result that the rank of an idempotent matrix is equal to its trace (see Graybill, 1961, Theorem 1.63). Also (ii) P and Q are orthogonal, i.e. $PQ = 0$ and (iii) they sum to the identity matrix, $P + Q = I_{NT}$. In fact, any two of these properties imply the third (see Graybill, 1961, Theorem 1.68).

2.2 THE FIXED EFFECTS MODEL

In this case, the μ_i are assumed to be fixed parameters to be estimated and the remainder disturbances stochastic with ν_{it} independent and identically distributed $\text{IID}(0, \sigma_\nu^2)$. The X_{it} are assumed independent of the ν_{it} for all i and t. The fixed effects model is an appropriate specification if we are focusing on a specific set of N firms, say IBM, GE, Westinghouse, etc. and our inference is restricted to the behavior of these sets of firms. Alternatively, it could be a set of N OECD countries, or N American states. Inference in this case is conditional on the particular N firms, countries or states that are observed. One can substitute the disturbances given by (2.4) into (2.3) to get

$$y = \alpha\iota_{NT} + X\beta + Z_\mu\mu + \nu = Z\delta + Z_\mu\mu + \nu \tag{2.5}$$

and then perform ordinary least squares (OLS) on (2.5) to get estimates of α, β and μ. Note that Z is $NT \times (K+1)$ and Z_μ, the matrix of individual dummies, is $NT \times N$. If N is large, (2.5) will include too many individual dummies, and the matrix to be inverted by OLS is large and of dimension $(N+K)$. In fact, since α and β are the parameters of interest, one can obtain the LSDV (least squares dummy variables) estimator from (2.5) by premultiplying the model by

Q and performing OLS on the resulting transformed model:

$$Qy = QX\beta + Q\nu \tag{2.6}$$

This uses the fact that $QZ_\mu = Q\iota_{NT} = 0$, since $PZ_\mu = Z_\mu$. In other words, the Q matrix wipes out the individual effects. This is a regression of $\widetilde{y} = Qy$ with typical element $(y_{it} - \bar{y}_{i.})$ on $\widetilde{X} = QX$ with typical element $(X_{it,k} - \bar{X}_{i.,k})$ for the kth regressor, $k = 1, 2, \ldots, K$. This involves the inversion of a $(K \times K)$ matrix rather than $(N + K) \times (N + K)$ as in (2.5). The resulting OLS estimator is

$$\widetilde{\beta} = \left(X'QX\right)^{-1} X'Qy \tag{2.7}$$

with $\text{var}(\widetilde{\beta}) = \sigma_\nu^2(X'QX)^{-1} = \sigma_\nu^2(\widetilde{X}'\widetilde{X})^{-1}$. $\widetilde{\beta}$ could have been obtained from (2.5) using results on partitioned inverse or the Frisch–Waugh–Lovell theorem discussed in Davidson and MacKinnon (1993, p. 19). This uses the fact that P is the projection matrix on Z_μ and $Q = I_{NT} - P$ (see problem 2.1). In addition, generalized least squares (GLS) on (2.6), using the generalized inverse, will also yield $\widetilde{\beta}$ (see problem 2.2).

Note that for the simple regression

$$y_{it} = \alpha + \beta x_{it} + \mu_i + \nu_{it} \tag{2.8}$$

and averaging over time gives

$$\bar{y}_{i.} = \alpha + \beta \bar{x}_{i.} + \mu_i + \bar{\nu}_{i.} \tag{2.9}$$

Therefore, subtracting (2.9) from (2.8) gives

$$y_{it} - \bar{y}_{i.} = \beta(x_{it} - \bar{x}_{i.}) + (\nu_{it} - \bar{\nu}_{i.}) \tag{2.10}$$

Also, averaging across all observations in (2.8) gives

$$\bar{y}_{..} = \alpha + \beta \bar{x}_{..} + \bar{\nu}_{..} \tag{2.11}$$

where we utilized the restriction that $\sum_{i=1}^N \mu_i = 0$. This is an arbitrary restriction on the dummy variable coefficients to avoid the dummy variable trap, or perfect multicollinearity; see Suits (1984) for alternative formulations of this restriction. In fact only β and $(\alpha + \mu_i)$ are estimable from (2.8), and not α and μ_i separately, unless a restriction like $\sum_{i=1}^N \mu_i = 0$ is imposed. In this case, $\widetilde{\beta}$ is obtained from regression (2.10), $\widetilde{\alpha} = \bar{y}_{..} - \widetilde{\beta}\bar{x}_{..}$ can be recovered from (2.11) and $\widetilde{\mu}_i = \bar{y}_{i.} - \widetilde{\alpha} - \widetilde{\beta}\bar{x}_{i.}$ from (2.9). For large labor or consumer panels, where N is very large, regressions like (2.5) may not be feasible, since one is including $(N - 1)$ dummies in the regression. This fixed effects (FE) least squares, also known as least squares dummy variables (LSDV), suffers from a large loss of degrees of freedom. We are estimating $(N-1)$ extra parameters, and too many dummies may aggravate the problem of multicollinearity among the regressors. In addition, this FE estimator cannot estimate the effect of any time-invariant variable like sex, race, religion, schooling or union participation. These time-invariant variables are wiped out by the Q transformation, the deviations from means transformation (see (2.10)). Alternatively, one can see that these time-invariant variables are spanned by the individual dummies in (2.5) and therefore any regression package attempting (2.5) will fail, signaling perfect multicollinearity. If (2.5) is the true model, LSDV is the best linear unbiased estimator (BLUE) as long as ν_{it} is the standard classical disturbance with mean 0 and variance–covariance matrix $\sigma_\nu^2 I_{NT}$. Note that as $T \to \infty$, the FE estimator is consistent. However, if T is fixed and $N \to \infty$ as is typical in short labor panels, then only the FE estimator of β is consistent; the FE estimators of the individual effects $(\alpha + \mu_i)$ are not consistent since the number of these parameters increases as N increases. This is the incidental parameter problem discussed by Neyman and Scott (1948) and reviewed more recently by Lancaster (2000). Note that when the true model is fixed effects as in (2.5), OLS on (2.1) yields biased and inconsistent estimates of the regression parameters. This is an omission variables bias due to the fact that OLS deletes the individual dummies when in fact they are relevant.

(1) *Testing for fixed effects*. One could test the joint significance of these dummies, i.e. H_0: $\mu_1 = \mu_2 = \cdots = \mu_{N-1} = 0$, by performing an F-test. (Testing for individual effects will be extensively treated in Chapter 4.) This is a simple Chow test with the restricted residual sums of squares (RRSS) being that of OLS on the pooled model and the unrestricted residual sums of squares (URSS) being that of the LSDV regression. If N is large, one can perform the Within transformation described in (2.10) and use that residual sum of squares as the URSS. In this case

$$F_0 = \frac{(\text{RRSS} - \text{URSS})/(N-1)}{\text{URSS}/(NT - N - K)} \overset{H_0}{\sim} F_{N-1,N(T-1)-K} \tag{2.12}$$

(2) *Computational warning*. One computational caution for those using the Within regression given by (2.10). The s^2 of this regression as obtained from a typical regression package divides the residual sums of squares by $NT - K$ since the intercept and the dummies are not included. The proper s^2, say s^{*2} from the LSDV regression in (2.5), would divide the same residual sums of squares by $N(T-1) - K$. Therefore, one has to adjust the variances obtained from the Within regression (2.10) by multiplying the variance–covariance matrix by (s^{*2}/s^2) or simply by multiplying by $[NT - K]/[N(T-1) - K]$.

(3) *Robust estimates of the standard errors*. For the Within estimator, Arellano (1987) suggests a simple method for obtaining robust estimates of the standard errors that allow for a general variance–covariance matrix on the ν_{it} as in White (1980). One would stack the panel as an equation for each individual:

$$y_i = Z_i\delta + \mu_i \iota_T + \nu_i \tag{2.13}$$

where y_i is $T \times 1$, $Z_i = [\iota_T, X_i]$, X_i is $T \times K$, μ_i is a scalar, $\delta' = (\alpha, \beta')$, ι_T is a vector of ones of dimension T and ν_i is $T \times 1$. In general, $E(\nu_i \nu_i') = \Omega_i$ for $i = 1, 2, \ldots, N$, where Ω_i is a positive definite matrix of dimension T. We still assume $E(\nu_i \nu_j') = 0$, for $i \neq j$. T is assumed small and N large as in household or company panels, and the asymptotic results are performed for $N \to \infty$ and T fixed. Performing the Within transformation on this set of equations (2.13) one gets

$$\widetilde{y}_i = \widetilde{X}_i\beta + \widetilde{\nu}_i \tag{2.14}$$

where $\widetilde{y} = Qy$, $\widetilde{X} = QX$ and $\widetilde{\nu} = Q\nu$, with $\widetilde{y} = (\widetilde{y}_1', \ldots, \widetilde{y}_N')'$ and $\widetilde{y}_i = (I_T - \bar{J}_T)y_i$. Computing robust least squares on this system, as described by White (1980), under the restriction that each equation has the same β one gets the Within estimator of β which has the following asymptotic distribution:

$$N^{1/2}(\widetilde{\beta} - \beta) \sim N(0, M^{-1}VM^{-1}) \tag{2.15}$$

where $M = \text{plim}(\widetilde{X}'\widetilde{X})/N$ and $V = \text{plim}\sum_{i=1}^{N}(\widetilde{X}_i' \, \Omega_i \widetilde{X}_i)/N$. Note that $\widetilde{X}_i = (I_T - \bar{J}_T)X_i$ and $\widetilde{X}'Q \text{ diag}[\Omega_i]Q\widetilde{X} = \widetilde{X}' \text{ diag}[\Omega_i]\widetilde{X}$ (see problem 2.3). In this case, V is estimated by $\widetilde{V} = \sum_{i=1}^{N} \widetilde{X}_i'\widetilde{u}_i\widetilde{u}_i'\widetilde{X}_i/N$, where $\widetilde{u}_i = \widetilde{y}_i - \widetilde{X}_i\widetilde{\beta}$. Therefore, the robust asymptotic variance–covariance matrix of β is estimated by

$$\text{var}(\widetilde{\beta}) = (\widetilde{X}'\widetilde{X})^{-1} \left[\sum_{i=1}^{N} \widetilde{X}_i'\widetilde{u}_i\widetilde{u}_i'\widetilde{X}_i \right] (\widetilde{X}'\widetilde{X})^{-1} \tag{2.16}$$

2.3 THE RANDOM EFFECTS MODEL

There are too many parameters in the fixed effects model and the loss of degrees of freedom can be avoided if the μ_i can be assumed random. In this case $\mu_i \sim \text{IID}(0, \sigma_\mu^2)$, $\nu_{it} \sim \text{IID}(0, \sigma_\nu^2)$ and the μ_i are independent of the ν_{it}. In addition, the X_{it} are independent of the μ_i and ν_{it}, for all i and t. The random effects model is an appropriate specification if we are drawing N individuals randomly from a large population. This is usually the case for household panel studies. Care is taken in the design of the panel to make it "representative" of the population we are trying to make inferences about. In this case, N is usually large and a fixed effects model would lead to an enormous loss of degrees of freedom. The individual effect is characterized as random and inference pertains to the population from which this sample was randomly drawn. But what is the population in this case? Nerlove and Balestra (1996) emphasize Haavelmo's (1944) view that the population "consists *not* of an infinity of individuals, in general, but of an infinity of *decisions*" that each individual might make. This view is consistent with a random effects specification. From (2.4), one can compute the variance–covariance matrix

$$\begin{aligned} \Omega = E(uu') &= Z_\mu E(\mu\mu')Z_\mu' + E(\nu\nu') \\ &= \sigma_\mu^2(I_N \otimes J_T) + \sigma_\nu^2(I_N \otimes I_T) \end{aligned} \tag{2.17}$$

This implies a homoskedastic variance $\text{var}(u_{it}) = \sigma_\mu^2 + \sigma_\nu^2$ for all i and t, and an equicorrelated block-diagonal covariance matrix which exhibits serial correlation over time only between the disturbances of the same individual. In fact

$$\begin{aligned} \text{cov}(u_{it}, u_{js}) &= \sigma_\mu^2 + \sigma_\nu^2 \quad &&\text{for } i = j,\ t = s \\ &= \sigma_\mu^2 &&\text{for } i = j,\ t \neq s \end{aligned}$$

and zero otherwise. This also means that the correlation coefficient between u_{it} and u_{js} is

$$\begin{aligned} \rho = \text{correl}(u_{it}, u_{js}) &= 1 && \text{for } i = j,\ t = s \\ &= \sigma_\mu^2/(\sigma_\mu^2 + \sigma_\nu^2) && \text{for } i = j,\ t \neq s \end{aligned}$$

and zero otherwise. In order to obtain the GLS estimator of the regression coefficients, we need Ω^{-1}. This is a huge matrix for typical panels and is of dimension $(NT \times NT)$. No brute force inversion should be attempted even if the researcher's application has a small N and T.[1] We will follow a simple trick devised by Wansbeek and Kapteyn (1982b, 1983) that allows the derivation of Ω^{-1} and $\Omega^{-1/2}$.[2] Essentially, one replaces J_T by $T\bar{J}_T$ and I_T by $(E_T + \bar{J}_T)$ where E_T is by definition $(I_T - \bar{J}_T)$. In this case

$$\Omega = T\sigma_\mu^2(I_N \otimes \bar{J}_T) + \sigma_\nu^2(I_N \otimes E_T) + \sigma_\nu^2(I_N \otimes \bar{J}_T)$$

Collecting terms with the same matrices, we get

$$\Omega = (T\sigma_\mu^2 + \sigma_\nu^2)(I_N \otimes \bar{J}_T) + \sigma_\nu^2(I_N \otimes E_T) = \sigma_1^2 P + \sigma_\nu^2 Q \tag{2.18}$$

where $\sigma_1^2 = T\sigma_\mu^2 + \sigma_\nu^2$. (2.18) is the spectral decomposition representation of Ω, with σ_1^2 being the first unique characteristic root of Ω of multiplicity N and σ_ν^2 the second unique characteristic root of Ω of multiplicity $N(T-1)$. It is easy to verify, using the properties of P and Q, that

$$\Omega^{-1} = \frac{1}{\sigma_1^2}P + \frac{1}{\sigma_\nu^2}Q \tag{2.19}$$

and

$$\Omega^{-1/2} = \frac{1}{\sigma_1}P + \frac{1}{\sigma_\nu}Q \tag{2.20}$$

In fact, $\Omega^r = (\sigma_1^2)^r P + (\sigma_\nu^2)^r Q$ where r is an arbitrary scalar. Now we can obtain GLS as a weighted least squares. Fuller and Battese (1973, 1974) suggested premultiplying the regression equation given in (2.3) by $\sigma_\nu\Omega^{-1/2} = Q + (\sigma_\nu/\sigma_1)P$ and performing OLS on the resulting transformed regression. In this case, $y^* = \sigma_\nu\Omega^{-1/2}y$ has a typical element $(y_{it} - \theta\bar{y}_{i.})$ where $\theta = 1 - (\sigma_\nu/\sigma_1)$ (see problem 2.4). This transformed regression inverts a matrix of dimension $(K+1)$ and can be easily implemented using any regression package.

The best quadratic unbiased (BQU) estimators of the variance components arise naturally from the spectral decomposition of Ω. In fact, $Pu \sim (0, \sigma_1^2 P)$ and $Qu \sim (0, \sigma_\nu^2 Q)$ and

$$\widehat{\sigma}_1^2 = \frac{u'Pu}{\text{tr}(P)} = T\sum_{i=1}^{N}\bar{u}_{i.}^2/N \tag{2.21}$$

and

$$\widehat{\sigma}_\nu^2 = \frac{u'Qu}{\text{tr}(Q)} = \frac{\sum_{i=1}^N\sum_{t=1}^T(u_{it} - \bar{u}_{i.})^2}{N(T-1)} \tag{2.22}$$

provide the BQU estimators of σ_1^2 and σ_ν^2, respectively (see Balestra, 1973 and problem 2.5).

These are analyses of variance-type estimators of the variance components and are minimum variance unbiased under normality of the disturbances (see Graybill, 1961). The true disturbances are not known and therefore (2.21) and (2.22) are not feasible. Wallace and Hussain (1969) suggest substituting the OLS residual $\widehat{u}_{\text{OLS}}$ instead of the true u. After all, under the random effects model, the OLS estimates are still unbiased and consistent, but no longer efficient. Amemiya (1971) shows that these estimators of the variance components have a different asymptotic distribution from that knowing the true disturbances. He suggests using the LSDV residuals instead of the OLS residuals. In this case $\widetilde{u} = y - \tilde{\alpha}\iota_{NT} - X\widetilde{\beta}$ where $\widetilde{\alpha} = \bar{y}_{..} - \bar{X}'_{..}\widetilde{\beta}$ and $\bar{X}'_{..}$ is a $1 \times K$ vector of averages of all regressors. Substituting these $\widetilde{u}$ for u in (2.21) and (2.22) we get the Amemiya-type estimators of the variance components. The resulting estimates of the variance components have the same asymptotic distribution as that knowing the true disturbances:

$$\begin{pmatrix} \sqrt{NT}(\widehat{\sigma}_\nu^2 - \sigma_\nu^2) \\ \sqrt{N}(\widehat{\sigma}_\mu^2 - \sigma_\mu^2) \end{pmatrix} \sim N\left(0, \begin{pmatrix} 2\sigma_\nu^4 & 0 \\ 0 & 2\sigma_\mu^4 \end{pmatrix}\right) \tag{2.23}$$

where $\widehat{\sigma}_\mu^2 = (\widehat{\sigma}_1^2 - \widehat{\sigma}_\nu^2)/T$.[3]

Swamy and Arora (1972) suggest running two regressions to get estimates of the variance components from the corresponding mean square errors of these regressions. The first regression is the Within regression, given in (2.10), which yields the following s^2:

$$\widehat{\widehat{\sigma}}_\nu^2 = [y'Qy - y'QX(X'QX)^{-1}X'Qy]/[N(T-1) - K] \tag{2.24}$$

The second regression is the Between regression which runs the regression of averages across time, i.e.

$$\bar{y}_{i.} = \alpha + \bar{X}'_{i.}\beta + \bar{u}_{i.} \qquad i = 1, \ldots, N \tag{2.25}$$

This is equivalent to premultiplying the model in (2.5) by P and running OLS. The only caution is that the latter regression has NT observations because it repeats the averages T times for each individual, while the cross-section regression in (2.25) is based on N observations. To remedy this, one can run the cross-section regression

$$\sqrt{T}\bar{y}_{i.} = \alpha\sqrt{T} + \sqrt{T}\bar{X}'_{i.}\beta + \sqrt{T}\bar{u}_{i.} \tag{2.26}$$

where one can easily verify that $\text{var}(\sqrt{T}\bar{u}_{i.}) = \sigma_1^2$. This regression will yield an s^2 given by

$$\widehat{\widehat{\sigma}}_1^2 = [y'Py - y'PZ(Z'PZ)^{-1}Z'Py]/(N - K - 1) \tag{2.27}$$

Note that stacking the following two transformed regressions we just performed yields

$$\begin{pmatrix} Qy \\ Py \end{pmatrix} = \begin{pmatrix} QZ \\ PZ \end{pmatrix}\delta + \begin{pmatrix} Qu \\ Pu \end{pmatrix} \tag{2.28}$$

and the transformed error has mean 0 and variance–covariance matrix given by

$$\begin{pmatrix} \sigma_\nu^2 Q & 0 \\ 0 & \sigma_1^2 P \end{pmatrix}$$

Problem 2.7 asks the reader to verify that OLS on this system of $2NT$ observations yields OLS on the pooled model (2.3). Also, GLS on this system yields GLS on (2.3). Alternatively, one could get rid of the constant α by running the following stacked regressions:

$$\begin{pmatrix} Qy \\ (P - \bar{J}_{NT})y \end{pmatrix} = \begin{pmatrix} QX \\ (P - \bar{J}_{NT})X \end{pmatrix} \beta + \begin{pmatrix} Qu \\ (P - \bar{J}_{NT})u \end{pmatrix} \tag{2.29}$$

This follows from the fact that $Q\iota_{NT} = 0$ and $(P - \bar{J}_{NT})\iota_{NT} = 0$. The transformed error has zero mean and variance–covariance matrix

$$\begin{pmatrix} \sigma_\nu^2 Q & 0 \\ 0 & \sigma_1^2 (P - \bar{J}_{NT}) \end{pmatrix}$$

OLS on this system yields OLS on (2.3) and GLS on (2.29) yields GLS on (2.3). In fact

$$\begin{aligned} \widehat{\beta}_{\text{GLS}} &= [(X'QX/\sigma_\nu^2) + X'(P - \bar{J}_{NT})X/\sigma_1^2]^{-1} \\ &\quad \times [(X'Qy/\sigma_\nu^2) + X'(P - \bar{J}_{NT})y/\sigma_1^2] \\ &= [W_{XX} + \phi^2 B_{XX}]^{-1}[W_{Xy} + \phi^2 B_{Xy}] \end{aligned} \tag{2.30}$$

with $\text{var}(\widehat{\beta}_{\text{GLS}}) = \sigma_\nu^2[W_{XX} + \phi^2 B_{XX}]^{-1}$. Note that $W_{XX} = X'QX$, $B_{XX} = X'(P - \bar{J}_{NT})X$ and $\phi^2 = \sigma_\nu^2/\sigma_1^2$. Also, the Within estimator of β is $\widetilde{\beta}_{\text{Within}} = W_{XX}^{-1}W_{Xy}$ and the Between estimator of β is $\widehat{\beta}_{\text{Between}} = B_{XX}^{-1}B_{Xy}$. This shows that $\widehat{\beta}_{\text{GLS}}$ is a matrix-weighted average of $\widetilde{\beta}_{\text{Within}}$ and $\widehat{\beta}_{\text{Between}}$ weighing each estimate by the inverse of its corresponding variance. In fact

$$\widehat{\beta}_{\text{GLS}} = W_1 \widetilde{\beta}_{\text{Within}} + W_2 \widehat{\beta}_{\text{Between}} \tag{2.31}$$

where

$$W_1 = [W_{XX} + \phi^2 B_{XX}]^{-1} W_{XX}$$

and

$$W_2 = [W_{XX} + \phi^2 B_{XX}]^{-1}(\phi^2 B_{XX}) = I - W_1$$

This was demonstrated by Maddala (1971). Note that (i) if $\sigma_\mu^2 = 0$ then $\phi^2 = 1$ and $\widehat{\beta}_{\text{GLS}}$ reduces to $\widehat{\beta}_{\text{OLS}}$. (ii) If $T \to \infty$, then $\phi^2 \to 0$ and $\widehat{\beta}_{\text{GLS}}$ tends to $\widetilde{\beta}_{\text{Within}}$. Also, if W_{XX} is huge compared to B_{XX} then $\widehat{\beta}_{\text{GLS}}$ will be close to $\widetilde{\beta}_{\text{Within}}$. However, if B_{XX} dominates W_{XX} then $\widehat{\beta}_{\text{GLS}}$ tends to $\widehat{\beta}_{\text{Between}}$. In other words, the Within estimator ignores the Between variation, and the Between estimator ignores the Within variation. The OLS estimator gives equal weight to the Between and Within variations. From (2.30), it is clear that $\text{var}(\widetilde{\beta}_{\text{Within}}) - \text{var}(\widehat{\beta}_{\text{GLS}})$ is a positive semidefinite matrix, since ϕ^2 is positive. However, as $T \to \infty$ for any fixed N, $\phi^2 \to 0$ and both $\widehat{\beta}_{\text{GLS}}$ and $\widetilde{\beta}_{\text{Within}}$ have the same asymptotic variance.

Another estimator of the variance components was suggested by Nerlove (1971a). His suggestion is to estimate σ_μ^2 as $\sum_{i=1}^{N}(\widehat{\mu}_i - \overline{\widehat{\mu}})^2/(N-1)$ where $\widehat{\mu}_i$ are the dummy coefficient estimates from the LSDV regression. σ_ν^2 is estimated from the Within residual sums of squares divided by NT without correction for degrees of freedom.[4]

Note that, except for Nerlove's (1971a) method, one has to retrieve $\widehat{\sigma}_\mu^2$ as $(\widehat{\sigma}_1^2 - \widehat{\sigma}_\nu^2)/T$. In this case, there is no guarantee that the estimate of $\widehat{\sigma}_\mu^2$ would be non-negative. Searle (1971) has an extensive discussion of the problem of negative estimates of the variance components in the biometrics literature. One solution is to replace these negative estimates by zero. This in fact is the suggestion of the Monte Carlo study by Maddala and Mount (1973). This study finds that negative estimates occurred only when the true σ_μ^2 was small and close to zero. In these cases OLS is still a viable estimator. Therefore, replacing negative $\widehat{\sigma}_\mu^2$ by zero is not a bad sin after all, and the problem is dismissed as not being serious.[5]

How about the properties of the various feasible GLS estimators of β? Under the random effects model, GLS based on the true variance components is BLUE, and all the feasible GLS estimators considered are asymptotically efficient as either N or $T \to \infty$. Maddala and Mount (1973) compared OLS, Within, Between, feasible GLS methods, MINQUE, Henderson's method III, true GLS and maximum likelihood estimation using their Monte Carlo study. They found little to choose among the various feasible GLS estimators in small samples and argued in favor of methods that were easier to compute. MINQUE was dismissed as more difficult to compute and the applied researcher given one shot at the data was warned to compute at least two methods of estimation, like an ANOVA feasible GLS and maximum likelihood to ensure that they do not yield drastically different results. If they do give different results, the authors diagnose misspecification.

Taylor (1980) derived exact finite sample results for the one-way error component model. He compared the Within estimator with the Swamy–Arora feasible GLS estimator. He found the following important results:

(1) Feasible GLS is more efficient than LSDV for all but the fewest degrees of freedom.
(2) The variance of feasible GLS is never more than 17% above the Cramer–Rao lower bound.
(3) More efficient estimators of the variance components do not necessarily yield more efficient feasible GLS estimators.

These finite sample results are confirmed by the Monte Carlo experiments carried out by Maddala and Mount (1973) and Baltagi (1981a).

Bellmann, Breitung and Wagner (1989) consider the bias in estimating the variance components using the Wallace and Hussain (1969) method due to the replacement of the true disturbances by OLS residuals, also the bias in the regression coefficients due to the use of estimated variance components rather than the true variance components. The magnitude of this bias is estimated using bootstrap methods for two economic applications. The first application relates product innovations, import pressure and factor inputs using a panel at the industry level. The second application estimates the earnings of 936 full-time working German males based on the first and second wave of the German Socio-Economic Panel. Only the first application revealed considerable bias in estimating σ_μ^2. However, this did not affect the bias much in the corresponding regression coefficients.

2.3.1 Fixed vs Random

Having discussed the fixed effects and the random effects models and the assumptions underlying them, the reader is left with the daunting question, which one to choose? This is not as easy a choice as it might seem. In fact, the fixed vs random effects issue has generated a hot debate in the biometrics and statistics literature which has spilled over into the panel data econometrics literature. Mundlak (1961) and Wallace and Hussain (1969) were early proponents of the fixed effects model and Balestra and Nerlove (1966) were advocates of the random error component model.[6] In Chapter 4, we will study a specification test proposed by Hausman (1978) which is based on the difference between the fixed and random effects estimators. Unfortunately, applied researchers have interpreted a rejection as an adoption of the fixed effects model and nonrejection as an adoption of the random effects model.[7] Chamberlain (1984) showed that the fixed effects model imposes testable restrictions on the parameters of the reduced form model and one should check the validity of these restrictions before adopting the fixed effects model (see Chapter 4). Mundlak (1978) argued that the random effects model assumes exogeneity of *all* the regressors with the random individual effects. In contrast, the fixed effects model allows for endogeneity of *all* the regressors with these individual effects. So, it is an "all" or "nothing" choice of exogeneity of the regressors and the individual effects, see Chapter 7 for a more formal discussion of this subject. Hausman and Taylor (1981) allowed for *some* of the regressors to be correlated with the individual effects, as opposed to the all or nothing choice. These overidentification restrictions are testable using a Hausman-type test (see Chapter 7). For the applied researcher, performing fixed effects and random effects and the associated Hausman test reported in standard packages like STATA, LIMDEP, TSP, etc. the message is clear: Do not stop here. Test the restrictions implied by the fixed effects model derived by Chamberlain (1984) (see Chapter 4) and check whether a Hausman and Taylor (1981) specification might be a viable alternative (see Chapter 7).

2.4 MAXIMUM LIKELIHOOD ESTIMATION

Under normality of the disturbances, one can write the likelihood function as

$$L(\alpha, \beta, \phi^2, \sigma_\nu^2) = \text{constant} - \frac{NT}{2}\log\sigma_\nu^2 + \frac{N}{2}\log\phi^2 - \frac{1}{2\sigma_\nu^2}u'\Sigma^{-1}u \quad (2.32)$$

where $\Omega = \sigma_\nu^2\Sigma$, $\phi^2 = \sigma_\nu^2/\sigma_1^2$ and $\Sigma = Q + \phi^{-2}P$ from (2.18). This uses the fact that $|\Omega|$ = a product of its characteristic roots $= (\sigma_\nu^2)^{N(T-1)}(\sigma_1^2)^N = (\sigma_\nu^2)^{NT}(\phi^2)^{-N}$. Note that there is a one-to-one correspondence between ϕ^2 and σ_μ^2. In fact, $0 \leqslant \sigma_\mu^2 < \infty$ translates into $0 < \phi^2 \leqslant 1$. Brute force maximization of (2.32) leads to nonlinear first-order conditions (see Amemiya, 1971). Instead, Breusch (1987) concentrates the likelihood with respect to α and σ_ν^2. In this case, $\widehat{\alpha}_{\text{mle}} = \bar{y}_{..} - \bar{X}'_{..}\widehat{\beta}_{\text{mle}}$ and $\widehat{\sigma}^2_{\nu,\text{mle}} = (1/NT)\widehat{u}'\widehat{\Sigma}^{-1}\widehat{u}$ where $\widehat{u}$ and $\widehat{\Sigma}$ are based on maximum likelihood estimates of β, ϕ^2 and α. Let $d = y - X\widehat{\beta}_{\text{mle}}$, then $\widehat{\alpha}_{\text{mle}} = (1/NT)\iota'_{NT}d$ and $\widehat{u} = d - \iota_{NT}\widehat{\alpha}_{\text{mle}} = d - \bar{J}_{NT}d$. This implies that $\widehat{\sigma}^2_{\nu,\text{mle}}$ can be rewritten as

$$\widehat{\sigma}^2_{\nu,\text{mle}} = d'[Q + \phi^2(P - \bar{J}_{NT})]d/NT \tag{2.33}$$

and the concentrated likelihood becomes

$$L_C(\beta, \phi^2) = \text{constant} - \frac{NT}{2}\log\{d'[Q + \phi^2(P - \bar{J}_{NT})]d\} + \frac{N}{2}\log\phi^2 \tag{2.34}$$

Maximizing (2.34) over ϕ^2, given β (see problem 2.9), yields

$$\widehat{\phi}^2 = \frac{d'Qd}{(T-1)d'(P - \bar{J}_{NT})d} = \frac{\sum\sum(d_{it} - \bar{d}_{i.})^2}{T(T-1)\sum(\bar{d}_{i.} - \bar{d}_{..})^2} \tag{2.35}$$

Maximizing (2.34) over β, given ϕ^2, yields

$$\widehat{\beta}_{\text{mle}} = [X'(Q + \phi^2(P - \bar{J}_{NT}))X]^{-1}X'[Q + \phi^2(P - \bar{J}_{NT})]y \tag{2.36}$$

One can iterate between β and ϕ^2 until convergence. Breusch (1987) shows that provided $T > 1$, any ith iteration β, call it β_i, gives $0 < \phi^2_{i+1} < \infty$ in the $(i+1)$th iteration. More importantly, Breusch (1987) shows that these ϕ_i^2 have a "remarkable property" of forming a monotonic sequence. In fact, starting from the Within estimator of β, for $\phi^2 = 0$, the next ϕ^2 is finite and positive and starts a monotonically increasing sequence of ϕ^2. Similarly, starting from the Between estimator of β, for $\phi^2 \to \infty$ the next ϕ^2 is finite and positive and starts a monotonically decreasing sequence of ϕ^2. Hence, to guard against the possibility of a local maximum, Breusch (1987) suggests starting with $\widehat{\beta}_{\text{Within}}$ and $\widehat{\beta}_{\text{Between}}$ and iterating. If these two sequences converge to the same maximum, then this is the global maximum. If one starts with $\widehat{\beta}_{\text{OLS}}$ for $\phi^2 = 1$ and the next iteration obtains a larger ϕ^2, then we have a local maximum at the boundary $\phi^2 = 1$. Maddala (1971) finds that there are at most two maxima for the likelihood $L(\phi^2)$ for $0 < \phi^2 \leqslant 1$. Hence, we have to guard against one local maximum.

2.5 PREDICTION

Suppose we want to predict S periods ahead for the ith individual. For the GLS model, knowing the variance–covariance structure of the disturbances, Goldberger (1962) showed that the best linear unbiased predictor (BLUP) of $y_{i,T+S}$ is

$$\widehat{y}_{i,T+S} = Z'_{i,T+S}\widehat{\delta}_{\text{GLS}} + w'\Omega^{-1}\widehat{u}_{\text{GLS}} \quad \text{for } s \geqslant 1 \tag{2.37}$$

where $\widehat{u}_{\text{GLS}} = y - Z\widehat{\delta}_{\text{GLS}}$ and $w = E(u_{i,T+S}u)$. Note that for period $T+S$

$$u_{i,T+S} = \mu_i + \nu_{i,T+S} \tag{2.38}$$

and $w = \sigma_\mu^2(l_i \otimes \iota_T)$ where l_i is the ith column of I_N, i.e. l_i is a vector that has one in the ith position and zero elsewhere. In this case

$$w'\Omega^{-1} = \sigma_\mu^2(l'_i \otimes \iota'_T)\left[\frac{1}{\sigma_1^2}P + \frac{1}{\sigma_\nu^2}Q\right] = \frac{\sigma_\mu^2}{\sigma_1^2}(l'_i \otimes \iota'_T) \tag{2.39}$$

since $(l'_i \otimes \iota'_T)P = (l'_i \otimes \iota'_T)$ and $(l'_i \otimes \iota'_T)Q = 0$. Using (2.39), the typical element of $w'\Omega^{-1}\widehat{u}_{\text{GLS}}$ becomes $((T\sigma_\mu^2/\sigma_1^2)\overline{\widehat{u}}_{i.,\text{GLS}})$ where $\overline{\widehat{u}}_{i.,\text{GLS}} = \sum_{t=1}^{T}\widehat{u}_{it,\text{GLS}}/T$. Therefore, in (2.37), the BLUP for $y_{i,T+S}$ corrects the GLS prediction by a fraction of the mean of the GLS residuals corresponding to that ith individual. This predictor was considered by Wansbeek and Kapteyn (1978), Lee and Griffiths (1979) and Taub (1979).

Baillie and Baltagi (1999) consider the practical situation of prediction from the error component regression model when the variance components are not known. They derive both theoretical and simulation evidence as to the relative efficiency of four alternative predictors: (i) an ordinary predictor, based on the optimal predictor given in (2.37), but with MLEs replacing population parameters; (ii) a truncated predictor that ignores the error component correction, given by the last term in (2.37), but uses MLEs for its regression parameters; (iii) a misspecified predictor which uses OLS estimates of the regression parameters; and (iv) a fixed effects predictor which assumes that the individual effects are fixed parameters that can be estimated. The asymptotic formulae for MSE prediction are derived for all four predictors. Using numerical and simulation results, these are shown to perform adequately in realistic sample sizes ($N = 50$ and 500 and $T = 10$ and 20). Both the analytical and sampling results show that there are substantial gains in mean square error prediction by using the ordinary predictor instead of the misspecified or the truncated predictors, especially with increasing $\rho = \sigma_\mu^2/(\sigma_\mu^2 + \sigma_\nu^2)$ values. The reduction in MSE is about tenfold for $\rho = 0.9$ and a little more than twofold for $\rho = 0.6$ for various values of N and T. The fixed effects predictor performs remarkably well, being a close second to the ordinary predictor for all experiments. Simulation evidence confirms the importance of taking into account the individual effects when making predictions. The ordinary predictor and the fixed effects predictor outperform the truncated and misspecified predictors and are recommended in practice.

For an application in actuarial science to the problem of predicting future claims of a risk class, given past claims of that and related risk classes, see Frees, Young and Luo (1999). See also Chamberlain and Hirano (1999) who suggest optimal ways of combining an individual's personal earnings history with panel data on the earnings trajectories of other individuals to provide a conditional distribution of this individual's earnings.

2.6 EXAMPLES

2.6.1 Example 1

Grunfeld (1958) considered the following investment equation:

$$I_{it} = \alpha + \beta_1 F_{it} + \beta_2 C_{it} + u_{it} \tag{2.40}$$

where I_{it} denotes real gross investment for firm i in year t, F_{it} is the real value of the firm (shares outstanding) and C_{it} is the real value of the capital stock. These panel data consist of 10 large US manufacturing firms over 20 years, 1935–54, and are available on the Wiley web site as Grunfeld.fil. This data set, even though dated, is of manageable size for classroom use and has been used by Zellner (1962) and Taylor (1980). Table 2.1 gives the OLS, Between and Within estimators for the slope coefficients along with their standard errors. The Between estimates are different from the Within estimates and a Hausman (1978) test based on their difference is given in Chapter 4. OLS and feasible GLS are matrix-weighted combinations of these two estimators. These weights depend

Table 2.1 Grunfeld's Data. One-way Error Component Results

	β_1	β_2	θ
OLS	0.116	0.231	0
	(0.006)*	(0.025)*	
Between	0.135	0.032	∞
	(0.029)	(0.191)	
Within	0.110	0.310	1
	(0.012)	(0.017)	
WALHUS	0.110	0.307	0.837
	(0.011)	(0.018)	
AMEMIYA	0.110	0.308	0.856
	(0.010)	(0.017)	
SWAR	0.110	0.308	0.861
	(0.010)	(0.017)	
NERLOVE	0.110	0.308	0.868
	(0.010)	(0.017)	
IMLE	0.110	0.308	0.855
	(0.010)	(0.017)	

*These are biased standard errors when the true model has error component disturbances (see Moulton, 1986)

on θ. Table 2.1 reports four feasible GLS estimates of the regression coefficients along with the corresponding estimates of θ. These are WALHUS, AMEMIYA, SWAR and NERLOVE, respectively. Next, Breusch's (1987) iterative maximum likelihood estimation is performed (IMLE). This procedure converged to a global maximum in three to four iterations depending on whether one started from the Between or Within estimators. There is not much difference among the feasible GLS estimates or the iterative MLE and they are all close to the Within estimates. This is understandable given that $\widehat{\theta}$ for these estimators varies between 0.84 and 0.99, which is close to 1.

2.6.2 Example 2

Baltagi and Griffin (1983) considered the following gasoline demand equation:

$$\ln\frac{\text{Gas}}{\text{Car}} = \alpha + \beta_1 \ln\frac{Y}{N} + \beta_2 \ln\frac{P_{\text{MG}}}{P_{\text{GDP}}} + \beta_3 \ln\frac{\text{Car}}{N} + u \qquad (2.41)$$

where Gas/Car is motor gasoline consumption per auto, Y/N is real per capita income, $P_{\text{MG}}/P_{\text{GDP}}$ is real motor gasoline price and Car$/N$ denotes the stock of cars per capita. This panel consists of annual observations across 18 OECD countries, covering the period 1960–78. The data for this example are given as Gasoline.dat on the Wiley web site. Table 2.2 gives the parameter estimates for OLS, Between, Within and four feasible GLS estimates of the slope coefficients along with their standard errors, and the corresponding estimate of θ. Breusch's

Table 2.2 Gasoline Demand Data. One-way Error Component Results

	β_1	β_2	β_3	θ
OLS	0.890	−0.892	−0.763	0
	(0.036)*	(0.030)*	(0.019)*	
Between	0.968	−0.964	−0.795	∞
	(0.156)	(0.133)	(0.082)	
Within	0.662	−0.322	−0.640	1
	(0.073)	(0.044)	(0.030)	
WALHUS	0.543	−0.471	−0.606	0.848
	(0.064)	(0.046)	(0.028)	
AMEMIYA	0.601	−0.366	−0.620	0.938
	(0.065)	(0.041)	(0.027)	
SWAR	0.555	−0.420	−0.607	0.892
	(0.057)	(0.039)	(0.025)	
NERLOVE	0.606	−0.362	−0.622	0.941
	(0.064)	(0.040)	(0.027)	
IMLE	0.580	−0.386	−0.614	0.921
	(0.063)	(0.041)	(0.026)	

*These are biased standard errors when the true model has error component disturbances (see Moulton, 1986)

Source: Baltagi and Griffin (1983). Reproduced by permission of Elsevier Science Publishers B.V. (North-Holland)

(1987) iterative maximum likelihood converged to a global maximum in four to six iterations depending on whether one starts from the Between or Within estimators. Once again the estimates of θ are closer to 1 than 0, which explains why feasible GLS is closer to the Within estimator than the OLS estimator. The Between and OLS price elasticity estimates of gasoline demand are more than double those for the Within and feasible GLS estimators.

2.6.3 Example 3

Following Munnell (1990), Baltagi and Pinnoi (1995) considered the following Cobb–Douglas production function relationship investigating the productivity of public capital in private production:

$$\ln Y = \alpha + \beta_1 \ln K_1 + \beta_2 \ln K_2 + \beta_3 \ln L + \beta_4 \text{ Unemp} + u \tag{2.42}$$

where Y is gross state product, K_1 is public capital which includes highways and streets, water and sewer facilities and other public buildings and structures, K_2 is the private capital stock based on the Bureau of Economic Analysis national stock estimates, L is labor input measured as employment in nonagricultural payrolls. Unemp is the state unemployment rate included to capture business cycle effects. This panel consists of annual observations for 48 contiguous states over the period 1970–86. This data set was provided by Munnell (1990) and is given as Produc.prn on the Wiley web site. Table 2.3 gives the estimates for a one-way error component model. Note that both OLS and the Between estimators report that public capital is productive and significant in the state's private production. In contrast, the Within and feasible GLS estimators find that public capital is insignificant. This result was also reported by Holtz-Eakin (1994) who found

Table 2.3 Public Capital Productivity Data. One-way Error Component Results

	β_1	β_2	β_3	β_4	θ
OLS	0.155	0.309	0.594	−0.007	0
	(0.017)*	(0.010)*	(0.014)*	(0.001)*	
Between	0.179	0.302	0.576	−0.004	∞
	(0.072)	(0.042)	(0.056)	(0.010)	
Within	−0.026	0.292	0.768	−0.005	1
	(0.029)	(0.025)	(0.030)	(0.001)	
WALHUS	0.009	0.313	0.724	−0.006	0.878
	(0.024)	(0.020)	(0.025)	(0.001)	
AMEMIYA	0.001	0.309	0.734	−0.006	0.897
	(0.024)	(0.020)	(0.025)	(0.001)	
SWAR	0.004	0.311	0.730	−0.006	0.889
	(0.023)	(0.020)	(0.025)	(0.001)	
NERLOVE	−0.001	0.308	0.736	−0.006	0.902
	(0.023)	(0.020)	(0.025)	(0.001)	
IMLE	0.003	0.310	0.731	−0.006	0.892
	(0.023)	(0.020)	(0.025)	(0.001)	

*These are biased standard errors when the true model has error component disturbances (see Moulton, 1986)

that after controlling for state-specific effects, the public-sector capital has no role in affecting private production.

2.7 SELECTED APPLICATIONS

There are far too many applications of the error component model in economics to be exhaustive and here we only want to refer the reader to a few applications. These include:

(1) Weiss (1985) who studied the determinants of loss reserving error of 16 large automobile liability insurers over the period 1955–76.
(2) Owusu-Gyapong (1986) who studied the strike activity of 60 Canadian manufacturing industries over the period 1967–79.
(3) Lichtenberg (1988) who used a fixed effects model to study the internal costs associated with the introduction of new plant and equipment into manufacturing. The panel consisted of 1092 manufacturing plants contained in the Census Bureau's Longitudinal Establishment Data File and observed annually over the period 1973–81.
(4) Cardellichio (1990) who modeled the production behavior of 1147 sawmills in the state of Washington, observed biennially over the period 1972–84.
(5) Behrman and Deolalikar (1990) who estimated the effect of per capita income on the calorie intake using the panel data collected by the International Crops Research Institute for the Semi-Arid Tropics Village level studies in rural south India.
(6) Johnson and Lahiri (1992) who estimated a production function for ambulatory care using panel data on 30 health care centers in New York state over the years 1984–87.
(7) Conway and Kniesner (1992) who used the Panel Study of Income Dynamics to study the sensitivity of male labor supply function estimates to how the wage is measured and how the researcher models individual heterogeneity.
(8) Cornwell and Rupert (1997) who used panel data from the NLSY to show that much of the wage premium normally attributed to marriage is associated with unobservable individual effects that are correlated with marital status and wages.

For an application from political science, see Stimson (1985) who used an error component model to study the regional dynamics of party polarization over issues of racial desegregation in the US House of Representatives. For an application from sociology, see England et al. (1988) who used a fixed effects model to test whether predominantly female occupations have advantages that compensate for their lower average wages. For an application from finance, see Chang and Lee (1977) who examined the impact of changes in dividends and retained earnings on price per share. For an application from marketing, see Palda and Blair (1970) who estimated a fixed effects demand model for toothpaste.

2.8 COMPUTATIONAL NOTE

There is no magical software written explicitly for all panel data estimation and testing procedures. For a software review of LIMDEP, RATS, SAS, TSP and GAUSS with special attention to the panel data procedures presented in this book, see Blanchard (1996). My students use SAS or STATA especially when large database management is needed. For hard to program estimation or testing methods GAUSS has the comparative advantage. Simple panel data estimators can be done with LIMDEP, TSP or STATA.

NOTES

1. For example, if we observe $N = 20$ firms over $T = 5$ time periods, Ω will be 100 by 100.
2. See also Searle and Henderson (1979) for a systematic method for deriving the characteristic roots and vectors of Ω for any balanced error component model.
3. It is important to note that once one substitutes OLS or LSDV residuals in (2.21) and (2.22), the resulting estimators of the variance components are no longer unbiased. The degrees of freedom corrections required to make these estimators unbiased involve traces of matrices that depend on the data. These correction terms are given in Wallace and Hussain (1969) and Amemiya (1971), respectively. Alternatively, one can infer these correction terms from the more general unbalanced error component model considered in Chapter 9.
4. One can also apply Rao's (1970, 1972) MINQUE (minimum norm quadratic unbiased estimation) procedure or Henderson's method III as described by Fuller and Battese (1973). These methods are studied in detail in Baltagi (1995b, Appendix 3) for the two-way error component model and in Chapter 9 for the unbalanced error component model. Unfortunately, these methods have not been widely used in the empirical economics literature.
5. Berzeg (1979) generalizes the one-way error component model to the case where the individual effects (μ_i) and the remainder disturbances (ν_{it}) are correlated for the same individual i. This specification ensures a non-negative estimate of the error component variance. This is applied to the estimation of US demand for motor gasoline (see Berzeg, 1982).
6. Recently, Nerlove (2000b) revisited this debate and gave his candid views on the subject. Once again, he argues in favor of the random effects model.
7. Hsiao and Sun (2000) argue that fixed vs random effects specification is better treated as an issue of model selection rather than hypothesis testing. They suggest a recursive predictive density ratio as well as the Akaike and Schwartz information criteria for model selection. Monte Carlo results indicate that all three criteria perform well in finite samples. However, the Schwartz criterion was found to be the more reliable of the three.

PROBLEMS

2.1 Prove that $\widetilde{\beta}$ given in (2.7) can be obtained from OLS on (2.5) using results on the partitioned inverse. This can easily be obtained using the Frisch–Waugh–Lovell theorem of Davidson and MacKinnon (1993, p. 19).

Hint: This theorem states that the OLS estimate of β from (2.5) will be identical to the OLS estimate of β from (2.6). Also, the least squares residuals will be the same.

2.2 (a) Using the generalized inverse, show that OLS or GLS on (2.6) yields $\widetilde{\beta}$, the Within estimator given in (2.7).

(b) Show that (2.6) satisfies the necessary and sufficient condition for OLS to be equivalent to GLS (see Baltagi, 1989b). Hint: Show that $\text{var}(Q\nu) = \sigma_\nu^2 Q$ which is positive semidefinite and then use the fact that Q is idempotent and is its own generalized inverse.

2.3 Verify that by stacking the panel as an equation for each individual in (2.13) and performing the Within transformation as in (2.14) one gets the Within estimator as OLS on this system. Verify that the robust asymptotic $\text{var}(\widetilde{\beta})$ is the one given by (2.16).

2.4 (a) Verify (2.17) and check that $\Omega^{-1}\Omega = I$ using (2.18).

(b) Verify that $\Omega^{-1/2}\Omega^{-1/2} = \Omega^{-1}$ using (2.20) and (2.19).

(c) Premultiply y by $\sigma_\nu \Omega^{-1/2}$ from (2.20), and show that the typical element is $(y_{it} - \theta \bar{y}_{i.})$ where $\theta = 1 - (\sigma_\nu/\sigma_1)$.

2.5 Using (2.21) and (2.22), show that $E(\widehat{\sigma}_1^2) = \sigma_1^2$ and $E(\widehat{\sigma}_\nu^2) = \sigma_\nu^2$. Hint: $E(u'Qu) = E\{\text{tr}(u'Qu)\} = E\{\text{tr}(uu'Q)\} = \text{tr}\{E(uu')Q\} = \text{tr}(\Omega Q)$.

2.6 (a) Show that $\widehat{\widehat{\sigma}}_\nu^2$ given in (2.24) is unbiased for σ_ν^2.

(b) Show that $\widehat{\widehat{\sigma}}_1^2$ given in (2.27) is unbiased for σ_1^2.

2.7 (a) Perform OLS on the system of equations given in (2.28) and show that the resulting estimator is $\widehat{\delta}_{\text{OLS}} = (Z'Z)^{-1}Z'y$.

(b) Perform GLS on the system of equations given in (2.28) and show that the resulting estimator is $\widehat{\delta}_{\text{GLS}} = (Z'\Omega^{-1}Z)^{-1}Z'\Omega^{-1}y$ where Ω^{-1} is given in (2.19).

2.8 Using the $\text{var}(\widehat{\beta}_{\text{GLS}})$ expression below (2.30) and $\text{var}(\widetilde{\beta}_{\text{Within}}) = \sigma_\nu^2 W_{XX}^{-1}$, show that

$$(\text{var}(\widehat{\beta}_{\text{GLS}}))^{-1} - (\text{var}(\widetilde{\beta}_{\text{Within}}))^{-1} = \phi^2 B_{XX}/\sigma_\nu^2$$

which is positive semidefinite. Conclude that $\text{var}(\widetilde{\beta}_{\text{Within}}) - \text{var}(\widehat{\beta}_{\text{GLS}})$ is positive semidefinite.

2.9 (a) Using the concentrated likelihood function in (2.34), solve $\partial L_C/\partial\phi^2 = 0$ and verify (2.35).

(b) Solve $\partial L_C/\partial\beta = 0$ and verify (2.36).

2.10 (a) For the predictor $y_{i,T+S}$ given in (2.37), compute $E(u_{i,T+S}u_{it})$ for $t = 1, 2, \ldots, T$ and verify that $w = E(u_{i,T+S}u) = \sigma_\mu^2(l_i \otimes \iota_T)$ where l_i is the ith column of I_N.

(b) Verify (2.39) by showing that $(l_i' \otimes \iota_T')P = (l_i' \otimes \iota_T')$.

2.11 Using Grunfeld's data, given as Grunfeld.fil on the Wiley web site, reproduce Table 2.1.

2.12 Using the gasoline demand data of Baltagi and Griffin (1983), given as Gasoline.dat on the Wiley web site, reproduce Table 2.2.

2.13 Using the Monte Carlo setup for the one-way error component model given in Maddala and Mount (1973), compare the various estimators of the variance components and regression coefficients studied in this chapter.

2.14 For the random one-way error component model given in (2.1) and (2.2), consider the OLS estimator of $\text{var}(u_{it}) = \sigma^2$, which is given by $s^2 = \widehat{u}'_{\text{OLS}}\widehat{u}_{\text{OLS}}/(n - K')$, where $n = NT$ and $K' = K + 1$.
(a) Show that $E(s^2) = \sigma^2 + \sigma_\mu^2[K' - \text{tr}(I_N \otimes J_T)P_x]/(n - K')$.
(b) Consider the inequalities given by Kiviet and Krämer (1992) which state that

$$0 \leqslant \text{mean of } (n - K') \text{ smallest roots of } \Omega \leqslant E(s^2)$$
$$\leqslant \text{mean of } (n - K') \text{ largest roots of } \Omega \leqslant \text{tr}(\Omega)/(n - K')$$

where $\Omega = E(uu')$. Show that for the one-way error component model, these bounds are

$$0 \leqslant \sigma_\nu^2 + (n - TK')\sigma_\mu^2/(n - K') \leqslant E(s^2) \leqslant \sigma_\nu^2 + n\sigma_\mu^2/(n - K')$$
$$\leqslant n\sigma^2/(n - K')$$

As $n \to \infty$, both bounds tend to σ^2 and s^2 is asymptotically unbiased, irrespective of the particular evolution of X. See Baltagi and Krämer (1994) for a proof of this result.

2.15 Using the public capital productivity data of Munnell (1990), given as Produc.prn on the Wiley web site, reproduce Table 2.3.

2.16 Using the Monte Carlo design of Baillie and Baltagi (1999), compare the four predictors described in section 2.5.

2.17 *Heteroskedastic fixed effects models*. This is based on problem 96.5.1 in *Econometric Theory* by Baltagi (1996b). Consider the fixed effects model

$$y_{it} = \alpha_i + u_{it} \quad i = 1, 2, \ldots, N;\ t = 1, 2, \ldots, T_i$$

where y_{it} denotes output in industry i at time t and α_i denotes the industry fixed effect. The disturbances u_{it} are assumed to be independent with heteroskedastic variances σ_i^2. Note that the data are unbalanced with different number of observations for each industry.
(a) Show that OLS and GLS estimates of α_i are identical.
(b) Let $\sigma^2 = \sum_{i=1}^N T_i\sigma_i^2/n$, where $n = \sum_{i=1}^N T_i$, be the average disturbance variance. Show that the GLS estimator of σ^2 is unbiased, whereas the OLS estimator of σ^2 is biased. Also show that this bias disappears if the data are balanced or the variances are homoskedastic.
(c) Define $\lambda_i^2 = \sigma_i^2/\sigma^2$ for $i = 1, 2, \ldots, N$. Show that for $\alpha' = (\alpha_1, \alpha_2, \ldots, \alpha_N)$

$$E[\text{estimated var}(\widehat{\alpha}_{\text{OLS}}) - \text{ true var}(\widehat{\alpha}_{\text{OLS}})]$$
$$= \sigma^2[(n - \sum_{i=1}^N \lambda_i^2)/(n - N)]\,\text{diag}(1/T_i) - \sigma^2\,\text{diag}(\lambda_i^2/T_i)$$

This problem shows that in case there are no regressors in the unbalanced panel data model, fixed effects with heteroskedastic disturbances can be estimated by OLS, but one has to correct the standard errors. See solution 96.5.1 in *Econometric Theory* by Kleiber (1997).

3 The Two-way Error Component Regression Model

3.1 INTRODUCTION

Wallace and Hussain (1969), Nerlove (1971b) and Amemiya (1971), among others, considered the regression model given by (2.1), but with two-way error component disturbances:

$$u_{it} = \mu_i + \lambda_t + \nu_{it} \qquad i = 1, \ldots, N;\ t = 1, \ldots, T \tag{3.1}$$

where μ_i denotes the unobservable individual effect discussed in Chapter 2, λ_t denotes the unobservable time effect and ν_{it} is the remainder stochastic disturbance term. Note that λ_t is individual-invariant and accounts for any time-specific effect that is not included in the regression. For example, it could account for strike year effects that disrupt production, oil embargo effects that disrupt the supply of oil and affect its price, Surgeon General reports on the ill-effects of smoking, or government laws restricting smoking in public places, all of which could affect consumption behavior. In vector form, (3.1) can be written as

$$u = Z_\mu \mu + Z_\lambda \lambda + \nu \tag{3.2}$$

where Z_μ, μ and ν were defined earlier. $Z_\lambda = \iota_N \otimes I_T$ is the matrix of time dummies that one may include in the regression to estimate the λ_t if they are fixed parameters, and $\lambda' = (\lambda_1, \ldots, \lambda_T)$. Note that $Z_\lambda Z_\lambda' = J_N \otimes I_T$ and the projection on Z_λ is $Z_\lambda(Z_\lambda' Z_\lambda)^{-1} Z_\lambda' = \bar{J}_N \otimes I_T$. This last matrix averages the data over individuals, i.e. $(\bar{J}_N \otimes I_T)u$ has a typical element $\bar{u}_{.t} = \sum_{i=1}^{N} u_{it}/N$.

3.2 THE FIXED EFFECTS MODEL

If the μ_i *and* λ_t are assumed to be fixed parameters to be estimated and the remainder disturbances are stochastic with $\nu_{it} \sim \text{IID}(0, \sigma_\nu^2)$, then (3.1) represents a two-way fixed effects error component model. The X_{it} are assumed independent of the ν_{it} for all i and t. Inference in this case is conditional on the particular N individuals and over the specific time periods observed. Recall that Z_λ, the matrix of time dummies, is $NT \times T$. If N or T is large, there will be too many dummy variables in the regression $[(N-1)+(T-1)]$ of them, and this causes an enormous loss in degrees of freedom. In addition, this attenuates the problem of multicollinearity among the regressors. Rather than invert a large $(N+T+K-1)$ matrix, one can obtain the fixed effects estimates of β by performing the following Within transformation given by Wallace and Hussain (1969):

$$Q = E_N \otimes E_T = I_N \otimes I_T - I_N \otimes \bar{J}_T - \bar{J}_N \otimes I_T + \bar{J}_N \otimes \bar{J}_T \tag{3.3}$$

This transformation "sweeps" the μ_i and λ_t effects. In fact, $\widetilde{u} = Qu$ has a typical element $\widetilde{u}_{it} = (u_{it} - \bar{u}_{i.} - \bar{u}_{.t} + \bar{u}_{..})$ where $\bar{u}_{..} = \sum_i \sum_t u_{it}/NT$ and one would perform the regression of $\widetilde{y} = Qy$ on $\widetilde{X} = QX$ to get the Within estimator $\widetilde{\beta} = (X'QX)^{-1}X'Qy$.

Note that by averaging over individuals the simple regression given in (2.8) with disturbances given by (3.1). We get

$$\bar{y}_{.t} = \alpha + \beta\bar{x}_{.t} + \lambda_t + \bar{\nu}_{.t} \tag{3.4}$$

where we have utilized the restriction that $\sum_i \mu_i = 0$ to avoid the dummy variable trap. Similarly the averages defined in (2.9) and (2.11) still hold using $\sum_t \lambda_t = 0$, and one can deduce that

$$(y_{it} - \bar{y}_{i.} - \bar{y}_{.t} + \bar{y}_{..}) = (x_{it} - \bar{x}_{i.} - \bar{x}_{.t} + \bar{x}_{..})\beta + (\nu_{it} - \bar{\nu}_{i.} - \bar{\nu}_{.t} + \bar{\nu}_{..}) \tag{3.5}$$

OLS on this model gives $\widetilde{\beta}$, the Within estimator for the two-way model. Once again, the Within estimate of the intercept can be deduced from $\widetilde{\alpha} = \bar{y}_{..} - \widetilde{\beta}\bar{x}_{..}$ and those of μ_i and λ_t are given by

$$\widetilde{\mu}_i = (\bar{y}_{i.} - \bar{y}_{..}) - \widetilde{\beta}(\bar{x}_{i.} - \bar{x}_{..}) \tag{3.6}$$

$$\widetilde{\lambda}_t = (\bar{y}_{.t} - \bar{y}_{..}) - \widetilde{\beta}(\bar{x}_{.t} - \bar{x}_{..}) \tag{3.7}$$

Note that the Within estimator cannot estimate the effect of time-invariant and individual-invariant variables because the Q transformation wipes out these variables.

3.2.1 Testing for Fixed Effects

As in the one-way error component model case, one can test for joint significance of the dummy variables:

$$H_0\colon \mu_1 = \ldots = \mu_{N-1} = 0 \qquad \text{and} \qquad \lambda_1 = \ldots = \lambda_{T-1} = 0$$

The restricted residual sums of squares (RRSS) is that of pooled OLS and the unrestricted residual sums of squares (URSS) is that from the Within regression in (3.5). In this case

$$F_1 = \frac{(\text{RRSS} - \text{URSS})/(N+T-2)}{\text{URSS}/((N-1)(T-1)-K)} \overset{H_0}{\sim} F_{(N+T-2),(N-1)(T-1)-K} \tag{3.8}$$

Next, one can test for the existence of individual effects given time effects, i.e.

$$H_2\colon \mu_1 = \ldots = \mu_{N-1} = 0 \qquad \text{given} \qquad \lambda_t \neq 0 \text{ for } t = 1, \ldots, T-1$$

The URSS is still the Within residual sum of squares. However, the RRSS is the regression with time-series dummies only, or the regression based upon

$$(y_{it} - \bar{y}_{.t}) = (x_{it} - \bar{x}_{.t})\beta + (u_{it} - \bar{u}_{.t}) \tag{3.9}$$

In this case the resulting F-statistic is $F_2 \overset{H_0}{\sim} F_{(N-1),(N-1)(T-1)-K}$. Note that F_2 differs from F_0 in (2.12) in testing for $\mu_i = 0$. The latter tests $H_0\colon \mu_i = 0$ assuming that $\lambda_t = 0$, whereas the former tests $H_2\colon \mu_i = 0$ knowing that $\lambda_t \neq 0$ for $t = 1, \ldots, T-1$. Similarly, one can test for the existence of time effects given individual effects, i.e.

$$H_3\colon \lambda_1 = \ldots = \lambda_{T-1} = 0 \qquad \text{given} \qquad \mu_i \neq 0 \quad \text{for } i = 1, \ldots, N-1$$

The RRSS is given by the regression in (2.10), while the URSS is obtained from the regression (3.5). In this case, the resulting F-statistic is $F_3 \overset{H_0}{\sim} F_{(T-1),(N-1)(T-1)-K}$.

Computational Warning

As in the one-way model, s^2 from the regression in (3.5) as obtained from any standard regression package has to be adjusted for loss of degrees of freedom. In this case, one divides by $(N-1)(T-1) - K$ and multiplies by $(NT - K)$ to get the proper variance–covariance matrix of the Within estimator.

3.3 THE RANDOM EFFECTS MODEL

If $\mu_i \sim \text{IID}(0, \sigma_\mu^2)$, $\lambda_t \sim \text{IID}(0, \sigma_\lambda^2)$ and $\nu_{it} \sim \text{IID}(0, \sigma_\nu^2)$ independent of each other, then this is the two-way *random* effects model. In addition, X_{it} is independent of μ_i, λ_t and ν_{it} for all i and t. Inference in this case pertains to the large population from which this sample was randomly drawn.[1] From (3.2), one can compute the variance–covariance matrix

$$\begin{aligned} \Omega = E(uu') &= Z_\mu E(\mu\mu')Z_\mu' + Z_\lambda E(\lambda\lambda')Z_\lambda' + \sigma_\nu^2 I_{NT} \\ &= \sigma_\mu^2(I_N \otimes J_T) + \sigma_\lambda^2(J_N \otimes I_T) + \sigma_\nu^2(I_N \otimes I_T) \end{aligned} \tag{3.10}$$

The disturbances are homoskedastic with $\text{var}(u_{it}) = \sigma_\mu^2 + \sigma_\lambda^2 + \sigma_\nu^2$ for all i and t

$$\begin{aligned} \text{cov}(u_{it}, u_{js}) &= \sigma_\mu^2 \quad i = j,\ t \neq s \\ &= \sigma_\lambda^2 \quad i \neq j,\ t = s \end{aligned} \tag{3.11}$$

and zero otherwise. This means that the correlation coefficient

$$\begin{aligned} \text{correl}(u_{it}, u_{js}) &= \sigma_\mu^2/(\sigma_\mu^2 + \sigma_\lambda^2 + \sigma_\nu^2) & i = j,\ t \neq s \\ &= \sigma_\lambda^2/(\sigma_\mu^2 + \sigma_\lambda^2 + \sigma_\nu^2) & i \neq j,\ t = s \\ &= 1 & i = j,\ t = s \\ &= 0 & i \neq j,\ t \neq s \end{aligned} \tag{3.12}$$

In order to get Ω^{-1}, we replace J_N by $N\bar{J}_N$, I_N by $E_N + \bar{J}_N$, J_T by $T\bar{J}_T$ and I_T by $E_T + \bar{J}_T$ and collect terms with the same matrices. This gives

$$\Omega = \sum_{i=1}^{4} \lambda_i Q_i \tag{3.13}$$

where $\lambda_1 = \sigma_\nu^2$, $\lambda_2 = T\sigma_\mu^2 + \sigma_\nu^2$, $\lambda_3 = N\sigma_\lambda^2 + \sigma_\nu^2$ and $\lambda_4 = T\sigma_\mu^2 + N\sigma_\lambda^2 + \sigma_\nu^2$. Correspondingly, $Q_1 = E_N \otimes E_T$, $Q_2 = E_N \otimes \bar{J}_T$, $Q_3 = \bar{J}_N \otimes E_T$ and $Q_4 = \bar{J}_N \otimes \bar{J}_T$, respectively. The λ_i are the distinct characteristic roots of Ω and the Q_i are the corresponding matrices of eigenprojectors. λ_1 is of multiplicity $(N-1)(T-1)$, λ_2 is of multiplicity $(N-1)$, λ_3 is of multiplicity $(T-1)$ and λ_4 is of multiplicity 1.[2] Each Q_i is symmetric and idempotent with its rank equal to its trace. Moreover, the Q_i are pairwise orthogonal and sum to the identity matrix. The advantages of this spectral decomposition are that

$$\Omega^r = \sum_{i=1}^{4} \lambda_i^r Q_i \tag{3.14}$$

where r is an arbitrary scalar so that

$$\sigma_\nu \Omega^{-1/2} = \sum_{i=1}^{4} (\sigma_\nu/\lambda_i^{1/2}) Q_i \tag{3.15}$$

and the typical element of $y^* = \sigma_\nu \Omega^{-1/2} y$ is given by

$$y_{it}^* = y_{it} - \theta_1 \bar{y}_{i.} - \theta_2 \bar{y}_{.t} + \theta_3 \bar{y}_{..} \tag{3.16}$$

where $\theta_1 = 1 - (\sigma_\nu/\lambda_2^{1/2})$, $\theta_2 = 1 - (\sigma_\nu/\lambda_3^{1/2})$ and $\theta_3 = \theta_1 + \theta_2 + (\sigma_\nu/\lambda_4^{1/2}) - 1$.[3] As a result, GLS can be obtained as OLS of y^* on Z^*, where $Z^* = \sigma_\nu \Omega^{-1/2} Z$.

The best quadratic unbiased (BQU) estimators of the variance components arise naturally from the fact that $Q_i u \sim (0, \lambda_i Q_i)$. Hence

$$\widehat{\lambda}_i = u' Q_i u / \text{tr}(Q_i) \tag{3.17}$$

is the BQU estimator of λ_i for $i = 1, 2, 3$ (see Balestra, 1973). These ANOVA estimators are minimum variance unbiased (MVU) under normality of the disturbances (see Graybill, 1961). As in the one-way error component model, one can obtain feasible estimates of the variance components by replacing the true disturbances by OLS residuals (see Wallace and Hussain, 1969). Alternatively, one could substitute the Within residuals with $\widetilde{u} = y - \widetilde{\alpha}\iota_{NT} - X\widetilde{\beta}$, where $\widetilde{\alpha} = \bar{y}_{..} - \bar{X}'_{..}\widetilde{\beta}$ and $\widetilde{\beta}$ is obtained by the regression in (3.5). This is the method proposed by Amemiya (1971). In fact, Amemiya (1971) shows that the Wallace and

Hussain (1969) estimates of the variance components have a different asymptotic distribution from that knowing the true disturbances, while the Amemiya (1971) estimates of the variance components have the same asymptotic distribution as that knowing the true disturbances:

$$\begin{pmatrix} \sqrt{NT}(\widehat{\sigma}_\nu^2 - \sigma_\nu^2) \\ \sqrt{N}(\widehat{\sigma}_\mu^2 - \sigma_\mu^2) \\ \sqrt{T}(\widehat{\sigma}_\lambda^2 - \sigma_\lambda^2) \end{pmatrix} \sim N\left(0, \begin{pmatrix} 2\sigma_\nu^4 & 0 & 0 \\ 0 & 2\sigma_\mu^4 & 0 \\ 0 & 0 & 2\sigma_\lambda^4 \end{pmatrix}\right) \quad (3.18)$$

Substituting OLS or Within residuals instead of the true disturbances in (3.17) introduces bias in the corresponding estimates of the variance components. The degrees of freedom corrections that make these estimates unbiased depend upon traces of matrices that involve the matrix of regressors X. These corrections are given in Wallace and Hussain (1969) and Amemiya (1971), respectively. Alternatively, one can infer these correction terms from the more general unbalanced error component model considered in Chapter 9.

Swamy and Arora (1972) suggest running three least squares regressions and estimating the variance components from the corresponding mean square errors of these regressions. The first regression corresponds to the Within regression which transforms the original model by $Q_1 = E_N \otimes E_T$. This is equivalent to the regression in (3.5), and yields the following estimate of σ_ν^2:

$$\widehat{\widehat{\lambda}}_1 = \widehat{\widehat{\sigma}}_\nu^2 = [y'Q_1y - y'Q_1X(X'Q_1X)^{-1}X'Q_1y]/[(N-1)(T-1) - K] \quad (3.19)$$

The second regression is the Between individuals regression which transforms the original model by $Q_2 = E_N \otimes \bar{J}_T$. This is equivalent to the regression of $(\bar{y}_{i.} - \bar{y}_{..})$ on $(\bar{X}_{i.} - \bar{X}_{..})$ and yields the following estimate of $\lambda_2 = T\sigma_\mu^2 + \sigma_\nu^2$:

$$\widehat{\widehat{\lambda}}_2 = [y'Q_2y - y'Q_2X(X'Q_2X)^{-1}X'Q_2y]/[(N-1) - K] \quad (3.20)$$

from which one obtains $\widehat{\widehat{\sigma}}_\mu^2 = (\widehat{\widehat{\lambda}}_2 - \widehat{\widehat{\sigma}}_\nu^2)/T$. The third regression is the Between time periods regression which transforms the original model by $Q_3 = \bar{J}_N \otimes E_T$. This is equivalent to the regression of $(\bar{y}_{.t} - \bar{y}_{..})$ on $(\bar{X}_{.t} - \bar{X}_{..})$ and yields the following estimate of $\lambda_3 = N\sigma_\lambda^2 + \sigma_\nu^2$:

$$\widehat{\widehat{\lambda}}_3 = [y'Q_3y - y'Q_3X(X'Q_3X)^{-1}X'Q_3y]/[(T-1) - K] \quad (3.21)$$

from which one obtains $\widehat{\widehat{\sigma}}_\lambda^2 = (\widehat{\widehat{\lambda}}_3 - \widehat{\widehat{\sigma}}_\nu^2)/N$. Stacking the three transformed regressions just performed yields

$$\begin{pmatrix} Q_1y \\ Q_2y \\ Q_3y \end{pmatrix} = \begin{pmatrix} Q_1X \\ Q_2X \\ Q_3X \end{pmatrix} \beta + \begin{pmatrix} Q_1u \\ Q_2u \\ Q_3u \end{pmatrix} \quad (3.22)$$

since $Q_i\iota_{NT} = 0$ for $i = 1, 2, 3$ and the transformed error has mean 0 and variance–covariance matrix given by diag$[\lambda_i Q_i]$ with $i = 1, 2, 3$. Problem 3.4 asks the reader to show that OLS on this system of $3NT$ observations yields the same estimator of β as OLS on the pooled model (2.3). Also, GLS on this system of equations (3.22) yields the same estimator of β as GLS on (2.3). In fact

$$\begin{aligned}\widehat{\beta}_{\text{GLS}} &= [(X'Q_1X)/\sigma_\nu^2 + (X'Q_2X)/\lambda_2 + (X'Q_3X)/\lambda_3]^{-1} \\ &\quad \times [(X'Q_1y)/\sigma_\nu^2 + (X'Q_2y)/\lambda_2 + (X'Q_3y)/\lambda_3] \\ &= [W_{XX} + \phi_2^2 B_{XX} + \phi_3^2 C_{XX}]^{-1}[W_{Xy} + \phi_2^2 B_{Xy} + \phi_3^2 C_{Xy}]\end{aligned} \tag{3.23}$$

with $\text{var}(\widehat{\beta}_{\text{GLS}}) = \sigma_\nu^2[W_{XX} + \phi_2^2 B_{XX} + \phi_3^2 C_{XX}]^{-1}$. Note that $W_{XX} = X'Q_1X$, $B_{XX} = X'Q_2X$ and $C_{XX} = X'Q_3X$ with $\phi_2^2 = \sigma_\nu^2/\lambda_2$, $\phi_3^2 = \sigma_\nu^2/\lambda_3$. Also, the Within estimator of β is $\widetilde{\beta}_{\text{W}} = W_{XX}^{-1}W_{Xy}$, the Between individuals estimator of β is $\widehat{\beta}_{\text{B}} = B_{XX}^{-1}B_{Xy}$ and the Between time periods estimator of β is $\widehat{\beta}_{\text{C}} = C_{XX}^{-1}C_{Xy}$. This shows that $\widehat{\beta}_{\text{GLS}}$ is a matrix-weighted average of $\widetilde{\beta}_{\text{W}}$, $\widehat{\beta}_{\text{B}}$ and $\widehat{\beta}_{\text{C}}$. In fact

$$\widehat{\beta}_{\text{GLS}} = W_1\widetilde{\beta}_{\text{W}} + W_2\widehat{\beta}_{\text{B}} + W_3\widehat{\beta}_{\text{C}} \tag{3.24}$$

where

$$\begin{aligned}W_1 &= [W_{XX} + \phi_2^2 B_{XX} + \phi_3^2 C_{XX}]^{-1} W_{XX} \\ W_2 &= [W_{XX} + \phi_2^2 B_{XX} + \phi_3^2 C_{XX}]^{-1}(\phi_2^2 B_{XX}) \\ W_3 &= [W_{XX} + \phi_2^2 B_{XX} + \phi_3^2 C_{XX}]^{-1}(\phi_3^2 C_{XX})\end{aligned}$$

This was demonstrated by Maddala (1971). Note that (i) if $\sigma_\mu^2 = \sigma_\lambda^2 = 0$, $\phi_2^2 = \phi_3^2 = 1$ and $\widehat{\beta}_{\text{GLS}}$ reduces to $\widehat{\beta}_{\text{OLS}}$; (ii) as T and $N \to \infty$, ϕ_2^2 and $\phi_3^2 \to 0$ and $\widehat{\beta}_{\text{GLS}}$ tends to $\widetilde{\beta}_{\text{W}}$; (iii) if $\phi_2^2 \to \infty$ with ϕ_3^2 finite, then $\widehat{\beta}_{\text{GLS}}$ tends to $\widehat{\beta}_{\text{B}}$; (iv) if $\phi_3^2 \to \infty$ with ϕ_2^2 finite, then $\widehat{\beta}_{\text{GLS}}$ tends to $\widehat{\beta}_{\text{C}}$.

Wallace and Hussain (1969) compare $\widehat{\beta}_{\text{GLS}}$ and $\widetilde{\beta}_{\text{Within}}$ in the case of nonstochastic (repetitive) X and find that both are (i) asymptotically normal, (ii) consistent and unbiased and that (iii) $\widehat{\beta}_{\text{GLS}}$ has a smaller generalized variance (i.e. more efficient) in finite samples. In the case of nonstochastic (nonrepetitive) X they find that both $\widehat{\beta}_{\text{GLS}}$ and $\widetilde{\beta}_{\text{Within}}$ are consistent, asymptotically unbiased and have equivalent asymptotic variance–covariance matrices, as both N and $T \to \infty$. The last statement can be proved as follows: the limiting variance of the GLS estimator is

$$\frac{1}{NT}\lim_{\substack{N\to\infty\\T\to\infty}}(X'\Omega^{-1}X/NT)^{-1} = \frac{1}{NT}\lim_{\substack{N\to\infty\\T\to\infty}}\left[\sum_{i=1}^{3}\frac{1}{\lambda_i}(X'Q_iX/NT)\right]^{-1} \tag{3.25}$$

But the limit of the inverse is the inverse of the limit, and

$$\lim_{\substack{N\to\infty\\T\to\infty}}\frac{X'Q_iX}{NT} \quad \text{for } i = 1, 2, 3 \tag{3.26}$$

all exist and are positive semidefinite, since $\lim_{\substack{N\to\infty\\T\to\infty}}(X'X/NT)$ is assumed finite and positive definite. Hence

$$\lim_{\substack{N\to\infty\\T\to\infty}}\frac{1}{(N\sigma_\lambda^2 + \sigma_\nu^2)}\left(\frac{X'Q_3X}{NT}\right) = 0$$

and

$$\lim_{\substack{N\to\infty\\T\to\infty}} \frac{1}{(T\sigma_\mu^2+\sigma_\nu^2)}\left(\frac{X'Q_2X}{NT}\right)=0$$

Therefore the limiting variance of the GLS estimator becomes

$$\frac{1}{NT}\lim_{\substack{N\to\infty\\T\to\infty}} \sigma_\nu^2\left(\frac{X'Q_1X}{NT}\right)^{-1}$$

which is the limiting variance of the Within estimator.

One can extend Nerlove's (1971a) method for the one-way model by estimating $\widehat{\sigma_\mu^2}$ as $\sum_{i=1}^N(\widehat{\mu}_i-\overline{\widehat{\mu}})^2/(N-1)$ and σ_λ^2 as $\sum_{t=1}^T(\widehat{\lambda}_t-\overline{\widehat{\lambda}})^2/(T-1)$ where the $\widehat{\mu}_i$ and $\widehat{\lambda}_t$ are obtained as coefficients from the least squares dummy variables regression (LSDV). σ_ν^2 is estimated from the Within residual sums of squares divided by NT. Baltagi (1995b, Appendix 3) develops two other methods of estimating the variance components. The first is Rao's (1970) minimum norm quadratic unbiased estimation (MINQUE) and the second is Henderson's method III as described by Fuller and Battese (1973). These methods require more notation and development and may be skipped in a brief course on this subject. Chapter 9 studies these estimation methods in the context of an unbalanced error component model.

Baltagi (1981a) performed a Monte Carlo study on a simple regression equation with two-way error component disturbances and studied the properties of the following estimators: ordinary least squares (OLS), the Within estimator, and six feasible GLS estimators denoted by WALHUS, AMEMIYA, SWAR, MINQUE, FUBA and NERLOVE corresponding to the methods developed by Wallace and Hussain (1969), Amemiya (1971), Swamy and Arora (1972), Rao (1972), Fuller and Battese (1974) and Nerlove (1971a), respectively. The mean square error (MSE) of these estimators was computed relative to that of true GLS, i.e. GLS knowing the true variance components.

To review some of the properties of these estimators: OLS is unbiased, but asymptotically inefficient, and its standard errors are biased; see Moulton (1986) for the extent of this bias in empirical applications. In contrast, the Within estimator is unbiased whether or not prior information about the variance components is available. It is also asymptotically equivalent to the GLS estimator in case of weakly nonstochastic exogenous variables. Early in the literature, Wallace and Hussain (1969) recommended the Within estimator for the practical researcher, based on theoretical considerations but more importantly for its ease of computation. In Wallace and Hussain's (1969, p. 66) words the "covariance estimators come off with a surprisingly clear bill of health". True GLS is BLUE, but the variance components are usually not known and have to be estimated. All of the feasible GLS estimators considered are asymptotically efficient. In fact, Prucha (1984) showed that as long as the estimate of σ_ν^2 is consistent, and the probability limits of the estimates σ_μ^2 and σ_λ^2 are finite, the corresponding feasible GLS estimator is asymptotically efficient. Also, Swamy and Arora (1972) proved the existence of a family of asymptotically efficient two-stage feasible GLS estimators of the regression coefficients. Therefore, based on asymptotics only, one cannot differentiate among these two-stage GLS estimators. This leaves undecided the question of which estimator is the best to use. Some analytical results were obtained by Swamy (1971) and Swamy and Arora (1972). These studies derived the relative efficiencies of (i) SWAR with respect to OLS, (ii) SWAR with respect to Within, and (iii) Within with respect to OLS. Then, for various values of N, T, the variance components, the Between groups, Between time periods and Within groups sums of squares of the independent variable, they tabulated these relative efficiency values (see Swamy, 1971, Chapters II and III; Swamy and Arora, 1972, p. 272). Among their basic findings is the fact that, for small samples, SWAR is less efficient than OLS if σ_μ^2 and σ_λ^2 are small. Also, SWAR is less efficient than Within if σ_μ^2 and σ_λ^2 are large. The latter result is disconcerting, since Within which uses only a part of the available data is more efficient than SWAR, a feasible GLS estimator, which uses all of the available data.

3.3.1 Design of the Experiment

Baltagi (1981a) considered the following simple regression equation:

$$y_{it} = \alpha + \beta x_{it} + u_{it} \tag{3.27}$$

with

$$u_{it} = \mu_i + \lambda_t + \nu_{it} \quad i = 1, \ldots, N; \; t = 1, \ldots, T \tag{3.28}$$

The exogenous variable x was generated by a similar method to that of Nerlove (1971a). Throughout the experiment $\alpha = 5, \beta = 0.5, N = 25, T = 10$ and $\sigma^2 = 20$. However, $\rho = \sigma_\mu^2/\sigma^2$ and $\omega = \sigma_\lambda^2/\sigma^2$ were varied over the set $(0, 0.01, 0.2, 0.4, 0.6, 0.8)$ such that $(1 - \rho - \omega)$ is always positive. In each experiment 100 replications were performed. For every replication $(NT + N + T)$ independent and identically distributed normal IIN(0, 1) random numbers were generated. The first N numbers were used to generate the μ_i as $\text{IIN}(0, \sigma_\mu^2)$. The second T numbers were used to generate the λ_t as $\text{IIN}(0, \sigma_\lambda^2)$. The last NT numbers were used to generate the ν_{it} as $\text{IIN}(0, \sigma_\nu^2)$. For the estimation methods considered, the Monte Carlo results show the following:

(1) For the two-way model, the researcher should not label the problem of negative variance estimates "not serious" as in the one-way model. This is because we cannot distinguish between the case where the model is misspecified (i.e. with at least one of the variance components actually equal to zero) and the case where the model is properly specified (i.e. with at least one of the variance components relatively small but different from zero). Another important reason is that we may not be able to distinguish between a case where OLS is equivalent to GLS according to the MSE criterion and a case where it is not. For these cases, the practical solution seems to be the replacement of a negative estimate by zero. Of course, this will affect the properties of the variance components estimates, especially if the actual variances are different from zero. The Monte Carlo results

of Baltagi (1981a) report that the performance of the two-stage GLS methods is not seriously affected by this substitution.

(2) As long as the variance components are not relatively small and close to zero, there is always gain according to the MSE criterion in performing feasible GLS rather than least squares or least squares with dummy variables.

(3) All the two-stage GLS methods considered performed reasonably well according to the relative MSE criteria. However, none of these methods could claim to be the best for all the experiments performed. Most of these methods had relatively close MSEs which therefore made it difficult to choose among them. This same result was obtained in the one-way model by Maddala and Mount (1973).

(4) Better estimates of the variance components do not necessarily give better second-round estimates of the regression coefficients. This confirms the finite sample results obtained by Taylor (1980) and extends them from the one-way to the two-way model.[4]

Finally, the recommendation given in Maddala and Mount (1973) is still valid, i.e. always perform more than one of the two-stage GLS procedures to see whether the estimates obtained differ widely.

3.4 MAXIMUM LIKELIHOOD ESTIMATION

In this case, the normality assumption is needed on our error structure. The log-likelihood function is given by

$$\log L = \text{constant} - \frac{1}{2}\log|\Omega| - \frac{1}{2}(y - Z\gamma)'\Omega^{-1}(y - Z\gamma) \tag{3.29}$$

where Ω and Ω^{-1} were given in (3.13) and (3.14). The maximum likelihood estimators of $\gamma, \sigma_\nu^2, \sigma_\mu^2$ and σ_λ^2 are obtained by simultaneously solving the following normal equations:

$$\begin{aligned}
\frac{\partial \log L}{\partial \gamma} &= Z'\Omega^{-1}y - (Z'\Omega^{-1}Z)\gamma = 0 \\
\frac{\partial \log L}{\partial \sigma_\nu^2} &= -\frac{1}{2}\,\text{tr}\,\Omega^{-1} + \frac{1}{2}u'\Omega^{-2}u = 0 \\
\frac{\partial \log L}{\partial \sigma_\mu^2} &= -\frac{1}{2}\,\text{tr}\,\Omega^{-1}(I_N \otimes J_T) + \frac{1}{2}u'\Omega^{-2}(I_N \otimes J_T)u = 0 \\
\frac{\partial \log L}{\partial \sigma_\lambda^2} &= -\frac{1}{2}\,\text{tr}\,\Omega^{-1}(J_N \otimes I_T) + \frac{1}{2}u'\Omega^{-2}(J_N \otimes I_T)u = 0
\end{aligned} \tag{3.30}$$

Even if the u were observable, these would still be highly nonlinear and difficult to solve explicitly. However, Amemiya (1971) suggests an iterative scheme to solve (3.30). The resulting maximum likelihood estimates of the variance components are shown to be consistent and asymptotic normal with an asymptotic distribution given by (3.18).

Following Breusch (1987) one can write the likelihood for the two-way model as

$$L(\alpha, \beta, \sigma_v^2, \phi_2^2, \phi_3^2) = \text{constant} \; - (NT/2)\log\sigma_v^2 + (N/2)\log\phi_2^2 + (T/2)\log\phi_3^2$$
$$-(1/2)\log[\phi_2^2 + \phi_3^2 - \phi_2^2\phi_3^2] - (1/2\sigma_v^2)u'\Sigma^{-1}u \qquad (3.31)$$

where $\Omega = \sigma_v^2\Sigma = \sigma_v^2(\sum_{i=1}^4 Q_i/\phi_i^2)$ from (3.13) with $\phi_i^2 = \sigma_v^2/\lambda_i$ for $i = 1, \ldots, 4$. The likelihood (3.31) uses the fact that $|\Omega|^{-1} = (\sigma_v^2)^{-NT}(\phi_2^2)^{N-1}(\phi_3^2)^{T-1}\phi_4^2$. The feasibility conditions $\infty > \lambda_i \geqslant \sigma_v^2$ are equivalent to $0 < \phi_i^2 \leqslant 1$ for $i = 1, 2, 3, 4$. Following Breusch (1987), we define $d = y - X\beta$, therefore $u = d - \iota_{NT}\alpha$. Given arbitrary values of β, ϕ_2^2, ϕ_3^2, one can concentrate this likelihood function with respect to α and σ_v^2. Estimates of α and σ_v^2 are obtained later as $\widehat{\alpha} = \iota'_{NT}d/NT$ and $\widehat{\sigma}_v^2 = (u'\Sigma^{-1}u/NT)$. Substituting the maximum value of α in u one gets $u = d - \iota_{NT}\widehat{\alpha} = (I_{NT} - \bar{J}_{NT})d$. Also, using the fact that

$$(I_{NT} - \bar{J}_{NT})\Sigma^{-1}(I_{NT} - \bar{J}_{NT}) = Q_1 + \phi_2^2 Q_2 + \phi_3^2 Q_3$$

one gets $\widehat{\sigma}_v^2 = d'[Q_1 + \phi_2^2 Q_2 + \phi_3^2 Q_3]d/NT$, given β, ϕ_2^2 and ϕ_3^2. The concentrated likelihood function becomes

$$L_C(\beta, \phi_2^2, \phi_3^2) = \text{constant} \; - (NT/2)\log[d'(Q_1 + \phi_2^2 Q_2 + \phi_3^2 Q_3)d]$$
$$+(N/2)\log\phi_2^2 + (T/2)\log\phi_3^2 \qquad (3.32)$$
$$-(1/2)\log[\phi_2^2 + \phi_3^2 - \phi_2^2\phi_3^2]$$

Maximizing L_C over β, given ϕ_2^2 and ϕ_3^2, Baltagi and Li (1992b) get

$$\widehat{\beta} = [X'(Q_1 + \phi_2^2 Q_2 + \phi_3^2 Q_3)X]^{-1}X'(Q_1 + \phi_2^2 Q_2 + \phi_3^2 Q_3)y \qquad (3.33)$$

which is the GLS estimator knowing ϕ_2^2 and ϕ_3^2. Similarly, maximizing L_C over ϕ_2^2, given β and ϕ_3^2, one gets[5]

$$\frac{\partial L_C}{\partial \phi_2^2} = -\frac{NT}{2}\frac{d'Q_2 d}{d'[Q_1 + \phi_2^2 Q_2 + \phi_3^2 Q_3]d} + \frac{N}{2}\frac{1}{\phi_2^2} - \frac{1}{2}\frac{(1-\phi_3^2)}{[\phi_2^2 + \phi_3^2 - \phi_2^2\phi_3^2]} = 0 \qquad (3.34)$$

which can be written as

$$a\phi_2^4 + b\phi_2^2 + c = 0 \qquad (3.35)$$

where $a = -[N(T-1)+1](1-\phi_3^2)(d'Q_2 d)$, $b = (1-\phi_3^2)(N-1)d'[Q_1 + \phi_3^2 Q_3]d - \phi_3^2(T-1)N(d'Q_2 d)$ and $c = N\phi_3^2 d'[Q_1 + \phi_3^2 Q_3]d$. We will *fix* ϕ_3^2, where $0 < \phi_3^2 < 1$ and focus on iterating between β and ϕ_2^2.[6] For a fixed ϕ_3^2, if $\phi_2^2 = 0$, then (3.33) becomes $\widehat{\beta}_{\text{BW}} = [X'(Q_1 + \phi_3^2 Q_3)X]^{-1}X'(Q_1 + \phi_3^2 Q_3)y$, which is a matrix-weighted average of the Within estimator $\widehat{\beta}_{\text{W}} = (X'Q_1X)^{-1}X'Q_1y$ and the Between time periods estimator $\widehat{\beta}_{\text{C}} = (X'Q_3X)^{-1}X'Q_3y$. If $\phi_2^2 \to \infty$, with ϕ_3^2 fixed, then (3.33) reduces to the Between individuals estimator $\widehat{\beta}_{\text{B}} = (X'Q_2X)^{-1}X'Q_2y$. Using standard assumptions, Baltagi and Li (1992b) show that $a < 0$ and $c > 0$ in (3.35). Hence $b^2 - 4ac > b^2 > 0$, and the unique positive root of (3.35) is

$$\widehat{\phi}_2^2 = \left[-b - \sqrt{b^2 - 4ac}\right]/2a = \left[b + \sqrt{b^2 + 4|a|c}\right]/2|a| \tag{3.36}$$

Since ϕ_3^2 is fixed, we let $\bar{Q}_1 = Q_1 + \phi_3^2 Q_3$, then (3.33) becomes

$$\widehat{\beta} = [X'(\bar{Q}_1 + \phi_2^2 Q_2)X]^{-1} X'(\bar{Q}_1 + \phi_2^2 Q_2)y \tag{3.37}$$

Iterated GLS can be obtained through the successive application of (3.36) and (3.37). Baltagi and Li (1992b) show that the update of $\phi_2^2(i+1)$ in the $(i+1)$th iteration will be positive and finite even if the initial $\beta(i)$ value is $\widehat{\beta}_{\text{BW}}$ (from $\phi_2^2(i) = 0$) or $\widehat{\beta}_{\text{B}}$ (from the limit as $\phi_2^2(i) \to \infty$). More importantly, Breusch's (1987) "remarkable property" extends to the two-way error component model in the sense that the ϕ_2^2 form a monotonic sequence. Therefore, if one starts with $\widehat{\beta}_{\text{BW}}$, which corresponds to $\phi_2^2 = 0$, the sequence of ϕ_2^2 is strictly increasing. On the other hand, starting with $\widehat{\beta}_{\text{B}}$, which corresponds to $\phi_2^2 \to \infty$, the sequence of ϕ_2^2 is strictly decreasing. This remarkable property allows the applied researcher to check for the possibility of multiple local maxima. For a fixed ϕ_3^2, starting with *both* $\widehat{\beta}_{\text{BW}}$ and $\widehat{\beta}_{\text{B}}$ as initial values, there is a single maximum if and only if both sequences of iterations converge to the same ϕ_2^2 estimate.[7] Since this result holds for any arbitrary ϕ_3^2 between zero and one, a search over ϕ_3^2 in this range will guard against multiple local maxima.

The problem with the above search procedure is that it is relatively costly. Baltagi and Li (1992b) propose another computationally more efficient algorithm. This can be summarized as follows:

Step 1: Using an initial value for ϕ_2^2, obtain the convergent $(\widehat{\phi}_3^2, \widehat{\beta})$ using Breusch's monotonic algorithm.

Step 2: Compute $\widehat{\phi}_2^2$ from (3.36) using the values of $(\widehat{\phi}_3^2, \widehat{\beta})$ from Step 1.

Step 3: Iterate until convergence. Since this procedure maximizes the likelihood at each step, it will converge to a local maximum. Additionally, one can reverse the roles of $\widehat{\phi}_3^2$ and $\widehat{\phi}_2^2$ in this algorithm. In practice, one should try it both ways to ensure that the same answer is obtained.

3.5 PREDICTION

How does the best linear unbiased predictor (BLUP) look for the ith individual, S periods ahead for the two-way model? From (3.1), for period $T+S$

$$u_{i,T+S} = \mu_i + \lambda_{T+S} + \nu_{i,T+S} \tag{3.38}$$

and

$$\begin{aligned} E(u_{i,T+S}u_{jt}) &= \sigma_\mu^2 \quad \text{for } i = j \\ &= 0 \quad\ \ \text{for } i \neq j \end{aligned} \tag{3.39}$$

and $t = 1, 2, \ldots, T$. Hence, for the BLUP given in (2.37), $w = E(u_{i,T+S}u) = \sigma_\mu^2(l_i \otimes \iota_T)$ remains the same where l_i is the ith column of I_N. However, Ω^{-1} is given by (3.14) and

$$w'\Omega^{-1} = \sigma_\mu^2(l_i' \otimes \iota_T')\left[\sum_{i=1}^{4} \frac{1}{\lambda_i} Q_i\right] \tag{3.40}$$

Using the fact that

$$\begin{aligned} (l_i' \otimes \iota_T')Q_1 &= 0 \qquad (l_i' \otimes \iota_T')Q_2 = (l_i' \otimes \iota_T') - \iota_{NT}'/N \\ (l_i' \otimes \iota_T')Q_3 &= 0 \qquad (l_i' \otimes \iota_T')Q_4 = \iota_{NT}'/N \end{aligned} \tag{3.41}$$

one gets

$$w'\Omega^{-1} = \frac{\sigma_\mu^2}{\lambda_2}[(l_i' \otimes \iota_T') - \iota_{NT}'/N] + \frac{\sigma_\mu^2}{\lambda_4}(\iota_{NT}'/N) \tag{3.42}$$

Therefore, the typical element of $w'\Omega^{-1}\widehat{u}_{\text{GLS}}$ where $\widehat{u}_{\text{GLS}} = y - Z\widehat{\delta}_{\text{GLS}}$ is

$$\frac{T\sigma_\mu^2}{(T\sigma_\mu^2 + \sigma_\nu^2)}(\overline{\widehat{u}}_{i.,\text{GLS}} - \overline{\widehat{u}}_{..,\text{GLS}}) + \frac{T\sigma_\mu^2}{(T\sigma_\mu^2 + N\sigma_\lambda^2 + \sigma_\nu^2)}\overline{\widehat{u}}_{..,\text{GLS}} \tag{3.43}$$

or

$$\frac{T\sigma_\mu^2}{(T\sigma_\mu^2 + \sigma_\nu^2)}\overline{\widehat{u}}_{i.,\text{GLS}} + T\sigma_\mu^2\left[\frac{1}{\lambda_4} - \frac{1}{\lambda_2}\right]\overline{\widehat{u}}_{..,\text{GLS}}$$

where $\overline{\widehat{u}}_{i.,\text{GLS}} = \sum_{t=1}^{T} \widehat{u}_{it,\text{GLS}}/T$ and $\overline{\widehat{u}}_{..,\text{GLS}} = \sum_i \sum_t \widehat{u}_{it,\text{GLS}}/NT$. See problem 88.1.1 in *Econometric Theory* by Baltagi (1988a) and its solution 88.1.1 by Koning (1989). In general, $\overline{\widehat{u}}_{..,\text{GLS}}$ is not necessarily zero. The GLS normal equations are $Z'\Omega^{-1}\widehat{u}_{\text{GLS}} = 0$. However, if Z contains a constant, then $\iota_{NT}'\Omega^{-1}\widehat{u}_{\text{GLS}} = 0$, and using the fact that $\iota_{NT}'\Omega^{-1} = \iota_{NT}'/\lambda_4$ from (3.14), one gets $\overline{\widehat{u}}_{..,\text{GLS}} = 0$. Hence, for the two-way model, if there is a constant in the model, the BLUP for $y_{i,T+S}$ corrects the GLS prediction by a fraction of the mean of the GLS residuals corresponding to that ith individual:

$$\widehat{y}_{i,T+S} = Z_{i,T+S}'\widehat{\delta}_{\text{GLS}} + \left(\frac{T\sigma_\mu^2}{T\sigma_\mu^2 + \sigma_\nu^2}\right)\overline{\widehat{u}}_{i.,\text{GLS}} \tag{3.44}$$

This looks exactly like the BLUP for the one-way model but with a different Ω. If there is no constant in the model, the last term in (3.44) should be replaced by (3.43).

3.6 EXAMPLES

3.6.1 Example 1

For Grunfeld's (1958) example considered in Chapter 2, the investment equation is estimated using a two-way error component model. Table 3.1 gives OLS, Within, four feasible GLS estimates and the iterative MLE for the slope

Table 3.1 Grunfeld's Data. Two-way Error Component Results

	β_1	β_2	θ_1	θ_2	θ_3
OLS	0.116	0.231	0	0	0
	(0.006)*	(0.025)*			
Within	0.118	0.358	1	1	1
	(0.014)	(0.023)			
WALHUS	0.110	0.308	0.843	0	0
	(0.010)	(0.017)			
AMEMIYA	0.112	0.325	0.875	0.297	0.296
	(0.011)	(0.019)			
SWAR	0.110	0.308	0.864	0	0
	(0.011)	(0.017)			
NERLOVE	0.113	0.334	0.885	0.455	0.453
	(0.011)	(0.020)			
IMLE	0.110	0.309	0.856	0.026	0.026
	(0.010)	(0.017)			

*These are biased standard errors when the true model has error component disturbances (see Moulton, 1986)

coefficients. The Within estimator yields a $\widetilde{\beta}_1$ estimate at 0.118 (0.014) and a $\widetilde{\beta}_2$ estimate at 0.358 (0.023). Both SWAR and WALHUS report negative estimates of σ_λ^2 which in turn yield $\theta_2 = \theta_3 = 0$. These estimates are different from OLS because $\widehat{\sigma}_\mu^2 \neq 0$. The iterative maximum likelihood method yields a $\widehat{\beta}_1$ estimate at 0.110 (0.010) and a $\widehat{\beta}_2$ estimate at 0.309 (0.017). A search procedure yields a maximum value of the log-likelihood of -1341.293 obtained at $\widehat{\phi_2^2} = 0.02$ and $\widehat{\phi_3^2} = 0.95$. This search procedure guards against local maxima, but is relatively costly. Applying the algorithm described above, the procedure converged at $\widehat{\phi_2^2} = 0.021$ and $\widehat{\phi_3^2} = 0.948$ after 13 iterations (starting from $\phi_3^2 = 1$) and 28 iterations (starting from $\phi_2^2 = 0$).

3.6.2 Example 2

For the motor gasoline data in Baltagi and Griffin (1983) considered in Chapter 2, the gasoline demand equation is estimated using a two-way error component model. Table 3.2 gives OLS, Within, four feasible GLS estimates and iterative MLE for the slope coefficients. The Within estimator is drastically different from OLS. The WALHUS and SWAR methods yield negative estimates of σ_λ^2 and iterative MLE yields $\widehat{\phi_2^2} = 0.0027$ and $\widehat{\phi_3^2} = 0.0399$ after 13 iterations.

3.6.3 Example 3

For the Munnell (1990) public capital data considered by Baltagi and Pinnoi (1995) in Chapter 2, the Cobb–Douglas production function is estimated using a two-way error component model. Table 3.3 gives OLS, Within and four feasible GLS estimates of the slope coefficients. With the exception of OLS, estimates of

Table 3.2 Gasoline Demand Data. Two-way Error Component Results

	β_1	β_2	β_3	θ_1	θ_2	θ_3
OLS	0.889	−0.892	−0.763	0	0	0
	(0.036)*	(0.030)*	(0.019)*			
Within	0.051	−0.193	−0.593	1	1	1
	(0.091)	(0.043)	(0.028)			
WALHUS	0.543	−0.467	−0.606	0.852	0	0
	(0.055)	(0.039)	(0.024)			
AMEMIYA	0.168	−0.232	−0.602	0.957	0.857	0.855
	(0.080)	(0.041)	(0.026)			
SWAR	0.565	−0.405	−0.609	0.905	0	0
	(0.061)	(0.040)	(0.026)			
NERLOVE	0.157	−0.228	−0.602	0.959	0.866	0.864
	(0.081)	(0.041)	(0.026)			
IMLE	0.230	−0.254	−0.606	0.948	0.800	0.799
	(0.078)	(0.041)	(0.026)			

*These are biased standard errors when the true model has error component disturbances (see Moulton, 1986)

Table 3.3 Public Capital Productivity Data. Two-way Error Component Results

	β_1	β_2	β_3	β_4	θ_1	θ_2	θ_3
OLS	0.155	0.309	0.594	−0.007	0	0	0
	(0.017)*	(0.010)*	(0.014)*	(0.001)*			
Within	−0.030	0.169	0.769	−0.004	1	1	1
	(0.027)	(0.028)	(0.028)	(0.001)			
WALHUS	0.028	0.260	0.738	−0.005	0.890	0.696	0.690
	(0.023)	(0.021)	(0.023)	(0.001)			
AMEMIYA	0.002	0.216	0.770	−0.004	0.947	0.816	0.814
	(0.025)	(0.024)	(0.026)	(0.001)			
SWAR	0.018	0.266	0.745	−0.005	0.900	0.551	0.549
	(0.023)	(0.021)	(0.024)	(0.001)			
NERLOVE	0.0005	0.213	0.771	−0.004	0.949	0.826	0.824
	(0.025)	(0.025)	(0.026)	(0.001)			

*These are biased standard errors when the true model has error component disturbances (see Moulton, 1986)

the public capital coefficient are insignificant in this production function. Also, none of the feasible GLS estimators yield negative estimates of the variance components.

3.7 SELECTED APPLICATIONS

(1) Chang (1979) used the two-way error component model to study the determinants of cotton textile industry location in the USA using a panel of 12 states that reported active cotton-system spindles over the period 1951–60.

(2) For an application of the two-way fixed effects model to a study of the effects of foreign aid on public sector budgets of 46 developing countries observed over the period 1975–80, see Cashel-Cordo and Craig (1990).

(3) For an application of the two-way random effects model to study the determinants of secondary market prices for developing country syndicated loans, see Boehmer and Megginson (1990). Their panel consisted of 10 countries observed over 32 months beginning in July 1985 and ending in July 1988.

(4) Carpenter, Fazzari and Petersen (1998) estimate a two-way fixed effects model to provide evidence of the importance of the firm's financing constraints in explaining the dramatic cycles in inventory investments. Using quarterly firm panel data obtained from the Compustat tapes, they conclude that cash flow is much more successful than cash stocks or coverage in explaining inventory investment across firm size, different inventory cycles and different manufacturing sectors.

NOTES

1. The random effects model across time and individuals could be justified using Haavelmo's (1944) views, discussed in Chapter 2.
2. These characteristic roots and eigenprojectors were first derived by Nerlove (1971b) for the two-way error component model. More details are given in Appendix 1.
3. This transformation was first derived by Fuller and Battese (1974). See also Baltagi (1993b).
4. At two crucial choices of the explanatory variable, one where OLS is least efficient with respect to GLS and another where an arbitrary feasible GLS is least efficient with respect to GLS, Baltagi (1990) shows that a better guess of a certain variance components ratio leads to better estimates of the regression coefficients.
5. Alternatively, one can maximize L_C over ϕ_3^2, given β and ϕ_2^2. The results are symmetric and are left as an exercise. In fact, one can show (see problem 3.6) that ϕ_3^2 will satisfy a quadratic equation like (3.35) with N exchanging places with T, ϕ_2^2 replacing ϕ_3^2 and Q_2 exchanging places with Q_3 in a, b and c, respectively.
6. The case where $\phi_3^2 = 1$ corresponds to $\sigma_\lambda^2 = 0$, i.e. the one-way error component model where Breusch's (1987) results apply.
7. There will be no local maximum interior to $0 < \phi_2^2 \leqslant 1$ if starting from $\widehat{\beta}_{\mathrm{BW}}$ we violate the non-negative variance component requirement, $\phi_2^2 \leqslant 1$. In this case, one should set $\phi_2^2 = 1$.

PROBLEMS

3.1 (a) Prove that the Within estimator $\widetilde{\beta} = (X'QX)^{-1}X'Qy$ with Q defined in (3.3) can be obtained from OLS on the panel regression model (2.3) with disturbances defined in (3.2). Hint: Use the Frisch–Waugh–Lovell theorem of Davidson and MacKinnon (1993, p. 19). Also, the generalized inverse matrix result given in problem 9.6.

(b) *Within two-way is equivalent to two Withins one-way*. This is based on problem 98.5.2 in *Econometric Theory* by Baltagi (1998). Show that the Within two-way estimator of β can be obtained by applying two Within (one-way) transformations. The first is the Within transformation ignoring the time effects followed by the Within transformation ignoring the individual effects. Show that the order of these two Within (one-way) transformations is unimportant. Give an intuitive explanation for this result. See solution 98.5.2 in *Econometric Theory* by Li (1999).

3.2 (a) Using the generalized inverse, show that OLS or GLS on (2.6) with Q defined in (3.3) yields $\widetilde{\beta}$, the Within estimator.
(b) Show that (2.6) with Q defined in (3.3) satisfies the necessary and sufficient condition for OLS to be equivalent to GLS (see Baltagi, 1989b).

3.3 (a) Verify (3.10) and (3.13) and check that $\Omega^{-1}\Omega = I$ using (3.14).
(b) Verify that $\Omega^{-1/2}\Omega^{-1/2} = \Omega^{-1}$ using (3.14).
(c) Premultiply y by $\sigma_\nu \Omega^{-1/2}$ from (3.15) and show that the typical element is given by (3.16).

3.4 (a) Perform OLS on the system of equations given in (3.22) and show that the resulting estimate is $\widehat{\beta}_{\text{OLS}} = [X(I_{NT} - \bar{J}_{NT})X]^{-1}X'(I_{NT} - \bar{J}_{NT})y$.
(b) Perform GLS on this system of equations and show that $\widehat{\beta}_{\text{GLS}}$ reduces to the expression given by (3.23).

3.5 Show that the Swamy and Arora (1972) estimators of λ_1, λ_2 and λ_3 given by (3.19), (3.20) and (3.21) are unbiased for σ_ν^2, λ_2 and λ_3, respectively.

3.6 (a) Using the concentrated likelihood function in (3.32), solve $\partial L_C/\partial\beta = 0$, given ϕ_2^2 and ϕ_3^2, and verify (3.33).
(b) Solve $\partial L_C/\partial\phi_2^2 = 0$, given ϕ_3^2 and β, and verify (3.34).
(c) Solve $\partial L_C/\partial\phi_3^2 = 0$, given ϕ_2^2 and β, and show that the solution ϕ_3^2 satisfies

$$\overline{a}\phi_3^4 + \overline{b}\phi_3^2 + \overline{c} = 0$$

where

$$\overline{a} = -[T(N-1)+1](1-\phi_2^2)(d'Q_3 d)$$
$$\overline{b} = (1-\phi_2^2)(T-1)d'[Q_1 + \phi_2^2 Q_2]d - \phi_2^2 T(N-1)d'Q_3 d$$

and

$$\overline{c} = T\phi_2^2 d'(Q_1 + \phi_2^2 Q_2)d$$

Note that this is analogous to (3.35), with ϕ_2^2 replacing ϕ_3^2, N replacing T, and Q_2 replacing Q_3 and vice versa, wherever they occur.

3.7 *Predicting* $y_{i,T+S}$.
(a) For the two-way error component model in (3.1), verify (3.39) and (3.42).
(b) Also, show that if there is a constant in the regression $\iota'_{NT}\Omega^{-1}\widehat{u}_{\text{GLS}} = 0$ and $\overline{\widehat{u}}_{..,\text{GLS}} = 0$.

3.8 Using Grunfeld's data, given on the Wiley web site as Grunfeld.fil, reproduce Table 3.1.

3.9 Using the gasoline demand data of Baltagi and Griffin (1983), given as Gasoline.dat on the Wiley web site, reproduce Table 3.2.

3.10 Using the public capital data of Munnell (1990), given as Produc.prn on the Wiley web site, reproduce Table 3.3.

3.11 Using the Monte Carlo setup for the two-way error component model given in (3.27) and (3.28) (see Baltagi, 1981a), compare the various estimators of the variance components and regression coefficients studied in this chapter.

3.12 *Variance component estimation under misspecification.* This is based on problem 91.3.3 in *Econometric Theory* by Baltagi and Li (1991c). This problem investigates the consequences of under- or overspecifying the error component model on the variance components estimates. Since the one-way and two-way error component models are popular in economics, we focus on the following two cases.

(1) *Underspecification*: In this case, the true model is two-way, see (3.1):

$$u_{it} = \mu_i + \lambda_t + \nu_{it} \qquad i = 1, \ldots, N;\ t = 1, \ldots, T$$

while the estimated model is one-way, see (2.2):

$$u_{it} = \mu_i + \nu_{it}$$

$\mu_i \sim \text{IID}(0, \sigma_\mu^2)$, $\lambda_t \sim \text{IID}(0, \sigma_\lambda^2)$, $\nu_{it} \sim \text{IID}(0, \sigma_\nu^2)$ independent of each other and among themselves.

(a) Knowing the true disturbances (u_{it}), show that the BQUE of σ_ν^2 for the misspecified one-way model is biased upwards, while the BQUE of σ_μ^2 remains unbiased.

(b) Show that if the u_{it} are replaced by the one-way least squares dummy variables (LSDV) residuals, the variance component estimate of σ_ν^2 given in part (a) is inconsistent, while that of σ_μ^2 is consistent.

(2) *Overspecification*: In this case, the true model is one-way, given by (2.2), while the estimated model is two-way, given by (3.1).

(c) Knowing the true disturbances (u_{it}), show that the BQUE of σ_μ^2, σ_λ^2 and σ_ν^2 for the misspecified two-way model remain unbiased.

(d) Show that if the u_{it} are replaced by the two-way (LSDV) residuals, the variance components estimates given in part (c) remain consistent. (Hint: See solution 91.3.3 in *Econometric Theory* by Baltagi and Li (1992a). See also Deschamps (1991) who shows that an underspecified error component model yields inconsistent estimates of the coefficient variances.)

3.13 For the random two-way error component model described by (2.1) and (3.1), consider the OLS estimator of $\text{var}(u_{it}) = \sigma^2$, which is given by $s^2 = \widehat{u}'_{\text{OLS}}\widehat{u}_{\text{OLS}}/(n - K')$ where $n = NT$ and $K' = K + 1$.

(a) Show that

$$E(s^2) = \sigma^2 - \sigma_\mu^2[\text{tr}(I_N \otimes J_T)P_x - K']/(n - K')$$
$$-\sigma_\lambda^2[\text{tr}(J_N \otimes I_T)P_x - K']/(n - K')$$

(b) Consider the inequalities given by Kiviet and Krämer (1992) which are reproduced in problem 2.14, part (b). Show that for the two-way error component model, these bounds are given by the following two cases:
(1) For $T\sigma_\mu^2 < N\sigma_\lambda^2$:

$$0 \leqslant \sigma_\nu^2 + \sigma_\mu^2(n-T)/(n-K') + \sigma_\lambda^2(n-NK')/(n-K') \leqslant E(s^2)$$
$$\leqslant \sigma_\nu^2 + \sigma_\mu^2[n/(n-K')] + \sigma_\lambda^2[n/(n-K')] \leqslant \sigma^2(n/(n-K'))$$

(2) For $T\sigma_\mu^2 > N\sigma_\lambda^2$:

$$0 \leqslant \sigma_\nu^2 + \sigma_\mu^2(n-TK')/(n-K') + \sigma_\lambda^2(n-N)/(n-K') \leqslant E(s^2)$$
$$\leqslant \sigma_\nu^2 + \sigma_\mu^2[n/(n-K')] + \sigma_\lambda^2[n/(n-K')] \leqslant \sigma^2(n/(n-K'))$$

In either case, as $n \to \infty$, both bounds tend to σ^2 and s^2 is asymptotically unbiased, irrespective of the particular evolution of X. See Baltagi and Krämer (1994) for a proof of this result.

3.14 *Nested effects*. This is based on problem 93.4.2 in *Econometric Theory* by Baltagi (1993a). In many economic applications, the data may contain nested groupings. For example, data on firms may be grouped by industry, data on states by region and data on individuals by profession. In this case, one can control for unobserved industry and firm effects using a nested error component model. Consider the regression equation

$$y_{ijt} = x'_{ijt}\beta + u_{ijt} \quad \text{for } i = 1, \ldots, M;\; j = 1, \ldots, N;\; t = 1, 2, \ldots, T$$

where y_{ijt} could denote the output of the jth firm in the ith industry for the tth time period. x_{ijt} denotes a vector of k inputs, and the disturbance is given by

$$u_{ijt} = \mu_i + \nu_{ij} + \epsilon_{ijt}$$

where $\mu_i \sim \text{IID}(0, \sigma_\mu^2)$, $\nu_{ij} \sim \text{IID}(0, \sigma_\nu^2)$ and $\epsilon_{ijt} \sim \text{IID}(0, \sigma_\epsilon^2)$, independent of each other and among themselves. This assumes that there are M industries with N firms in each industry observed over T periods.
(1) Derive $\Omega = E(uu')$ and obtain Ω^{-1} and $\Omega^{-1/2}$.
(2) Show that $y^* = \sigma_\epsilon \Omega^{-1/2} y$ has a typical element

$$y^*_{ijt} = (y_{ijt} - \theta_1 \bar{y}_{ij.} + \theta_2 \bar{y}_{i..})$$

where $\theta_1 = 1 - (\sigma_\epsilon/\sigma_1)$ with $\sigma_1^2 = (T\sigma_\nu^2 + \sigma_\epsilon^2)$; $\theta_2 = -(\sigma_\epsilon/\sigma_1) + (\sigma_\epsilon/\sigma_2)$ with $\sigma_2^2 = (NT\sigma_\mu^2 + T\sigma_\nu^2 + \sigma_\epsilon^2)$; $\bar{y}_{ij.} = \sum_{t=1}^T y_{ijt}/T$ and $\bar{y}_{i..} = \sum_{j=1}^N \sum_{t=1}^T y_{ijt}/NT$. See solution 93.4.2 in *Econometric Theory* by Xiong (1995).

3.15 Ghosh (1976) considered the following error component model:

$$u_{itq} = \mu_i + \lambda_t + \eta_q + \nu_{itq}$$

where $i = 1, \ldots, N$; $T = 1, \ldots, T$; $q = 1, \ldots, M$. Ghosh (1976) argued that in international or inter-regional studies, there might be two rather than one cross-sectional components; for example, i might denote countries and q might be regions within that country. These four *independent* components are assumed to be random with $\mu_i \sim \text{IID}(0, \sigma_\mu^2)$, $\lambda_t \sim \text{IID}(0, \sigma_\lambda^2)$, $\eta_q \sim \text{IID}(0, \sigma_\eta^2)$ and $\nu_{itq} \sim \text{IID}(0, \sigma_\nu^2)$. Order the observations such that the faster index is q, while the slowest index is t, so that

$$u' = (u_{111}, \ldots, u_{11M}, u_{121}, \ldots, u_{12M}, \ldots, u_{1N1}, \ldots,$$
$$u_{1NM}, \ldots, u_{T11}, \ldots, u_{T1M}, \ldots, u_{TN1}, \ldots, u_{TNM})$$

(a) Show that the error has mean zero and variance–covariance matrix

$$\Omega = E(uu') = \sigma_\nu^2(I_T \otimes I_N \otimes I_M) + \sigma_\lambda^2(I_T \otimes J_N \otimes J_M)$$
$$+ \sigma_\mu^2(J_T \otimes I_N \otimes J_M) + \sigma_\eta^2(J_T \otimes J_N \otimes I_M)$$

(b) Using the Wansbeek and Kapteyn (1982b) trick, show that $\Omega = \sum_{j=1}^{5} \xi_j V_j$ where $\xi_1 = \sigma_\nu^2$, $\xi_2 = NM\sigma_\lambda^2 + \sigma_\nu^2$, $\xi_3 = TM\sigma_\mu^2 + \sigma_\nu^2$, $\xi_4 = NT\sigma_\eta^2 + \sigma_\nu^2$ and $\xi_5 = NM\sigma_\lambda^2 + TM\sigma_\mu^2 + NT\sigma_\eta^2 + \sigma_\nu^2$. Also

$$V_1 = I_T \otimes I_N \otimes I_M - I_T \otimes \bar{J}_N \otimes \bar{J}_M - \bar{J}_T \otimes I_N \otimes \bar{J}_M$$
$$- \bar{J}_T \otimes \bar{J}_N \otimes I_M + 2\bar{J}_T \otimes \bar{J}_N \otimes \bar{J}_M$$
$$V_2 = E_T \otimes \bar{J}_N \otimes \bar{J}_M \quad \text{where} \quad E_T = I_T - \bar{J}_T$$
$$V_3 = \bar{J}_T \otimes E_N \otimes \bar{J}_M$$
$$V_4 = \bar{J}_T \otimes \bar{J}_N \otimes E_M \quad \text{and} \quad V_5 = \bar{J}_T \otimes \bar{J}_N \otimes \bar{J}_M$$

are all symmetric and idempotent and sum to the identity matrix.

(c) Conclude that $\Omega^{-1} = \sum_{j=1}^{5}(1/\xi_j)V_j$, $\sigma_\nu \Omega^{-1/2} = \sum_{j=1}^{5}(\sigma_\nu/\sqrt{\xi_j})V_j$ with the typical element of $\sigma_\nu \Omega^{-1/2}$ being

$$y_{tiq} - \theta_1 \bar{y}_{t..} - \theta_2 \bar{y}_{.i.} - \theta_3 \bar{y}_{..q} - \theta_4 \bar{y}_{...}$$

where the dot indicates a sum over that index and a bar means an average. Here, $\theta_j = 1 - \sigma_\nu/\sqrt{\xi_{j+1}}$ for $j = 1, 2, 3$ while $\theta_4 = \theta_1 + \theta_2 + \theta_3 - 1 + (\sigma_\nu/\sqrt{\xi_5})$.

(d) Show that the BQU estimator of ξ_j is given by $u'V_j u/\text{tr}(V_j)$ for $j = 1, 2, 3, 4$. Show that BQU estimators of $\sigma_\nu^2, \sigma_\mu^2, \sigma_\eta^2$ and σ_λ^2 can be obtained using the one-to-one correspondence between the ξ_j and σ^2.

This problem is based on Baltagi (1987). For a generalization of this four-component model as well as an alternative class of decompositions of the variance–covariance matrix, see Wansbeek and Kapteyn (1982a). More recently, Davis (2001) gave an elegant generalization to the multiway unbalanced error component model, see Chapter 9.

3.16 *A mixed-error component model.* This is based on problem 95.1.4 in *Econometric Theory* by Baltagi and Krämer (1995). Consider the panel data regression equation with a two-way mixed error component model described by (3.1) where the individual specific effects are assumed to be random, with $\mu_i \sim (0, \sigma_\mu^2)$ and $\nu_{it} \sim (0, \sigma_\nu^2)$ independent of each other and among themselves. The time-specific effects, i.e. the λ_t's, are assumed to be fixed parameters to be estimated. In vector form, this can be written as

$$y = X\beta + Z_\lambda \lambda + w \tag{1}$$

where $Z_\lambda = \iota_N \otimes I_T$ and

$$w = Z_\mu \mu + \nu \tag{2}$$

with $Z_\mu = I_N \otimes \iota_T$. By applying the Frisch–Waugh–Lovell (FWL) theorem, one gets

$$Q_\lambda y = Q_\lambda X\beta + Q_\lambda w \tag{3}$$

where $Q_\lambda = E_N \otimes I_T$ with $E_N = I_N - \bar{J}_N$ and $\bar{J}_N = \iota_N \iota_N'/N$. This is the familiar Within time effects transformation, with the typical element of $Q_\lambda y$ being $y_{it} - \bar{y}_{.t}$ and $\bar{y}_{.t} = \sum_{i=1}^N y_{it}/N$. Let $\Omega = E(ww')$, this is the familiar one-way error component variance–covariance matrix given in (2.17).

(a) Show that the GLS estimator of β obtained from (1) by premultiplying by $\Omega^{-1/2}$ first and then applying the FWL theorem yields the same estimator as GLS on (3) using the generalized inverse of $Q_\lambda \Omega Q_\lambda$. This is a special case of a more general result proved by Fiebig, Bartels and Krämer (1996).

(b) Show that pseudo-GLS on (3) using Ω rather than $Q_\lambda \Omega Q_\lambda$ for the variance of the disturbances yields the same estimator of β as found in part (a). In general, pseudo-GLS may not be the same as GLS, but Fiebig, Bartels and Krämer (1996) provided a necessary and sufficient condition for this equivalence that is easy to check in this case. In fact, this amounts to checking whether $X'Q_\lambda \Omega^{-1} Z_\lambda = 0$. See solution 95.1.4 in *Econometric Theory* by Xiong (1996a).

For computational purposes, these results imply that one can perform the Within time effects transformation to wipe out the matrix of time dummies and then do the usual Fuller–Battese (1974) transformation without worrying about the loss in efficiency of not using the proper variance–covariance matrix of the transformed disturbances.

4

Test of Hypotheses with Panel Data

4.1 TESTS FOR POOLABILITY OF THE DATA

The question of whether to pool the data or not naturally arises with panel data. The restricted model is the pooled model given by (2.3) representing a behavioral equation with the same parameters over time and across regions. The unrestricted model, however, is the same behavioral equation but with different parameters across time or across regions. For example, Balestra and Nerlove (1966) considered a dynamic demand equation for natural gas across 36 states over six years. In this case, the question of whether to pool or not to pool boils down to the question of whether the parameters of this demand equation vary from one year to the other over the six years of available data. One can have a behavioral equation whose parameters may vary across regions. For example, Baltagi and Griffin (1983) considered panel data on motor gasoline demand for 18 OECD countries. In this case, one is interested in testing whether the behavioral relationship predicting demand is the same across the 18 OECD countries, i.e. the parameters of the prediction equation do not vary from one country to the other.

These are but two examples of many economic applications where time-series and cross-section data may be pooled. Generally, most economic applications tend to be of the first type, i.e. with a large number of observations on individuals, firms, economic sectors, regions, industries and countries but only over a few time periods. In what follows, we study the tests for the poolability of the data for the case of pooling across regions keeping in mind that the other case of pooling over time can be obtained in a similar fashion.

For the unrestricted model, we have a regression equation for each region given by

$$y_i = Z_i\delta_i + u_i \qquad \text{for } i = 1, 2, \ldots, N \tag{4.1}$$

where $y_i' = (y_{i1}, \ldots, y_{iT})$, $Z_i = [\iota_T, X_i]$ and X_i is $T \times K$. δ_i' is $1 \times (K+1)$ and u_i is $T \times 1$. The important thing to notice is that δ_i is different for every regional equation. We want to test the hypothesis H_0: $\delta_i = \delta$ for all i, so that under H_0

we can write the restricted model given in (4.1) as

$$y = Z\delta + u \tag{4.2}$$

where $Z' = (Z_1', Z_2', \ldots, Z_N')$ and $u' = (u_1', u_2', \ldots, u_N')$. The unrestricted model can also be written as

$$y = \begin{pmatrix} Z_1 & 0 & \ldots & 0 \\ 0 & Z_2 & \ldots & 0 \\ \vdots & & \ddots & \vdots \\ 0 & 0 & \ldots & Z_N \end{pmatrix} \begin{pmatrix} \delta_1 \\ \delta_2 \\ \vdots \\ \delta_N \end{pmatrix} + u = Z^*\delta^* + u \tag{4.3}$$

where $\delta^{*\prime} = (\delta_1', \delta_2', \ldots, \delta_N')$ and $Z = Z^* I^*$ with $I^* = (\iota_N \otimes I_{K'})$, an $NK' \times K'$ matrix, with $K' = K + 1$. Hence the variables in Z are all linear combinations of the variables in Z^*.

4.1.1 Test for Poolability under $u \sim N(0, s^2 I_{NT})$

Assumption 4.1 $u \sim N(0, \sigma^2 I_{NT})$

Under assumption 4.1, the minimum variance unbiased (MVU) estimator for δ in (4.2) is

$$\widehat{\delta}_{\text{OLS}} = \widehat{\delta}_{\text{mle}} = (Z'Z)^{-1}Z'y \tag{4.4}$$

and therefore

$$y = Z\widehat{\delta}_{\text{OLS}} + e \tag{4.5}$$

implying that $e = (I_{NT} - Z(Z'Z)^{-1}Z')y = My = M(Z\delta + u) = Mu$ since $MZ = 0$. Similarly, under assumption 4.1, the MVU for δ_i is given by

$$\widehat{\delta}_{i,\text{OLS}} = \widehat{\delta}_{i,\text{mle}} = (Z_i'Z_i)^{-1}Z_i'y_i \tag{4.6}$$

and therefore

$$y_i = Z_i\widehat{\delta}_{i,\text{OLS}} + e_i \tag{4.7}$$

implying that $e_i = (I_T - Z_i(Z_i'Z_i)^{-1}Z_i')y_i = M_i y_i = M_i(Z_i\delta_i + u_i) = M_i u_i$ since $M_i Z_i = 0$, and this is true for $i = 1, 2, \ldots, N$. Also, let

$$M^* = I_{NT} - Z^*(Z^{*\prime}Z^*)^{-1}Z^{*\prime} = \begin{pmatrix} M_1 & 0 & \ldots & 0 \\ 0 & M_2 & \ldots & 0 \\ \vdots & & \ddots & \vdots \\ 0 & 0 & \ldots & M_N \end{pmatrix}$$

One can easily deduce that $y = Z^*\widehat{\delta}^* + e^*$ with $e^* = M^*y = M^*u$ and $\widehat{\delta}^* = (Z^{*\prime}Z^*)^{-1}Z^{*\prime}y$. Note that both M and M^* are symmetric and idempotent with $MM^* = M^*$. This easily follows since

$$\begin{aligned} Z(Z'Z)^{-1}Z'Z^*(Z^{*\prime}Z^*)^{-1}Z^{*\prime} &= Z(Z'Z)^{-1}I^{*\prime}Z^{*\prime}Z^*(Z^{*\prime}Z^*)^{-1}Z^{*\prime} \\ &= Z(Z'Z)^{-1}Z' \end{aligned}$$

This uses the fact that $Z = Z^*I^*$. Under assumption 4.1, $e'e - e^{*\prime}e^* = u'(M - M^*)u$ and $e^{*\prime}e^* = u'M^*u$ are independent since $(M - M^*)M^* = 0$. Also, both quadratic forms when divided by σ^2 are distributed as χ^2 since $(M - M^*)$ and M^* are idempotent. Dividing these quadratic forms by their respective degrees of freedom and taking their ratio leads to the following test statistic:[1]

$$F_{\text{obs}} = \frac{(e'e - e^{*\prime}e^*)/(\text{tr}(M) - \text{tr}(M^*))}{e^{*\prime}e^*/\text{tr}(M^*)} \tag{4.8}$$

$$F_{\text{obs}} = \frac{(e'e - e_1'e_1 - e_2'e_2 - \cdots - e_N'e_N)/(N-1)K'}{(e_1'e_1 + e_2'e_2 + \cdots + e_N'e_N)/N(T-K')}$$

Under H_0, F_{obs} is distributed as $F((N-1)K', N(T-K'))$. Hence the critical region for this test is defined as

$$\{F_{\text{obs}} > F((N-1)K', NT - NK'; \alpha_0)\}$$

where α_0 denotes the level of significance of the test. This is exactly the Chow test presented by Chow (1960) extended to the case of N linear regressions. Therefore if an economist has reason to believe that assumption 4.1 is true, and wants to pool his data across regions, then it is recommended that he or she test for the poolability of the data using the Chow test given in (4.8). However, for the variance component model, $u \sim (0, \Omega)$ and not $(0, \sigma^2 I_{NT})$. Therefore, even if we assume normality on the disturbances two questions remain. (1) Is the Chow test still the right test to perform when $u \sim N(0, \Omega)$? (2) Does the Chow statistic still have an F-distribution when $u \sim N(0, \Omega)$? The answer to the first question is no, the Chow test given in (4.8) is not the right test to perform. However, as will be shown later, a generalized Chow test will be the right test to perform. As for the second question, it is still relevant to ask because it highlights the problem of economists using the Chow test assuming erroneously that u is $N(0, \sigma^2 I_{NT})$ when in fact it is not. For example, Toyoda (1974), in treating the case where the u_i are heteroskedastic, found that the Chow statistic given by (4.8) has an approximate F-distribution where the degree of freedom of the denominator depends upon the true variances. Hence for specific values of these variances, Toyoda demonstrates how wrong it is to apply the Chow test in case of heteroskedastic variances.

Having posed the two questions above, we can proceed along two lines: the first is to find the approximate distribution of the Chow statistic (4.8) in case $u \sim N(0, \Omega)$ and therefore show how erroneous it is to use the Chow test in this case (this is not pursued in this book). The second route, and the more fruitful, is to derive the right test to perform for pooling the data in case $u \sim N(0, \Omega)$. This is done in the next section.

4.1.2 Test for Poolability under the General Assumption $u \sim N(0, \Omega)$

Assumption 4.2 $u \sim N(0, \Omega)$

In case Ω is known up to a scalar factor, the test statistic employed for the poolability of the data would be simple to derive. All we need to do is transform our model (under both the null and alternative hypotheses) such that the transformed disturbances have a variance of $\sigma^2 I_{NT}$, then apply the Chow test on the transformed model. The latter step is legitimate because the transformed disturbances have homoskedastic variances and the analysis of the previous section applies in full. Given $\Omega = \sigma^2\Sigma$, we premultiply the restricted model given in (4.2) by $\Sigma^{-1/2}$ and call $\Sigma^{-1/2}y = \dot{y}$, $\Sigma^{-1/2}Z = \dot{Z}$ and $\Sigma^{-1/2}u = \dot{u}$. Hence

$$\dot{y} = \dot{Z}\delta + \dot{u} \tag{4.9}$$

with $E(\dot{u}\dot{u}') = \Sigma^{-1/2}E(uu')\Sigma^{-1/2'} = \sigma^2 I_{NT}$. Similarly, we premultiply the unrestricted model given in (4.3) by $\Sigma^{-1/2}$ and call $\Sigma^{-1/2}Z^* = \dot{Z}^*$. Therefore

$$\dot{y} = \dot{Z}^*\delta^* + \dot{u} \tag{4.10}$$

with $E(\dot{u}\dot{u}') = \sigma^2 I_{NT}$.

At this stage, we can test H_0: $\delta_i = \delta$ for every $i = 1, 2, \ldots, N$, simply by using the Chow statistic, only now on the transformed models (4.9) and (4.10) since they satisfy assumption 4.1 of homoskedasticity of the normal disturbances. Note that $\dot{Z} = \dot{Z}^* I^*$ which is simply obtained from $Z = Z^* I^*$ by premultiplying by $\Sigma^{-1/2}$. Defining $\dot{M} = I_{NT} - \dot{Z}(\dot{Z}'\dot{Z})^{-1}\dot{Z}'$ and $\dot{M}^* = I_{NT} - \dot{Z}^*(\dot{Z}^{*\prime}\dot{Z}^*)^{-1}\dot{Z}^{*\prime}$, it is easy to show that $\dot{M}$ and $\dot{M}^*$ are both symmetric, idempotent and such that $\dot{M}\dot{M}^* = \dot{M}^*$. Once again the conditions for lemma 2.2 of Fisher (1970) are satisfied, and the test statistic

$$\dot{F}_{\text{obs}} = \frac{(\dot{e}'\dot{e} - \dot{e}^{*\prime}\dot{e}^*)/(\text{tr}(\dot{M}) - \text{tr}(\dot{M}^*))}{\dot{e}^{*\prime}\dot{e}^*/\text{tr}(\dot{M}^*)} \sim F((N-1)K', N(T-K')) \tag{4.11}$$

where $\dot{e} = \dot{y} - \dot{Z}\hat{\dot{\delta}}_{\text{OLS}}$ and $\hat{\dot{\delta}}_{\text{OLS}} = (\dot{Z}'\dot{Z})^{-1}\dot{Z}'\dot{y}$ implying that $\dot{e} = \dot{M}\dot{y} = \dot{M}\dot{u}$. Similarly, $\dot{e}^* = \dot{y} - \dot{Z}^*\hat{\dot{\delta}}^*_{\text{OLS}}$ and $\hat{\dot{\delta}}^*_{\text{OLS}} = (\dot{Z}^{*\prime}\dot{Z}^*)^{-1}\dot{Z}^{*\prime}\dot{y}$ implying that $\dot{e}^* = \dot{M}^*\dot{y} = \dot{M}^*\dot{u}$. Using the fact that $\dot{M}$ and $\dot{M}^*$ are symmetric and idempotent, we can rewrite (4.11) as

$$\begin{aligned}\dot{F}_{\text{obs}} &= \frac{(\dot{y}'\dot{M}\dot{y} - \dot{y}'\dot{M}^*\dot{y})/(N-1)K'}{\dot{y}'\dot{M}^*\dot{y}/N(T-K')} \\ &= \frac{(y'\Sigma^{-1/2}\dot{M}\Sigma^{-1/2}y - y'\Sigma^{-1/2}\dot{M}^*\Sigma^{-1/2}y)/(N-1)K'}{y'\Sigma^{-1/2}\dot{M}^*\Sigma^{-1/2}y/N(T-K')}\end{aligned} \tag{4.12}$$

But

$$\dot{M} = I_{NT} - \Sigma^{-1/2}Z(Z'\Sigma^{-1}Z)^{-1}Z'\Sigma^{-1/2'}$$

and

$$\dot{M}^* = I_{NT} - \Sigma^{-1/2}Z^*(Z^{*\prime}\Sigma^{-1}Z^*)^{-1}Z^{*\prime}\Sigma^{-1/2'}$$

so that

$$\Sigma^{-1/2}\dot{M}\Sigma^{-1/2} = \Sigma^{-1} - \Sigma^{-1}Z(Z'\Sigma^{-1}Z)^{-1}Z'\Sigma^{-1}$$

and

$$\Sigma^{-1/2}\dot{M}^*\Sigma^{-1/2} = \Sigma^{-1} - \Sigma^{-1}Z^*(Z^{*\prime}\Sigma^{-1}Z^*)^{-1}Z^{*\prime}\Sigma^{-1}$$

Hence we can write (4.12) in the form

$$\dot{F}_{\text{obs}} = \frac{y'[\Sigma^{-1}(Z^*(Z^{*\prime}\Sigma^{-1}Z^*)^{-1}Z^{*\prime} - Z(Z'\Sigma^{-1}Z)^{-1}Z')\Sigma^{-1}]y/(N-1)K'}{(y'\Sigma^{-1}y - y'\Sigma^{-1}Z^*(Z^{*\prime}\Sigma^{-1}Z^*)^{-1}Z^{*\prime}\Sigma^{-1}y)/N(T-K')} \tag{4.13}$$

and $\dot{F}_{\text{obs}}$ has an F-distribution with $((N-1)K', N(T-K'))$ degrees of freedom. It is important to emphasize that (4.13) is operational only when Σ is known. This test is a special application of a general test for linear restrictions described in Roy (1957) and used by Zellner (1962) to test for aggregation bias in a set of seemingly unrelated regressions. In case Σ is unknown, we replace Σ in (4.13) by a consistent estimator (say $\widehat{\Sigma}$) and call the resulting test statistic $\widehat{F}_{\text{obs}}$.

One of the main motivations behind pooling a time series of cross-sections is to widen our database in order to get better and more reliable estimates of the parameters of our model. Using the Chow test, the question of whether "to pool or not to pool" reduced to a test of the validity of the null hypothesis H_0: $\delta_i = \delta$ for all i. Imposing these restrictions (true or false) will reduce the variance of the pooled estimator, but may introduce bias if these restrictions are false. This motivated Toro-Vizcarrondo and Wallace (1968, p. 560) to write "if one is willing to accept some bias in trade for a reduction in variance, then even if the restriction is not true one might still prefer the restricted estimator". Baltagi (1995b, pp. 54–58) discusses three mean square error (MSE) criteria used in the literature to test whether the pooled estimator restricted by H_0 is better than the unrestricted estimator of δ^*. It is important to emphasize that these MSE criteria do not test whether H_0 is true or false, but help us to choose on "pragmatic grounds" between two sets of estimators of δ^* and hence achieve, in a sense, one of the main motivations behind pooling. A summary table of these MSE criteria is given by Wallace (1972, p. 697). McElroy (1977) extends these MSE criteria to the case where $u \sim N(0, \sigma^2\Sigma)$.

Monte Carlo Evidence

In the Monte Carlo study by Baltagi (1981a), the Chow test is performed given that the data are poolable and the model is generated as a two-way error component model. This test gave a high frequency of rejecting the null hypothesis when true. The reason for the poor performance of the Chow test is that it is applicable only under assumption 4.1 on the disturbances. This is violated under a random effects model with large variance components. For example, in testing the stability of cross-section regressions over time, the high frequency of type I error occurred whenever the variance components due to the time effects are not relatively small. Similarly, in testing the stability of time-series regressions across regions, the high frequency of type I error occurred whenever the variance components due to the cross-section effects are not relatively small.

Under this case of nonspherical disturbances, the proper test to perform is the Roy–Zellner test given by (4.13). Applying this test knowing the true variance components or using the Amemiya (1971) and the Wallace and Hussain (1969) estimates of the variance components leads to low frequencies of committing a type I error. Therefore, if pooling is contemplated using an error component model, then the Roy–Zellner test should be used rather than the Chow test.

The alternative MSE criteria, developed by Toro-Vizcarrondo and Wallace (1968) and Wallace (1972), were applied to the error component model in order to choose between the pooled and unpooled estimators. These weaker criteria gave a lower frequency of committing a type I error than the Chow test, but their performance was still poor when compared to the Roy–Zellner test. McElroy's (1977) extension of these weaker MSE criteria to the case of nonspherical disturbances performed well when compared with the Roy–Zellner test, and is recommended.

4.1.3 Examples

Example 1

For the Grunfeld data, Chow's test for poolability across firms as in (4.1) gives an observed F-statistic of 27.75 and is distributed as $F(27, 170)$ under H_0: $\delta_i = \delta$ for $i = 1, \ldots, N$. The RRSS $= 1\,755\,850.48$ is obtained from pooled OLS and the URSS $= 324\,728.47$ is obtained from summing the RSS from 10 individual firm OLS regressions, each with 17 degrees of freedom. There are 27 restrictions and the test rejects poolability across firms for all coefficients. One can test for poolability of slopes only, allowing for varying intercepts. The restricted model is the Within regression with firm dummies. The RRSS $= 523\,478$, while the unrestricted regression is the same as above. The observed F-statistic is 5.78 which is distributed as $F(18, 170)$ under H_0: $\beta_i = \beta$ for $i = 1, \ldots, N$. This again is significant at the 5% level and rejects poolability of the slopes across firms. Note that one could have tested poolability across time. The Chow test gives an observed value of 1.12 which is distributed as $F(57, 140)$. This does not reject poolability across time, but the unrestricted model is based on 20 regressions each with only seven degrees of freedom. As is clear from the numerator degrees of freedom, this F-statistic tests 57 restrictions. The Roy–Zellner test for poolability across firms, allowing for one-way error component disturbances, yields an observed F-value of 4.35 which is distributed as $F(27, 170)$ under H_0: $\delta_i = \delta$ for $i = 1, \ldots, N$. This still rejects poolability across firms even after allowing for one-way error component disturbances. The Roy–Zellner test for poolability over time, allowing for a one-way error component model, yields an F-value of 2.72 which is distributed as $F(57, 140)$ under H_0: $\delta_t = \delta$ for $t = 1, \ldots, T$.

Example 2

For the gasoline demand data in Baltagi and Griffin (1983), Chow's test for poolability across countries yields an observed F-statistic of 129.38 and is distributed as $F(68, 270)$ under H_0: $\delta_i = \delta$ for $i = 1, \ldots, N$. This tests the stability of four time-series regression coefficients across 18 countries. The unrestricted SSE is based upon 18 OLS time-series regressions, one for each country. For the stability of the slope coefficients only, H_0: $\beta_i = \beta$, an observed F-value of 27.33 is obtained which is distributed as $F(51, 270)$ under the null. Chow's test for poolability across time yields an F-value of 0.276 which is distributed as $F(72, 266)$ under H_0: $\delta_t = \delta$ for $t = 1, \ldots, T$. This tests the stability of four cross-section regression coefficients across 19 time periods. The unrestricted SSE is based upon 19 OLS cross-section regressions, one for each year. This does not reject poolability across time periods. The Roy–Zellner test for poolability across countries, allowing for a one-way error component model, yields an F-value of 21.64 which is distributed as $F(68, 270)$ under H_0: $\delta_i = \delta$ for $i = 1, \ldots, N$. The Roy–Zellner test for poolability across time yields an F-value of 1.66 which is distributed as $F(72, 266)$ under H_0: $\delta_t = \delta$ for $t = 1, \ldots, T$. This rejects H_0 at the 5% level.

4.1.4 Other Tests for Poolability

Ziemer and Wetzstein (1983) suggest comparing pooled estimators (like $\widehat{\delta}_{\text{OLS}}$) with nonpooled estimators (like $\widehat{\delta}_{i,\text{OLS}}$) according to their forecast risk performance. Using a wilderness recreation demand model, they show that a Stein rule estimator gives a better forecast risk performance than the pooled or individual cross-section estimators. The Stein rule estimator for δ_i in (4.1) is given by

$$\widehat{\delta}_i^* = \widehat{\delta}_{\text{OLS}} + \left(1 - \frac{c}{F_{\text{obs}}}\right)\left(\widehat{\delta}_{i,\text{OLS}} - \widehat{\delta}_{\text{OLS}}\right) \tag{4.14}$$

where $\widehat{\delta}_{i,\text{OLS}}$ is given in (4.6) and $\widehat{\delta}_{\text{OLS}}$ is given in (4.4). F_{obs} is the F-statistic to test H_0: $\delta_i = \delta$, given in (4.8), and the constant c is given by $c = ((N-1)K' - 2)/(NT - NK' + 2)$. Note that $\widehat{\delta}_i^*$ shrinks $\widehat{\delta}_{i,\text{OLS}}$ towards the pooled estimator $\widehat{\delta}_{\text{OLS}}$. More recently, Maddala (1991) argued that shrinkage estimators appear to be better than either the pooled estimator or the individual cross-section estimators.

Brown, Durbin and Evans (1975) derived cumulative sum and cumulative sum of squares tests for structural change based on recursive residuals in a time-series regression. Han and Park (1989) extended these tests of structural change to the panel data case. They applied these tests to a study of US foreign trade of manufacturing goods. They found no evidence of structural change over the period 1958–76. Baltagi, Hidalgo and Li (1996) derived a nonparametric test for poolability which is robust to functional form misspecification. In particular, they considered the following nonparametric panel data model:

$$y_{it} = g_t(x_{it}) + \epsilon_{it} \qquad i = 1, \ldots, N; \; t = 1, \ldots, T$$

where $g_t(\cdot)$ is an unspecified functional form that may vary over time. x_{it} is a $k \times 1$ column vector of predetermined explanatory variables with $p \geqslant 1$ variables being continuous and $k - p \geqslant 0$. Poolability of the data over time is equivalent to testing that $g_t(x) = g_s(x)$ almost everywhere for all t and $s = 1, 2, \ldots, T$ vs $g_t(x) \neq g_s(x)$ for some $t \neq s$ with probability greater than zero. The test statistic is shown to be consistent and asymptotically normal and is applied to an earnings equation using data from the PSID.

4.2 TESTS FOR INDIVIDUAL AND TIME EFFECTS

4.2.1 The Breusch–Pagan Test

For the random two-way error component model, Breusch and Pagan (1980) derived a Lagrange multiplier (LM) test to test H_0: $\sigma_\mu^2 = \sigma_\lambda^2 = 0$. The log-likelihood function under normality of the disturbances is given by (3.29) as

$$L(\delta, \theta) = \text{constant} - \frac{1}{2}\log|\Omega| - \frac{1}{2}u'\Omega^{-1}u \tag{4.15}$$

where $\theta' = (\sigma_\mu^2, \sigma_\lambda^2, \sigma_\nu^2)$ and Ω is given by (3.10) as

$$\Omega = \sigma_\mu^2(I_N \otimes J_T) + \sigma_\lambda^2(J_N \otimes I_T) + \sigma_\nu^2 I_{NT} \tag{4.16}$$

The information matrix is block-diagonal between θ and δ. Since H_0 involves only θ, the part of the information matrix due to δ is ignored. In order to reconstruct the Breusch and Pagan (1980) LM statistic, we need the score $D(\widetilde{\theta}) = (\partial L/\partial\theta)|_{\widetilde{\theta}_{\text{mle}}}$, the first derivative of the likelihood with respect to θ, evaluated at the restricted MLE of θ under H_0, which is denoted by $\widetilde{\theta}_{\text{mle}}$. Hartley and Rao (1967) or Hemmerle and Hartley (1973) give a useful general formula to obtain $D(\theta)$:

$$\partial L/\partial\theta_r = \frac{1}{2}\text{tr}[\Omega^{-1}(\partial\Omega/\partial\theta_r)] + \frac{1}{2}[u'\Omega^{-1}(\partial\Omega/\partial\theta_r)\Omega^{-1}u] \tag{4.17}$$

for $r = 1, 2, 3$. Also, from (4.16), $(\partial\Omega/\partial\theta_r) = (I_N \otimes J_T)$ for $r = 1$, $(J_N \otimes I_T)$ for $r = 2$ and I_{NT} for $r = 3$. The restricted MLE of Ω under H_0 is $\widetilde{\Omega} = \widetilde{\sigma}_\nu^2 I_{NT}$ where $\widetilde{\sigma}_\nu^2 = \widetilde{u}'\widetilde{u}/NT$ and $\widetilde{u}$ are the OLS residuals. Using $\text{tr}(I_N \otimes J_T) = \text{tr}(J_N \otimes I_T) = \text{tr}(I_{NT}) = NT$, one gets

$$D(\widetilde{\theta}) = \begin{bmatrix} -\frac{1}{2}\text{tr}[(I_N \otimes J_T)/\widetilde{\sigma}_\nu^2] + \frac{1}{2}[\widetilde{u}'(I_N \otimes J_T)\widetilde{u}/\widetilde{\sigma}_\nu^4] \\ -\frac{1}{2}\text{tr}[(J_N \otimes I_T)/\widetilde{\sigma}_\nu^2] + \frac{1}{2}[\widetilde{u}'(J_N \otimes I_T)\widetilde{u}/\widetilde{\sigma}_\nu^4] \\ -\frac{1}{2}\text{tr}[I_{NT}/\widetilde{\sigma}_\nu^2] + \frac{1}{2}[\widetilde{u}'\widetilde{u}/\widetilde{\sigma}_\nu^4] \end{bmatrix}$$

$$= \frac{-NT}{2\widetilde{\sigma}_\nu^2}\begin{bmatrix} 1 - \dfrac{\widetilde{u}'(I_N \otimes J_T)\widetilde{u}}{\widetilde{u}'\widetilde{u}} \\ 1 - \dfrac{\widetilde{u}'(J_N \otimes I_T)\widetilde{u}}{\widetilde{u}'\widetilde{u}} \\ 0 \end{bmatrix} \tag{4.18}$$

The information matrix for this model is

$$J(\theta) = E\left[-\frac{\partial^2 L}{\partial\theta\partial\theta'}\right] = [J_{rs}] \quad \text{for } r, s = 1, 2, 3$$

where

$$J_{rs} = E[-\partial^2 L/\partial\theta_r\partial\theta_s] = \frac{1}{2}\text{tr}[\Omega^{-1}(\partial\Omega/\partial\theta_r)\Omega^{-1}(\partial\Omega/\partial\theta_s)] \tag{4.19}$$

(see Harville, 1977). Using $\widetilde{\Omega}^{-1} = (1/\widetilde{\sigma}_\nu^2)I_{NT}$ and $\mathrm{tr}[(I_N \otimes J_T)(J_N \otimes I_T)] = \mathrm{tr}(J_{NT}) = NT$, $\mathrm{tr}(I_N \otimes J_T)^2 = NT^2$ and $\mathrm{tr}(J_N \otimes I_T)^2 = N^2T$, one gets

$$\begin{aligned}
\widetilde{J} &= \frac{1}{2\widetilde{\sigma}_\nu^4}\begin{bmatrix} \mathrm{tr}(I_N \otimes J_T)^2 & \mathrm{tr}(J_{NT}) & \mathrm{tr}(I_N \otimes J_T) \\ \mathrm{tr}(J_{NT}) & \mathrm{tr}(J_N \otimes I_T)^2 & \mathrm{tr}(J_N \otimes I_T) \\ \mathrm{tr}(I_N \otimes J_T) & \mathrm{tr}(J_N \otimes I_T) & \mathrm{tr}(I_{NT}) \end{bmatrix} \\
&= \frac{NT}{2\widetilde{\sigma}_\nu^4}\begin{bmatrix} T & 1 & 1 \\ 1 & N & 1 \\ 1 & 1 & 1 \end{bmatrix}
\end{aligned} \tag{4.20}$$

with

$$\widetilde{J}^{-1} = \frac{2\widetilde{\sigma}_\nu^4}{NT(N-1)(T-1)}\begin{bmatrix} (N-1) & 0 & (1-N) \\ 0 & (T-1) & (1-T) \\ (1-N) & (1-T) & (NT-1) \end{bmatrix} \tag{4.21}$$

Therefore

$$\begin{aligned}
\mathrm{LM} &= \widetilde{D}'\widetilde{J}^{-1}\widetilde{D} \\
&= \frac{NT}{2(N-1)(T-1)}\left[(N-1)\left[1 - \frac{\widetilde{u}'(I_N \otimes J_T)\widetilde{u}}{\widetilde{u}'\widetilde{u}}\right]^2 \right. \\
&\quad \left. + (T-1)\left[1 - \frac{\widetilde{u}'(J_N \otimes I_T)\widetilde{u}}{\widetilde{u}'\widetilde{u}}\right]^2\right] \\
\mathrm{LM} &= \mathrm{LM}_1 + \mathrm{LM}_2
\end{aligned} \tag{4.22}$$

where

$$\mathrm{LM}_1 = \frac{NT}{2(T-1)}\left[1 - \frac{\widetilde{u}'(I_N \otimes J_T)\widetilde{u}}{\widetilde{u}'\widetilde{u}}\right]^2 \tag{4.23}$$

and

$$\mathrm{LM}_2 = \frac{NT}{2(N-1)}\left[1 - \frac{\widetilde{u}'(J_N \otimes I_T)\widetilde{u}}{\widetilde{u}'\widetilde{u}}\right]^2 \tag{4.24}$$

Under H_0, LM is asymptotically distributed as χ_2^2. This LM test requires only OLS residuals and is easy to compute. This may explain its popularity. In addition, if one wants to test H_0^a: $\sigma_\mu^2 = 0$, following the derivation given above, one gets LM_1 which is asymptotically distributed under H_0^a as χ_1^2. Similarly, if one wants to test H_0^b: $\sigma_\lambda^2 = 0$, by symmetry, one gets LM_2 which is asymptotically distributed as χ_1^2 under H_0^b. This LM test performed well in Monte Carlo studies (see Baltagi, 1981a), except for small values of σ_μ^2 and σ_λ^2 close to zero. These are precisely the cases where negative estimates of the variance components are most likely to occur.[2]

4.2.2 King and Wu, Honda and the Standardized Lagrange Multiplier Tests

One problem with the Breusch–Pagan test is that it assumes that the alternative hypothesis is two-sided when we know that the variance components are non-negative. This means that the alternative hypotheses should be one-sided. Honda (1985) suggests a *uniformly most powerful* test for H_0^a: $\sigma_\mu^2 = 0$ which is based upon

$$\text{HO} \equiv A = \sqrt{\frac{NT}{2(T-1)}}\left[\frac{\widetilde{u}'(I_N \otimes J_T)\widetilde{u}}{\widetilde{u}'\widetilde{u}} - 1\right] \overset{H_0^a}{\rightarrow} N(0, 1) \tag{4.25}$$

Note that the square of this $N(0, 1)$ statistic is the Breusch and Pagan (1980) LM_1 test statistic given in (4.23). Honda (1985) finds that this test statistic is robust to non-normality.[3] Moulton and Randolph (1989) showed that the asymptotic $N(0, 1)$ approximation for this one-sided LM statistic can be poor even in large samples. This occurs when the number of regressors is large or the intra-class correlation of some of the regressors is high. They suggest an alternative standardized Lagrange multiplier (SLM) test whose asymptotic critical values are generally closer to the exact critical values than those of the LM test. This SLM test statistic centers and scales the one-sided LM statistic so that its mean is zero and its variance is one:

$$\text{SLM} = \frac{\text{HO} - E(\text{HO})}{\sqrt{\text{var}(\text{HO})}} = \frac{d - E(d)}{\sqrt{\text{var}(d)}} \tag{4.26}$$

where $d = \widetilde{u}'D\widetilde{u}/\widetilde{u}'\widetilde{u}$ and $D = (I_N \otimes J_T)$. Using the results on moments of quadratic forms in regression residuals (see e.g. Evans and King, 1985), we get

$$E(d) = \text{tr}(D\bar{P}_Z)/p \tag{4.27}$$

and

$$\text{var}(d) = 2\{p\ \text{tr}(D\bar{P}_Z)^2 - [\text{tr}(D\bar{P}_Z)]^2\}/p^2(p+2) \tag{4.28}$$

where $p = n - (K+1)$ and $\bar{P}_Z = I_n - Z(Z'Z)^{-1}Z'$. Under the null hypothesis H_0^a, SLM has an asymptotic $N(0, 1)$ distribution. King and Wu (1997) suggest a locally mean most powerful (LMMP) one-sided test, which for H_0^a coincides with Honda's (1985) uniformly most powerful test (see Baltagi, Chang and Li, 1992b).

Similarly, for H_0^b: $\sigma_\lambda^2 = 0$, the one-sided Honda-type LM test statistic is

$$B = \sqrt{\frac{NT}{2(N-1)}}\left[\frac{\widetilde{u}'(J_N \otimes I_T)\widetilde{u}}{\widetilde{u}'\widetilde{u}} - 1\right] \tag{4.29}$$

which is asymptotically distributed as $N(0, 1)$. Note that the square of this statistic is the corresponding two-sided LM test given by LM_2 in (4.24). This can be standardized as in (4.26) with $D = (J_N \otimes I_T)$. Also, the King and Wu (1997) LMMP test for H_0^b coincides with Honda's uniformly most powerful test given in (4.29).

For H_0^c: $\sigma_\mu^2 = \sigma_\lambda^2 = 0$, the two-sided LM test given by Breusch and Pagan (1980) is $A^2 + B^2 \sim \chi^2(2)$. Honda (1985) does not derive a uniformly most powerful one-sided test for H_0^c, but suggests a "handy" one-sided test given by $(A+B)/\sqrt{2}$ which is distributed as $N(0, 1)$ under H_0^c. Following King and Wu (1997), Baltagi, Chang and Li (1992b) derived the LMMP one-sided test for H_0^c. This is given by

$$\mathrm{KW} = \frac{\sqrt{T-1}}{\sqrt{N+T-2}}A + \frac{\sqrt{N-1}}{\sqrt{N+T-2}}B \tag{4.30}$$

which is distributed as $N(0, 1)$ under H_0^c. See problem 4.6.

Following the Moulton and Randolph (1989) standardization of the LM test for the one-way error component model, Honda (1991) suggested a standardization of his "handy" one-sided test for the two-way error component model. In fact, for $\mathrm{HO} = (A+B)/\sqrt{2}$, the SLM test is given by (4.26) with $d = \widetilde{u}'D\widetilde{u}/\widetilde{u}'\widetilde{u}$ and

$$D = \frac{1}{2}\sqrt{\frac{NT}{(T-1)}}(I_N \otimes J_T) + \frac{1}{2}\sqrt{\frac{NT}{(N-1)}}(J_N \otimes I_T) \tag{4.31}$$

Also, one can similarly standardize the KW test given in (4.30) by subtracting its mean and dividing by its standard deviation, as in (4.26), with $d = \widetilde{u}'D\widetilde{u}/\widetilde{u}'\widetilde{u}$ and

$$D = \frac{\sqrt{NT}}{\sqrt{2}\sqrt{N+T-2}}[(I_N \otimes J_T) + (J_N \otimes I_T)] \tag{4.32}$$

With this new D matrix, $E(d)$ and $\mathrm{var}(d)$ can be computed using (4.27) and (4.28). Under H_0^c: $\sigma_\mu^2 = \sigma_\lambda^2 = 0$, these SLM statistics are asymptotically $N(0, 1)$ and their asymptotic critical values should be closer to the exact critical values than those of the corresponding unstandardized tests.

4.2.3 Gourieroux, Holly and Monfort and Two Other Lagrange Multiplier Tests

Note that A or B can be negative for a specific application, especially when one or both variance components are small and close to zero. Following Gourieroux, Holly and Monfort (1982), hereafter GHM, Baltagi, Chang and Li (1992b) proposed the following test for H_0^c:

$$\chi_{\mathrm{m}}^2 = \begin{cases} A^2 + B^2 & \text{if } A > 0, B > 0 \\ A^2 & \text{if } A > 0, B \leqslant 0 \\ B^2 & \text{if } A \leqslant 0, B > 0 \\ 0 & \text{if } A \leqslant 0, B \leqslant 0 \end{cases} \tag{4.33}$$

where χ_{m}^2 denotes the mixed χ^2 distribution. Under the null hypothesis

$$\chi_{\mathrm{m}}^2 \sim \left(\tfrac{1}{4}\right)\chi^2(0) + \left(\tfrac{1}{2}\right)\chi^2(1) + \left(\tfrac{1}{4}\right)\chi^2(2)$$

where $\chi^2(0)$ equals zero with probability one.[4] The weights $\left(\frac{1}{4}\right)$, $\left(\frac{1}{2}\right)$ and $\left(\frac{1}{4}\right)$ follow from the fact that A and B are asymptotically independent of each other and the results in Gourieroux, Holly and Monfort (1982). This proposed test has the advantage over the Honda and KW tests in that it is immune to the possible negative values of A and B.

Two More Lagrange Multiplier Tests

When one uses HO given in (4.25) to test $H_0^a\colon \sigma_\mu^2 = 0$ one implicitly assumes that the time-specific effects do not exist. This may lead to incorrect decisions especially when the variance of the time effects (assumed to be zero) is large. To overcome this problem, Baltagi, Chang and Li (1992b) suggest testing the individual effects assuming that the time-specific effects are present (i.e. assuming $\sigma_\lambda^2 > 0$). The corresponding new LM test for testing $H_0^d\colon \sigma_\mu^2 = 0$ (assuming $\sigma_\lambda^2 > 0$) is derived in Appendix 2 of Baltagi, Chang and Li (1992b) and is given by

$$\text{LM}_\mu = \frac{\sqrt{2}\widetilde{\sigma}_2^2\widetilde{\sigma}_\nu^2}{\sqrt{T(T-1)[\widetilde{\sigma}_\nu^4 + (N-1)\widetilde{\sigma}_2^4]}}\widetilde{D}_\mu \tag{4.34}$$

where

$$\widetilde{D}_\mu = \frac{T}{2}\left\{\frac{1}{\widetilde{\sigma}_2^2}\left[\frac{\widetilde{u}'(\bar{J}_N \otimes \bar{J}_T)\widetilde{u}}{\widetilde{\sigma}_2^2} - 1\right] + \frac{(N-1)}{\widetilde{\sigma}_\nu^2}\left[\frac{\widetilde{u}'(E_N \otimes \bar{J}_T)\widetilde{u}}{(N-1)\widetilde{\sigma}_\nu^2} - 1\right]\right\} \tag{4.35}$$

with $\widetilde{\sigma}_2^2 = \widetilde{u}'(\bar{J}_N \otimes I_T)\widetilde{u}/T$ and $\widetilde{\sigma}_\nu^2 = \widetilde{u}'(E_N \otimes I_T)\widetilde{u}/T(N-1)$. LM_μ is asymptotically distributed as $N(0,1)$ under H_0^d. The estimated disturbances $\widetilde{u}$ denote the one-way GLS residuals using the maximum likelihood estimates $\widetilde{\sigma}_\nu^2$ and $\widetilde{\sigma}_2^2$. One can easily check that if $\widetilde{\sigma}_\lambda^2 \to 0$, then $\widetilde{\sigma}_2^2 \to \widetilde{\sigma}_\nu^2$ and LM_μ given in (4.34) tends to the one-sided Honda test given in (4.25).

Similarly, the alternative LM test statistic for testing $H_0^e\colon \sigma_\lambda^2 = 0$ (assuming $\sigma_\mu^2 > 0$) can be obtained as follows:

$$\text{LM}_\lambda = \frac{\sqrt{2}\widetilde{\sigma}_1^2\widetilde{\sigma}_\nu^2}{\sqrt{N(N-1)[\widetilde{\sigma}_\nu^4 + (T-1)\widetilde{\sigma}_1^4]}}\widetilde{D}_\lambda \tag{4.36}$$

where

$$\widetilde{D}_\lambda = \frac{N}{2}\left\{\frac{1}{\widetilde{\sigma}_1^2}\left[\frac{\widetilde{u}'(\bar{J}_N \otimes \bar{J}_T)\widetilde{u}}{\widetilde{\sigma}_1^2} - 1\right] + \frac{(T-1)}{\widetilde{\sigma}_\nu^2}\left[\frac{\widetilde{u}'(\bar{J}_N \otimes E_T)\widetilde{u}}{(T-1)\widetilde{\sigma}_\nu^2} - 1\right]\right\} \tag{4.37}$$

with $\widetilde{\sigma}_1^2 = \widetilde{u}'(I_N \otimes \bar{J}_T)\widetilde{u}/N$, $\widetilde{\sigma}_\nu^2 = \widetilde{u}'(I_N \otimes E_T)\widetilde{u}/N(T-1)$. The test statistic LM_λ is asymptotically distributed as $N(0,1)$ under H_0^e.

4.2.4 ANOVA F and the Likelihood Ratio Tests

Moulton and Randolph (1989) found that the ANOVA F-test which tests the significance of the fixed effects performs well for the one-way error component model. The ANOVA F-test statistics have the following familiar general form:

$$F = \frac{y'MD(D'MD)^{-}D'My/(p-r)}{y'Gy/[NT-(\widetilde{k}+p-r)]} \tag{4.38}$$

Under the null hypothesis, this statistic has a central F-distribution with $p-r$ and $NT-(\widetilde{k}+p-r)$ degrees of freedom. For H_0^a: $\sigma_\mu^2 = 0$, $D = I_N \otimes \iota_T$, $M = \bar{P}_Z$, $\widetilde{k} = K'$, $p = N$, $r = K' + N-$ rank(Z, D) and $G = \bar{P}_{(Z,D)}$ where $\bar{P}_Z = I - P_Z$ and $P_Z = Z(Z'Z)^{-1}Z'$. For details regarding other hypotheses, see Baltagi, Chang and Li (1992b).

The one-sided likelihood ratio (LR) tests all have the following form:

$$\text{LR} = -2 \log \frac{l(\text{res})}{l(\text{unres})} \tag{4.39}$$

where l(res) denotes the restricted maximum likelihood value (under the null hypothesis), while l(unres) denotes the unrestricted maximum likelihood value. The LR tests require MLE estimators of the one-way and the two-way models and are comparatively more expensive than their LM counterparts. Under the null hypotheses considered, the LR test statistics have the same asymptotic distributions as their LM counterparts (see Gourieroux, Holly and Monfort, 1982). More specifically, for H_0^a, H_0^b, H_0^d and H_0^e, LR $\sim (\frac{1}{2})\chi^2(0) + (\frac{1}{2})\chi^2(1)$ and for H_0^c, LR $\sim (\frac{1}{4})\chi^2(0) + (\frac{1}{2})\chi^2(1) + (\frac{1}{4})\chi^2(2)$.

4.2.5 Monte Carlo Results

Baltagi, Chang and Li (1992b) compared the performance of the above tests using Monte Carlo experiments on the two-way error component model described in Baltagi (1981a). Each experiment involved 1000 replications. For each replication, the following test statistics were computed: BP, Honda, KW, SLM, LR, GHM and the F-test statistics. The results can be summarized as follows: when H_0^a: $\sigma_\mu^2 = 0$ is true but σ_λ^2 is large, all the usual tests for H_0^a perform badly since they ignore the fact that $\sigma_\lambda^2 > 0$. In fact, the two-sided BP test performs the worst, over-rejecting the null, while HO, SLM, LR and F underestimate the nominal size. As σ_μ^2 gets large, all the tests perform well in rejecting the null hypothesis H_0^a. But for small $\sigma_\mu^2 > 0$, the power of all the tests considered deteriorates as σ_λ^2 increases.

For testing H_0^d: $\sigma_\mu^2 = 0$ (assuming $\sigma_\lambda^2 > 0$), LM$_\mu$, LR and F perform well with their estimated size not significantly different from their nominal size. Also, for large σ_μ^2 all these tests have high power, rejecting the null hypothesis in 98–100% of the cases. The results also suggest that overspecifying the model, i.e. assuming the model is two-way ($\sigma_\lambda^2 > 0$) when in fact it is one-way ($\sigma_\lambda^2 = 0$) does not seem to hurt the power of these tests. Finally, the power of all the tests improves as σ_λ^2 increases. This is in sharp contrast to the performance of the tests that ignore the fact that $\sigma_\lambda^2 > 0$. The Monte Carlo results strongly support the fact that one should not ignore the possibility that $\sigma_\lambda^2 > 0$ when testing $\sigma_\mu^2 = 0$. In fact, it may be better to overspecify the model rather than underspecify it in testing the variance components.

For the joint test H_0^c: $\sigma_\mu^2 = \sigma_\lambda^2 = 0$, the BP, HO, KW and LR significantly underestimate the nominal size, while GHM and the F-test have estimated sizes that are not significantly different from the nominal size. Negative values of A and B make the estimated size for HO and KW underestimate the nominal size. For these cases, the GHM test is immune to negative values of A and B, and performs well in the Monte Carlo experiments. Finally, the ANOVA F-tests perform reasonably well when compared to the LR and LM tests, for both the one-way and two-way models, and are recommended. This confirms similar results on the F-statistic by Moulton and Randolph (1989) for the one-way error component model.

4.2.6 An Illustrative Example

The Monte Carlo results show that the test statistics A and/or B take on large negative values quite often under some designs. A natural question is whether a large negative A and/or B is possible for real data. In this subsection, we apply

Table 4.1 Test Results for the Grunfeld Example*

Null Hypothesis Tests	H_0^a $\sigma_\mu^2 = 0$	H_0^b $\sigma_\lambda^2 = 0$	H_0^c $\sigma_\mu^2 = \sigma_\lambda^2 = 0$	H_0^d $\sigma_\mu^2 = 0/\sigma_\lambda^2 > 0$	H_0^e $\sigma_\lambda^2 = 0/\sigma_\mu^2 > 0$
BP	798.162 (3.841)	6.454 (3.841)	804.615 (5.991)	—	—
HO	28.252 (1.645)	−2.540 (1.645)	18.181 (1.645)	—	—
KW	28.252 (1.645)	−2.540 (1.645)	21.832 (1.645)	—	—
SLM	32.661 (1.645)	−2.433 (1.645)	—	—	—
GHM	—	—	798.162 (4.231)	—	—
F	49.177 (1.930)	0.235 (1.645)	17.403 (1.543)	52.672 (1.648)	1.412 (1.935)
LR	193.091 (2.706)	0 (2.706)	193.108 (4.231)	193.108 (2.706)	0.017 (2.706)
LM_μ	—	—	—	28.252 (2.706)	—
LM_λ	—	—	—	—	0.110 (2.706)

*Numbers in parentheses are asymptotic critical values at the 5% level

Source: Baltagi, Chang and Li (1992b). Reproduced by permission of Elsevier Science Publishers B.V. (North-Holland)

the tests considered above to the Grunfeld (1958) investment equation. Table 4.1 gives the observed test statistics. The null hypotheses H_0^c: $\sigma_\mu^2 = \sigma_\lambda^2 = 0$ as well as H_0^a: $\sigma_\mu^2 = 0$ and H_0^d: $\sigma_\mu^2 = 0$ (assuming $\sigma_\lambda^2 > 0$) are rejected by all tests considered. Clearly, all the tests strongly suggest that there are individual specific effects. However, for testing time-specific effects, except for the two-sided LM (BP) test which rejects H_0^b: $\sigma_\lambda^2 = 0$, all the tests suggest that there are no time-specific effects for this data. The conflict occurs because B takes on a large negative value (−2.540) for this data set. This means that the two-sided LM test is $B^2 = 6.454$ which is larger than the χ_1^2 critical value (3.841). In contrast, the one-sided LM, SLM, LR and F-tests for this hypothesis do not reject H_0^b. In fact, the LM$_\lambda$ test proposed by Baltagi, Chang and Li (1992b) for testing H_0^e: $\sigma_\lambda^2 = 0$ (assuming $\sigma_\mu^2 > 0$) as well as the LR and F-tests for this hypothesis do not reject H_0^e. These data clearly support the use of the one-sided test in empirical applications.

4.3 HAUSMAN'S SPECIFICATION TEST

A critical assumption in the error component regression model is that $E(u_{it}/X_{it}) = 0$. This is important given that the disturbances contain individual invariant effects (the μ_i) which are unobserved and may be correlated with the X_{it}. For example, in an earnings equation these μ_i may denote unobservable ability of the individual and this may be correlated with the schooling variable included on the right-hand side of this equation. In this case, $E(u_{it}/X_{it}) \neq 0$ and the GLS estimator $\widehat{\beta}_{\text{GLS}}$ becomes biased and inconsistent for β. However, the Within transformation wipes out these μ_i and leaves the Within estimator $\widetilde{\beta}_{\text{Within}}$ unbiased and consistent for β. Hausman (1978) suggests comparing $\widehat{\beta}_{\text{GLS}}$ and $\widetilde{\beta}_{\text{Within}}$, both of which are consistent under the null hypothesis H_0: $E(u_{it}/X_{it}) = 0$, but which will have different probability limits if H_0 is not true. In fact, $\widetilde{\beta}_{\text{Within}}$ is consistent whether H_0 is true or not, while $\widehat{\beta}_{\text{GLS}}$ is BLUE, consistent and asymptotically efficient under H_0, but is inconsistent when H_0 is false. A natural test statistic would be based on $\widetilde{q}_1 = \widehat{\beta}_{\text{GLS}} - \widetilde{\beta}_{\text{Within}}$. Under H_0, $\text{plim}\,\widehat{q}_1 = 0$ and $\text{cov}(\widehat{q}_1, \widehat{\beta}_{\text{GLS}}) = 0$.

Using the fact that $\widehat{\beta}_{\text{GLS}} - \beta = (X'\Omega^{-1}X)^{-1}X'\Omega^{-1}u$ and $\widetilde{\beta}_{\text{Within}} - \beta = (X'QX)^{-1}X'Qu$, one gets $E(\widehat{q}_1) = 0$ and

$$\begin{aligned}\text{cov}(\widehat{\beta}_{\text{GLS}}, \widehat{q}_1) &= \text{var}(\widehat{\beta}_{\text{GLS}}) - \text{cov}(\widehat{\beta}_{\text{GLS}}, \widetilde{\beta}_{\text{Within}})\\ &= (X'\Omega^{-1}X)^{-1} - (X'\Omega^{-1}X)^{-1}X\Omega^{-1}E(uu')QX(X'QX)^{-1}\\ &= (X'\Omega^{-1}X)^{-1} - (X'\Omega^{-1}X)^{-1} = 0\end{aligned}$$

Using the fact that $\widetilde{\beta}_{\text{Within}} = \widehat{\beta}_{\text{GLS}} - \widehat{q}_1$, one gets

$$\text{var}(\widetilde{\beta}_{\text{Within}}) = \text{var}(\widehat{\beta}_{\text{GLS}}) + \text{var}(\widehat{q}_1)$$

since $\text{cov}(\widehat{\beta}_{\text{GLS}}, \widehat{q}_1) = 0$. Therefore

$$\text{var}(\widehat{q}_1) = \text{var}(\widetilde{\beta}_{\text{Within}}) - \text{var}(\widehat{\beta}_{\text{GLS}}) = \sigma_\nu^2(X'QX)^{-1} - (X'\Omega^{-1}X)^{-1} \tag{4.40}$$

Hence, the Hausman test statistic is given by

$$m_1 = \hat{q}_1'[\text{var}(\widehat{q}_1)]^{-1}\widehat{q}_1 \tag{4.41}$$

and under H_0 is asymptotically distributed as χ_K^2 where K denotes the dimension of slope vector β. In order to make this test operational, Ω is replaced by a consistent estimator $\widehat{\Omega}$, and GLS by its corresponding feasible GLS.

An alternative asymptotically equivalent test can be obtained from the augmented regression

$$y^* = X^*\beta + \widetilde{X}\gamma + w \tag{4.42}$$

where $y^* = \sigma_\nu\Omega^{-1/2}y$, $X^* = \sigma_\nu\Omega^{-1/2}X$ and $\widetilde{X} = QX$. Hausman's test is now equivalent to testing whether $\gamma = 0$. This is a standard Wald test for the omission of the variables $\widetilde{X}$ from (4.42).[5] It is worthwhile to rederive this test. In fact, performing OLS on (4.42) yields

$$\begin{pmatrix} \widehat{\beta} \\ \widehat{\gamma} \end{pmatrix} = \begin{bmatrix} X'(Q+\phi^2P)X & X'QX \\ X'QX & X'QX \end{bmatrix}^{-1} \begin{pmatrix} X'(Q+\phi^2P)y \\ X'Qy \end{pmatrix} \tag{4.43}$$

where $\sigma_\nu\Omega^{-1/2} = Q+\phi P$ and $\phi = \sigma_\nu/\sigma_1$ (see (2.20)). Using partitioned inverse formulae, one can show that

$$\begin{pmatrix} \widehat{\beta} \\ \widehat{\gamma} \end{pmatrix} = \begin{bmatrix} E & -E \\ -E & (X'QX)^{-1} + E \end{bmatrix} \begin{pmatrix} X'(Q+\phi^2P)y \\ X'Qy \end{pmatrix} \tag{4.44}$$

where $E = (X'PX)^{-1}/\phi^2$. This reduces to

$$\widehat{\beta} = \widehat{\beta}_{\text{Between}} = (X'PX)^{-1}X'Py \tag{4.45}$$

and

$$\widehat{\gamma} = \widetilde{\beta}_{\text{Within}} - \widehat{\beta}_{\text{Between}} \tag{4.46}$$

Substituting the Within and Between estimators of β into (4.46) one gets

$$\widehat{\gamma} = (X'QX)^{-1}X'Q\nu - (X'PX)^{-1}X'Pu \tag{4.47}$$

It is easy to show that $E(\widehat{\gamma}) = 0$ and

$$\begin{aligned}\text{var}(\widehat{\gamma}) = E(\widehat{\gamma}\widehat{\gamma}') &= \sigma_\nu^2(X'QX)^{-1} + \sigma_1^2(X'PX)^{-1} \\ &= \text{var}(\widetilde{\beta}_{\text{Within}}) + \text{var}(\widehat{\beta}_{\text{Between}})\end{aligned} \tag{4.48}$$

since the cross-product terms are zero. The test for $\gamma = 0$ is based on $\widehat{\gamma} = \widetilde{\beta}_{\text{Within}} - \widehat{\beta}_{\text{Between}} = 0$ and the corresponding test statistic would therefore be $\widehat{\gamma}'(\text{var}(\widehat{\gamma}))^{-1}\widehat{\gamma}$, which looks different from the Hausman m_1 statistic given in (4.41). These tests are numerically exactly identical (see Hausman and Taylor, 1981). In fact, Hausman and Taylor (1981) showed that H_0 can be tested using any of the following three paired differences: $\widehat{q}_1 = \widehat{\beta}_{\text{GLS}} - \widetilde{\beta}_{\text{Within}}$; $\widehat{q}_2 = \widehat{\beta}_{\text{GLS}} - \widehat{\beta}_{\text{Between}}$; or $\widehat{q}_3 = \widetilde{\beta}_{\text{Within}} - \widehat{\beta}_{\text{Between}}$. The corresponding test statistics can be computed as $m_i = \widehat{q}_i' V_i^{-1} \widehat{q}_i$, where $V_i = \text{var}(\widehat{q}_i)$. These are asymptotically distributed as χ^2_K for $i = 1, 2, 3$ under H_0.[6] Hausman and Taylor (1981) proved that these three tests differ from each other by nonsingular matrices. This easily follows from the fact that

$$\widehat{\beta}_{\text{GLS}} = W_1 \widetilde{\beta}_{\text{Within}} + (I - W_1)\widehat{\beta}_{\text{Between}}$$

derived in (2.31). So $\widehat{q}_1 = \widehat{\beta}_{\text{GLS}} - \widetilde{\beta}_{\text{Within}} = (I - W_1)(\widehat{\beta}_{\text{Between}} - \widetilde{\beta}_{\text{Within}}) = \Gamma \widehat{q}_3$, where $\Gamma = W_1 - I$. Also, $\text{var}(\widehat{q}_1) = \Gamma \ \text{var}(\widehat{q}_3)\Gamma'$ and

$$\begin{aligned} m_1 &= \widehat{q}_1'[\text{var}(\widehat{q}_1)]^{-1}\widehat{q}_1 = \widehat{q}_3'\Gamma'[\Gamma \ \text{var}(\widehat{q}_3)\Gamma']^{-1}\Gamma\widehat{q}_3 \\ &= \widehat{q}_3'[\text{var}(\widehat{q}_3)]^{-1}\widehat{q}_3 = m_3 \end{aligned}$$

This proves that m_1 and m_3 are numerically exactly identical. Similarly one can show that m_2 is numerically exactly identical to m_1 and m_3. In fact, Baltagi (1989a) showed that these m_i are also exactly numerically identical to $m_4 = \widehat{q}_4' V_4^{-1} \widehat{q}_4$ where $\widehat{q}_4 = \widehat{\beta}_{\text{GLS}} - \widehat{\beta}_{\text{OLS}}$ and $V_4 = \text{var}(\widehat{q}_4)$. In the Monte Carlo study by Baltagi (1981a), the Hausman test is performed given that the exogeneity assumption is true. This test performed well with a low frequency of type I errors.

More recently, Arellano (1993) provided an alternative variable addition test to the Hausman test which is robust to autocorrelation and heteroskedasticity of arbitrary form. In particular, Arellano (1993) suggests constructing the following regression:

$$\begin{pmatrix} y_i^+ \\ \bar{y}_i \end{pmatrix} = \begin{bmatrix} X_i^+ & 0 \\ \bar{X}_i' & \bar{X}_i' \end{bmatrix} \begin{pmatrix} \beta \\ \gamma \end{pmatrix} + \begin{pmatrix} u_i^+ \\ \bar{u}_i \end{pmatrix} \tag{4.49}$$

where $y_i^+ = (y_{i1}^+, \ldots, y_{iT}^+)'$ and $X_i^+ = (X_{i1}^+, \ldots, X_{iT}^+)'$ is a $T \times K$ matrix and $u_i^+ = (u_{i1}^+, \ldots, u_{iT}^+)'$. Also

$$y_{it}^+ = \left[\frac{T-t}{T-t+1}\right]^{1/2} \left[y_{it} - \frac{1}{(T-t)}(y_{i,t+1} + \cdots + y_{iT})\right] \quad t = 1, 2, \ldots, T-1$$

defines the forward orthogonal deviations operator, $\bar{y}_i = \sum_{t=1}^{T} y_{it}/T$, X_{it}^+, $\bar{X}_i$, u_{it}^+ and $\bar{u}_i$ are similarly defined. OLS on this model yields $\widehat{\beta} = \widetilde{\beta}_{\text{Within}}$ and $\widehat{\gamma} = \widehat{\beta}_{\text{Between}} - \widetilde{\beta}_{\text{Within}}$. Therefore, Hausman's test can be obtained from the artificial regression (4.49) by testing for $\gamma = 0$. If the disturbances are heteroskedastic and/or serially correlated, then neither $\widetilde{\beta}_{\text{Within}}$ nor $\widehat{\beta}_{\text{GLS}}$ are optimal under the null or alternative. Also, the standard formulae for the asymptotic variances of these estimators are no longer valid. Moreover, these estimators cannot be ranked in terms of efficiency so that the var(q) is not the difference of the two variances $\text{var}(\widetilde{\beta}_{\text{W}}) - \text{var}(\widehat{\beta}_{\text{GLS}})$. Arellano (1993) suggests using White's (1984) robust variance–covariance matrix from OLS on (4.49) and applying a standard Wald test for $\gamma = 0$ using these robust standard errors. This can easily be calculated using any standard regression package that computes White robust standard errors. This test is asymptotically distributed as χ^2_K under the null.

Chamberlain (1982) showed that the fixed effects specification imposes testable restrictions on the coefficients from regressions of all leads and lags of dependent variables on all leads and lags of independent variables. Chamberlain specified the relationship between the unobserved individual effects and X_{it} as follows:

$$\mu_i = X'_{i1}\lambda_1 + \cdots + X'_{iT}\lambda_T + \epsilon_i \tag{4.50}$$

where each λ_t is of dimension $K \times 1$ for $t = 1, 2, \ldots, T$. Let $y'_i = (y_{i1}, \ldots, y_{iT})$ and $X'_i = (X'_{i1}, \ldots, X'_{iT})$ and denote the "reduced form" regression of y'_i on X'_i by

$$y'_i = X'_i\pi + \eta_i \tag{4.51}$$

The restrictions between the reduced form and structural parameters are given by

$$\pi = (I_T \otimes \beta) + \lambda\iota'_T \tag{4.52}$$

with $\lambda' = (\lambda'_1, \ldots, \lambda'_T)$.[7] Chamberlain (1982) suggested estimation and testing be carried out using the minimum chi-square method where the minimand is a χ^2 goodness of fit statistic for the restrictions on the reduced form. However, Angrist and Newey (1991) showed that this minimand can be obtained as the sum of T terms. Each term of this sum is simply the degrees of freedom times the R^2 from a regression of the Within residuals for a particular period on all leads and lags of the independent variables. Angrist and Newey (1991) illustrate this test using two examples. The first example estimates and tests a number of models for the union–wage effect using five years of data from the National Longitudinal Survey of Youth (NLSY). They find that the assumption of fixed effects in an equation for union–wage effects is not at odds with the data. The second example considers a conventional human capital earnings function. They find that the fixed effects estimates of the return to schooling in the NLSY are roughly twice those of ordinary least squares. However, the overidentification test suggests that the fixed effects assumption may be inappropriate for this model.

Modifying the set of additional variables in (4.49) so that the set of K additional regressors is replaced by KT additional regressors, Arellano (1993) obtains

$$\begin{pmatrix} y_i^+ \\ \bar{y}_i \end{pmatrix} = \begin{bmatrix} X_i^+ & 0 \\ \bar{X}'_i & X'_i \end{bmatrix} \begin{pmatrix} \beta \\ \lambda \end{pmatrix} + \begin{pmatrix} u_i^+ \\ \bar{u}_i \end{pmatrix} \tag{4.53}$$

where $X_i = (X'_{i1}, \ldots, X'_{iT})'$ and λ is $KT \times 1$. Chamberlain's (1982) test of correlated effects based on the reduced form approach turns out to be equivalent to testing for $\lambda = 0$ in (4.53). Once again this can be made robust to an arbitrary form of serial correlation and heteroskedasticity by using a Wald test for $\lambda = 0$ using White's (1984) robust standard errors. This test is asymptotically distributed as χ^2_{TK}. Note that this clarifies the relationship between the Hausman specification test and the Chamberlain omnibus goodness of fit test. In fact, both tests can be computed as Wald tests from the artificial regressions in (4.49) and (4.53). Hausman's test can be considered as a special case of the Chamberlain test for $\lambda_1 = \lambda_2 = \cdots = \lambda_T = \gamma/T$. Arellano (1993) extends this analysis to dynamic models and to the case where some of the explanatory variables are known to be uncorrelated or weakly correlated with the individual effects.

Recently, Ahn and Low (1996) showed that Hausman's test statistic can be obtained from the artificial regression of the GLS residuals $(y^*_{it} - X^{*\prime}_{it}\widehat{\beta}_{GLS})$ on

$\widetilde{X}$ and $\bar{X}$, where $\widetilde{X}$ has typical element $\widetilde{X}_{it,k}$ and $\bar{X}$ is the matrix of regressors averaged over time. The test statistic is NT times the R^2 of this regression. Using (4.42), one can test H_0: $\gamma = 0$ by running the Gauss–Newton regression (GNR) evaluated at the restricted estimators under the null. Knowing θ, the restricted estimates yield $\widehat{\beta} = \widehat{\beta}_{\text{GLS}}$ and $\widehat{\gamma} = 0$. Therefore, the GNR on (4.42) regresses the GLS residuals $(y_{it}^* - X_{it}^{*\prime}\widehat{\beta}_{\text{GLS}})$ on the derivatives of the regression function with respect to β and γ evaluated at $\widehat{\beta}_{\text{GLS}}$ and $\widehat{\gamma} = 0$. These regressors are X_{it}^* and $\widetilde{X}_{it}$, respectively. But X_{it}^* and $\widetilde{X}_{it}$ span the same space as $\widetilde{X}_{it}$ and $\bar{X}_{i.}$. This follows immediately from the definition of X_{it}^* and $\widetilde{X}_{it}$ given above. Hence, this GNR yields the same regression sums of squares and therefore the same Hausman test statistic as that proposed by Ahn and Low (1996), see problem 97.4.1 in *Econometric Theory* by Baltagi (1997c).

Ahn and Low (1996) argue that Hausman's test can be generalized to test that each X_{it} is uncorrelated with μ_i and not simply that $\bar{X}_i$ is uncorrelated with μ_i. In this case, one computes NT times R^2 of the regression of GLS residuals $(y_{it}^* - X_{it}^{*\prime}\widehat{\beta}_{\text{GLS}})$ on $\widetilde{X}_{it}$ and $[X_{i1}', \ldots, X_{iT}']$. This LM statistic is identical to Arellano's (1993) Wald statistic described earlier if the same estimates of the variance components are used. Ahn and Low (1996) argue that this test is recommended for testing the joint hypothesis of exogeneity of the regressors and the stability of the regression parameters over time. If the regression parameters are nonstationary over time, both $\widehat{\beta}_{\text{GLS}}$ and $\widetilde{\beta}_{\text{Within}}$ are inconsistent even though the regressors are exogenous. Monte Carlo experiments were performed that showed that both the Hausman test and the Ahn and Low (1996) test have good power in detecting endogeneity of the regressors. However, the latter test dominates if the coefficients of the regressors are nonstationary. For Ahn and Low (1996), rejection of the null does not necessarily favor the Within estimator since the latter estimator may be inconsistent. In this case, the authors recommend performing Chamberlain's (1982) test or the equivalent test proposed by Angrist and Newey (1991).

4.3.1 Example 1

For the Grunfeld data, the Within estimates are given by $(\widetilde{\beta}_1, \widetilde{\beta}_2) = (0.1101238, 0.310065)$ with a variance–covariance matrix:

$$\text{var}(\widetilde{\beta}_{\text{Within}}) = \begin{bmatrix} 0.14058 & -0.077468 \\ & 0.3011788 \end{bmatrix} \times 10^{-3}$$

The Between estimates are given by $(0.1346461, 0.03203147)$ with variance–covariance matrix:

$$\text{var}(\widehat{\beta}_{\text{Between}}) = \begin{bmatrix} 0.82630142 & -3.7002477 \\ & 36.4572431 \end{bmatrix} \times 10^{-3}$$

The resulting Hausman χ_2^2 test statistic is $m_3 = 2.131$ which is not significant at the 5% level. Hence we do not reject the null hypothesis of no correlation between the individual effects and the X_{it}. Based on the SWAR feasible GLS estimates, one can similarly compute $m_2 = 2.131$ and $m_1 = 2.330$. These give the same decision. The augmented regression, given in (4.42) based on the SWAR feasible GLS estimates of θ, yields the following estimates: $\widehat{\beta} = (0.135, 0.032)$ and $\widehat{\gamma} = (-0.025, 0.278)$ with an observed F-value for H_0: $\gamma = 0$ equal to 1.066. This is distributed under H_0 as $F(2, 195)$. This is again not significant at the 5% level and leads to nonrejection of H_0.

4.3.2 Example 2

For the Baltagi and Griffin (1983) gasoline data, the Within estimates are given by $(\widetilde{\beta}_1, \widetilde{\beta}_2, \widetilde{\beta}_3) = (0.66128, -0.32130, -0.64015)$ with variance–covariance matrix:

$$\text{var}(\widetilde{\beta}_{\text{Within}}) = \begin{bmatrix} 0.539 & 0.029 & -0.205 \\ & 0.194 & 0.009 \\ & & 0.088 \end{bmatrix} \times 10^{-2}$$

The Between estimates are given by $(0.96737, -0.96329, -0.79513)$ with variance–covariance matrix:

$$\text{var}(\widehat{\beta}_{\text{Between}}) = \begin{bmatrix} 2.422 & -1.694 & -1.056 \\ & 1.766 & 0.883 \\ & & 0.680 \end{bmatrix} \times 10^{-2}$$

The resulting Hausman χ_3^2 test statistic is $m_3 = 26.507$ which is significant. Hence we reject the null hypothesis of no correlation between the individual effects and the X_{it}. One can similarly compute $m_2 = 27.465$, based on the SWAR feasible GLS estimator, and $m_1 = 9.292$ based on the AMEMIYA feasible GLS estimator. These give different values of the asymptotic χ_3^2 statistic, but they all lead to the same decision. The augmented regression, given in (4.42) based on the iterative MLE estimate of θ, yields the following estimates: $\widehat{\beta}_{\text{Between}} = (0.967, -0.963, -0.795)$ and $\widehat{\gamma} = \widetilde{\beta}_{\text{Within}} - \widehat{\beta}_{\text{Between}} = (-0.306, 0.642, 0.155)$ with an observed F-value for H_0: $\gamma = 0$ equal to 4.821. This is distributed under H_0 as $F(3, 335)$ and leads to the rejection of H_0.

4.3.3 Example 3

Owusu-Gyapong (1986) considered panel data on strike activity in 60 Canadian manufacturing industries for the period 1967–79. A one-way error component model is used and OLS, Within and GLS estimates are obtained. With $K' = 12$ regressors, $N = 60$ and $T = 13$, an F-test for the significance of industry-specific effects described in (2.12) yields an F-value of 5.56. This is distributed as $F_{59,709}$ under the null hypothesis of zero industry-specific effects. The null is soundly rejected and the Within estimator is preferred to the OLS estimator. Next, H_0: $\sigma_\mu^2 = 0$ is tested using the Breusch and Pagan (1980) two-sided LM test given as LM_1 in (4.23). This yields a χ^2 value of 21.4, which is distributed as χ_1^2 under the null hypothesis of zero random effects. The null is soundly rejected and the GLS estimator is preferred to the OLS estimator. Finally, for a choice between the Within and GLS estimators, the author performs a Hausman (1978) type test to test H_0: $E(\mu_i/X_{it}) = 0$. This is based on the difference between the Within and GLS estimators as described in (4.41) and yields a χ^2 value equal to 3.84. This is distributed as χ^2_{11} under the null and is not significant. The Hausman test was also run as an augmented regression-type test described in (4.42). This also did not reject the null of no correlation between the μ_i and the regressors. Based on these results, Owusu-Gyapong (1986) chose GLS as the preferred estimator.

4.3.4 Example 4

Cardellichio (1990) estimated the production behavior of 1147 sawmills in the state of Washington observed biennially over the period 1972–84. A one-way error component model is used and OLS, Within and GLS estimates are presented. With $K' = 21$ regressors, $N = 1147$ and $T = 7$, an F-test for the stability of the slope parameters over time was performed which was not significant at the 5% level. In addition, an F-test for the significance of sawmill effects described in (2.12) was performed which rejected the null at the 1% significance level. Finally, a Hausman test was performed and it rejected the null at the 1% significance level. Cardellichio (1990) concluded that the regression slopes are stable over time, sawmill dummies should be included and the Within estimator is preferable to OLS and GLS since the orthogonality assumption between the regressors and the sawmill effects is rejected.

4.3.5 Example 5

Cornwell and Rupert (1997) estimated the wage premium attributed to marriage using the 1971, 1976, 1978 and 1980 waves of the NLSY. They found that the Within estimates of the marriage premium are smaller than those obtained from feasible GLS. A Hausman test based on the difference between these two estimators rejects the null hypothesis. This indicates the possibility of important omitted individual specific characteristics which are correlated with both marriage and the wage rate. They conclude that the marriage premium is purely an intercept shift and no more than 5% to 7%. They also cast doubt on the interpretation that marriage enhances productivity through specialization.

4.3.6 Hausman's Test for the Two-way Model

For the two-way error component model, Hausman's (1978) test can still be based on the difference between the fixed effects estimator (with both time and individual dummies) and the two-way random effects GLS estimator. Also, the augmented regression, given in (4.42), can still be used as long as the Within and GLS transformations used are those for the two-way error component model. But what about the equivalent tests described for the one-way model? Do they extend to the two-way model? Not quite. Kang (1985) showed that a similar equivalence for the Hausman test does not hold for the two-way error component model, since there would be two Between estimators, one between time periods $\widehat{\beta}_{\mathrm{T}}$ and one between cross-sections $\widehat{\beta}_{\mathrm{C}}$. Also, $\widehat{\beta}_{\mathrm{GLS}}$ is a weighted combination of $\widehat{\beta}_{\mathrm{T}}$, $\widehat{\beta}_{\mathrm{C}}$ and the Within estimator $\widetilde{\beta}_{\mathrm{W}}$. Kang (1985) shows that the Hausman test based on $(\widetilde{\beta}_{\mathrm{W}} - \widehat{\beta}_{\mathrm{GLS}})$ is not equivalent to that based on $(\widehat{\beta}_{\mathrm{C}} - \widehat{\beta}_{\mathrm{GLS}})$ or that based on $(\widehat{\beta}_{\mathrm{T}} - \widehat{\beta}_{\mathrm{GLS}})$. But there are other types of equivalencies (see Kang's Table 2). More importantly, Kang classifies five testable hypotheses:

(1) Assume the μ_i are fixed and test $E(\lambda_t/X_{it}) = 0$ based upon $\widetilde{\beta}_{\mathrm{W}} - \widehat{\beta}_{\mathrm{T}}$.
(2) Assume the μ_i are random and test $E(\lambda_t/X_{it}) = 0$ based upon $\widehat{\beta}_{\mathrm{T}} - \widehat{\beta}_{\mathrm{GLS}}$.
(3) Assume the λ_t are fixed and test $E(\mu_i/X_{it}) = 0$ based upon $\widetilde{\beta}_{\mathrm{W}} - \widehat{\beta}_{\mathrm{C}}$.
(4) Assume the λ_t are random and test $E(\mu_i/X_{it}) = 0$ based upon $\widehat{\beta}_{\mathrm{C}} - \widehat{\beta}_{\mathrm{GLS}}$.
(5) Compare two estimators, one which assumes both the μ_i and λ_T are fixed, and another that assumes both are random such that $E(\lambda_t/X_{it}) = E(\mu_i/X_{it}) = 0$. This test is based upon $\widehat{\beta}_{\mathrm{GLS}} - \widetilde{\beta}_{\mathrm{W}}$.

4.4 FURTHER READING

Li and Stengos (1992) proposed a Hausman specification test based on root-N consistent semiparametric estimators. Also, Baltagi and Chang (1996) proposed a simple ANOVA F-statistic based on recursive residuals to test for random individual effects and studied its size and power using Monte Carlo experiments. Chesher (1984) derived a score test for neglected heterogeneity, which is viewed as causing parameter variation. Also, Hamerle (1990) and Orme (1993) suggest a score test for neglected heterogeneity for qualitative limited dependent variable panel data models.

The normality assumption on the error components disturbances may be untenable. Horowitz and Markatou (1996) show how to carry out nonparametric estimation of the densities of the error components. Using data from the Current Population Survey, they estimate an earnings model and show that the probability that individuals with low earnings will become high earners in the future is much lower than that obtained under the assumption of normality. One drawback of this nonparametric estimator is its slow convergence at a rate of $1/(\log N)$, where N is the number of individuals. Monte Carlo results suggest that this estimator should be used for N larger than 1000. Blanchard and Mátyás (1996) performed Monte Carlo simulations to study the robustness of several tests for individual effects with respect to non-normality of the disturbances. The alternative distributions considered are the exponential, lognormal, $t(5)$ and Cauchy distributions. The main findings are that the F-test is robust against non-normality while the one-sided and two-sided LM and LR tests are sensitive to non-normality.

Davidson and MacKinnon (1993) showed that the double-length artificial regression (DLR) can be very useful in choosing between and testing the specification of models that are linear or log-linear in the dependent variable. Baltagi

(1997a) extends this DLR to panel data regressions, where the choice between linear and log-linear models is complicated by the presence of error components. This DLR can easily be extended to test jointly for functional form and random individual effects; see problem 97.1.3 in *Econometric Theory* by Baltagi (1997b) and its solution by Li (1998).

NOTES

1. An elegant presentation of this F-statistic is given in Fisher (1970).
2. Baltagi (1996a) shows that testing for random individual and time effects can be obtained from a variable addition test using two extra variables. One that involves the average of least squares residuals over time and another that involves the average of these residuals across individuals. In fact, this test applies to *nonlinear* regression models with error component disturbances. This variable addition test is an application of the Gauss–Newton regression (GNR) described in detail in Davidson and MacKinnon (1993). For other applications of the GNR in panel data, see Baltagi (1999a).
3. Häggström (2000) studies the properties of Honda's tests for random individual effects in nonlinear regression models. Two corrections for Honda's test statistic are suggested when random time effects are present.
4. Critical values for the mixed χ^2_{m} are 7.289, 4.321 and 2.952 for $\alpha = 0.01, 0.05$ and 0.1, respectively.
5. Hausman (1978) tests $\gamma = 0$ from (4.42) using an F-statistic. The restricted regression yields OLS of y^* on X^*. This is the Fuller and Battese (1973) regression yielding GLS as described below (2.20). The unrestricted regression adds the matrix of Within regressors $\widetilde{X}$ as in (4.42).
6. For an important discussion of what null hypothesis is actually being tested using the Hausman test, see Holly (1982).
7. For more on the Chamberlain approach, read Crépon and Mairesse (1996).

PROBLEMS

4.1 Verify the relationship between M and M^*, i.e. $MM^* = M^*$, given below (4.7). Hint: Use the fact that $Z = Z^*I^*$ with $I^* = (\iota_N \otimes I_{K'})$.

4.2 Verify that $\dot{M}$ and $\dot{M}^*$ defined below (4.10) are both symmetric, idempotent and satisfy $\dot{M}\dot{M}^* = \dot{M}^*$.

4.3 For Grunfeld's data, given as Grunfeld.fil on the Wiley web site, verify the testing for poolability results given in example 1, section 4.1.3.

4.4 For the gasoline data, given as Gasoline.dat on the Wiley web site, verify the testing for poolability results given in example 2, section 4.1.3.

4.5 Under normality of the disturbances, show that for the likelihood function given in (4.15):

(a) The information matrix is block-diagonal between $\theta' = (\sigma^2_\mu, \sigma^2_\lambda, \sigma^2_\nu)$ and δ.

(b) For H^c_0: $\sigma^2_\mu = \sigma^2_\lambda = 0$, verify (4.18), (4.20) and (4.22).

4.6 Using the results of Baltagi, Chang and Li (1992b) verify that the King–Wu (1997) test for H^c_0: $\sigma^2_\mu = \sigma^2_\lambda = 0$ is given by (4.30).

4.7 For H_0^c: $\sigma_\mu^2 = \sigma_\lambda^2 = 0$:
(a) Verify that the standardized Lagrange multiplier (SLM) test statistic for Honda's (1991) $(A + B)/\sqrt{2}$ statistic is as described by (4.26) and (4.31).
(b) Also, verify that the King and Wu (1997) standardized test statistic is as described by (4.26) and (4.32).

4.8 Using the Monte Carlo setup for the two-way error component model described in Baltagi (1981a):
(a) Compare the performance of the Chow F-test and the Roy–Zellner test for various values of the variance components.
(b) Compare the performance of the BP, KW, SLM, LR, GHM and F-test statistics as done in Baltagi, Chang and Li (1992b).
(c) Perform Hausman's specification test and discuss its size for the various experiments conducted.

4.9 For the Grunfeld data, replicate Table 4.1.

4.10 For the gasoline data, derive a similar table to test the hypotheses given in Table 4.1.

4.11 For the public capital data, derive a similar table to test the hypotheses given in Table 4.1.

4.12 Using the partitioned inverse on (4.43), verify (4.44) and deduce (4.45) and (4.46).

4.13 (a) Verify that m_2 is numerically exactly identical to m_1 and m_3, where $m_i = \widehat{q}_i' V_i^{-1} \widehat{q}_i$ defined below (4.48).
(b) Verify that these are also exactly numerically identical to $m_4 = \widehat{q}_4'$ $V_4^{-1}\widehat{q}_4$ where $\widehat{q}_4 = \widehat{\beta}_{\text{GLS}} - \widehat{\beta}_{\text{OLS}}$ and $V_4 = \text{var}(\widehat{q}_4)$. Hint: See the solution in Koning (1990).

4.14 *Testing for correlated effects in panels.* This is based on problem 95.2.5 in *Econometric Theory* by Baltagi (1995c). This problem asks the reader to show that Hausman's test, studied in section 4.3, can be derived from Arellano's (1993) extended regression by using an alternative transformation of the data. In particular, consider the transformation given by $H = (C', \iota_T/T)'$ where C is the first $T - 1$ rows of the Within transformation $E_T = I_T - \bar{J}_T$, I_T is an identity matrix of dimension T and $\bar{J}_T = \iota_T \iota_T'/T$ with ι_T a vector of ones of dimension T.
(a) Show that the matrix C satisfies the following properties: $C\iota_T = 0$, $C'(CC')^{-1}C = I_T - \bar{J}_T$; see Arellano and Bover (1995).
(b) For the transformed model $y_i^+ = Hy_i = (y_i^{*\prime}, \bar{y}_i)'$, where $y_i^* = Cy_i$ and $\bar{y}_i = \sum_{t=1}^T y_{it}/T$. The typical element of y_i^* is given by $y_{it}^* = (y_{it} - \bar{y}_i)$ for $t = 1, 2, \ldots, T - 1$. Consider the extended regression similar to (4.49)

$$\begin{pmatrix} y_i^* \\ \bar{y}_i \end{pmatrix} = \begin{pmatrix} X_i^{*\prime} & 0 \\ \bar{X}_i' & \bar{X}_i' \end{pmatrix} \begin{pmatrix} \beta \\ \gamma \end{pmatrix} + \begin{pmatrix} u_i^* \\ \bar{u}_i \end{pmatrix}$$

and show that GLS on this extended regression yields $\widehat{\beta} = \widetilde{\beta}_{\text{Within}}$ and $\widehat{\gamma} = \widehat{\beta}_{\text{Between}} - \widetilde{\beta}_{\text{Within}}$, where $\widetilde{\beta}_{\text{Within}}$ and $\widehat{\beta}_{\text{Between}}$ are the familiar panel data estimators. Conclude that Hausman's test for H_0: $E(\mu_i/X_i) = 0$ can be based on a test for $\gamma = 0$, as shown by Arellano (1993). See solution 95.2.5 in *Econometric Theory* by Xiong (1996b).

4.15 For the Grunfeld data, replicate the Hausman test results given in example 1 of section 4.3.

4.16 For the gasoline demand data, replicate the Hausman test results given in example 2 of section 4.3.

4.17 Perform Hausman's test for the public capital data.

4.18 *The relative efficiency of the Between estimator with respect to the Within estimator.* This is based on problem 99.4.3 in *Econometric Theory* by Baltagi (1999b). Consider the simple panel data regression model

$$y_{it} = \alpha + \beta x_{it} + u_{it} \quad i = 1, 2, \ldots, N; \; t = 1, 2, \ldots, T \qquad (1)$$

where α and β are scalars. Subtract the mean equation to get rid of the constant

$$y_{it} - \bar{y}_{..} = \beta(x_{it} - \bar{x}_{..}) + u_{it} - \bar{u}_{..} \qquad (2)$$

where $\bar{x}_{..} = \sum_{i=1}^{N} \sum_{t=1}^{T} x_{it}/NT$ and $\bar{y}_{..}$ and $\bar{u}_{..}$ are similarly defined. Add and subtract $\bar{x}_{i.}$ from the regressor in parentheses and rearrange

$$y_{it} - \bar{y}_{..} = \beta(x_{it} - \bar{x}_{i.}) + \beta(\bar{x}_{i.} - \bar{x}_{..}) + u_{it} - \bar{u}_{..} \qquad (3)$$

where $\bar{x}_{i.} = \sum_{t=1}^{T} x_{it}/T$. Now run the unrestricted least squares regression

$$y_{it} - \bar{y}_{..} = \beta_w(x_{it} - \bar{x}_{i.}) + \beta_b(\bar{x}_{i.} - \bar{x}_{..}) + u_{it} - \bar{u}_{..} \qquad (4)$$

where β_w is not necessarily equal to β_b.

(a) Show that the least squares estimator of β_w from (4) is the Within estimator and that of β_b is the Between estimator.

(b) Show that if $u_{it} = \mu_i + \nu_{it}$ where $\mu_i \sim \text{IID}(0, \sigma_\mu^2)$ and $\nu_{it} \sim \text{IID}(0, \sigma_\nu^2)$ independent of each other and among themselves, then ordinary least squares (OLS) is equivalent to generalized least squares (GLS) on (4).

(c) Show that for model (1), the relative efficiency of the Between estimator with respect to the Within estimator is equal to $(B_{XX}/W_{XX})[(1 - \rho)/(T\rho + (1 - \rho))]$, where $W_{XX} = \sum_{i=1}^{N} \sum_{t=1}^{T} (x_{it} - \bar{x}_{i.})^2$ denotes the Within variation and $B_{XX} = T \sum_{i=1}^{N} (\bar{x}_{i.} - \bar{x}_{..})^2$ denotes the Between variation. Also, $\rho = \sigma_\mu^2/(\sigma_\mu^2 + \sigma_\nu^2)$ denotes the equicorrelation coefficient.

(d) Show that the square of the t-statistic used to test H_0: $\beta_w = \beta_b$ in (4) yields exactly Hausman's (1978) specification test. See solution 99.4.3 in *Econometric Theory* by Gurmu (2000).

5 Heteroskedasticity and Serial Correlation in the Error Component Model

5.1 HETEROSKEDASTICITY

The standard error component model given by (2.1) and (2.2) assumes that the regression disturbances are homoskedastic with the same variance across time and individuals. This may be a restrictive assumption for panels, where the cross-sectional units may be of varying size and as a result may exhibit different variation. For example, when dealing with gasoline demand across OECD countries, steam electric generation across various size utilities, or estimating cost functions for various US airline firms, one should expect to find heteroskedasticity in the disturbance term. Assuming homoskedastic disturbances when heteroskedasticity is present will still result in consistent estimates of the regression coefficients, but these estimates will not be efficient. Also, the standard errors of these estimates will be biased unless one computes robust standard errors correcting for the possible presence of heteroskedasticity. In this section, we relax the assumption of homoskedasticity of the disturbances and introduce heteroskedasticity through the μ_i as first suggested by Mazodier and Trognon (1978). Next, we suggest an alternative heteroskedastic error component specification, where only the ν_{it} are heteroskedastic. We illustrate these methods using the gasoline demand study of Baltagi and Griffin (1988a).

Mazodier and Trognon (1978) generalized the homoskedastic error component model to the case where the μ_i are heteroskedastic, i.e. $\mu_i \sim (0, w_i^2)$ for $i = 1, \ldots, N$, but $\nu_{it} \sim \text{IID}(0, \sigma_\nu^2)$. In vector form, $\mu \sim (0, \Sigma_\mu)$ where $\Sigma_\mu = \text{diag}[w_i^2]$ is a diagonal matrix of dimension $N \times N$ and $\nu \sim (0, \sigma_\nu^2 I_{NT})$. Therefore, using (2.4), one gets

$$\Omega = E(uu') = Z_\mu \Sigma_\mu Z_\mu' + \sigma_\nu^2 I_{NT} \tag{5.1}$$

This can be written as

$$\Omega = \text{diag}[w_i^2] \otimes J_T + \text{diag}[\sigma_\nu^2] \otimes I_T \tag{5.2}$$

where $\text{diag}[\sigma_\nu^2]$ is also of dimension $N \times N$. Using the Wansbeek and Kapteyn (1982b, 1983) trick, Baltagi and Griffin (1988a) derived the corresponding Fuller and Battese (1974) transformation as follows:

$$\Omega = \text{diag}[Tw_i^2 + \sigma_\nu^2] \otimes \bar{J}_T + \text{diag}[\sigma_\nu^2] \otimes E_T \tag{5.3}$$

Therefore

$$\Omega^r = \text{diag}[(\tau_i^2)^r] \otimes \bar{J}_T + \text{diag}[(\sigma_\nu^2)^r] \otimes E_T \tag{5.4}$$

where $\tau_i^2 = Tw_i^2 + \sigma_\nu^2$ and r is any arbitrary scalar. The Fuller–Battese transformation for the heteroskedastic case premultiplies the model by

$$\sigma_\nu \Omega^{-1/2} = \text{diag}[\sigma_\nu/\tau_i] \otimes \bar{J}_T + (I_N \otimes E_T)$$

Hence, $y^* = \sigma_\nu \Omega^{-1/2} y$ has a typical element $y_{it}^* = (y_{it} - \theta_i \bar{y}_{i.})$ where $\theta_i = 1 - (\sigma_\nu/\tau_i)$ for $i = 1, \ldots, N$.

Feasible GLS requires estimates of σ_ν^2 and the w_i^2 for $i = 1, \ldots, N$. It is immediately clear that this procedure requires large T and preferably small N with $T \gg N$. This is not the typical labor or consumer panel data situation, but it is likely to be the case when pooling a few countries, states or regions over a long time period. As in the homoskedastic case, the Within residuals MSE given in (2.24) still estimate σ_ν^2 consistently; call it $\widehat{\sigma}_\nu^2$. Note also that

$$\text{var}(u_{it}) = E(u_{it}^2) = w_i^2 + \sigma_\nu^2 = \sigma_i^2 \quad \text{for } i = 1, \ldots, N$$

Therefore, one can estimate

$$\widehat{\sigma}_i^2 = \sum_{t=1}^{T} (\widehat{u}_{it} - \bar{\widehat{u}}_{i.})^2/(T-1) \quad \text{for } i = 1, \ldots, N$$

using the OLS residuals $\widehat{u}_{it}$ and then obtain

$$\widehat{w}_i^2 = \widehat{\sigma}_i^2 - \widehat{\sigma}_\nu^2 \quad \text{for } i = 1, \ldots, N$$

In this case, the OLS regression coefficient estimates are still consistent, but not efficient. Next, we form $\widehat{\tau}_i^2 = T\widehat{w}_i^2 + \widehat{\sigma}_\nu^2$, $\widehat{\theta}_i = 1 - (\widehat{\sigma}_\nu/\widehat{\tau}_i)$ and compute $\widehat{y}_{it}^* = (y_{it} - \widehat{\theta}_i \bar{y}_{i.})$. Feasible GLS can now be performed as OLS on the transformed model. Consistency of the variance components requires $T \to \infty$ and N to be finite. Of course, one can iterate, using feasible GLS residuals rather than OLS residuals in estimating $\widehat{\sigma}_i^2$. In all cases, one has to guard against negative variance estimates of $\widehat{w}_i^2$. Other estimates of the variance components include maximum likelihood under normality; see Magnus (1982) and Rao's (1970, 1972) MINQUE estimates considered by Baltagi and Griffin (1988a). With consistent estimates of the variance components, the feasible GLS estimates in the next step are asymptotically efficient. In small samples, corrections for degrees of freedom in estimating $\widehat{\sigma}_i^2$ may be important and may affect the estimates of the resulting feasible GLS regression coefficients.

5.1.1 Empirical Illustration

For the Baltagi and Griffin (1983) gasoline demand example given in (2.41) utilizing a pooled data set for 18 OECD countries for the period 1964–78, the estimated model was generalized to allow for a distributed lag on real gasoline prices as follows:

$$\ln \frac{\text{GAS}}{\text{CAR}_{it}} = \alpha_0 + \alpha_1 \ln \frac{Y}{N_{it}} + \beta \sum_{j=1}^{n} \omega_j \left(\ln \frac{P_{\text{MG}}}{P_{\text{GDP}}} \right)_{it-j} + \phi \ln \frac{\text{CAR}}{N_{it}} + u_{it}$$

Table 5.1 reproduces the Baltagi and Griffin (1988a) results comparing the standard homoskedastic error components model with the heteroskedastic estimates. The following estimates are reported: OLS, Within and two feasible GLS estimators (the Swamy and Arora (1972) SWAR estimator and Rao's (1970, 1972) MINQUE) assuming homoskedasticity. The heteroskedastic error components estimator described above is computed and iterated, but only the first and last iterations are reported. Also, MINQUE assuming heteroskedasticity is computed. In order to avoid unnecessary detail, only the long-run price elasticities are reported.

Using N sample variances s_i^2 with f_i degrees of freedom, and assuming normality, one can test the hypothesis of homoskedasticity by employing Bartlett's test (see Kmenta, 1986, p. 297). Under homoskedasticity, the Bartlett statistic is χ^2 distributed with $N-1$ degrees of freedom. The observed value of this χ^2 is 244.96 which decisively rejects homoskedasticity. Baltagi and Griffin (1988a)

Table 5.1 Parameter Estimates under Heteroskedasticity*

Estimation Technique	$\ln Y/N$	$\ln P_{\text{MG}}/P_{\text{GDP}}$	$\ln \text{CAR}/N$	$\bar{R}^2$	SE
OLS	0.891	−0.904	−0.772	0.86	0.191
	(0.037)	(0.030)	(0.020)		
Within	0.540	−0.549	−0.655	0.83	0.066
	(0.080)	(0.069)	(0.032)		
Error Components (homoskedasticity)					
SWAR	0.545	−0.607	−0.662	0.83	0.069
	(0.060)	(0.052)	(0.028)		
MINQUE	0.553	−0.618	−0.666	0.83	0.070
	(0.057)	(0.050)	(0.028)		
Error Components (heteroskedasticity)					
Iterative Estimator:					
First Iteration	0.534	−0.587	−0.657	0.98	0.068
	(0.057)	(0.049)	(0.027)		
Last Iteration†	0.576	−0.592	−0.676	0.99	0.068
	(0.022)	(0.020)	(0.015)		
MINQUE†	0.507	−0.774	−0.639	0.99	0.076
	(0.036)	(0.024)	(0.012)		

*Numbers in parentheses are standard errors

†Negative variance estimates were replaced by zero

Source: Baltagi and Griffin (1988a). Reproduced by permission of *International Economic Review*

report the estimates of the w_i^2 and the corresponding $\widehat{\theta}_i$ and show that it is more likely to get negative variance components estimates when one is estimating N of these w_i^2 ($N = 18$ in this case). The first iteration did not yield negative estimates of the variance components, but subsequent iterations did. These negative variance estimates were replaced by zero.

The empirical example is supportive of the heteroskedastic error component estimator. Homoskedasticity was rejected and there is a substantial reduction in standard errors as we move from the homoskedastic to the heteroskedastic error components estimators. The presence of negative variances suggests that these procedures do not uniformly give precise estimates of θ_i. In effect, by allowing θ_i to vary, one is capturing the efficiency gains by allowing for differential θ but acknowledging that for some subset the estimates may be imprecise.

5.1.2 An Alternative Heteroskedastic Error Component Model

Alternatively, one could keep the μ_i homoskedastic with $\mu_i \sim \text{IID}(0, \sigma_\mu^2)$ and impose the heteroskedasticity on the ν_{it}, i.e. $\nu_{it} \sim (0, w_i^2)$ (see the problem by Baltagi (1988b) and the solution by Wansbeek (1989) in *Econometric Theory*). In this case, using (2.4) one obtains

$$\Omega = E(uu') = \text{diag}[\sigma_\mu^2] \otimes J_T + \text{diag}[w_i^2] \otimes I_T \qquad (5.5)$$

Replacing J_T by $T\bar{J}_T$ and I_T by $E_T + \bar{J}_T$, we get

$$\Omega = \text{diag}[T\sigma_\mu^2 + w_i^2] \otimes \bar{J}_T + \text{diag}[w_i^2] \otimes E_T \qquad (5.6)$$

and

$$\Omega^r = \text{diag}[(\tau_i^2)^r] \otimes \bar{J}_T + \text{diag}[(w_i^2)^r] \otimes E_T \qquad (5.7)$$

where $\tau_i^2 = T\sigma_\mu^2 + w_i^2$ and r is an arbitrary scalar. Therefore

$$\Omega^{-1/2} = \text{diag}[1/\tau_i] \otimes \bar{J}_T + \text{diag}[1/w_i] \otimes E_T$$

and $y^* = \Omega^{-1/2} y$ has a typical element

$$y_{it}^* = (\bar{y}_{i.}/\tau_i) + (y_{it} - \bar{y}_{i.})/w_i$$

Upon rearranging terms, we get

$$y_{it}^* = \frac{1}{w_i}(y_{it} - \theta_i \bar{y}_{i.}) \quad \text{where} \quad \theta_i = 1 - (w_i/\tau_i)$$

In this case $E(u_{it}^2) = \sigma_i^2 = \sigma_\mu^2 + w_i^2$ for $i = 1, \ldots, N$. Using the OLS residuals, say $\widehat{u}_{it}$, one obtains $\widehat{\sigma}_i^2 = \sum_{t=1}^T (\widehat{u}_{it} - \overline{\widehat{u}}_{i.})^2/(T-1)$. Also, using the Within residuals, say $\widetilde{u}_{it}$, one can compute $\widetilde{w}_i^2 = \sum_{t=1}^T (\widetilde{u}_{it} - \overline{\widetilde{u}}_{i.})^2/(T-1)$. In this case, N estimates of σ_μ^2 result from $(\widehat{\sigma}_i^2 - \widetilde{w}_i^2)$. Therefore, a consistent estimator σ_μ^2 is $\widehat{\sigma}_\mu^2 = \sum_{i=1}^N (\widehat{\sigma}_i^2 - \widetilde{w}_i^2)/N$, the average of the N estimators of σ_μ^2. The next step is to compute the corresponding $\widehat{\theta}_i = 1 - (\widetilde{w}_i/\widehat{\tau}_i)$, where $\widehat{\tau}_i^2 = T\widehat{\sigma}_\mu^2 + \widetilde{w}_i^2$, perform the transformation $\hat{y}_{it}^* = (1/\widetilde{w}_i)(y_{it} - \widehat{\theta}_i \bar{y}_{i.})$ and run OLS on the transformed model.

A more general heteroskedastic model is given by Randolph (1988) where both the μ_i and the ν_{it} are assumed heteroskedastic in the context of an unbalanced panel. In this case, $\text{var}(\mu_i) = \sigma_i^2$ and $E(\nu\nu') = \text{diag}[\sigma_{it}^2]$ for $i = 1, \ldots, N$ and $t = 1, \ldots, T_i$. Also, Griffiths and Anderson (1982) utilize a heteroskedastic error component model to estimate a production function for wool in the pastoral zone of eastern Australia. The specification of the production function is Cobb–Douglas that allows for the estimation of positive or negative marginal risks. Li and Stengos (1994) propose estimating a one-way error component model with the remainder error heteroskedastic of unknown form using adaptive estimation techniques. They also suggest a modified Breusch and Pagan test for significance of the random individual effects. Holly and Gardiol (2000) derive a score test for heteroskedasticity in a one-way error component model where the μ_i's are independent and distributed as $N(0, \sigma_\mu^2 h(z_i'\gamma))$. Here, z_i is a $p \times 1$ vector of explanatory variables such that $z_i'\gamma$ does not contain a constant term and h is a strictly positive twice-differentiable function satisfying $h(0) = 1$ with $h'(0) \neq 0$ and $h''(0) \neq 0$. This score test statistic is one half the explained sum of squares of the OLS regression of $(\hat{s}/\bar{s}) - \iota_N$ against the p regressors in Z as in the Breusch and Pagan test for heteroskedasticity. Here $\hat{s}_i = \hat{u}_i' \bar{J}_T \hat{u}_i$ and $\bar{s} = \sum_{i=1}^N \hat{s}_i/N$ where $\widehat{u}_i$ denote the maximum likelihood residuals from the restricted model under H_0: $\gamma = 0$. This is a one-way error component model without heteroskedasticity, i.e. $\mu_i \sim (0, \sigma_\mu^2)$.

5.2 SERIAL CORRELATION

The classical error component disturbances given by (2.2) assume that the only correlation over time is due to the presence of the same individual across the panel. In Chapter 2, this equicorrelation coefficient was shown to be $\text{correl}(u_{it}, u_{is}) = \sigma_\mu^2/(\sigma_\mu^2 + \sigma_\nu^2)$ for $t \neq s$. Note that it is the same no matter how far t is from s. This may be a restrictive assumption for economic relationships, like investment or consumption, where an unobserved shock this period will affect the behavioral relationship for at least the next few periods. This type of serial correlation is not allowed for in the simple error component model. Ignoring serial correlation when it is present results in consistent but inefficient estimates of the regression coefficients and biased standard errors. This section introduces serial correlation in the ν_{it}. First as an autoregressive process of order one, AR(1), as in the Lillard and Willis (1978) study on earnings. Next, as a second-order autoregressive process AR(2). Also, as a special fourth-order autoregressive process AR(4) for quarterly data and finally as a first-order moving average MA(1) process. For all these serial correlation specifications, a simple generalization of the Fuller and Battese (1973) transformation is derived and the implications for predictions are given. Testing for individual effects and serial correlation is taken up in the last subsection.

5.2.1 The AR(1) Process

Lillard and Willis (1978) generalized the error component model to the serially correlated case, by assuming that the remainder disturbances (the ν_{it}) follow an AR(1) process. In this case $\mu_i \sim \text{IID}(0, \sigma_\mu^2)$, whereas

$$\nu_{it} = \rho \nu_{i,t-1} + \epsilon_{it} \tag{5.8}$$

$|\rho| < 1$ and $\epsilon_{it} \sim \text{IID}(0, \sigma_\epsilon^2)$. The μ_i are independent of the ν_{it} and $\nu_{i0} \sim (0, \sigma_\epsilon^2/(1-\rho^2))$. Baltagi and Li (1991a) derived the corresponding Fuller and Battese (1974) transformation for this model. First, one applies the Prais–Winsten (PW) transformation matrix

$$C = \begin{bmatrix} (1-\rho^2)^{1/2} & 0 & 0 & \cdots & 0 & 0 & 0 \\ -\rho & 1 & 0 & \cdots & 0 & 0 & 0 \\ \cdot & \cdot & \cdot & \cdots & \cdot & \cdot & \cdot \\ \cdot & \cdot & \cdot & \cdots & \cdot & \cdot & \cdot \\ 0 & 0 & 0 & \cdots & -\rho & 1 & 0 \\ 0 & 0 & 0 & \cdots & 0 & -\rho & 1 \end{bmatrix}$$

to transform the remainder AR(1) disturbances into serially uncorrelated classical errors. For panel data, this has to be applied for N individuals. The transformed regression disturbances are in vector form

$$u^* = (I_N \otimes C)u = (I_N \otimes C\iota_T)\mu + (I_N \otimes C)\nu \tag{5.9}$$

Using the fact that $C\iota_T = (1-\rho)\iota_T^\alpha$, where $\iota_T^{\alpha\prime} = (\alpha, \iota_{T-1}')$ and $\alpha = \sqrt{(1+\rho)/(1-\rho)}$, one can rewrite (5.9) as

$$u^* = (1-\rho)(I_N \otimes \iota_T^\alpha)\mu + (I_N \otimes C)\nu \tag{5.10}$$

Therefore, the variance–covariance matrix of the transformed disturbances is

$$\Omega^* = E(u^* u^{*\prime}) = \sigma_\mu^2 (1-\rho)^2 [I_N \otimes \iota_T^\alpha \iota_T^{\alpha\prime}] + \sigma_\epsilon^2 (I_N \otimes I_T)$$

since $(I_N \otimes C)E(\nu\nu')(I_N \otimes C') = \sigma_\epsilon^2 (I_N \otimes I_T)$. Alternatively, this can be rewritten as

$$\Omega^* = d^2 \sigma_\mu^2 (1-\rho)^2 [I_N \otimes \iota_T^\alpha \iota_T^{\alpha\prime}/d^2] + \sigma_\epsilon^2 (I_N \otimes I_T) \tag{5.11}$$

where $d^2 = \iota_T^{\alpha\prime}\iota_T^\alpha = \alpha^2 + (T-1)$. This replaces $J_T^\alpha = \iota_T^\alpha \iota_T^{\alpha\prime}$ by $d^2 \bar{J}_T^\alpha$, its idempotent counterpart, where $\bar{J}_T^\alpha = \iota_T^\alpha \iota_T^{\alpha\prime}/d^2$. Extending the Wansbeek and Kapteyn (1982b) trick, we replace I_T by $E_T^\alpha + \bar{J}_T^\alpha$, where $E_T^\alpha = I_T - \bar{J}_T^\alpha$. Collecting terms with the same matrices, one obtains the spectral decomposition of Ω^*:

$$\Omega^* = \sigma_\alpha^2 (I_N \otimes \bar{J}_T^\alpha) + \sigma_\epsilon^2 (I_N \otimes E_T^\alpha) \tag{5.12}$$

where $\sigma_\alpha^2 = d^2 \sigma_\mu^2 (1-\rho)^2 + \sigma_\epsilon^2$. Therefore

$$\sigma_\epsilon \Omega^{*-1/2} = (\sigma_\epsilon/\sigma_\alpha)(I_N \otimes \bar{J}_T^\alpha) + (I_N \otimes E_T^\alpha) = I_N \otimes I_T - \theta_\alpha (I_N \otimes \bar{J}_T^\alpha) \tag{5.13}$$

where $\theta_\alpha = 1 - (\sigma_\epsilon/\sigma_\alpha)$.

Premultiplying the PW transformed observations $y^* = (I_N \otimes C)y$ by $\sigma_\epsilon \Omega^{*-1/2}$ one gets $y^{**} = \sigma_\epsilon \Omega^{*-1/2} y^*$. The typical elements of $y^{**} = \sigma_\epsilon \Omega^{*-1/2} y^*$ are given by

$$(y^*_{i1} - \theta_\alpha \alpha b_i, y^*_{i2} - \theta_\alpha b_i, \ldots, y^*_{iT} - \theta_\alpha b_i)' \tag{5.14}$$

where $b_i = [(\alpha y^*_{i1} + \sum_2^T y^*_{it})/d^2]$ for $i = 1, \ldots, N$.[1] The first observation gets special attention in the AR(1) error component model. First, the PW transformation gives it a special weight $\sqrt{1-\rho^2}$ in y^*. Second, the Fuller and Battese transformation gives it a special weight $\alpha = \sqrt{(1+\rho)/(1-\rho)}$ in computing the weighted average b_i and the pseudo-difference in (5.14). Note that (i) if $\rho = 0$, then $\alpha = 1, d^2 = T, \sigma^2_\alpha = \sigma^2_1$ and $\theta_\alpha = \theta$. Therefore, the typical element of y^{**}_{it} reverts to the familiar $(y_{it} - \theta \bar{y}_{i.})$ transformation for the one-way error component model with no serial correlation. (ii) If $\sigma^2_\mu = 0$, then $\sigma^2_\alpha = \sigma^2_\epsilon$ and $\theta_\alpha = 0$. Therefore, the typical element of y^{**}_{it} reverts to the PW transformation y^*_{it}.

The BQU estimators of the variance components arise naturally from the spectral decomposition of Ω^*. In fact, $(I_N \otimes E^\alpha_T)u^* \sim (0, \sigma^2_\epsilon[I_N \otimes E^\alpha_T])$ and $(I_N \otimes \bar{J}^\alpha_T)u^* \sim (0, \sigma^2_\alpha[I_N \otimes \bar{J}^\alpha_T])$ and

$$\widehat{\sigma}^2_\epsilon = u^{*\prime}(I_N \otimes E^\alpha_T)u^*/N(T-1) \quad \text{and} \quad \widehat{\sigma}^2_\alpha = u^{*\prime}(I_N \otimes \bar{J}^\alpha_T)u^*/N \tag{5.15}$$

provide the BQU estimators of σ^2_ϵ and σ^2_α, respectively. Baltagi and Li (1991a) suggest estimating ρ from Within residuals $\widetilde{\nu}_{it}$ as $\widetilde{\rho} = \sum_{i=1}^N \sum_{t=1}^T \widetilde{\nu}_{it}\widetilde{\nu}_{i,t-1} / \sum_{i=1}^N \sum_{t=2}^T \widetilde{\nu}^2_{i,t-1}$. Then, $\widehat{\sigma}^2_\epsilon$ and $\widehat{\sigma}^2_\alpha$ are estimated from (5.15) by substituting OLS residuals $\hat{u}^*$ from the PW transformed equation using $\widetilde{\rho}$. Using Monte Carlo experiments, Baltagi and Li (1997) found that $\widetilde{\rho}$ performs poorly for small T and recommended an alternative estimator of ρ which is based on the autocovariance function $Q_s = E(u_{it}u_{i,t-s})$. For the AR(1) model given in (5.8), it is easy to show that $Q_s = \sigma^2_\mu + \sigma^2_\nu \rho^s$. From Q_0, Q_1 and Q_2, one can easily show that $\rho + 1 = (Q_0 - Q_2)/(Q_0 - Q_1)$. Hence, a consistent estimator of ρ (for large N) is given by

$$\widehat{\rho} = \frac{\widetilde{Q}_0 - \widetilde{Q}_2}{\widetilde{Q}_0 - \widetilde{Q}_1} - 1 = \frac{\widetilde{Q}_1 - \widetilde{Q}_2}{\widetilde{Q}_0 - \widetilde{Q}_1}$$

where $\widetilde{Q}_s = \sum_{i=1}^N \sum_{t=s+1}^T \widehat{u}_{it}\widehat{u}_{i,t-s}/N(T-s)$ and $\widehat{u}_{it}$ denotes the OLS residuals on (2.1). $\widehat{\sigma}^2_\epsilon$ and $\widehat{\sigma}^2_\alpha$ are estimated from (5.15) by substituting OLS residuals $\hat{u}^*$ from the PW transformed equation using $\widehat{\rho}$ rather than $\widetilde{\rho}$.

Therefore, the estimation of an AR(1) serially correlated error component model is considerably simplified by (i) applying the PW transformation in the first step, as is usually done in the time-series literature, and (ii) subtracting a pseudo-average from these transformed data as in (5.14) in the second step.

Empirical Applications

Lillard and Weiss (1979) applied the first-order autoregressive error component model to study the sources of variation in the earnings of American scientists over the decade 1960–70. The disturbances are assumed to be of the form

$$u_{it} = \mu_i + \xi_i(t - \bar{t}) + \nu_{it}$$

with $\nu_{it} = \rho\nu_{i,t-1} + \epsilon_{it}$ as in (5.8), $\epsilon_{it} \sim \text{IID}(0, \sigma_\epsilon^2)$ and

$$\begin{pmatrix} \mu_i \\ \xi_i \end{pmatrix} \sim (0, \Sigma_{\mu\xi})$$

Unlike the individual effect μ_i which represents unmeasured characteristics like ability that affect the levels of earnings and persist throughout the period of observation, ξ_i represents the effect of omitted variables which affect the growth in earnings. ξ_i could be the individual's learning ability, so it is highly likely that μ_i and ξ_i are correlated. Lillard and Weiss (1979) derived the MLE and GLS for this model and offered two generalizations for the error structure.

Berry, Gottschalk and Wissoker (1988) applied the one-way error component model with first-order autoregressive remainder disturbances to study the impact of plant closing on the mean and variance of log earnings. The data are drawn from the Panel Study of Income Dynamics (PSID) and include male heads of households who were less than 65 years old and not retired. The sample period considered spans seven years (1975–81) and allows observation over the pre- and postdisplacement earnings histories. The sample is not limited only to displaced workers and therefore naturally provides a control group. Their findings show that during the period of displacement, mean earnings decline while the variance of earnings increases sharply. This causes a dramatic increase in the proportion of persons earning less than \$10 000. However, this is temporary, as the mean earnings increase in the postdisplacement period and the variance of earnings declines back to its predisplacement level.

5.2.2 The AR(2) Process

This simple transformation can be extended to allow for an AR(2) process on the ν_{it}, i.e.

$$\nu_{it} = \rho_1\nu_{i,t-1} + \rho_2\nu_{i,t-2} + \epsilon_{it} \tag{5.16}$$

where $\epsilon_{it} \sim \text{IIN}(0, \sigma_\epsilon^2)$, $|\rho_2| < 1$ and $|\rho_1| < (1 - \rho_2)$. Let $E(\nu_i\nu_i') = \sigma_\epsilon^2 V$, where $\nu_i' = (\nu_{i1}, \ldots, \nu_{iT})$ and note that V is invariant to $i = 1, \ldots, N$. The unique $T \times T$ lower triangular matrix C with positive diagonal elements which satisfies $CVC' = I_T$ is given by

$$C = \begin{bmatrix} \gamma_0 & 0 & 0 & 0 & \ldots & 0 & 0 & 0 & 0 \\ -\gamma_2 & \gamma_1 & 0 & 0 & \ldots & 0 & 0 & 0 & 0 \\ -\rho_2 & -\rho_1 & 1 & 0 & \ldots & 0 & 0 & 0 & 0 \\ \cdot & \cdot & \cdot & \cdot & & \cdot & \cdot & \cdot & \cdot \\ \cdot & \cdot & \cdot & \cdot & & \cdot & \cdot & \cdot & \cdot \\ 0 & 0 & 0 & 0 & \ldots & -\rho_2 & -\rho_1 & 1 & 0 \\ 0 & 0 & 0 & 0 & \ldots & 0 & -\rho_2 & -\rho_1 & 1 \end{bmatrix}$$

where $\gamma_0 = \sigma_\epsilon/\sigma_\nu$, $\gamma_1 = \sqrt{1-\rho_2^2}$, $\gamma_2 = \gamma_1[\rho_1/(1-\rho_2)]$ and $\sigma_\nu^2 = \sigma_\epsilon^2(1-\rho_2)/(1+\rho_2)[(1-\rho_2)^2 - \rho_1^2]$. The transformed disturbances are given by

$$u^* = (I_N \otimes C)u = (1-\rho_1-\rho_2)(I_N \otimes \iota_T^\alpha)\mu + (I_N \otimes C)\nu \tag{5.17}$$

Using the fact that $C\iota_T = (1-\rho_1-\rho_2) \times$ (the new ι_T^α) where $\iota_T^{\alpha\prime} = (\alpha_1, \alpha_2, \iota_{T-2}^\prime)$, $\alpha_1 = \sigma_\epsilon/\sigma_\nu(1-\rho_1-\rho_2)$ and $\alpha_2 = \sqrt{(1+\rho_2)/(1-\rho_2)}$.

Similarly, one can define

$$d^2 = \iota_T^{\alpha\prime}\iota_T^\alpha = \alpha_1^2 + \alpha_2^2 + (T-2)$$

$$J_T^\alpha, E_T^\alpha$$

etc. as in section 5.2.1 to obtain

$$\Omega^* = d^2\sigma_\mu^2(1-\rho_1-\rho_2)^2[I_N \otimes \bar{J}_T^\alpha] + \sigma_\epsilon^2[I_N \otimes I_T] \tag{5.18}$$

as in (5.11). The only difference is that $(1-\rho_1-\rho_2)$ replaces $(1-\rho)$ and ι_T^α is defined in terms of α_1 and α_2 rather than α. Similarly, one can obtain $\sigma_\epsilon\Omega^{*-1/2}$ as in (5.13) with $\sigma_\alpha^2 = d^2\sigma_\mu^2(1-\rho_1-\rho_2)^2 + \sigma_\epsilon^2$. The typical elements of $y^{**} = \sigma_\epsilon\Omega^{*-1/2}y^*$ are given by

$$(y_{i1}^* - \theta_\alpha\alpha_1 b_i, y_{i2}^* - \theta_\alpha\alpha_2 b_i, y_{i3}^* - \theta_\alpha b_i, \ldots, y_{iT}^* - \theta_\alpha b_i) \tag{5.19}$$

where $b_i = [(\alpha_1 y_{i1}^* + \alpha_2 y_{i2}^* + \sum_3^T y_{it}^*)/d^2]$. The first two observations get special attention in the AR(2) error component model. First in the matrix C defined above (5.17) and second in computing the average b_i and the Fuller–Battese transformation in (5.19). Therefore, one can obtain GLS on this model by (i) transforming the data as in the time-series literature by the C matrix defined above (5.17) and (ii) subtracting a pseudo-average in the second step as in (5.19).

5.2.3 The AR(4) Process for Quarterly Data

Consider the specialized AR(4) process for quarterly data, i.e. $\nu_{it} = \rho\nu_{i,t-4} + \epsilon_{it}$, where $|\rho| < 1$ and $\epsilon_{it} \sim \text{IIN}(0, \sigma_\epsilon^2)$. The C matrix for this process can be defined as follows: $u_i^* = Cu_i$ where

$$\begin{aligned} u_{it}^* &= \sqrt{1-\rho^2}\, u_{it} \quad \text{for } t = 1,2,3,4 \\ &= u_{it} - \rho u_{i,t-4} \quad \text{for } t = 5,6,\ldots,T \end{aligned} \tag{5.20}$$

This means that the μ_i component of u_{it} gets transformed as $\sqrt{1-\rho^2}\mu_i$ for $t = 1,2,3,4$ and as $(1-\rho)\mu_i$ for $t = 5,6,\ldots,T$. This can be rewritten as $\alpha(1-\rho)\mu_i$ for $t = 1,2,3,4$ where $\alpha = \sqrt{(1+\rho)/(1-\rho)}$ and $(1-\rho)\mu_i$ for $t = 5,\ldots,T$. So that $u^* = (I_N \otimes C)u$ is given by (5.9) with a new C, the same α, but $\iota_T^{\alpha\prime} = (\alpha, \alpha, \alpha, \alpha, \iota_{T-4}^\prime)$, $d^2 = \iota_T^{\alpha\prime}\iota_T^\alpha = 4\alpha^2 + (T-4)$ and the derivations Ω^* and $\sigma_\epsilon\Omega^{*-1/2}$ in (5.12) and (5.13) are the same. The typical elements of $y^{**} = \sigma_\epsilon\Omega^{*-1/2}y^*$ are given by

$$(y_{i1}^* - \theta_\alpha\alpha b_i, \ldots, y_{i4}^* - \theta\alpha b_i, y_{i5}^* - \theta_\alpha b_i, \ldots, y_{iT}^* - \theta_\alpha b_i) \tag{5.21}$$

where $b_i = [(\alpha(\sum_{t=1}^{4} y_{it}^*) + \sum_{t=5}^{T} y_{it}^*)/d^2]$. Once again, GLS can easily be computed by applying (5.20) to the data in the first step and (5.21) in the second step.

5.2.4 The MA(1) Process

For the MA(1) model, defined by

$$\nu_{it} = \epsilon_{it} + \lambda\epsilon_{i,t-1} \tag{5.22}$$

where $\epsilon_{it} \sim \text{IIN}(0, \sigma_\epsilon^2)$ and $|\lambda| < 1$, Balestra (1980) gives the following C matrix, $C = D^{-1/2}P$ where $D = \text{diag}\{a_t, a_{t-1}\}$ for $t = 1, \ldots, T$:

$$P = \begin{bmatrix} 1 & 0 & 0 & \ldots & 0 \\ \lambda & a_1 & 0 & \ldots & 0 \\ \lambda^2 & a_1\lambda & a_2 & \ldots & 0 \\ \vdots & \vdots & \vdots & & \vdots \\ \lambda^{T-1} & a_1\lambda^{T-2} & a_2\lambda^{T-3} & \ldots & a_{T-1} \end{bmatrix}$$

and $a_t = 1+\lambda^2+\ldots+\lambda^{2t}$ with $a_0 = 1$. For this C matrix, one can show that the new $\iota_T^\alpha = C\iota_T = (\alpha_1, \alpha_2, \ldots, \alpha_T)'$ where these α_t can be solved for recursively as follows:

$$\begin{aligned} \alpha_1 &= (a_0/a_1)^{1/2} \\ \alpha_t &= \lambda(a_{t-2}/a_{t-1})^{1/2}\alpha_{t-1} + (a_{t-1}/a_t)^{1/2} \qquad t = 2, \ldots, T \end{aligned} \tag{5.23}$$

Therefore, $d^2 = \iota_T^{\alpha\prime}\iota_T^\alpha = \sum_{t=1}^{T} \alpha_t^2$, $\sigma_\alpha^2 = d^2\sigma_\mu^2 + \sigma_\epsilon^2$ and the spectral decomposition of Ω^* is the same as that given in (5.12), with the newly defined ι_T^α and σ_α^2. The typical elements of $y^{**} = \sigma_\epsilon\Omega^{*-1/2}y^*$ are given by

$$(y_{i1}^* - \theta_\alpha\alpha_1 b_i, \ldots, y_{iT}^* - \theta_\alpha\alpha_T b_i) \tag{5.24}$$

where $b_i = [\sum_{t=1}^{T} \alpha_t y_{it}^*/d^2]$. Therefore, for an MA(1) error component model, one applies the recursive transformation given in (5.23) in the first step and subtracts a pseudo-average described in (5.24) in the second step; see Baltagi and Li (1992c) for more details. In order to implement the estimation of an error component model with MA(1) remainder errors, Baltagi and Li (1997) proposed an alternative transformation that is simple to compute and requires only least squares. This can be summarized as follows:

Let $\gamma_s = E(\nu_{it}\nu_{i,t-s})$ denote the autocovariance function of ν_{it} and $r = \gamma_1/\gamma_0$. Note that when ν_{it} follows an MA(1) process, we have $Q_s = \sigma_\mu^2 + \gamma_s$ for $s = 0, 1$ and $Q_s = \sigma_\mu^2$ for $s > 1$. Hence we have $\gamma_\tau = Q_\tau - Q_s$ ($\tau = 0, 1$) for some $s > 1$.

Step 1: Compute $y_{i1}^* = y_{i1}/\sqrt{g_1}$ and $y_{it}^* = [y_{it} - (ry_{i,t-1}^*)/\sqrt{g_{t-1}}]/\sqrt{g_t}$ for $t = 2, \ldots, T$, where $g_1 = 1$ and $g_t = 1 - r^2/g_{t-1}$ for $t = 2, \ldots, T$. Note that this transformation depends only on r, which can be estimated by $\widehat{r} = \widehat{\gamma}_1/\widehat{\gamma}_0 = (\widetilde{Q}_1 - \widetilde{Q}_s)/(\widetilde{Q}_0 - \widetilde{Q}_s)$ for some $s > 1$.

Step 2: Compute y^{**} using the result that $\iota_T^\alpha = C\iota_T = (\alpha_1, \ldots, \alpha_T)'$ with $\alpha_1 = 1$ and $\alpha_t = [1 - r/\sqrt{g_{t-1}}]/\sqrt{g_t}$ for $t = 2, \ldots, T$. Note that in this case $\sigma^2 = \gamma_0$. The estimators of σ_α^2 and σ^2 are simply given by $\widehat{\sigma}_\alpha^2 = (\sum_{t=1}^T \widehat{\alpha}_t^2)\widehat{\sigma}_\mu^2 + \widehat{\sigma}^2$ and $\widehat{\sigma}^2 = \widehat{\gamma}_0 = \widetilde{Q}_0 - \widetilde{Q}_s$ for some $s > 1$ with $\widehat{\sigma}_\mu^2 = \widetilde{Q}_s$ for some $s > 1$. Finally $\widehat{\delta} = 1 - \sqrt{\widehat{\gamma}_0/\widehat{\sigma}_\alpha^2}$. Again, the OLS estimator on the (**) transformed equation is equivalent to GLS on (2.1).

The advantages of this approach are by now evident: $\widehat{\sigma}^2 = \widehat{\gamma}_0$ is trivially obtained from OLS residuals. This is because we did not choose $\sigma_\epsilon^2 = \sigma^2$ as in Baltagi and Li (1991a). Next we estimated γ's rather than the moving average parameter λ. The $\widehat{\gamma}$'s require only linear least squares, whereas $\widehat{\lambda}$ requires nonlinear least squares. Finally, our proposed estimation procedure requires simple recursive transformations that are very easy to program. This should prove useful for panel data users.

In summary, a simple transformation for the one-way error component model with serial correlation can easily be generalized to any error process generating the remainder disturbances ν_{it} as long as there exists a *simple* $(T \times T)$ matrix C such that the transformation $(I_N \otimes C)\nu$ has zero mean and variance $\sigma^2 I_{NT}$.

Step 1: Perform the C transformation on the observations of each individual $y_i' = (y_{i1}, \ldots, y_{iT})$ to obtain $y_i^* = Cy_i$ free of serial correlation.

Step 2: Perform another transformation on the y_{it}^*'s, obtained in Step 1, which subtracts from y_{it}^* a fraction of a weighted average of observations on y_{it}^*, i.e.

$$y_{it}^{**} = y_{it}^* - \theta_\alpha \alpha_t \left(\sum_{s=1}^T \alpha_s y_{is}^*\right) \Big/ \left(\sum_{s=1}^T \alpha_s^2\right)$$

where the α_t's are the elements of $\iota_T^\alpha = C\iota_T \equiv (\alpha_1, \alpha_2, \ldots, \alpha_T)'$ and $\theta_\alpha = 1 - (\sigma/\sigma_\alpha)$ with $\sigma_\alpha^2 = \sigma_\mu^2(\sum_{t=1}^T \alpha_t^2) + \sigma^2$. See Baltagi and Li (1994) for an extension to the MA(q) case and Galbraith and Zinde-Walsh (1995) for an extension to the ARMA(p, q) case.

5.2.5 Unequally Spaced Panels with AR(1) Disturbances

Some panel data sets cannot be collected every period due to lack of resources or cuts in funding. Instead, these panels are collected over unequally spaced time intervals. For example, a panel of households could be collected over unequally spaced years rather than annually. This is also likely when collecting data on countries, states or firms where in certain years the data are not recorded, are hard to obtain, or are simply missing. Other common examples are panel data sets using daily data from the stock market, including stock prices, commodity prices, futures, etc. These panel data sets are unequally spaced when the market closes on weekends and holidays. This is also common for housing resale data where the pattern of resales for each house occurs at different time periods and the panel is unbalanced because we observe different numbers of resales for each house. Baltagi and Wu (1999) extended Baltagi and Li's (1991a) results to the estimation of an unequally spaced panel data regression model with AR(1) remainder disturbances. A feasible generalized least squares procedure is proposed as a weighted least squares that can handle a wide range of unequally spaced panel data patterns. This procedure is simple to compute and provides natural estimates of the serial correlation and variance components parameters. Baltagi and Wu (1999) also provided a locally best invariant test for zero first-order serial correlation against positive or negative serial correlation in case of unequally spaced panel data. Details are given in that paper. This is programmed in STATA. Unbalanced panels arising from randomly missing observations are studied in Chapter 9.

5.2.6 Prediction

In section 2.5 we derived Goldberger's (1962) BLUP of $y_{i,T+S}$ for the one-way error component model without serial correlation. For ease of reference, we reproduce (2.37) for predicting one period ahead for the ith individual:

$$\widehat{y}_{i,T+1} = Z'_{i,T+1}\widehat{\delta}_{\text{GLS}} + w'\Omega^{-1}\widehat{u}_{\text{GLS}} \tag{5.25}$$

where $\widehat{u}_{\text{GLS}} = y - Z\widehat{\delta}_{\text{GLS}}$ and $w = E(u_{i,T+1}u)$. For the AR(1) model with no error components, a standard result is that the last term in (5.25) reduces to $\rho\widehat{u}_{i,T}$, where $\widehat{u}_{i,T}$ is the Tth GLS residual for the ith individual. For the one-way error component model without serial correlation (see Taub, 1979 or section 2.5), the last term of (5.25) reduces to $[T\sigma_\mu^2/(T\sigma_\mu^2+\sigma_\nu^2)]\overline{\widehat{u}}_{i.}$, where $\overline{\widehat{u}}_{i.} = \sum_{t=1}^{T}\widehat{u}_{it}/T$ is the average of the ith individual's GLS residuals. This section summarizes the Baltagi and Li (1992c) derivation of the last term of (5.25) when *both* error components and serial correlation are present. This provides the applied researcher with a simple way of augmenting the GLS predictions obtained from the Fuller and Battese (1973) transformation described above.

For the one-way error component model with AR(1) remainder disturbances, considered in section 5.2.1, Baltagi and Li (1992c) find that

$$w'\Omega^{-1}\widehat{u}_{\text{GLS}} = \rho\widehat{u}_{i,T} + \left(\frac{(1-\rho)^2\sigma_\mu^2}{\sigma_\alpha^2}\right)\left[\alpha\hat{u}_{i1}^* + \sum_{t=2}^{T}\hat{u}_{it}^*\right] \tag{5.26}$$

Note that the first PW transformed GLS residual receives an α weight in averaging across the ith individual's residuals in (5.26). (i) If $\sigma_\mu^2 = 0$, so that only serial correlation is present, (5.26) reduces to $\rho\widehat{u}_{i,T}$. Similarly, (ii) if $\rho = 0$, so that only error components are present, (5.26) reduces to $[T\sigma_\mu^2/(T\sigma_\mu^2+\sigma_\nu^2)]\overline{\widehat{u}}_{i.}$.

For the one-way error component model with remainder disturbances following an AR(2) process, considered in section 5.2.2, Baltagi and Li (1992c) find that

$$\begin{aligned} w'\Omega^{-1}\widehat{u}_{\text{GLS}} &= \rho_1\widehat{u}_{i,T-1} + \rho_2\widehat{u}_{i,T-2} \\ &\quad + \left[\frac{(1-\rho_1-\rho_2)^2\sigma_\mu^2}{\sigma_\alpha^2}\right]\left[\alpha_1\hat{u}_{i1}^* + \alpha_2\hat{u}_{i2}^* + \sum_{t=3}^{T}\hat{u}_{it}^*\right] \end{aligned} \tag{5.27}$$

where

$$\alpha_1 = \sigma_\epsilon/\sigma_\nu(1-\rho_1-\rho_2) \quad \alpha_2 = \sqrt{(1+\rho_2)/(1-\rho_2)}$$
$$\sigma_\alpha^2 = d^2\sigma_\mu^2(1-\rho_1-\rho_2)^2 + \sigma_\epsilon^2$$
$$d^2 = \alpha_1^2 + \alpha_2^2 + (T-2)$$

and

$$\hat{u}_{i1}^* = (\sigma_\epsilon/\sigma_\nu)\widehat{u}_{i1}$$
$$\hat{u}_{i2}^* = \sqrt{1-\rho_2^2}\,[\widehat{u}_{i2} - (\rho_1/(1-\rho_2))\widehat{u}_{i1}]$$
$$\hat{u}_{it}^* = \widehat{u}_{it} - \rho_1\widehat{u}_{i,t-1} - \rho_2\widehat{u}_{i,t-2} \quad \text{for } t = 3, \ldots, T$$

Note that if $\rho_2 = 0$, this predictor reduces to (5.26). Also, note that for this predictor the first two residuals are weighted differently when averaging across the ith individual's residuals in (5.27).

For the one-way error component model with remainder disturbances following the specialized AR(4) process for quarterly data, considered in section 5.2.3, Baltagi and Li (1992c) find that

$$w'\Omega^{-1}\widehat{u}_{\text{GLS}} = \rho\widehat{u}_{i,T-3} + \left[\frac{(1-\rho)^2\sigma_\mu^2}{\sigma_\alpha^2}\right]\left[\alpha\sum_{t=1}^{4}\hat{u}_{it}^* + \sum_{t=5}^{T}\hat{u}_{it}^*\right] \tag{5.28}$$

where $\alpha = \sqrt{(1+\rho)/(1-\rho)}$, $\sigma_\alpha^2 = d^2(1-\rho)^2\sigma_\mu^2 + \sigma_\epsilon^2$, $d^2 = 4\alpha^2 + (T-4)$ and

$$u_{it}^* = \sqrt{1-\rho^2}\,u_{it} \qquad \text{for } t = 1, 2, 3, 4$$
$$= u_{it} - \rho u_{i,t-4} \qquad \text{for } t = 5, 6, \ldots, T$$

Note, for this predictor, that the first four quarterly residuals are weighted by α when averaging across the ith individual's residuals in (5.28).

Finally, for the one-way error component model with remainder disturbances following an MA(1) process, considered in section 5.2.4, Baltagi and Li (1992c) find that

$$w'\Omega^{-1}\widehat{u}_{\text{GLS}} = -\lambda\left(\frac{a_{T-1}}{a_T}\right)^{1/2}\hat{u}_{iT}^* + \left[1 + \lambda\left(\frac{a_{T-1}}{a_T}\right)^{1/2}\alpha_T\right]\left(\frac{\sigma_\mu^2}{\sigma_\alpha^2}\right)\left[\sum_{t=1}^{T}\alpha_t\hat{u}_{it}^*\right] \tag{5.29}$$

where the $\hat{u}_{it}^*$ can be solved for recursively as follows:

$$\hat{u}_{i1}^* = (a_0/a_1)^{1/2}\hat{u}_{i1}$$
$$\hat{u}_{it}^* = \lambda(a_{t-2}/a_{t-1})^{1/2}\hat{u}_{i,t-1}^* + (a_{t-1}/a_t)^{1/2}\hat{u}_{it} \quad t = 2, \ldots, T$$

If $\lambda = 0$, then from (5.23) $a_t = \alpha_t = 1$ for all t and (5.29) reduces to the predictor for the error component model with no serial correlation. If $\sigma_\mu^2 = 0$, the second term in (5.29) drops out and the predictor reduces to that of the MA(1) process.

5.2.7 Testing for Serial Correlation and Individual Effects

In this section, we address the problem of *jointly* testing for serial correlation and individual effects. Baltagi and Li (1995) derived three LM statistics for an error component model with first-order serially correlated errors. The first LM statistic jointly tests for zero first-order serial correlation and random individual effects. The second LM statistic tests for zero first-order serial correlation assuming fixed individual effects, and the third LM statistic tests for zero first-order serial correlation assuming random individual effects. In all three cases, Baltagi and Li (1995) showed that the corresponding LM statistic is the *same* whether the alternative is AR(1) or MA(1). Also, Baltagi and Li (1995) derived two extensions of the Burke, Godfrey and Termayne (1990) AR(1) vs MA(1) test from the time-series to the panel data literature. The first extension tests the null of AR(1) disturbances against MA(1) disturbances, and the second the null of MA(1) disturbances against AR(1) disturbances in an error component model. These tests are computationally simple, requiring only OLS or Within residuals. In what follows, we briefly review the basic ideas behind these tests.

Consider the panel data regression given in (2.3):

$$y_{it} = Z_{it}'\delta + u_{it} \qquad i = 1, 2, \ldots, N; \; t = 1, 2, \ldots, T \tag{5.30}$$

where δ is a $(K+1) \times 1$ vector of regression coefficients including the intercept. The disturbance follows a one-way error component model

$$u_{it} = \mu_i + \nu_{it} \tag{5.31}$$

where $\mu_i \sim \text{IIN}(0, \sigma_\mu^2)$ and the remainder disturbance follows a stationary AR(1) process: $\nu_{it} = \rho\nu_{i,t-1} + \epsilon_{it}$ with $|\rho| < 1$ or an MA(1) process: $\nu_{it} = \epsilon_{it} + \lambda\epsilon_{i,t-1}$ with $|\lambda| < 1$ and $\epsilon_{it} \sim \text{IIN}(0, \sigma_\epsilon^2)$. In what follows, we will show that the joint LM test statistic for H_1^a: $\sigma_\mu^2 = 0$; $\lambda = 0$ is the same as that for H_1^b: $\sigma_\mu^2 = 0$; $\rho = 0$.

A Joint LM Test for Serial Correlation and Random Individual Effects

Let us consider the joint LM test for the error component model where the remainder disturbances follow an MA(1) process. In this case, the variance–covariance matrix of the disturbances is given by

$$\Omega = E(uu') = \sigma_\mu^2 I_N \otimes J_T + \sigma_\epsilon^2 I_N \otimes V_\lambda \tag{5.32}$$

where

$$V_\lambda = \begin{pmatrix} 1+\lambda^2 & \lambda & 0 \ldots & 0 \\ \lambda & 1+\lambda^2 & \lambda \ldots & 0 \\ \vdots & \vdots & \vdots \ddots & \vdots \\ 0 & 0 & 0 \ldots & 1+\lambda^2 \end{pmatrix} \tag{5.33}$$

and the log-likelihood function is given by $L(\delta, \theta)$ in (4.15) with $\theta = (\lambda, \sigma_\mu^2, \sigma_\epsilon^2)'$. In order to construct the LM test statistic for H_1^a: $\sigma_\mu^2 = 0; \lambda = 0$, one needs $D(\theta) = \partial L(\theta)/\partial\theta$ and the information matrix $J(\theta) = E[-\partial^2 L(\theta)/\partial\theta\partial\theta']$ evaluated at the restricted maximum likelihood estimator $\widehat{\theta}$. Note that under the null hypothesis $\Omega^{-1} = (1/\sigma_\epsilon^2)I_{NT}$. Using the general Hemmerle and Hartley (1973) formula given in (4.17), one gets the scores

$$\partial L(\theta)/\partial\lambda = NT\sum_{i=1}^{N}\sum_{t=2}^{T}\widehat{u}_{it}\widehat{u}_{i,t-1}/\sum_{i=1}^{N}\sum_{t=2}^{T}\widehat{u}_{it}^2 \equiv NT(\widehat{u}'\widehat{u}_{-1}/\widehat{u}'\widehat{u})$$

$$\partial L(\theta)/\partial\sigma_\mu^2 = -(NT/2\widehat{\sigma}_\epsilon^2)[1 - \widehat{u}'(I_N \otimes J_T)\widehat{u}/(\widehat{u}'\widehat{u})] \tag{5.34}$$

where $\widehat{u}$ denotes the OLS residuals and $\widehat{\sigma}_\epsilon^2 = \widehat{u}'\widehat{u}/NT$. Using (4.19), see Harville (1977), one gets the information matrix

$$\widehat{J} = (NT/2\widehat{\sigma}_\epsilon^4)\begin{pmatrix} T & 2(T-1)\widehat{\sigma}_\epsilon^2/T & 1 \\ 2(T-1)\widehat{\sigma}_\epsilon^2/T & 2\widehat{\sigma}_\epsilon^4(T-1)/T & 0 \\ 1 & 0 & 1 \end{pmatrix} \tag{5.35}$$

Hence the LM statistic for the null hypothesis H_1^a: $\sigma_\mu^2 = 0$; $\lambda = 0$ is given by

$$\text{LM}_1 = \widehat{D}'\widehat{J}^{-1}\widehat{D} = \frac{NT^2}{2(T-1)(T-2)}[A^2 - 4AB + 2TB^2] \tag{5.36}$$

where $A = [\widehat{u}'(I_N \otimes J_T)\widehat{u}/(\widehat{u}'\widehat{u})] - 1$ and $B = (\widehat{u}'\widehat{u}_{-1}/\widehat{u}'\widehat{u})$. This is asymptotically distributed (for large N) as χ_2^2 under H_1^a.

It remains to show that LM_1 is exactly the same as the joint test statistic for H_1^b: $\sigma_\mu^2 = 0; \rho = 0$, where the remainder disturbances follow an AR(1) process (see Baltagi and Li, 1991b). In fact, if we repeat the derivation given in (5.32)–(5.36), the only difference is to replace the V_λ matrix by its AR(1) counterpart

$$V_\rho = \begin{pmatrix} 1 & \rho & \ldots & \rho^{T-1} \\ \rho & 1 & \ldots & \rho^{T-2} \\ \vdots & \vdots & \ddots & \vdots \\ \rho^{T-1} & \rho^{T-2} & \ldots & 1 \end{pmatrix}$$

Note that under the null hypothesis, we have $(V_\rho)_{\rho=0} = I_T = (V_\lambda)_{\lambda=0}$ and

$$(\partial V_\rho/\partial\rho)_{\rho=0} = G = (\partial V_\lambda/\partial\lambda)_{\lambda=0}$$

where G is the bidiagonal matrix with bidiagonal elements all equal to one. Using these results, problem 5.14 asks the reader to verify that the resulting joint LM test statistic is the same whether the residual disturbances follow an AR(1) or an MA(1) process. Hence, the joint LM test statistic for random individual effects and first-order serial correlation is independent of the form of serial correlation, whether it is AR(1) or MA(1). This extends the Breusch and Godfrey (1981) result from time-series regression to panel data regression using an error component model.

Note that the A^2 term is the basis for the LM test statistic for H_2: $\sigma_\mu^2 = 0$ assuming there is no serial correlation (see Breusch and Pagan, 1980). In fact, $\text{LM}_2 = \sqrt{NT/2(T-1)}A$ is asymptotically distributed (for large N) as $N(0,1)$ under H_2 against the one-sided alternative H_2': $\sigma_\mu^2 > 0$, see (4.25). Also, the B^2 term is the basis for the LM test statistic for H_3: $\rho = 0$ (or $\lambda = 0$) assuming there are no individual effects (see Breusch and Godfrey, 1981). In fact, $\text{LM}_3 = \sqrt{NT^2/(T-1)}B$ is asymptotically distributed (for large N) as $N(0,1)$ under H_3 against the one-sided alternative H_3': ρ (or λ) > 0. The presence of an interaction term in the joint LM test statistic, given in (5.36), emphasizes the importance of the joint test when both serial correlation and random individual effects are suspected. However, when T is large the interaction term becomes negligible.

Note that all the LM tests considered assume that the underlying null hypothesis is that of white noise disturbances. However, in panel data applications, especially with large labor panels, one is concerned with individual effects and guaranteed their existence. In this case, it is inappropriate to test for serial correlation assuming no individual effects as is done in H_3. In fact, if one uses LM_3 to test for serial correlation, one is very likely to reject the null hypothesis of H_3 even if the null is true. This is because the μ_i are correlated for the same individual across time and this will contribute to rejecting the null of no serial correlation.

An LM Test for First-order Serial Correlation in a Random Effects Model

Baltagi and Li (1995) derived an LM test for first-order serial correlation given the existence of random individual effects. In case of an AR(1) model, the null hypothesis is H_4^b: $\rho = 0$ (given $\sigma_\mu^2 > 0$) vs $H_4^{b\prime}$: $\rho \neq 0$ (given $\sigma_\mu^2 > 0$). The variance–covariance matrix (under the alternative) is

$$\Omega_1 = \sigma_\mu^2(I_N \otimes J_T) + \sigma_\nu^2(I_N \otimes V_\rho)$$

Under the null hypothesis H_4^b, we have

$$(\Omega_1^{-1})|_{\rho=0} = (1/\sigma_\epsilon^2)I_N \otimes E_T + (1/\sigma_1^2)I_N \otimes \bar{J}_T$$

$$(\partial\Omega_1/\partial\rho)|_{\rho=0} = \sigma_\epsilon^2(I_N \otimes G)$$

$$(\partial\Omega_1/\partial\sigma_\mu^2)|_{\rho=0} = (I_N \otimes J_T)$$

$$(\partial\Omega_1/\partial\sigma_\epsilon^2)|_{\rho=0} = (I_N \otimes I_T)$$

where $\bar{J}_T = \iota_T\iota_T'/T$, $E_T = I_T - \bar{J}_T$, G is a bidiagonal matrix with bidiagonal elements all equal to one and $\sigma_1^2 = T\sigma_\mu^2 + \sigma_\epsilon^2$. Substituting these into (4.17), one gets the score

$$D_\rho = (\partial L/\partial\rho)|_{\rho=0} = [N(T-1)/T]\frac{\sigma_1^2 - \sigma_\epsilon^2}{\sigma_1^2}$$
$$+(\sigma_\epsilon^2/2)u'\{I_N \otimes [(\bar{J}_T/\sigma_1^2 + E_T/\sigma_\epsilon^2)G(\bar{J}_T/\sigma_1^2 + E_T/\sigma_\epsilon^2)]\}u$$

Using (4.19) and the results for $(\partial\Omega_1/\partial\theta_r)|_{\rho=0}$ for $r = 1, 2, 3$ and $\theta = (\rho, \sigma_\mu^2, \sigma^2)'$, we get the information matrix

$$\widehat{J} = \begin{pmatrix} \widehat{J}_{\rho\rho} & N(T-1)\widehat{\sigma}_\epsilon^2/\widehat{\sigma}_1^4 & \frac{N(T-1)}{T}\widehat{\sigma}_\epsilon^2[1/\widehat{\sigma}_1^4 - 1/\widehat{\sigma}_\epsilon^4] \\ & (NT^2/2\widehat{\sigma}_1^4) & NT/2\widehat{\sigma}_1^4 \\ & & \frac{N}{2}\left[\frac{1}{\widehat{\sigma}_1^4} + \frac{T-1}{\widehat{\sigma}_\epsilon^4}\right] \end{pmatrix}$$

where $\widehat{J}_{\rho\rho} = N[2a^2(T-1)^2 + 2a(2T-3) + (T-1)]$ and $a = [(\widehat{\sigma}_\epsilon^2 - \widehat{\sigma}_1^2)/T\widehat{\sigma}_1^2]$. Thus the LM test statistic is

$$\text{LM} = \widehat{D}'\widehat{J}^{-1}\widehat{D} = (\widehat{D}_\rho)^2 \hat{J}^{11} \tag{5.37}$$

where $\hat{J}^{11} = N^2T^2(T-1)/\det(\widehat{J})4\widehat{\sigma}_1^4\widehat{\sigma}_\epsilon^4$. Under the null hypothesis H_4^b, LM is asymptotically distributed (for large N) as χ_1^2. $\widehat{\sigma}_\epsilon^2 = \widehat{u}'(I_N \otimes E_T)\widehat{u}/N(T-1)$ and $\widehat{\sigma}_1^2 = \widehat{u}'(I_N \otimes \bar{J}_T)\widehat{u}/N$, where $\widehat{u}$ are the maximum likelihood residuals under the null hypothesis.

The one-sided LM test for the hypothesis H_4^b (corresponding to the alternative $\rho > 0$) is

$$\text{LM}_4 = \widehat{D}_\rho\sqrt{\widehat{J}^{11}} \tag{5.38}$$

and this is asymptotically distributed (for large N) as $N(0, 1)$.

When the first-order serial correlation is of the MA(1) type, the null hypothesis becomes H_4^a: $\lambda = 0$ (given that $\sigma_\mu^2 > 0$) vs $H_4^{a'}$: $\lambda \neq 0$ (given that $\sigma_\mu^2 > 0$). In this case, the variance–covariance matrix is

$$\Omega_2 = \sigma_\mu^2(I_N \otimes J_T) + \sigma_\epsilon^2(I_N \otimes V_\lambda)$$

and under the null hypothesis H_4^a

$$(\Omega_2^{-1})|_{\lambda=0} = (1/\sigma_\epsilon^2)(I_N \otimes E_T) + (1/\sigma_1^2)(I_N \otimes \bar{J}_T) = (\Omega_1^{-1})|_{\rho=0}$$

$$(\partial\Omega_2/\partial\lambda)|_{\lambda=0} = \sigma_\epsilon^2(I_N \otimes G) = (\partial\Omega_1/\partial\rho)|_{\rho=0}$$

$$(\partial\Omega_2/\partial\sigma_\mu^2)|_{\lambda=0} = (I_N \otimes J_T) = (\partial\Omega_1/\partial\sigma_\mu^2)|_{\rho=0}$$

$$(\partial\Omega_2/\partial\sigma_\epsilon^2)|_{\lambda=0} = (I_N \otimes I_T) = (\partial\Omega_1/\partial\sigma_\epsilon^2)|_{\rho=0}$$

Using these results, problem 5.15 asks the reader to verify that the test statistic for H_4^a is the same as (5.37).

To summarize, the LM test statistics for testing first-order serial correlation, assuming random individual effects, are invariant to the form of serial correlation (i.e. whether it is AR(1) or MA(1)). Also, we see that the LM test in this case is no longer simple. This is due to the fact that under the null hypothesis, the model is a one-way error component model with individual effects, and GLS rather than OLS residuals are involved.

Bera, Sosa-Escudero and Yoon (2001) suggest an adjustment of the LM test that is robust to local misspecification. Instead of $\text{LM}_\mu = NTA^2/2(T-1)$ for testing H_2: $\sigma_\mu^2 = 0$, which ignores the possible presence of serial correlation, they suggest computing

$$\text{LM}_\mu^* = \frac{NT(2B - A)^2}{2(T-1)(1-(2/T))}$$

This test essentially modifies LM_μ by correcting the mean and variance of the score $\partial L/\partial\sigma_\mu^2$ for its asymptotic correlation with $\partial L/\partial\rho$. Under the null hypothesis, LM_μ^* is asymptotically distributed as χ_1^2. Under local misspecification, this adjusted test statistic is equivalent to Neyman's $C(\alpha)$ test and shares its optimality properties. Similarly, they suggest computing

$$\text{LM}_\rho^* = \frac{NT^2[B - (A/T)]^2}{(T-1)(1-(2/T))}$$

instead of $\text{LM}_\rho = NT^2B^2/(T-1)$ to test H_3: $\rho = 0$ against the alternative that $\rho \neq 0$, ignoring the presence of random individual effects. They also show that

$$\text{LM}_\mu^* + \text{LM}_\rho = \text{LM}_\rho^* + \text{LM}_\mu = \text{LM}_1$$

where LM_1 is the joint LM test given in (5.36). In other words, the two-directional LM test for σ_μ^2 and ρ can be decomposed into the sum of the adjusted one-directional test of one type of alternative and the unadjusted form of the other hypothesis. Bera, Sosa-Escudero and Yoon (2001) argue that these tests use only OLS residuals and are easier to compute than the conditional LM tests like LM_4 that tests H_4^b: $\rho = 0$ (given $\sigma_\mu^2 > 0$). The latter test, given in (5.38), uses MLE of a one-way error component model to compute the LM test statistic. Bera, Sosa-Escudero and Yoon (2001) perform Monte Carlo experiments that show the usefulness of these modified Rao–Score tests in guarding against *local* misspecification.

An LM Test for First-order Serial Correlation in a Fixed Effects Model

The model is the same as (5.30), and the null hypothesis is H_5^b: $\rho = 0$ given that the μ_i are fixed parameters. Writing each individual's variables in a $T \times 1$ vector form, we have

$$y_i = Z_i\delta + \mu_i\iota_T + \nu_i \tag{5.39}$$

where $y_i = (y_{i1}, y_{i2}, \ldots, y_{iT})'$, Z_i is $T \times (K+1)$ and ν_i is $T \times 1$. $\nu_i \sim N(0, \Omega_\rho)$ where $\Omega_\rho = \sigma_\epsilon^2 V_\rho$ for the AR(1) disturbances. The log-likelihood function is

$$L(\delta, \rho, \mu, \sigma_\epsilon^2) = \text{constant} - \frac{1}{2}\log|\Omega|$$
$$-\frac{1}{2\sigma_\epsilon^2}\sum_{i=1}^{N}[(y_i - Z_i\delta - \mu_i\iota_T)'V_\rho^{-1}(y_i - Z_i\delta - \mu_i\iota_T)] \tag{5.40}$$

where $\Omega = I_N \otimes \Omega_\rho$ is the variance–covariance matrix of $\nu' = (\nu_1', \ldots, \nu_N')$. One can easily check that the maximum likelihood estimator of μ_i is given by

$\widehat{\mu}_i = \{(\iota_T' V_\rho^{-1}\iota_T)^{-1}[\iota_T' V_\rho^{-1}(y_i - Z_i\widehat{\delta})]\}_{\rho=0} = \bar{y}_{i.} - \bar{Z}_{i.}'\widehat{\delta}$, where $\widehat{\delta}$ is the maximum likelihood estimator of δ, $\bar{y}_{i.} = \sum_{t=1}^{T} y_{it}/T$ and $\bar{Z}_{i.}$ is a $(K+1)\times 1$ vector of averages of Z_{it} across time.

Write the log-likelihood function in vector form of ν as

$$L(\delta, \mu, \theta) = \text{constant} - \frac{1}{2}\log|\Omega| - \frac{1}{2}\nu'\Omega^{-1}\nu \tag{5.41}$$

where $\theta' = (\rho, \sigma_\epsilon^2)$. Now (5.41) has a similar form to (4.15). By following a similar derivation as that given earlier, one can easily verify that the LM test statistic for testing H_5^b is

$$\text{LM} = [NT^2/(T-1)](\widehat{\nu}'\widehat{\nu}_{-1}/\widehat{\nu}'\widehat{\nu})^2 \tag{5.42}$$

which is asymptotically distributed (for large T) as χ_1^2 under the null hypothesis H_5^b. Note that $\widehat{\nu}_{it} = y_{it} - Z_{it}'\widehat{\delta} - \widehat{\mu}_i = (\widetilde{y}_{it} - \widetilde{Z}_{it}'\widehat{\delta}) + (\bar{y}_{i.} - \bar{Z}_{i.}'\widehat{\delta} - \widehat{\mu}_i)$ where $\widetilde{y}_{it} = y_{it} - \bar{y}_{i.}$ is the usual Within transformation. Under the null of $\rho = 0$, the last term in parentheses is zero since $\{\widehat{\mu}_i\}_{\rho=0} = \bar{y}_{i.} - \bar{Z}_{i.}'\widehat{\delta}$ and $\{\widehat{\nu}_{it}\}_{\rho=0} = \widetilde{y}_{it} - \widetilde{Z}_{it}\widehat{\delta} = \widetilde{\nu}_{it}$. Therefore, the LM statistic given in (5.42) can be expressed in terms of the usual Within residuals (the $\widetilde{\nu}$) and the one-sided test for H_5^b (corresponding to the alternative $\rho > 0$) is

$$\text{LM}_5 = \sqrt{NT^2/(T-1)}(\widetilde{\nu}'\widetilde{\nu}_{-1}/\widetilde{\nu}'\widetilde{\nu}) \tag{5.43}$$

This is asymptotically distributed (for large T) as $N(0, 1)$.

By a similar argument, one can show that the LM test statistic for H_5^a: $\lambda = 0$, in a fixed effects model with MA(1) residual disturbances, is identical to LM_5.

Note also that LM_5 differs from LM_3 only by the fact that the Within residuals $\widetilde{\nu}$ (in LM_5) replace the OLS residuals $\widehat{u}$ (in LM_3). Since the Within transformation wipes out the individual effects whether fixed or random, one can also use (5.43) to test for serial correlation in the random effects models.

The Durbin–Watson Statistic for Panel Data

For the fixed effects model described in (5.39) with ν_{it} following an AR(1) process, Bhargava, Franzini and Narendranathan (1982), hereafter BFN, suggested testing for H_0: $\rho = 0$ against the alternative that $|\rho| < 1$, using the Durbin–Watson statistic only based on the Within residuals (the $\widetilde{\nu}_{it}$) rather than OLS residuals:

$$d_\text{p} = \sum_{i=1}^{N}\sum_{t=2}^{T}(\widetilde{\nu}_{it} - \widetilde{\nu}_{i,t-1})^2 \Big/ \sum_{i=1}^{N}\sum_{t=1}^{T}\widetilde{\nu}_{it}^2 \tag{5.44}$$

BFN showed that for arbitrary regressors, d_p is a locally most powerful invariant test in the neighborhood of $\rho = 0$. They argued that exact critical values using the Imhof routine are both impractical and unnecessary for panel data since they involve the computation of the nonzero eigenvalues of a large $NT \times NT$ matrix. Instead, BFN show how one can easily compute upper and lower bounds of d_p, and they tabulate the 5% levels for $N = 50, 100, 150, 250, 500, 1000$, $T = 6, 10$

and $k = 1, 3, 5, 7, 9, 11, 13, 15$. BFN remark that d_p would be rarely inconclusive since the bounds will be very tight even for moderate values of N. Also, for very large N, BFN argue that it is not necessary to compute these bounds, but simply test whether d_p is less than two when testing against positive serial correlation.

BFN also suggested the Berenblut–Webb statistic to test H_0: $\rho = 0$ because it is a locally most powerful invariant test in the neighborhood of $\rho = 1$. This is given by

$$g_\text{p} = \sum_{i=1}^{N}\sum_{t=2}^{T} \Delta\widehat{u}_{it}^2 \Big/ \sum_{i=1}^{N}\sum_{t=1}^{T} \widetilde{\nu}_{it}^2 \tag{5.45}$$

where $\Delta\widehat{u}_{it}$ denote the OLS residuals obtained from the first-differenced version of the regression equation given in (5.30), and $\widetilde{\nu}_{it}$ denote the Within residuals. BFN show that g_p and d_p have similar exact powers when $N = 30, T = 10$, $k = 2$, $\alpha = 0.05$ and $\rho = 0.25, 0.40, 0.50$. Also, the two tests are equivalent if N is large.

BFN also suggest a test for random walk residuals, i.e. H_0: $\rho = 1$ vs the alternative that $|\rho| < 1$. This is based on the statistic

$$R_\text{p} = \frac{\Delta\widehat{u}'\Delta\widehat{u}}{(\Delta\widehat{u})'F^*(\Delta\widehat{u})} \tag{5.46}$$

where $\Delta\widehat{u}$ are the differenced OLS residuals used in g_p. $F^* = I_N \otimes F$ with F being a $(T-1) \times (T-1)$ symmetric matrix with elements given by

$$F_{js} = (T-j)s/T \quad \text{if } j \geqslant s \quad (j, s = 1, \ldots, T-1)$$

For general regressors, BFN show that $R_\text{p} \leqslant g_\text{p} \leqslant d_\text{p}$ where g_p and d_p are now being considered under the random walk null hypothesis. BFN also tabulate 5% lower and upper bounds for R_p and suggest that the bounds for R_p may be used in practice for g_p and d_p. However, when $N \to \infty$, as in typical panels, all three tests are equivalent, $R_\text{p} = g_\text{p} = d_\text{p}$, and BFN recommend only the Durbin–Watson d_p be calculated for testing the random walk hypothesis.

Testing AR(1) Against MA(1) in an Error Component Model

Testing AR(1) against MA(1) has been extensively studied in the time-series literature; see King and McAleer (1987) for a Monte Carlo comparison of non-nested, approximate point optimal, as well as LM tests.[3] In fact, King and McAleer (1987) found that the non-nested tests perform poorly in small samples, while King's (1983) point optimal test performs the best. Recently Burke, Godfrey and Termayne (1990) (hereafter BGT) derived a simple test to distinguish between AR(1) and MA(1) processes. Baltagi and Li (1995) proposed two extensions of the BGT test to the error component model. These tests are simple to implement, requiring Within or OLS residuals.

The basic idea of the BGT test is as follows: under the null hypothesis of an AR(1) process, the remainder error term ν_{it} satisfies

$$\text{correl}(\nu_{it}, \nu_{i,t-\tau}) = \rho_\tau = (\rho_1)^\tau \quad \tau = 1, 2, \ldots \tag{5.47}$$

Therefore, under the null hypothesis

$$\rho_2 - (\rho_1)^2 = 0 \tag{5.48}$$

Under the alternative hypothesis of an MA(1) process on ν_{it}, $\rho_2 = 0$ and hence $\rho_2 - (\rho_1)^2 < 0$. Therefore, BGT recommend a test statistic based on (5.48) using estimates of ρ obtained from OLS residuals. One problem remains. King (1983) suggests that any "good" test should have a size which tends to zero, asymptotically, for $\rho > 0.5$. The test based on (5.48) does not guarantee this property. To remedy this, BGT proposed supplementing (5.48) with the decision to accept the null hypothesis of AR(1) if $\widehat{\rho}_1 > \frac{1}{2} + 1/\sqrt{T}$.

In an error component model, the Within transformation wipes out the individual effects, and one can use the Within residuals of $\widetilde{u}_{it}(=\widetilde{\nu}_{it})$ instead of OLS residuals $\widehat{u}_{it}$ to construct the BGT test. Let

$$(\widetilde{\rho}_1)_i = \sum_{t=2}^{T} \widetilde{u}_{it}\widetilde{u}_{i,t-1} \bigg/ \sum_{t=1}^{T} \widetilde{u}_{it}^2$$

and

$$(\widetilde{\rho}_2)_i = \sum_{t=3}^{T} \widetilde{u}_{it}\widetilde{u}_{i,t-2} \bigg/ \sum_{t=1}^{T} \widetilde{u}_{it}^2 \quad \text{for } i = 1, \ldots, N$$

The following test statistic based on (5.48):

$$\widetilde{\gamma}_i = \sqrt{T}[(\widetilde{\rho}_2)_i - (\widetilde{\rho}_1^2)_i]/[1 - (\widetilde{\rho}_2)_i] \tag{5.49}$$

is asymptotically distributed (for large T) as $N(0, 1)$ under the null hypothesis of an AR(1). Using the data on all N individuals, we can construct a generalized BGT test statistic for the error component model

$$\widetilde{\gamma} = \sqrt{N}\left(\sum_{i=1}^{N} \widetilde{\gamma}_i/N\right) = \sqrt{NT}\sum_{i=1}^{N}\left[\frac{(\widetilde{\rho}_2)_i - (\widetilde{\rho}_1^2)_i}{1 - (\widetilde{\rho}_2)_i}\right]/N \tag{5.50}$$

$\widetilde{\gamma}_i$ are independent for different i since the $\widetilde{u}_i$ are independent. Hence $\widetilde{\gamma}$ is also asymptotically distributed (for large T) as $N(0, 1)$ under the null hypothesis of an AR(1) process. The test statistic (5.50) is supplemented by

$$\widetilde{r}_1 = \sum_{i=1}^{N} (\widetilde{r}_1)_i/N \equiv \frac{1}{N}\sum_{i=1}^{N}\left[\sum_{t=2}^{T} \widetilde{u}_{it}\widetilde{u}_{i,t-1} \bigg/ \sum_{t=1}^{T} \widetilde{u}_{it}^2\right] \tag{5.51}$$

and the Baltagi and Li (1995) proposed BGT$_1$ test can be summarized as follows:

(1) Use the Within residuals $\widetilde{u}_{it}$ to calculate $\widetilde{\gamma}$ and $\widetilde{r}_1$ from (5.50) and (5.51).
(2) Accept the AR(1) model if $\widetilde{\gamma} > c_\alpha$, or $\widetilde{r}_1 > \frac{1}{2} + 1/\sqrt{T}$, where $\Pr[N(0, 1) \leqslant c_\alpha] = \alpha$.

The bias in estimating ρ_s ($s = 1, 2$) by using Within residuals is of $O(1/T)$ as $N \to \infty$ (see Nickell, 1981). Therefore, BGT$_1$ may not perform well for small T. Since for typical labor panels N is large and T is small, it would be desirable if an alternative simple test can be derived which performs well for large N rather than large T. In the next section we will give such a test.

An Alternative BGT-type Test for Testing AR(1) vs MA(1)

Let the null hypothesis be H_7: $\nu_{it} = \epsilon_{it} + \lambda\epsilon_{i,t-1}$ and the alternative be H_7': $\nu_{it} = \rho\nu_{i,t-1} + \epsilon_{it}$, where $\epsilon_{it} \sim N(0, \sigma_\epsilon^2)$. Note that this test differs from the BGT_1 test in that the null hypothesis is MA(1) rather than AR(1). The alternative BGT-type test uses autocorrelation estimates derived from OLS residuals and can be motivated as follows. Let

$$Q_0 = \frac{\sum\sum u_{it}^2}{NT} = u'u/NT$$

and

$$Q_s = \frac{\sum\sum u_{it}u_{i,t-s}}{N(T-s)} = u'(I_N \otimes G_s)u/N(T-s) \quad \text{for } s = 1, \ldots, S$$

where $G_s = \frac{1}{2}$ Toeplitz(ι_s), ι_s is a vector of zeros with the $(s+1)$th element being one. $s = 1, \ldots, S$ with $S \leqslant (T-1)$ and S is finite.[4] Given the true residuals (the u) and assuming

$$\left[\frac{u'Au}{n} - E\left(\frac{u'Au}{n}\right)\right] \xrightarrow{P} 0$$

where $n = NT$ and A is an arbitrary symmetric matrix, Baltagi and Li (1995) proved the following results, as $N \to \infty$:

(1) For the MA(1) model

$$\begin{aligned}
\text{plim } Q_0 &= \sigma_\mu^2 + \sigma_\nu^2 = \sigma_\mu^2 + \sigma_\epsilon^2(1+\lambda^2) \\
\text{plim } Q_1 &= \sigma_\mu^2 + \lambda\sigma_\epsilon^2 \\
\text{plim } Q_s &= \sigma_\mu^2 \quad \text{for } s = 2, \ldots, S
\end{aligned} \tag{5.52}$$

(2) For the AR(1) model

$$\begin{aligned}
\text{plim } Q_0 &= \sigma_\mu^2 + \sigma_\nu^2 \\
\text{plim } Q_s &= \sigma_\mu^2 + \rho^s\sigma_\nu^2 \quad \text{for } s = 1, \ldots, S
\end{aligned} \tag{5.53}$$

See problem 5.17. Baltagi and Li (1995) showed that for large N one can distinguish the AR(1) process from the MA(1) process based on the information obtained from $Q_s - Q_{s+l}$, for $s \geqslant 2$ and $l \geqslant 1$. To see this, note that $\text{plim}(Q_s - Q_{s+l}) = 0$ for the MA(1) process and $\text{plim}(Q_s - Q_{s+l}) = \sigma_\nu^2\rho^s(1-\rho^l) > 0$ for the AR(1) process.

Hence, Baltagi and Li (1995) suggest an asymptotic test of H_7 against H_7' based upon

$$\gamma = \sqrt{N/V}(Q_2 - Q_3) \tag{5.54}$$

where $V = 2\ \mathrm{tr}\{[(\sigma_\mu^2 J_T + \sigma_\epsilon^2 V_\lambda)(G_2/(T-2) - G_3/(T-3))]^2\}$. Under some regularity conditions, γ is asymptotically distributed (for large N) as $N(0, 1)$ under the null hypothesis of an MA(1) process.[5] In order to calculate V, we note that for the MA(1) process, $\sigma_\nu^2 = \sigma_\epsilon^2(1+\lambda^2)$ and $\sigma_\epsilon^2 V_\lambda = \sigma_\nu^2 I_T + \sigma_\epsilon^2 \lambda G$. Therefore we do not need to estimate λ in order to compute the test statistic γ, all we need to get are some consistent estimators for σ_ν^2, $\lambda\sigma_\epsilon^2$ and σ_μ^2. These are obtained as follows:

$$\widehat{\sigma}_\nu^2 = \widehat{Q}_0 - \widehat{Q}_2$$
$$\lambda\widehat{\sigma}_\epsilon^2 = \widehat{Q}_0 - \widehat{Q}_1$$
$$\widehat{\sigma}_\mu^2 = \widehat{Q}_2$$

where $\widehat{Q}_s$ are obtained from Q_s by replacing u_{it} by the OLS residuals $\widehat{u}_{it}$. Substituting these consistent estimators into V we get $\widehat{V}$, and the test statistic γ becomes

$$\widehat{\gamma} = \sqrt{N/\widehat{V}}(\widehat{Q}_2 - \widehat{Q}_3) \tag{5.55}$$

where

$$(\widehat{Q}_2 - \widehat{Q}_3) = \sum_{i=1}^{N}\sum_{t=3}^{T} \widehat{u}_{it}\widehat{u}_{i,t-2}/N(T-2) - \sum_{i=1}^{N}\sum_{t=4}^{T} \widehat{u}_{it}\widehat{u}_{i,t-3}/N(T-3)$$

and

$$\widehat{V} = 2\ \mathrm{tr}\{[(\widehat{\sigma}_\mu^2 J_T + \widehat{\sigma}_\nu^2 I_T + \widehat{\sigma_\epsilon^2\lambda} G)(G_2/(T-2) + G_3/(T-3))]^2\}$$

$\widehat{\gamma}$ is asymptotically distributed (for large N) as $N(0, 1)$ under the null hypothesis H_7 and is referred to as the BGT_2 test.

Baltagi and Li (1995) performed extensive Monte Carlo experiments using the regression model setup considered in Chapter 4. However, the remainder disturbances are now allowed to follow the AR(1) or MA(1) process. Table 5.2 gives a summary of all tests considered. Their main results can be summarized as follows:

(1) The joint LM_1 test performs well in testing the null of H_1: $\rho = \sigma_\mu^2 = 0$. Its estimated size is not statistically different from its nominal size. Let $\omega = \sigma_\mu^2/\sigma^2$ denote the proportion of the total variance that is due to individual effects. Baltagi and Li (1995) find that in the presence of large individual effects ($\omega > 0.2$), or high serial correlation ρ (or λ) > 0.2, LM_1 has high power, rejecting the null in 99–100% of cases. It only has low power when $\omega = 0$ and ρ (or λ) $= 0.2$, or when $\omega = 0.2$ and ρ (or λ) $= 0$.

(2) The test statistic LM_2 for testing H_2: $\sigma_\mu^2 = 0$ implicitly assumes that ρ (or λ) $= 0$. When ρ is indeed equal to zero, this test performs well. However, as ρ moves away from zero and increases, this test tends to be biased in favor of rejecting the null. This is because a large serial correlation coefficient (i.e. large ρ) contributes to a large correlation among the individuals in the sample, even though $\sigma_\mu^2 = 0$. For example, when the null is true ($\sigma_\mu^2 = 0$) but $\rho = 0.9$, LM_2

Table 5.2 Testing for Serial Correlation and Individual Effects

Null Hypothesis H_0	Alternative Hypothesis H_A	Test Statistics	Asymptotic Distribution under H_0
1a. H_1^a: $\sigma_\mu^2 = 0; \lambda = 0$	σ_μ^2 or $\lambda \neq 0$	LM_1	χ_2^2
1b. H_1^b: $\sigma_\mu^2 = 0; \rho = 0$	σ_μ^2 or $\rho \neq 0$	LM_1	χ_2^2
2. H_2: $\sigma_\mu^2 = 0$	$\sigma_\mu^2 > 0$	LM_2	$N(0, 1)$
3a. H_3^a: $\lambda = 0$	$\lambda > 0$	LM_3	$N(0, 1)$
3b. H_3^b: $\rho = 0$	$\rho > 0$	LM_3	$N(0, 1)$
4a. H_4^a: $\lambda = 0$ ($\sigma_\mu^2 > 0$)	$\lambda > 0$ ($\sigma_\mu^2 > 0$)	LM_4	$N(0, 1)$
4b. H_4^b: $\rho = 0$ ($\sigma_\mu^2 > 0$)	$\rho > 0$ ($\sigma_\mu^2 > 0$)	LM_4	$N(0, 1)$
5a. H_5^a: $\lambda = 0$ (μ_i fixed)	$\lambda > 0$ (μ_i fixed)	LM_5	$N(0, 1)$
5b. H_5^b: $\rho = 0$ (μ_i fixed)	$\rho > 0$ (μ_i fixed)	LM_5	$N(0, 1)$
6 H_6: AR(1)	MA(1)	BGT_1	$N(0, 1)$
7 H_7: MA(1)	AR(1)	BGT_2	$N(0, 1)$

Source: Baltagi and Li (1995). Reproduced by permission of Elsevier Science Publishers B.V. (North-Holland)

rejects in 100% of the cases. Similar results are obtained in case ν_{it} follows an MA(1) process. In general, the presence of positive serial correlation tends to bias the case in favor of finding nonzero individual effects.

(3) Similarly, the LM_3 test for testing H_3: $\rho = 0$ implicitly assumes $\sigma_\mu^2 = 0$. This test performs well when $\sigma_\mu^2 = 0$. However, as σ_μ^2 increases, the performance of this test deteriorates. For example, when the null is true ($\rho = 0$) but $\omega = 0.9$, LM_3 rejects the null hypothesis in 100% of the cases. The large correlation among the μ_i contributes to the rejection of the null hypothesis of no serial correlation. These results strongly indicate that one should not ignore the individual effects when testing for serial correlation.

(4) In contrast to LM_3, both LM_4 and LM_5 take into account the presence of individual effects. For large values of ρ or λ (greater than 0.4), both LM_4 and LM_5 have high power, rejecting the null more than 99% of the time. However, the estimated size of LM_4 is closer to the 5% nominal value than that of LM_5. In addition, Baltagi and Li (1995) show that Bhargava, Franzini and Narendranathan's (1982) modified Durbin–Watson performs better than LM_5 and is recommended.

(5) The BGT_1 test, which uses Within residuals and tests the null of an AR(1) against the alternative of an MA(1), performs well if $T \geqslant 60$ and $T > N$. However, when T is small, or T is of moderate size but N is large, BGT_1 will tend to over-reject the null hypothesis. Therefore BGT_1 is not recommended for these cases. For typical labor panels, N is large and T is small. For these cases, Baltagi and Li (1995) recommend the BGT_2 test, which uses OLS residuals and tests the null of an MA(1) against the alternative of an AR(1). This test performs well when N is large and does not rely on T to achieve its asymptotic distribution.

The Monte Carlo results show that BGT_2's performance improves as either N or T increases.

Baltagi and Li (1997) performed Monte Carlo experiments to compare the finite sample relative efficiency of a number of pure and pretest estimators for an error component model with remainder disturbances that are generated by an AR(1) or an MA(1) process. These estimators are: (1) ordinary least squares (OLS); (2) the Within estimator; (3) conventional GLS which ignores the serial correlation in the remainder disturbances but accounts for the random error components structure, this is denoted by CGLS; (4) GLS assuming random error components with the remainder disturbances following an MA(1) process, this is denoted by GLSM; (5) GLS assuming random error components with the remainder disturbances following an AR(1) process, this is denoted by GLSA; (6) a pretest estimator which is based on the results of two tests, this is denoted by PRE. The first test is LM_4 which tests for the presence of serial correlation given the existence of random individual effects. If the null is not rejected, this estimator reduces to conventional GLS. In case serial correlation is found, the BGT_2 test is performed to distinguish between the AR(1) and MA(1) process and GLSA or GLSM is performed. (7) A generalized method of moments (GMM) estimator, where the error component structure of the disturbances is ignored and a general variance–covariance matrix is estimated across the time dimension. Finally (8) true GLS, which is denoted by TGLS, is obtained for comparison purposes. In fact, the relative efficiency of each estimator is obtained by dividing its MSE by that of TGLS. It is important to emphasize that all the estimators considered are consistent as long as the explanatory variables and the disturbances are uncorrelated, as $N \to \infty$, with T fixed. The primary concern here is with their small sample properties. The results show that the correct GLS procedure is always the best, but the researcher does not have perfect foresight on which one it is: GLSA for an AR(1) process, or GLSM for an MA(1) process. In this case, the pretest estimator is a viable alternative given that its performance is a close second to correct GLS whether the true serial correlation process is AR(1) or MA(1).

5.2.8 Extensions

Other extensions include the fixed effects model with AR(1) remainder disturbances considered by Bhargava, Franzini and Narendranathan (1982), and also Kiefer (1980) and Schmidt (1983) who extend the fixed effects model to cover cases with an arbitrary intertemporal covariance matrix. A Fourier transformation treatment of the autocorrelation in the ν_{it} is given by Silver (1982). There is an extension to the MA(q) case, by Baltagi and Li (1992e, 1993, 1994) and a treatment of the autoregressive moving average ARMA(p, q) case on the ν_{it} by Lee (1979), MaCurdy (1982) and more recently Galbraith and Zinde-Walsh (1995). For an extension to the two-way model with serially correlated disturbances, see Revankar (1979) who considers the case where the λ_t follow an AR(1) process. Also, Karlsson and Skoglund (2000) who propose a simple transformation à la Baltagi and Li (1991a) for this two-way model and derive the corresponding maximum likelihood estimator. Magnus and Woodland (1988) generalize this Revankar (1979) model to the multivariate error component model case and derive the corresponding maximum likelihood estimator. Chamberlain (1982, 1984) allows for arbitrary serial correlation and heteroskedastic patterns by viewing each time period as an equation and treating the panel as a multivariate setup. Testing for serial correlation in a dynamic error component model will be studied in Chapter 8. Li and Hsiao (1998) propose three test statistics in the context of a semiparametric partially linear panel data model

$$y_{it} = x'_{it}\beta + \theta(w_{it}) + u_{it}$$

with u_{it} satisfying $E(u_{it}/w_{it}, x_{it}) = 0$. The functional form of $\theta(\cdot)$ is unknown and $E(u_{it}^2/x_{it}, w_{it})$ is not specified. The first test statistic tests the null of zero first-order serial correlation. The second tests for the presence of higher order serial correlation and the third tests for the presence of individual effects. The asymptotics are carried out for $N \to \infty$ and fixed T. Monte Carlo experiments are performed to study the finite sample performance of these tests.

NOTES

1. An alternative derivation of this transformation is given by Wansbeek (1992). Bhargava, Franzini and Narendranathan (1982) give the corresponding transformation for the one-way error component model with fixed effects and first-order autoregressive disturbances.
2. Let $a = (a_1, a_2, \ldots, a_n)'$ denote an arbitrary $n \times 1$ vector, then Toeplitz(a) is an $n \times n$ symmetric matrix generated from the $n \times 1$ vector a with the diagonal elements all equal to a_1, second diagonal elements equal to a_2, etc.
3. Obviously, there are many different ways to construct such a test. For example, we can use $Q_2 + Q_3 - 2Q_4$ instead of $Q_2 - Q_3$ to define the γ test. In this case

$$V = 2\,\mathrm{tr}\{[(\sigma_\mu^2 J_T + \sigma_\epsilon^2 V_\lambda)(G_2/(T-2) + G_3/(T-3) - 2G_4/(T-4))]^2\}$$

PROBLEMS

5.1 (a) For the one-way error component model with heteroskedastic μ_i, i.e. $\mu_i \sim (0, w_i^2)$, verify that $\Omega = E(uu')$ is given by (5.1) and (5.2).
(b) Using the Wansbeek and Kapteyn (1982b) trick show that Ω can also be written as in (5.3).

5.2 (a) Using (5.3) and (5.4), verify that $\Omega\Omega^{-1} = I$ and that $\Omega^{-1/2}\Omega^{-1/2} = \Omega^{-1}$.
(b) Show that $y^* = \sigma_\nu \Omega^{-1/2} y$ has a typical element $y_{it}^* = (y_{it} - \theta_i \bar{y}_{i.})$ where $\theta_i = 1 - (\sigma_\nu/\tau_i)$ and $\tau_i^2 = Tw_i^2 + \sigma_\nu^2$ for $i = 1, \ldots, N$.

5.3 Using the data on gasoline demand given on the Wiley web site, estimate (2.41) using the heteroskedastic error described by (5.2).

5.4 (a) For the one-way error component model with heteroskedastic remainder disturbances, i.e. $\nu_{it} \sim (0, w_i^2)$, verify that $\Omega = E(uu')$ is given by (5.5).
(b) Using the Wansbeek and Kapteyn (1982b) trick show that Ω can also be written as in (5.6).

5.5 (a) Using (5.6) and (5.7), verify that $\Omega\Omega^{-1} = I$ and $\Omega^{-1/2}\Omega^{-1/2} = \Omega^{-1}$.
(b) Show that $y^* = \Omega^{-1/2}y$ has a typical element $y^*_{it} = (y_{it} - \theta_i \bar{y}_{i.})/w_i$ where $\theta_i = 1 - (w_i/\tau_i)$ and $\tau_i^2 = T\sigma_\mu^2 + w_i^2$ for $i = 1, \ldots, N$.
(c) Using the gasoline demand data given on the Wiley web site, estimate (2.41) using this alternative form of heteroskedasticity.

5.6 (a) For the one-way error component model with remainder disturbances ν_{it} following a stationary AR(1) process as in (5.8), verify that $\Omega^* = E(u^*u^{*\prime})$ is that given by (5.11).
(b) Using the Wansbeek and Kapteyn (1982b) trick show that Ω^* can be written as in (5.12).

5.7 (a) Using (5.12) and (5.13), verify that $\Omega^*\Omega^{*-1} = I$ and $\Omega^{*-1/2}\Omega^{*-1/2} = \Omega^{*-1}$.
(b) Show that $y^{**} = \sigma_\epsilon \Omega^{*-1/2}y^*$ has a typical element given by (5.14).
(c) Show that for $\rho = 0$, (5.14) reduces to $(y_{it} - \theta\bar{y}_{i.})$
(d) Show that for $\sigma_\mu^2 = 0$, (5.14) reduces to y^*_{it}.

5.8 Prove that $\widehat{\sigma}_\epsilon^2$ and $\widehat{\sigma}_\alpha^2$ given by (5.15) are unbiased for σ_ϵ^2 and σ_α^2, respectively.

5.9 (a) For the one-way error component model with remainder disturbances ν_{it} following a stationary AR(2) process as in (5.16), verify that $\Omega^* = E(u^*u^{*\prime})$ is that given by (5.18).
(b) Show that $y^{**} = \sigma_\epsilon \Omega^{*-1/2}y^*$ has a typical element given by (5.19).

5.10 For the one-way error component model with remainder disturbances ν_{it} following a specialized AR(4) process $\nu_{it} = \rho\nu_{i,t-4} + \epsilon_{it}$ with $|\rho| < 1$ and $\epsilon_{it} \sim \text{IIN}(0, \sigma_\epsilon^2)$, verify that $y^{**} = \sigma_\epsilon \Omega^{-1/2}y^*$ is given by (5.21).

5.11 For the one-way error component model with remainder disturbances ν_{it} following an MA(1) process given by (5.22), verify that $y^{**} = \sigma_\epsilon \Omega^{-1/2}y^*$ is given by (5.24).

5.12 For the BLU predictor of $y_{i,T+1}$ given in (5.25), show that when ν_{it} follows:
(a) the AR(1) process, the GLS predictor is corrected by the term in (5.26);
(b) the AR(2) process, the GLS predictor is corrected by the term given in (5.27);
(c) the specialized AR(4) process, the GLS predictor is corrected by the term given in (5.28);
(d) the MA(1) process, the GLS predictor is corrected by the term given in (5.29).

5.13 Using (4.17) and (4.19), verify (5.34) and (5.35) and derive the LM_1 statistic given in (5.36).

5.14 (a) Verify that $(\partial V_\rho/\partial\rho)_{\rho=0} = G = (\partial V_\lambda/\partial\lambda)_{\lambda=0}$ where G is the bidiagonal matrix with bidiagonal elements all equal to one.

(b) Using this result verify that the LM statistic (5.36) is the same whether the residual disturbances follow an AR(1) or an MA(1) process.

5.15 For H_4^b: $\rho = 0$ (given $\sigma_\mu^2 > 0$):
(a) Derive the score, the information matrix and the LM statistic given in (5.37).
(b) Verify that for H_4^a: $\lambda = 0$ (given $\sigma_\mu^2 > 0$) one obtains the same LM statistic as in (5.37).

5.16 For H_5^b: $\rho = 0$ (given the μ_i are fixed):
(a) Verify that the likelihood is given by (5.40) and derive the MLE of the μ_i.
(b) Using (5.34) and (5.35), verify that the LM statistic for H_5^b is given by (5.42).
(c) Verify that for H_5^a: $\lambda = 0$ (given the μ_i are fixed) one obtains the same LM statistic as in (5.42).

5.17 (a) Verify (5.52) for the MA(1) model. Hint: Use the fact that $\lim E(u'u)/(NT) = \lim \mathrm{tr}(\Omega)/(NT)$ for deriving plim Q_0. Similarly, use the fact that

$$\lim E(u'(I_N \otimes G_1)u)/N(T-1) = \lim \mathrm{tr}[\Omega(I_N \otimes G_1)]/N(T-1)$$

for deriving plim Q_1. Also

$$\lim E(u'(I_N \otimes G_s)u)/N(T-s) = \lim \mathrm{tr}[\Omega(I_N \otimes G_s)]/N(T-s)$$

for deriving plim Q_s for $s = 2, \ldots, S$.
(b) Verify (5.53) for the AR(1) model.

5.18 Using the Monte Carlo setup in Baltagi and Li (1995), study the performance of the tests proposed in Table 5.2.

5.19 For the Grunfeld data, perform the tests described in Table 5.2 and estimate this model assuming random firm effects and remainder disturbances that follow an AR(1) process.

5.20 For the gasoline data given on the Wiley web site, perform the tests described in Table 5.2.

5.21 For the public capital data given on the Wiley web site, perform the tests described in Table 5.2.

6 Seemingly Unrelated Regressions with Error Components

6.1 THE ONE-WAY MODEL

In several instances in economics, one needs to estimate a set of equations. This could be a set of demand equations, across different sectors, industries or regions. Other examples include the estimation of a translog cost function along with the corresponding cost share equations. In these cases, Zellner's (1962) seemingly unrelated regressions (SUR) approach is popular since it captures the efficiency due to the correlation of the disturbances across equations. Applications of the SUR procedure with time-series or cross-section data are too numerous to cite. In this chapter, we focus on the estimation of a set of SUR equations with panel data.

Avery (1977) seems to have been the first to consider the SUR model with error component disturbances. In this case, we have a set of M equations

$$y_j = Z_j\delta_j + u_j \quad j = 1, \ldots, M \tag{6.1}$$

where y_j is $NT \times 1$, Z_j is $NT \times k'_j$, $\delta'_j = (\alpha_j, \beta'_j)$, β_j is $k_j \times 1$ and $k'_j = k_j + 1$ with

$$u_j = Z_\mu \mu_j + \nu_j \quad j = 1, \ldots, M \tag{6.2}$$

where $Z_\mu = (I_N \otimes \iota_T)$ and $\mu'_j = (\mu_{1j}, \mu_{2j}, \ldots, \mu_{Nj})$ and $\nu'_j = (\nu_{11j}, \ldots, \nu_{1Tj}, \ldots, \nu_{N1j}, \ldots, \nu_{NTj})$ are random vectors with zero means and covariance matrix

$$E\begin{pmatrix}\mu_j \\ \nu_j\end{pmatrix}(\mu'_l, \nu'_l) = \begin{bmatrix}\sigma^2_{\mu_{jl}} I_N & 0 \\ 0 & \sigma^2_{\nu_{jl}} I_{NT}\end{bmatrix} \tag{6.3}$$

for $j, l = 1, 2, \ldots, M$. This can be justified as follows: $\mu \sim (0, \Sigma_\mu \otimes I_N)$ and $\nu \sim (0, \Sigma_\nu \otimes I_{NT})$ where $\mu' = (\mu'_1, \mu'_2, \ldots, \mu'_M)$, $\nu' = (\nu'_1, \nu'_2, \ldots, \nu'_M)$, $\Sigma_\mu = [\sigma^2_{\mu_{jl}}]$ and $\Sigma_\nu = [\sigma^2_{\nu_{jl}}]$ for $j, l = 1, 2, \ldots, M$. In other words, *each* error component follows the same standard Zellner (1962) SUR assumptions imposed on classical disturbances. Using (6.2), it follows that

$$\Omega_{jl} = E(u_j u_l') = \sigma^2_{\mu_{jl}}(I_N \otimes J_T) + \sigma^2_{\nu_{jl}}(I_N \otimes I_T) \tag{6.4}$$

In this case, the covariance matrix between the disturbances of different equations has the same one-way error component form. Except now, there are additional *cross-equations* variance components to be estimated. The variance–covariance matrix for the set of M equations is given by

$$\Omega = E(uu') = \Sigma_\mu \otimes (I_N \otimes J_T) + \Sigma_\nu \otimes (I_N \otimes I_T) \tag{6.5}$$

where $u' = (u_1', u_2', \ldots, u_M')$ is a $1 \times MNT$ vector of disturbances with u_j defined in (6.2) for $j = 1, 2, \ldots, M$. $\Sigma_\mu = [\sigma^2_{\mu_{jl}}]$ and $\Sigma_\nu = [\sigma^2_{\nu_{jl}}]$ are both $M \times M$ matrices. Replacing J_T by $T\bar{J}_T$ and I_T by $E_T + \bar{J}_T$ and collecting terms one gets

$$\begin{aligned}\Omega &= (T\Sigma_\mu + \Sigma_\nu) \otimes (I_N \otimes \bar{J}_T) + \Sigma_\nu \otimes (I_N \otimes E_T) \\ &= \Sigma_1 \otimes P + \Sigma_\nu \otimes Q\end{aligned} \tag{6.6}$$

where $\Sigma_1 = T\Sigma_\mu + \Sigma_\nu$. Also, $P = I_N \otimes \bar{J}_T$ and $Q = I_{NT} - P$ were defined below (2.4). (6.6) is the spectral decomposition of Ω derived by Baltagi (1980), which means that

$$\Omega^r = \Sigma_1^r \otimes P + \Sigma_\nu^r \otimes Q \tag{6.7}$$

where r is an arbitrary scalar (see also Magnus, 1982). For $r = -1$, one gets the inverse Ω^{-1} and for $r = -\frac{1}{2}$ one gets

$$\Omega^{-1/2} = \Sigma_1^{-1/2} \otimes P + \Sigma_\nu^{-1/2} \otimes Q \tag{6.8}$$

Kinal and Lahiri (1990) suggest obtaining the Cholesky decomposition of Σ_ν and Σ_1 in (6.8) to reduce the computation and simplify the transformation of the system.

One can estimate Σ_ν by $\widehat{\Sigma}_\nu = U'QU/N(T-1)$ and Σ_1 by $\widehat{\Sigma}_1 = U'PU/N$ where $U = [u_1, \ldots, u_M]$ is the $NT \times M$ matrix of disturbances for all M equations. Problem 6.7 asks the reader to verify that knowing U, $\widehat{\Sigma}_\nu$ and $\widehat{\Sigma}_1$ are unbiased estimates of Σ_ν and Σ_1, respectively. For feasible GLS estimates of the variance components, Avery (1977) following Wallace and Hussain (1969) in the single equation case recommends replacing U by OLS residuals, while Baltagi (1980) following Amemiya's (1971) suggestion for the single equation case recommends replacing U by Within-type residuals.

For this model, a block-diagonal Ω makes GLS on the whole system equivalent to GLS on each equation separately, see problem 6.3. However, when the same X appear in each equation, GLS on the whole system is not equivalent to GLS on each equation separately (see Avery, 1977). As in the single equation case, if N and $T \to \infty$, then the Within estimator of this system is asymptotically efficient and has the same asymptotic variance–covariance matrix as the GLS estimator. In fact, Prucha (1984) shows that as long as Σ_ν is estimated consistently and the estimate of Σ_μ has a finite positive definite limit then the corresponding feasible

SUR-GLS estimator is asymptotically efficient. This implies the existence of a large family of asymptotically efficient estimators of the regression coefficients.

6.2 THE TWO-WAY MODEL

It is easy to extend the analysis to a two-way error component structure across the system of equations. In this case (6.2) becomes

$$u_j = Z_\mu \mu_j + Z_\lambda \lambda_j + \nu_j \quad j = 1, \ldots, M \tag{6.9}$$

where $\lambda'_j = (\lambda_{1j}, \ldots, \lambda_{Tj})$ is a random vector with zero mean and covariance matrix given by the following:

$$E\begin{pmatrix}\mu_j \\ \lambda_j \\ \nu_j\end{pmatrix}(\mu'_l, \lambda'_l, \nu'_l) = \begin{bmatrix}\sigma^2_{\mu_{jl}} I_N & 0 & 0 \\ 0 & \sigma^2_{\lambda_{jl}} I_T & 0 \\ 0 & 0 & \sigma^2_{\nu_{jl}} I_{NT}\end{bmatrix} \tag{6.10}$$

for $j, l = 1, 2, \ldots, M$. In this case, $\lambda \sim (0, \Sigma_\lambda \otimes I_T)$ where $\lambda' = (\lambda_1, \lambda_2, \ldots, \lambda_T)$ and $\Sigma_\lambda = [\sigma^2_{\lambda_{jl}}]$ is $M \times M$. Like μ and ν, the λ follow a standard Zellner SUR-type assumption. Therefore

$$\Omega_{jl} = E(u_j u'_l) = \sigma^2_{\mu_{jl}}(I_N \otimes J_T) + \sigma^2_{\lambda_{jl}}(J_N \otimes I_T) + \sigma^2_{\nu_{jl}}(I_N \otimes I_T) \tag{6.11}$$

As in the one-way SUR model, the covariance between the disturbances of different equations has the same two-way error component form. Except now, there are additional cross-equations variance components to be estimated. The variance–covariance matrix of the system of M equations is given by

$$\Omega = E(uu') = \Sigma_\mu \otimes (I_N \otimes J_T) + \Sigma_\lambda \otimes (J_N \otimes I_T) + \Sigma_\nu \otimes (I_N \otimes I_T) \tag{6.12}$$

where $u' = (u'_1, u'_2, \ldots, u'_M)$ with u_j defined in (6.9). Using the Wansbeek and Kapteyn (1982b) trick one gets (see problem 6.5)

$$\Omega = \sum_{i=1}^{4} \Lambda_i \otimes Q_i \tag{6.13}$$

where $\Lambda_1 = \Sigma_\nu$, $\Lambda_2 = T\Sigma_\mu + \Sigma_\nu$, $\Lambda_3 = N\Sigma_\lambda + \Sigma_\nu$ and $\Lambda_4 = T\Sigma_\mu + N\Sigma_\lambda + \Sigma_\nu$, with Q_i defined below (3.13). This is the spectral decomposition of Ω (see Baltagi, 1980), with

$$\Omega^r = \sum_{i=1}^{4} \Lambda_i^r \otimes Q_i \tag{6.14}$$

for r an arbitrary scalar. When $r = -1$ one gets the inverse Ω^{-1} and when $r = -\frac{1}{2}$ one gets

$$\Omega^{-1/2} = \sum_{i=1}^{4} \Lambda_i^{-1/2} \otimes Q_i \tag{6.15}$$

Once again, the Cholesky decompositions of the Λ_i can be obtained in (6.15) to reduce the computation and simplify the transformation of the system (see Kinal and Lahiri, 1990). Knowing the true disturbances U, quadratic unbiased estimates of the variance components are obtained from

$$\widehat{\Sigma}_\nu = \frac{U'Q_1U}{(N-1)(T-1)} \quad \widehat{\Lambda}_2 = \frac{U'Q_2U}{(N-1)} \quad \text{and} \quad \widehat{\Lambda}_3 = \frac{U'Q_3U}{(T-1)} \tag{6.16}$$

see problem 6.7. Feasible estimates of (6.16) are obtained by replacing U by OLS residuals or Within-type residuals. One should check for positive definite estimates of Σ_μ and Σ_λ before proceeding. The Within estimator has the same asymptotic variance–covariance matrix as GLS when N and $T \to \infty$. Also, as long as the estimate of Σ_ν is consistent and the estimates of Σ_μ and Σ_λ have a finite positive definite probability limit, the corresponding feasible SUR-GLS estimate of the regression coefficients is asymptotically efficient.

6.3 APPLICATIONS AND EXTENSIONS

Verbon (1980) applied the SUR procedure with one-way error components to a set of four labor demand equations, using data from the Netherlands on 18 industries over 10 semiannual periods covering the period 1972–79. Verbon (1980) extended the above error component specification to allow for heteroskedasticity in the individual effects modeled as a simple function of p time-invariant variables. He applied a Breusch and Pagan (1979) LM test to check for the existence of heteroskedasticity.

Beierlein, Dunn and McConnon (1981) estimated the demand for electricity and natural gas in the northeastern United States using a SUR model with two-way error component disturbances. The data were collected for nine states comprising the Census Bureau's northeastern region of the USA for the period 1967–77. Six equations were considered corresponding to the various sectors considered. These were residential gas, residential electric, commercial gas, commercial electric, industrial gas and industrial electric. Comparison of the error components SUR estimates with those obtained from OLS and single equation error component procedures showed substantial improvement in the estimates and a sizeable reduction in the empirical standard errors.

Brown, Kleidon and Marsh (1983) applied the SUR model with error components to study the size-related anomalies in stock returns. Previous empirical evidence has shown that small firms tend to yield returns greater than those predicted by the capital asset pricing model. Brown, Kleidon and Marsh (1983) used a panel of 566 firms observed quarterly over the period June 1967 to December 1975. They found that size effects are sensitive to the time period studied.

Howrey and Varian (1984) applied the SUR with one-way error component disturbances to the estimation of a system of demand equations for electricity by time of day. Their data are based on the records of 60 households whose electricity usage was recorded over a five-month period in 1976 by the Arizona Public

Service Company. Using these panel data, the authors calculated the fraction of the population which would prefer such pricing policies to flat rate pricing.

Magnus (1982) derived the maximum likelihood estimator for the linear and nonlinear multivariate error component model under various assumptions on the errors. Sickles (1985) applied Magnus' multivariate nonlinear error components analysis to model the technology and specific factor productivity growth in the US airline industry.

Wan, Griffiths and Anderson (1992) applied a SUR model with two-way error component disturbances that are heteroskedastic to estimate the rice, maize and wheat production in China. These production functions allow for positive or negative marginal risks of output. The panel data cover 28 regions of China over the 1980–83 period. Their findings indicate that increases in chemical fertilizer and sown area generally increase the output variance. However, organic fertilizer and irrigation help stabilize Chinese cereal production.

PROBLEMS

6.1 Using the one-way error component structure on the disturbances of the jth equation given in (6.2) and (6.3), verify that Ω_{jl}, the variance–covariance matrix between the jth and lth equation disturbances, is given by (6.4).

6.2 Using (6.6) and (6.7), verify that $\Omega\Omega^{-1} = I$ and $\Omega^{-1/2}\Omega^{-1/2} = \Omega^{-1}$.

6.3 Consider a set of two equations with one-way error components disturbances.

(a) Show that if the variance–covariance matrix between the equations is block-diagonal, then GLS on the system is equivalent to GLS on each equation separately (see Avery, 1977; Baltagi, 1980).

(b) Show that if the explanatory variables are the same across the two equations, GLS on the system does not necessarily revert to GLS on each equation separately (see Avery, 1977; Baltagi, 1980).

(c) Does your answer to parts (a) and (b) change if the disturbances follow a two-way error component model?

6.4 Using the two-way error component structure on the disturbances of the jth equation given in (6.9) and (6.10), verify that Ω_{jl}, the variance–covariance matrix between the jth and lth equation disturbances, is given by (6.11).

6.5 Using the form of Ω given in (6.12) and the Wansbeek and Kapteyn (1982b) trick verify (6.13).

6.6 Using (6.13) and (6.14), verify that $\Omega\Omega^{-1} = I$ and $\Omega^{-1/2}\Omega^{-1/2} = \Omega^{-1}$.

6.7 (a) Using (6.6), verify that $\widehat{\Sigma}_\nu = U'QU/N(T-1)$ and $\widehat{\Sigma}_1 = U'PU/N$ yield unbiased estimates of Σ_ν and Σ_1, respectively.

(b) Using (6.13), verify that (6.16) results in unbiased estimates of Σ_ν, Λ_2 and Λ_3, respectively.

7 Simultaneous Equations with Error Components

7.1 SINGLE EQUATION ESTIMATION

Endogeneity of the right-hand regressors is a serious problem in econometrics. By endogeneity we mean the correlation of the right-hand side regressors and the disturbances. This may be due to the omission of relevant variables, measurement error, sample selectivity, self-selection or other reasons. Endogeneity causes inconsistency of the usual OLS estimates and requires instrumental variable methods like two-stage least squares (2SLS) to obtain consistent parameter estimates. The applied literature is full of examples of endogeneity: demand and supply equations for labor, money, goods and commodities to mention a few. Also, behavioral relationships like consumption, production, investment, import and export are just a few more examples in economics where endogeneity is suspected. We assume that the reader is familiar with the identification and estimation of a single equation and a system of simultaneous equations. In this chapter we focus on the estimation of simultaneous equations using panel data.

Consider the following first structural equation of a simultaneous equation model:

$$y_1 = Z_1\delta_1 + u_1 \tag{7.1}$$

where $Z_1 = [Y_1, X_1]$ and $\delta_1' = (\gamma_1', \beta_1')$. As in the standard simultaneous equation literature, Y_1 is the set of g_1 right-hand side endogenous variables and X_1 is the set of k_1 included exogenous variables. Let $X = [X_1, X_2]$ be the set of all exogenous variables in the system. This equation is identified with k_2, the number of excluded exogenous variables from the first equation (X_2) being larger than or equal to g_1.

Throughout this chapter we will focus on the one-way error component model

$$u_1 = Z_\mu \mu_1 + \nu_1 \tag{7.2}$$

where $Z_\mu = (I_N \otimes \iota_T)$ and $\mu_1' = (\mu_{11}, \ldots, \mu_{N1})$ and $\nu_1' = (\nu_{111}, \ldots, \nu_{NT1})$ are random vectors with zero means and covariance matrix

$$E\begin{pmatrix}\mu_1\\ \nu_1\end{pmatrix}(\mu_1', \nu_1') = \begin{bmatrix}\sigma^2_{\mu_{11}} I_N & 0\\ 0 & \sigma^2_{\nu_{11}} I_{NT}\end{bmatrix} \tag{7.3}$$

This differs from the SUR setup in Chapter 6 only in the fact that there are right-hand side endogenous variables in Z_1.[1] In this case

$$E(u_1 u_1') = \Omega_{11} = \sigma^2_{\nu_{11}} I_{NT} + \sigma^2_{\mu_{11}}(I_N \otimes J_T) \tag{7.4}$$

In other words, the first structural equation has the typical variance–covariance matrix of a one-way error component model described in Chapter 2. The only difference is that now a double subscript (1, 1) is attached to the variance components to specify that this is the first equation. One can transform (7.1) by $Q = I_{NT} - P$ with $P = I_N \otimes \bar{J}_T$, to get

$$Qy_1 = QZ_1\delta_1 + Qu_1 \tag{7.5}$$

Let $\widetilde{y}_1 = Qy_1$ and $\widetilde{Z}_1 = QZ_1$. Performing 2SLS on (7.5) with $\widetilde{X} = QX$ as the set of instruments, one gets Within 2SLS

$$\widetilde{\delta}_{1,\text{W2SLS}} = (\widetilde{Z}_1' P_{\widetilde{X}} \widetilde{Z}_1)^{-1} \widetilde{Z}_1' P_{\widetilde{X}} \widetilde{y}_1 \tag{7.6}$$

with $\text{var}(\widehat{\delta}_{1,\text{W2SLS}}) = \sigma^2_{\nu_{11}}(\widetilde{Z}_1' P_{\widetilde{X}} \widetilde{Z}_1)^{-1}$. Within 2SLS can also be obtained as GLS on

$$\widetilde{X}'\widetilde{y}_1 = \widetilde{X}'\widetilde{Z}_1\delta_1 + \widetilde{X}'\widetilde{u}_1 \tag{7.7}$$

see problem 7.1. Similarly, if we let $\bar{y}_1 = Py_1$ and $\bar{Z}_1 = PZ_1$, we can transform (7.1) by P and perform 2SLS with $\bar{X} = PX$ as the set of instruments. In this case, we get the Between 2SLS estimator of δ_1

$$\widehat{\delta}_{1,\text{B2SLS}} = (\bar{Z}_1' P_{\bar{X}} \bar{Z}_1)^{-1} \bar{Z}_1' P_{\bar{X}} \bar{y}_1 \tag{7.8}$$

with $\text{var}(\widehat{\delta}_{1,\text{B2SLS}}) = \sigma^2_{1_{11}}(\bar{Z}_1' P_{\bar{X}} \bar{Z}_1)^{-1}$ where $\sigma^2_{1_{11}} = T\sigma^2_{\mu_{11}} + \sigma^2_{\nu_{11}}$. Between 2SLS can also be obtained as GLS on

$$\bar{X}'\bar{y}_1 = \bar{X}'\bar{Z}_1\delta_1 + \bar{X}'\bar{u}_1 \tag{7.9}$$

Stacking these two transformed equations in (7.7) and (7.9) as a system, as in (2.28) and noting that δ_1 is the same for these two transformed equations, one gets

$$\begin{pmatrix}\widetilde{X}'\widetilde{y}_1\\ \bar{X}'\bar{y}_1\end{pmatrix} = \begin{pmatrix}\widetilde{X}'\widetilde{Z}_1\\ \bar{X}'\bar{Z}_1\end{pmatrix}\delta_1 + \begin{pmatrix}\widetilde{X}'\widetilde{u}_1\\ \bar{X}'\bar{u}_1\end{pmatrix} \tag{7.10}$$

where

$$E\begin{pmatrix}\widetilde{X}'\widetilde{u}_1\\ \bar{X}'\bar{u}_1\end{pmatrix} = 0 \quad \text{and} \quad \text{var}\begin{pmatrix}\widetilde{X}'\widetilde{u}_1\\ \bar{X}'\bar{u}_1\end{pmatrix} = \begin{bmatrix}\sigma^2_{\nu_{11}}\widetilde{X}'\widetilde{X} & 0\\ 0 & \sigma^2_{1_{11}}\bar{X}'\bar{X}\end{bmatrix}$$

Performing GLS on (7.10) yields the error component two-stage least squares (EC2SLS) estimator of δ_1 derived by Baltagi (1981b):

$$\widehat{\delta}_{1,\text{EC2SLS}} = \left[\frac{\widetilde{Z}_1' P_{\widetilde{X}} \widetilde{Z}_1}{\sigma^2_{\nu_{11}}} + \frac{\bar{Z}_1' P_{\bar{X}} \bar{Z}_1}{\sigma^2_{1_{11}}}\right]^{-1} \left[\frac{\widetilde{Z}_1' P_{\widetilde{X}} \widetilde{y}_1}{\sigma^2_{\nu_{11}}} + \frac{\bar{Z}_1' P_{\bar{X}} \bar{y}_1}{\sigma^2_{1_{11}}}\right] \tag{7.11}$$

with $\text{var}(\widehat{\delta}_{1,\text{EC2SLS}})$ given by the first inverted bracket in (7.11), see problem 7.2. Note that $\widehat{\delta}_{1,\text{EC2SLS}}$ can also be written as a matrix-weighted average of $\widetilde{\delta}_{1,\text{W2SLS}}$ and $\widehat{\delta}_{1,\text{B2SLS}}$ with the weights depending on their respective variance–covariance matrices:

$$\widehat{\delta}_{1,\text{EC2SLS}} = W_1\widetilde{\delta}_{1,\text{W2SLS}} + W_2\widehat{\delta}_{1,\text{B2SLS}} \tag{7.12}$$

with

$$W_1 = \left[\frac{\widetilde{Z}_1' P_{\widetilde{X}} \widetilde{Z}_1}{\sigma^2_{\nu_{11}}} + \frac{\bar{Z}_1' P_{\bar{X}} \bar{Z}_1}{\sigma^2_{1_{11}}}\right]^{-1} \left[\frac{\widetilde{Z}_1' P_{\widetilde{X}} \widetilde{Z}_1}{\sigma^2_{\nu_{11}}}\right]$$

and

$$W_2 = \left[\frac{\widetilde{Z}_1' P_{\widetilde{X}} \widetilde{Z}_1}{\sigma^2_{\nu_{11}}} + \frac{\bar{Z}_1' P_{\bar{X}} \bar{Z}_1}{\sigma^2_{1_{11}}}\right]^{-1} \left[\frac{\bar{Z}_1' P_{\bar{X}} \bar{Z}_1}{\sigma^2_{1_{11}}}\right]$$

Consistent estimates of $\sigma^2_{\nu_{11}}$ and $\sigma^2_{1_{11}}$ can be obtained from W2SLS and B2SLS residuals, respectively. In fact

$$\widehat{\sigma}^2_{\nu_{11}} = (y_1 - Z_1\widetilde{\delta}_{1,\text{W2SLS}})'Q(y_1 - Z_1\widetilde{\delta}_{1,\text{W2SLS}})/N(T-1) \tag{7.13}$$

$$\widehat{\sigma}^2_{1_{11}} = (y_1 - Z_1\widehat{\delta}_{1,\text{B2SLS}})'P(y_1 - Z_1\widehat{\delta}_{1,\text{B2SLS}})/N \tag{7.14}$$

Substituting these variance components estimates in (7.11) one gets a feasible estimate of EC2SLS. Note that unlike the usual 2SLS procedure, EC2SLS requires estimates of the variance components. One can correct for degrees of freedom in (7.13) and (7.14) especially for small samples, but the panel is assumed to have large N. Also, one should check that $\widehat{\sigma}^2_{\mu_{11}} = (\widehat{\sigma}^2_{1_{11}} - \widehat{\sigma}^2_{\nu_{11}})/T$ is positive.

Alternatively, one can premultiply (7.1) by $\Omega_{11}^{-1/2}$ where Ω_{11} is given in (7.4), to get

$$y_1^* = Z_1^*\delta_1 + u_1^* \tag{7.15}$$

with $y_1^* = \Omega_{11}^{-1/2}y_1$, $Z_1^* = \Omega_{11}^{-1/2}Z_1$ and $u_1^* = \Omega_{11}^{-1/2}u_1$. In this case, $\Omega_{11}^{-1/2}$ is given by (2.20) with the additional subscripts (1, 1) for the variance components, i.e.

$$\Omega_{11}^{-1/2} = (P/\sigma_{1_{11}}) + (Q/\sigma_{\nu_{11}}) \tag{7.16}$$

Therefore, the typical element of y_1^* is $y^*_{1_{it}} = (y_{1_{it}} - \theta_1\bar{y}_{1_{i.}})/\sigma_{\nu_{11}}$ where $\theta_1 = 1 - (\sigma_{\nu_{11}}/\sigma_{1_{11}})$ and $\bar{y}_{1_{i.}} = \sum_{t=1}^{T} y_{1_{it}}/T$.

Given a set of instruments A, then 2SLS on (7.15) using A gives

$$\widehat{\delta}_{1,\text{2SLS}} = (Z_1^{*\prime}P_A Z_1^*)^{-1}Z_1^{*\prime}P_A y_1^* \tag{7.17}$$

where $P_A = A(A'A)^{-1}A'$. Using the results in White (1986), the optimal set of instrumental variables in (7.15) is

$$X^* = \Omega_{11}^{-1/2}X = \frac{QX}{\sigma_{\nu_{11}}} + \frac{PX}{\sigma_{1_{11}}} = \frac{\widetilde{X}}{\sigma_{\nu_{11}}} + \frac{\bar{X}}{\sigma_{1_{11}}}$$

Using $A = X^*$, one gets the Balestra and Varadharajan-Krishnakumar (1987) generalized two-stage least squares (G2SLS):

$$\widehat{\delta}_{1,\mathrm{G2SLS}} = (Z_1^{*\prime} P_{X^*} Z_1^*)^{-1} Z_1^{*\prime} P_{X^*} y_1^* \tag{7.18}$$

Cornwell, Schmidt and Wyhowski (1992) showed that Baltagi's (1981b) EC2SLS can be obtained from (7.17), i.e. using a 2SLS package on the transformed equation (7.15) with the set of instruments $A = [QX, PX] = [\widetilde{X}, \bar{X}]$. In fact, QX is orthogonal to PX and $P_A = P_{\widetilde{X}} + P_{\bar{X}}$. This also means that

$$\begin{aligned} P_A Z_1^* &= (P_{\widetilde{X}} + P_{\bar{X}})[\Omega_{11}^{-1/2} Z_1] \\ &= (P_{\widetilde{X}} + P_{\bar{X}})\left[\frac{Q}{\sigma_{\nu_{11}}} + \frac{P}{\sigma_{1_{11}}}\right] Z_1 = \frac{P_{\widetilde{X}}\widetilde{Z}_1}{\sigma_{\nu_{11}}} + \frac{P_{\bar{X}}\bar{Z}_1}{\sigma_{1_{11}}} \end{aligned} \tag{7.19}$$

with

$$Z_1^{*\prime} P_A Z_1^* = \left(\frac{\widetilde{Z}_1' P_{\widetilde{X}} \widetilde{Z}_1}{\sigma_{\nu_{11}}^2} + \frac{\bar{Z}_1' P_{\bar{X}} \bar{Z}_1}{\sigma_{1_{11}}^2}\right)$$

and

$$Z_1^{*\prime} P_A y_1^* = \left(\frac{\widetilde{Z}_1' P_{\widetilde{X}} \widetilde{y}_1}{\sigma_{\nu_{11}}^2} + \frac{\bar{Z}_1' P_{\bar{X}} \bar{y}_1}{\sigma_{1_{11}}^2}\right)$$

Therefore, $\widehat{\delta}_{1,\mathrm{EC2SLS}}$ given by (7.11) is the same as (7.17) with $A = [\widetilde{X}, \bar{X}]$.

So, how is Baltagi's (1981b) EC2SLS given by (7.11) different from the Balestra and Varadharajan-Krishnakumar (1987) G2SLS given by (7.18)? It should be clear to the reader that the set of instruments used by Baltagi (1981b), i.e. $A = [\widetilde{X}, \bar{X}]$, spans the set of instruments used by Balestra and Varadharajan-Krishnakumar (1987), i.e. $X^* = [\widetilde{X}/\sigma_{\nu_{11}} + \bar{X}/\sigma_{1_{11}}]$. In fact, one can show that $A = [\widetilde{X}, \bar{X}]$, $B = [X^*, \widetilde{X}]$ and $C = [X^*, \bar{X}]$ yield the same projection, and therefore the same 2SLS estimator given by EC2SLS (see problem 7.3). Without going into proofs, we note that Baltagi and Li (1992d) showed that $\widehat{\delta}_{1,\mathrm{G2SLS}}$ and $\widetilde{\delta}_{1,\mathrm{EC2SLS}}$ yield the same asymptotic variance–covariance matrix. Therefore, using White's (1986) terminology, $\widetilde{X}$ in B and $\bar{X}$ in C are "redundant" with respect to X^*. Redundant instruments can be interpreted loosely as additional sets of instruments that do not yield extra gains in asymptotic efficiency; see White (1986) for the strict definition and Baltagi and Li (1992d) for the proof in this context.

For applications, it is easy to obtain EC2SLS using a standard 2SLS package:

Step 1: Run W2SLS and B2SLS using a standard 2SLS package on (7.5) and (7.9), i.e. run 2SLS of $\widetilde{y}$ on $\widetilde{Z}$ using $\widetilde{X}$ as instruments and run 2SLS of $\bar{y}$ on $\bar{Z}$ using $\bar{X}$ as instruments. This yields (7.6) and (7.8), respectively.[2]

Step 2: Compute $\widehat{\sigma}_{\nu_{11}}^2$ and $\widehat{\sigma}_{1_{11}}^2$ from (7.13) and (7.14) and obtain y_1^*, Z_1^* and X^* as described below (7.17). This transforms (7.1) by $\widehat{\Omega}_{11}^{-1/2}$ as in (7.15).

Step 3: Run 2SLS on this transformed equation (7.15) using the instrument set $A = X^*$ or $A = [QX, PX]$ as suggested above, i.e. run 2SLS of y_1^*

on Z_1^* using X_1^* or $[\widetilde{X}, \bar{X}]$ as instruments. This yields (7.18) and (7.11), respectively. These computations are easy and are programmed in STATA and in TSP. They involve simple transformations on the data and the application of 2SLS three times.

7.2 SYSTEM ESTIMATION

Consider the system of identified equations

$$y = Z\delta + u \tag{7.20}$$

where $y' = (y_1', \ldots, y_M')$, $Z = \text{diag}[Z_j]$, $\delta' = (\delta_1', \ldots, \delta_M')$ and $u' = (u_1', \ldots, u_M')$ with $Z_j = [Y_j, X_j]$ of dimension $NT \times (g_j + k_j)$, for $j = 1, \ldots, M$. In this case, there are g_j included right-hand side Y_j and k_j included right-hand side X_j. This differs from the SUR model only in the fact that there are right-hand side endogenous variables in the system of equations. For the one-way error component model, the disturbance of the jth equation u_j is given by (6.2) and $\Omega_{jl} = E(u_j u_l')$ is given by (6.4) as in the SUR case. Once again, the covariance matrix between the disturbances of different equations has the same error component form. Except now, there are additional cross-equations variance components to be estimated. The variance–covariance matrix of the set of M structural equations $\Omega = E(uu')$ is given by (6.5) and $\Omega^{-1/2}$ is given by (6.8). Premultiplying (7.20) by $(I_M \otimes Q)$ yields

$$\widetilde{y} = \widetilde{Z}\delta + \widetilde{u} \tag{7.21}$$

where $\widetilde{y} = (I_M \otimes Q)y$, $\widetilde{Z} = (I_M \otimes Q)Z$ and $\widetilde{u} = (I_M \otimes Q)u$. Performing 3SLS on (7.21) with $(I_M \otimes \widetilde{X})$ as the set of instruments, where $\widetilde{X} = QX$, one gets the Within 3SLS estimator:

$$\widetilde{\delta}_{\text{W3SLS}} = [\widetilde{Z}'(\Sigma_\nu^{-1} \otimes P_{\widetilde{X}})\widetilde{Z}]^{-1}[\widetilde{Z}'(\Sigma_\nu^{-1} \otimes P_{\widetilde{X}})\widetilde{y}] \tag{7.22}$$

Similarly, transforming (7.20) by $(I_M \otimes P)$ yields

$$\bar{y} = \bar{Z}\delta + \bar{u} \tag{7.23}$$

where $\bar{y} = (I_M \otimes P)y$, $\bar{Z} = (I_M \otimes P)Z$ and $\bar{u} = (I_M \otimes P)u$. Performing 3SLS on the transformed system (7.23) using $(I_M \otimes \bar{X})$ as the set of instruments, where $\bar{X} = PX$, one gets the Between 3SLS estimator:

$$\widehat{\delta}_{\text{B3SLS}} = [\bar{Z}'(\Sigma_1^{-1} \otimes P_{\bar{X}})\bar{Z}]^{-1}[\bar{Z}'(\Sigma_1^{-1} \otimes P_{\bar{X}})\bar{y}] \tag{7.24}$$

Next, we stack the two transformed systems given in (7.21) and (7.23) after premultiplying by $(I_M \otimes \widetilde{X}')$ and $(I_M \otimes \bar{X}')$, respectively. Then we perform GLS noting that δ is the same for these two transformed systems (see problem 7.5). The resulting estimator of δ is the error components three-stage least squares (EC3SLS) given by Baltagi (1981b):

$$\begin{aligned}\widehat{\delta}_{\text{EC3SLS}} = {} & [\widetilde{Z}'(\Sigma_\nu^{-1} \otimes P_{\widetilde{X}})\widetilde{Z} + \bar{Z}'(\Sigma_1^{-1} \otimes P_{\bar{X}})\bar{Z}]^{-1} \\ & \times[\widetilde{Z}'(\Sigma_\nu^{-1} \otimes P_{\widetilde{X}})\widetilde{y} + \bar{Z}'(\Sigma_1^{-1} \otimes P_{\bar{X}})\bar{y}]\end{aligned} \tag{7.25}$$

Note that $\widehat{\delta}_{\text{EC3SLS}}$ can also be written as a matrix-weighted average of $\widehat{\delta}_{\text{W3SLS}}$ and $\widehat{\delta}_{\text{B3SLS}}$ as follows:

$$\widehat{\delta}_{\text{EC3SLS}} = W_1 \widehat{\delta}_{\text{W3SLS}} + W_2 \widehat{\delta}_{\text{B3SLS}} \tag{7.26}$$

with

$$W_1 = [\widetilde{Z}'(\Sigma_\nu^{-1} \otimes P_{\widetilde{X}})\widetilde{Z} + \bar{Z}'(\Sigma_1^{-1} \otimes P_{\bar{X}})\bar{Z}]^{-1}[\widetilde{Z}'(\Sigma_\nu^{-1} \otimes P_{\widetilde{X}})\widetilde{Z}]$$

and

$$W_2 = [\widetilde{Z}'(\Sigma_\nu^{-1} \otimes P_{\widetilde{X}})\widetilde{Z} + \bar{Z}'(\Sigma_1^{-1} \otimes P_{\bar{X}})\bar{Z}]^{-1}[\bar{Z}'(\Sigma_1^{-1} \otimes P_{\bar{X}})\bar{Z}]$$

Consistent estimates of Σ_ν and Σ_1 can be obtained as in (7.13) and (7.14) using W2SLS and B2SLS residuals with

$$\widehat{\sigma}^2_{\nu_{jl}} = (y_j - Z_j \widetilde{\delta}_{j,\text{W2SLS}})' Q (y_l - Z_l \widetilde{\delta}_{l,\text{W2SLS}})/N(T-1) \tag{7.27}$$

$$\widehat{\sigma}^2_{1_{jl}} = (y_j - Z_j \widehat{\delta}_{j,\text{B2SLS}})' P (y_l - Z_l \widehat{\delta}_{l,\text{B2SLS}})/N \tag{7.28}$$

One should check whether $\widehat{\Sigma}_\mu = (\widehat{\Sigma}_1 - \widehat{\Sigma}_\nu)/T$ is positive definite.

Using $\Omega^{-1/2}$ from (6.8), one can transform (7.20) to get

$$y^* = Z^* \delta + u^* \tag{7.29}$$

with $y^* = \Omega^{-1/2} y$, $Z^* = \Omega^{-1/2} Z$ and $u^* = \Omega^{-1/2} u$. For an arbitrary set of instruments A, the 3SLS estimator of (7.29) becomes

$$\widehat{\delta}_{\text{3SLS}} = (Z^{*\prime} P_A Z^*)^{-1} Z^{*\prime} P_A y^* \tag{7.30}$$

Using the results of White (1986), the optimal set of instruments is

$$X^* = \Omega^{-1/2}(I_M \otimes X) = (\Sigma_\nu^{-1/2} \otimes QX) + (\Sigma_1^{-1/2} \otimes PX)$$

Substituting $A = X^*$ in (7.30), one gets the efficient three-stage least squares (E3SLS) estimator:

$$\widehat{\delta}_{\text{E3SLS}} = (Z^{*\prime} P_{X^*} Z^*)^{-1} Z^{*\prime} P_{X^*} y^* \tag{7.31}$$

This is not the G3SLS estimator suggested by Balestra and Varadharajan-Krishnakumar (1987). In fact, Balestra and Varadharajan-Krishnakumar (1987) suggest using

$$\begin{aligned} A &= \Omega^{1/2} \operatorname{diag}[\Omega_{jj}^{-1}](I_M \otimes X) \\ &= \Sigma_\nu^{1/2} \operatorname{diag}\left(\frac{1}{\sigma^2_{\nu_{jj}}}\right) \otimes \widetilde{X} + \Sigma_1^{1/2} \operatorname{diag}\left(\frac{1}{\sigma^2_{1_{jj}}}\right) \otimes \bar{X} \end{aligned} \tag{7.32}$$

Substituting this A in (7.30) yields the G3SLS estimator of δ. So, how are G3SLS, EC3SLS and E3SLS related? Baltagi and Li (1992d) show that Baltagi's (1981b) EC3SLS estimator can be obtained from (7.30) with $A = [I_M \otimes \widetilde{X}, I_M \otimes \bar{X}]$. From this it is clear that the set of instruments $[I_M \otimes \widetilde{X}, I_M \otimes \bar{X}]$ used by Baltagi (1981b) spans the set of instruments $[\Sigma_\nu^{-1/2} \otimes \widetilde{X} + \Sigma_1^{-1/2} \otimes \bar{X}]$ needed for E3SLS. In addition, we note without proof that Baltagi and Li (1992d) show that $\widehat{\delta}_{\text{EC3SLS}}$ and $\widehat{\delta}_{\text{E3SLS}}$ yield the same asymptotic variance–covariance matrix. Problem 7.6 shows that Baltagi's (1981b) EC3SLS estimator has redundant instruments with respect to those used by the E3SLS estimator. Therefore, using White's (1984) terminology, the extra instruments used by Baltagi (1981b) do not yield extra gains in asymptotic efficiency. However, Baltagi and Li (1992d) also show that both EC3SLS and E3SLS are asymptotically more efficient than the G3SLS estimator corresponding to the set of instruments given by (7.32). In applications, it is easy to obtain EC3SLS using a standard 3SLS package:

Step 1: Obtain W2SLS and B2SLS estimates of each structural equation as described in the first step of computing EC2SLS.
Step 2: Compute estimates of $\widehat{\Sigma}_1$ and $\widehat{\Sigma}_\nu$ as described in (7.27) and (7.28).
Step 3: Obtain the Cholesky decomposition of $\widehat{\Sigma}_1^{-1}$ and $\widehat{\Sigma}_\nu^{-1}$ and use those instead of $\widehat{\Sigma}_1^{-1/2}$ and $\widehat{\Sigma}_\nu^{-1/2}$ in the transformation described in (7.29), i.e. obtain y^*, Z^* and X^* as described below (7.30).
Step 4: Apply 3SLS to this transformed system (7.29) using as a set of instruments $A = X^*$ or $A = [I_M \otimes \widetilde{X}, I_M \otimes \bar{X}]$, i.e. run 3SLS of y^* on Z^* using as instruments X^* or $[I_M \otimes \widetilde{X}, I_M \otimes \bar{X}]$. These yield (7.31) and (7.25), respectively. The computations are again easy, requiring simple transformations and a 3SLS package.

Baltagi (1981b) shows that EC3SLS reduces to EC2SLS when the disturbances of the different structural equations are uncorrelated with each other, but not necessarily when all the structural equations are just identified. This is different from the analogous conditions between 2SLS and 3SLS in the classical simultaneous equations model (see problem 7.7).

Baltagi (1984) also performs Monte Carlo experiments on a two-equation simultaneous model with error components and demonstrates the efficiency gains in terms of mean squared error in performing EC2SLS and EC3SLS over the standard simultaneous equation counterparts, 2SLS and 3SLS. EC2SLS and EC3SLS also performed better than a two- or three-stage variance components method suggested by Maddala (1977) where right-hand side endogenous variables are replaced by their predicted values from the reduced form and the standard error component GLS is performed in the second step. Also, Baltagi (1984) demonstrates that better estimates of the variance components do not necessarily imply better estimates of the structural or reduced form parameters.[3] Mátyás and Lovrics (1990) performed Monte Carlo experiments on a just identified two-equation static model and compared OLS, Within-2SLS, true EC2SLS and a feasible EC2SLS for various generated exogenous variables and a variety of N and T. They recommend the panel data estimators as long as N and T are both larger than 15. Prucha (1985) derived the full information maximum likelihood (FIML) estimator of the simultaneous equation model with error components assuming normality of the disturbances. Prucha shows that this FIML estimator has an instrumental variable representation which generalizes Hausman's (1975) results for the standard simultaneous equation model. The instrumental variable form of the normal equations of the FIML estimator is used to generate a wide class of instrumental variable estimators. Prucha also establishes the existence of wide asymptotic equivalence classes of full and limited information estimators of which Baltagi's EC2SLS and EC3SLS are members. Balestra and Varadharajan-Krishnakumar (1987) derive the limiting distributions of both the coefficient estimators and covariance estimators of the FIML method for the SEM with error components. Krishnakumar (1988) provides a useful summary of this simultaneous equations with error components literature, which is updated in her chapter in Mátyás and Sevestre (1996).

For one of the early extensions of the error component model to the simultaneous equations context, see Chamberlain and Griliches (1975). They considered the problem of bias in estimating returns to schooling due to omitted ability and family background variables. Their basic idea is that omitted variables like ability must cause similar biases (proportional to each other) in different equations explaining, say, income, occupation and schooling. Taking advantage of this fact achieves identification of most of the coefficients of interest. MLE and GLS are derived and applied to the study of the economic experience of 156 pairs of brothers from Indiana, USA.

For an application of Within-2SLS to estimate regional supply and demand functions for the Southern Pine lumber industry, see Shim (1982). Nguyen and Bernier (1988) for an application of Within-2SLS to a system of simultaneous equations which examines the influence of a firm's market power on its risk level using Tobin's q. Cornwell and Trumbull (1994) for an application of Within-2SLS to the economics of crime across 90 North Carolina counties over seven time periods. Baltagi and Blien (1998) for an application of Within-2SLS to the estimation of a wage curve for Germany using data for 142 labor market regions over the period 1981–90. Briefly, the wage curve describes the negative relationship between the local unemployment rate and the level of wages. Baltagi and Blien (1998) find that ignoring endogeneity of the local employment rate yields results in favor of the wage curve only for younger and less qualified workers. Accounting for endogeneity of the unemployment rate yields evidence in favor of the wage curve across all types of workers. In particular, the wages of less qualified workers are more responsive to local unemployment rates than the wages of more qualified workers. Also, the wages of men are slightly more responsive to local unemployment rates than the wages of women. Applications of EC2SLS and EC3SLS include: (i) an econometric rational-expectations macroeconomic model for developing countries with capital controls (see Haque, Lahiri and Montiel, 1993), and (ii) an econometric model measuring income and price elasticities of foreign trade for developing countries (see Kinal and Lahiri, 1993).

7.3 ENDOGENOUS EFFECTS

Let us reconsider the single equation estimation case but now focus on endogeneity occurring through the unobserved individual effects. Examples where μ_i and the explanatory variables may be correlated include an earnings equation, where the unobserved individual ability may be correlated with schooling and experience; also a production function, where managerial ability may be correlated with the inputs. Mundlak (1978) considered the one-way error component regression model in (2.5) but with the additional auxiliary regression

$$\mu_i = \bar{X}'_{i.}\pi + \epsilon_i \tag{7.33}$$

where $\epsilon_i \sim \text{IIN}(0, \sigma_\epsilon^2)$ and $\bar{X}'_{i.}$ is a $1 \times K$ vector of observations on the explanatory variables averaged over time. In other words, Mundlak assumed that the individual effects are a linear function of the averages of *all* the explanatory variables across time. These effects are uncorrelated with the explanatory variables if and only if $\pi = 0$. Mundlak (1978) assumed, without loss of generality, that the X are deviations from their sample mean. In vector form, one can write (7.33) as

$$\mu = Z'_\mu X\pi/T + \epsilon \tag{7.34}$$

where $\mu' = (\mu_1, \ldots, \mu_N)$, $Z_\mu = I_N \otimes \iota_T$ and $\epsilon' = (\epsilon_1, \ldots, \epsilon_N)$. Substituting (7.34) in (2.5), with no constant, one gets

$$y = X\beta + PX\pi + (Z_\mu\epsilon + \nu) \tag{7.35}$$

where $P = I_N \otimes \bar{J}_T$. Using the fact that the ϵ and ν are uncorrelated, the new error in (7.35) has zero mean and variance–covariance matrix

$$V = E(Z_\mu\epsilon + \nu)(Z_\mu\epsilon + \nu)' = \sigma_\epsilon^2(I_N \otimes J_T) + \sigma_\nu^2 I_{NT} \tag{7.36}$$

Using the partitioned inverse, one can verify (see problem 7.8) that GLS on (7.35) yields

$$\widehat{\beta}_{\text{GLS}} = \widetilde{\beta}_{\text{Within}} = (X'QX)^{-1}X'Qy \tag{7.37}$$

and

$$\widehat{\pi}_{\text{GLS}} = \widehat{\beta}_{\text{Between}} - \widetilde{\beta}_{\text{Within}} = (X'PX)^{-1}X'Py - (X'QX)^{-1}X'Qy \tag{7.38}$$

with

$$\begin{aligned} \text{var}(\widehat{\pi}_{\text{GLS}}) &= \text{var}(\widehat{\beta}_{\text{Between}}) + \text{var}(\widetilde{\beta}_{\text{Within}}) \\ &= (T\sigma_\epsilon^2 + \sigma_\nu^2)(X'PX)^{-1} + \sigma_\nu^2(X'QX)^{-1} \end{aligned} \tag{7.39}$$

Therefore, Mundlak (1978) showed that the best linear unbiased estimator of (2.5) becomes the fixed effects (Within) estimator once these individual effects are modeled as a linear function of *all* the X_{it} as in (7.33). The random effects estimator on the other hand is biased because it ignores (7.33). Note that Hausman's test based on the Between minus Within estimators is basically a test for $H_0: \pi = 0$ and this turns out to be another natural derivation for the test considered in Chapter 4, namely

$$\widehat{\pi}'_{\text{GLS}}(\text{var}(\widehat{\pi}'_{\text{GLS}}))^{-1}\widehat{\pi}_{\text{GLS}} \stackrel{H_0}{\to} \chi_K^2$$

Mundlak's (1978) formulation in (7.35) assumes that all the explanatory variables are related to the individual effects. The random effects model on the other hand assumes no correlation between the explanatory variables and the individual effects. The random effects model generates the GLS estimator, whereas Mundlak's formulation produces the Within estimator. Instead of this "all or nothing" correlation among the X and the μ_i, Hausman and Taylor (1981) consider a model where some of the explanatory variables are related to the μ_i. In particular, they consider the following model:

$$y_{it} = X_{it}\beta + Z_i\gamma + \mu_i + \nu_{it} \tag{7.40}$$

where the Z_i are cross-sectional time-invariant variables. Hausman and Taylor (1981), hereafter HT, split X and Z into two sets of variables: $X = [X_1; X_2]$ and $Z = [Z_1; Z_2]$ where X_1 is $n \times k_1$, X_2 is $n \times k_2$, Z_1 is $n \times g_1$, Z_2 is $n \times g_2$ and $n = NT$. X_1 and Z_1 are assumed exogenous in that they are not correlated with μ_i and ν_{it}, while X_2 and Z_2 are endogenous because they are correlated with μ_i but not ν_{it}. The Within transformation would sweep the μ_i and remove the bias, but in the process it would also remove the Z_i and hence the Within estimator will not give an estimate of γ. To get around that, HT suggest premultiplying the model by $\Omega^{-1/2}$ and using the following set of instruments: $A_0 = [Q, X_1, Z_1]$, where $Q = I_{NT} - P$ and $P = (I_N \otimes \bar{J}_T)$. Breusch, Mizon and Schmidt (1989), hereafter BMS, show that this set of instruments yields the same projection and is therefore equivalent to another set, namely $A_{\text{HT}} = [QX_1, QX_2, PX_1, Z_1]$. The latter set of instruments A_{HT} is feasible, whereas A_0 is not.[4] The order condition for identification gives the result that k_1, the number of variables in X_1, must be at least as large as g_2, the number of variables in Z_2. Note that $\widetilde{X}_1 = QX_1$, $\widetilde{X}_2 = QX_2$, $\bar{X}_1 = PX_1$ and Z_1 are used as instruments. Therefore X_1 is used twice, once as averages and another time as deviations from these averages. This is an advantage of panel data allowing instruments from *within* the model. Note that the Within transformation wipes out the Z_i and does not allow the estimation of γ. In order to get consistent estimates of γ, HT propose obtaining the Within residuals and averaging them over time

$$\widehat{d}_i = \bar{y}_{i.} - \bar{X}'_{i.}\widetilde{\beta}_{\text{W}} \tag{7.41}$$

Then, (7.40) averaged over time can be estimated by running 2SLS of $\widehat{d}_i$ on Z_i with the set of instruments $A = [X_1, Z_1]$. This yields

$$\widehat{\gamma}_{\text{2SLS}} = (Z'P_AZ)^{-1}Z'P_A\widehat{d} \tag{7.42}$$

where $P_A = A(A'A)^{-1}A'$. It is clear that the order condition has to hold ($k_1 \geqslant g_2$) for $(Z'P_AZ)$ to be nonsingular. Next, the variance components estimates are obtained as follows:

$$\widetilde{\sigma}_\nu^2 = \widetilde{y}'\bar{P}_{\widetilde{X}}\widetilde{y}/N(T-1) \tag{7.43}$$

where $\widetilde{y} = Qy$, $\widetilde{X} = QX$, $\bar{P}_A = I - P_A$ and

$$\widetilde{\sigma}_1^2 = \frac{(y_{it} - X_{it}\widetilde{\beta}_{\text{W}} - Z_i\widehat{\gamma}_{\text{2SLS}})'P(y_{it} - X_{it}\widetilde{\beta}_{\text{W}} - Z_i\widehat{\gamma}_{\text{2SLS}})}{N} \tag{7.44}$$

This last estimate is based upon an NT vector of residuals. Once the variance components estimates are obtained, the model in (7.40) is transformed using

$\widehat{\Omega}^{-1/2}$ as follows:

$$\widehat{\Omega}^{-1/2}y_{it} = \widehat{\Omega}^{-1/2}X_{it}\beta + \widehat{\Omega}^{-1/2}Z_i\gamma + \widehat{\Omega}^{-1/2}u_{it} \tag{7.45}$$

The HT estimator is basically 2SLS on (7.45) using $A_{\text{HT}} = [\widetilde{X}, \bar{X}_1, Z_1]$ as a set of instruments.

(1) If $k_1 < g_2$, then the equation is underidentified. In this case $\widehat{\beta}_{\text{HT}} = \widetilde{\beta}_{\text{W}}$ and $\widehat{\gamma}_{\text{HT}}$ does not exist.
(2) If $k_1 = g_2$, then the equation is just-identified. In this case, $\widehat{\beta}_{\text{HT}} = \widetilde{\beta}_{\text{W}}$ and $\widehat{\gamma}_{\text{HT}} = \widehat{\gamma}_{\text{2SLS}}$ given by (7.42).
(3) If $k_1 > g_2$, then the equation is overidentified and the HT estimator obtained from (7.45) is more efficient than the Within estimator.

A test for overidentification is obtained by computing

$$\widehat{m} = \hat{q}'[\text{var}(\widetilde{\beta}_{\text{W}}) - \text{var}(\widehat{\beta}_{\text{HT}})]^{-}\widehat{q} \tag{7.46}$$

with $\widehat{q} = \widehat{\beta}_{\text{HT}} - \widetilde{\beta}_{\text{W}}$ and $\widehat{\sigma}_\nu^2\widehat{m} \overset{H_0}{\to} \chi_l^2$ where $l = \min[k_1 - g_2, NT - K]$.

Note that $y^* = \widehat{\sigma}_\nu\widehat{\Omega}^{-1/2}y$ has a typical element $y_{it}^* = (y_{it} - \widehat{\theta}\bar{y}_{i.})$ where $\widehat{\theta} = 1 - \widehat{\sigma}_\nu/\widehat{\sigma}_1$ and similar terms exist for X_{it}^* and Z_i^*. In this case 2SLS on (7.45) yields

$$\begin{pmatrix}\widehat{\beta}\\ \widehat{\gamma}\end{pmatrix} = \left[\begin{pmatrix}X^{*\prime}\\ Z^{*\prime}\end{pmatrix} P_A(X^*, Z^*)\right]^{-1}\begin{pmatrix}X^{*\prime}\\ Z^{*\prime}\end{pmatrix} P_A y^* \tag{7.47}$$

where P_A is the projection matrix on $A_{\text{HT}} = [\widetilde{X}, \bar{X}_1, Z_1]$.

Amemiya and MaCurdy (1986), hereafter AM, suggest a more efficient set of instruments $A_{\text{AM}} = [QX_1, QX_2, X_1^*, Z_1]$ where $X_1^* = X_1^0 \otimes \iota_T$ and

$$X_1^0 = \begin{bmatrix} X_{11} & X_{12} & \dots & X_{1T}\\ \vdots & \vdots & \dots & \vdots\\ X_{N1} & X_{N2} & \dots & X_{NT}\end{bmatrix} \tag{7.48}$$

is an $N \times k_1T$ matrix. So X_1 is used $T + 1$ times, once as $\widetilde{X}_1$ and T times as X_1^*. The order condition for identification is now more likely to be satisfied $(Tk_1 > g_2)$. However, this set of instruments requires a stronger exogeneity assumption than that of Hausman and Taylor (1981). The latter requires only uncorrelatedness of the mean of X_1 from the μ_i, i.e.

$$\text{plim}\left(\frac{1}{N}\sum_{i=1}^{N}\bar{X}_{1i.}\mu_i\right) = 0$$

while Amemiya and MaCurdy (1986) require

$$\text{plim}\left(\frac{1}{N}\sum_{i=1}^{N}X_{1it}\mu_i\right) = 0 \quad \text{for } t = 1, \dots, T$$

i.e. uncorrelatedness at each point in time. Breusch, Mizon and Schmidt (1989) suggest a yet more efficient set of instruments

$$A_{\mathrm{BMS}} = [QX_1, QX_2, PX_1, (QX_1)^*, (QX_2)^*, Z_1]$$

so that X_1 is used $T+1$ times and X_2 is used T times. This requires even more exogeneity assumptions, i.e. $\widetilde{X}_2 = QX_2$ should be uncorrelated with the μ_i effects. The BMS order condition becomes $Tk_1 + (T-1)k_2 \geqslant g_2$.

For the Hausman and Taylor (1981) model given in (7.40), Metcalf (1996) shows that using less instruments may lead to a more powerful Hausman specification test. Asymptotically, more instruments lead to more efficient estimators. However, the asymptotic bias of the less efficient estimator will also be greater as the null hypothesis of no correlation is violated. Metcalf argues that if the bias increases at the same rate as the variance (as the null is violated) for the less efficient estimator, then the power of the Hausman test will increase. This is due to the fact that the test statistic is linear in variance but quadratic in bias.

Computational Note

The number of instruments used by the AM and BMS procedures can increase rapidly as T and the number of variables in the equation get large. For large N panels, small T and reasonable k, this should not be a problem. However, even for $T = 7$, $k_1 = 4$ and $k_2 = 5$ as in the empirical illustration used in the next section, the number of additional instruments used by HT is four compared to 28 for AM and 58 for BMS.[5]

7.4 EMPIRICAL ILLUSTRATION

Cornwell and Rupert (1988) apply these three instrumental variable (IV) methods to a returns to schooling example based on a panel of 595 individuals observed over the period 1976–82 and drawn from the Panel Study of Income Dynamics (PSID). A description of the data is given in Cornwell and Rupert (1988) and is available on the Wiley web site as Wage.xls. In particular, log wage is regressed on years of education (ED), weeks worked (WKS), years of full-time work experience (EXP), occupation (OCC = 1 if the individual is in a blue-collar occupation), residence (SOUTH = 1, SMSA = 1 if the individual resides in the South or in a standard metropolitan statistical area), industry (IND = 1 if the individual works in a manufacturing industry), marital status (MS = 1 if the individual is married), sex and race (FEM = 1, BLK = 1 if the individual is female or black), union coverage (UNION = 1 if the individual's wage is set by a union contract) and time dummies to capture productivity and price level effects. Baltagi and Khanti-Akom (1990) replicate this study and their results are reproduced in Table 7.1. Std. Err. gives the standard error of each estimated equation. The conventional GLS indicates that an additional year of schooling produces a 6.98% wage gain. But conventional GLS does not account for the

Table 7.1 Dependent Variable: Log Wage* (Time Dummies Included)

	GLS	Within	HT†	AM†	BMS‡
Constant	0.645	—	0.384	0.495	0.521
	(0.014)		(0.057)	(0.043)	(0.039)
WKS	0.0007	0.0007	0.0008	0.0008	0.0008
	(0.0006)	(0.0006)	(0.0006)	(0.0006)	(0.0006)
SOUTH	−0.034	0.003	0.012	−0.007	−0.012
	(0.026)	(0.034)	(0.029)	(0.028)	(0.027)
SMSA	−0.007	−0.042	−0.039	−0.025	−0.022
	(0.017)	(0.019)	(0.019)	(0.018)	(0.018)
MS	−0.026	−0.029	−0.026	−0.027	−0.027
	(0.018)	(0.019)	(0.019)	(0.018)	(0.018)
EXP	0.027	—	0.042	0.038	0.038
	(0.003)		(0.011)	(0.007)	(0.007)
EXP^2	−0.0004	−0.0004	−0.0004	−0.0004	−0.0004
	(0.00005)	(0.00005)	(0.00005)	(0.00005)	(0.00005)
OCC	−0.028	−0.019	−0.019	−0.020	−0.022
	(0.013)	(0.014)	(0.014)	(0.013)	(0.013)
IND	0.023	0.021	0.021	0.021	0.021
	(0.014)	(0.015)	(0.015)	(0.015)	(0.015)
UNION	0.035	0.030	0.027	0.029	0.028
	(0.014)	(0.015)	(0.015)	(0.014)	(0.014)
FEM	−0.427	—	−0.404	−0.405	−0.401
	(0.067)		(0.080)	(0.072)	(0.070)
BLK	−0.147	—	0.016	−0.066	−0.091
	(0.080)		(0.107)	(0.090)	(0.085)
ED	0.070	—	0.224	0.154	0.135
	(0.008)		(0.041)	(0.027)	(0.022)
Std. Err.	0.144	0.151	0.151	0.146	0.146
		$\chi_8^2 = 18.9$	$\chi_3^2 = 4.86$	$\chi_{13}^2 = 9.16$	$\chi_{13}^2 = 2.38$

*X_2=(WKS, SOUTH, SMSA, MS), Z_1 = (FEM, BLK) and the estimates of the variance components are $\widehat{\sigma}_\nu^2 = 0.023$, $\widehat{\sigma}_\mu^2 = 0.256$ and $\widehat{\phi} = \widehat{\sigma}_\nu/\widehat{\sigma}_1 = 0.1122$

†This removes one of the time dummies from the set of instruments due to perfect collinearity

‡This removes EXP, EXP^2 from the set of additional instruments allowed by the BMS procedure due to singularity

Source: Baltagi and Khanti-Akom (1990). Reproduced by permission of John Wiley & Sons Ltd

possible correlation of the explanatory variables with the individual effects. The Within transformation eliminates the individual effects and all the Z_i variables, and the resulting Within estimator is consistent even if the individual effects are correlated with the explanatory variables. The Within estimates are quite different from those of GLS, and the Hausman test based on the difference between these two estimates yields $\chi_8^2 = 18.9$ which is significant at the 5% level. This rejects the hypothesis of no correlation between the individual effects and the explanatory variables. This justifies the use of the IV methods represented as HT, AM and BMS in Table 7.1. Following Cornwell and Rupert (1988), we let X_1 = (WKS, SOUTH, SMSA, MS), X_2 = (EXP, EXP^2, OCC, IND, UNION),

$Z_1 = $ (FEM, BLK) and $Z_2 = $ (ED). The coefficient of ED is estimated as 0.22, three times the estimate obtained using GLS (0.07). A Hausman test based on the difference between HT and the Within estimator yields $\chi_3^2 = 4.86$ which is not significant at the 5% level. There are three degrees of freedom since there are three overidentifying conditions (the number of X_1 variables minus the number of Z_2 variables).

Therefore, we cannot reject that the set of instruments X_1 and Z_1 chosen is legitimate. The AM estimates resemble the HT estimates whenever they are significant, except for the ED coefficient estimate which drops to 0.15 with a considerably lower standard error. The additional exogeneity assumptions needed for the AM estimator are not rejected using a Hausman test based on the difference between the HT and AM estimators. This yields $\chi_{13}^2 = 9.16$ which is not significant at the 5% level. The BMS estimates are similar to those of AM, whenever they are significant, but the ED coefficient estimate drops again to 0.135 with an even smaller standard error. Again, the additional exogeneity assumptions needed for the BMS estimator are not rejected using a Hausman test based on the difference between the AM and BMS estimators. This yields $\chi_{13}^2 = 2.38$ which is not significant at the 5% level. Therefore, there are empirical efficiency gains as one goes from the set of instruments A_{HT} to A_{AM} to A_{BMS} and they are most apparent in the coefficient of the time-invariant endogenous variables $Z_2 = $ (ED). Bowden and Turkington (1984) argue that canonical correlations are a useful device for comparing different sets of instruments. In fact, as far as asymptotic efficiency is concerned, one should use instruments for which the canonical correlations with the regressors are maximized. Baltagi and Khanti-Akom (1990) compute the canonical correlations for these three sets of instruments. The geometric average of the canonical correlations (which is a measure of the squared correlations between the set of instruments and the regressors) gives an idea of the gains in asymptotic efficiency for this particular data set as one moves from A_{HT} to A_{AM} to A_{BMS}. These are 0.682 for HT, 0.740 for AM and 0.770 for BMS.

For another application of the HT, AM and BMS estimators to a study of the impact of health on wages, see Contoyannis and Rice (2000). This paper considers the effect of self-assessed general and psychological health on hourly wages using longitudinal data from the six waves of the British Household Panel Survey. Contoyannis and Rice show that reduced psychological health reduces the hourly wage for males, while excellent self-assessed health increases the hourly wage for females.

7.5 EXTENSIONS

Cornwell, Schmidt and Wyhowski (1992) consider a simultaneous equation model with error components that distinguishes between two types of exogenous variables, namely *singly exogenous* and *doubly exogenous* variables. A singly exogenous variable is correlated with the individual effects but not with the remainder noise. These are given the subscript (2). On the other hand, a doubly exogenous variable is uncorrelated with both the effects and the remainder disturbance term. These are given the subscript (1). Cornwell, Schmidt and Wyhowski extend the results of HT, AM and BMS by transforming each structural equation by its $\Omega^{-1/2}$ and applying 2SLS on the transformed equation using $A = [QX, PB]$ as the set of instruments in (7.47). B is defined as follows:

(1) $B_{\text{HT}} = [X_{(1)}, Z_{(1)}]$ for the Hausman and Taylor (1981) type estimator. This B_{HT} is the set of all *doubly* exogenous variables in the system.
(2) $B_{\text{AM}} = [X^*_{(1)}, Z_{(1)}]$ for the Amemiya and MaCurdy (1986) type estimator. The (*) notation has been defined in (7.48).
(3) $B_{\text{BMS}} = [X^*_{(1)}, Z_{(1)}, (QX_{(2)})^*]$ for the Breusch, Mizon and Schmidt (1989) type estimator. They also derive a similar set of instruments for the 3SLS analogue and give a generalized method of moments interpretation to these estimators. Finally, they consider the possibility of a different set of instruments for each equation, say $A_j = [QX, PB_j]$ for the jth equation, where for the HT type estimator, B_j consists of all doubly exogenous variables of equation j (i.e. exogenous variables that are uncorrelated with the individual effects in equation j). Wyhowski (1994) extends the HT, AM and BMS approaches to the two-way error component model and gives the appropriate set of instruments. Revankar (1992) establishes conditions for exact equivalence of instrumental variables in a simultaneous two-way error component model.

Baltagi and Chang (2000) compare the performance of several single and system estimators of a two-equation simultaneous model with unbalanced panel data. The Monte Carlo design varies the degree of unbalancedness in the data and the variance components ratio due to the individual effects. Many of the results obtained for the simultaneous equation error component model with balanced data carry over to the unbalanced case. For example, both feasible EC2SLS estimators considered performed reasonably well and it is hard to choose between them. Simple ANOVA methods can still be used to obtain good estimates of the structural and reduced form parameters even in the unbalanced panel data case. Replacing negative estimates of the variance components by zero did not seriously affect the performance of the corresponding structural or reduced form estimates. Better estimates of the structural variance components do not necessarily imply better estimates of the structural coefficients. Finally, do not make the data balanced to simplify the computations. The loss in root mean squared error can be huge.

NOTES

1. The analysis in this chapter can easily be extended to the two-way error component model; see the problems at the end of this chapter and Baltagi (1981b).
2. As in the classical regression case, the variances of W2SLS have to be adjusted by the factor $(NT - k_1 - g_1 + 1)/[N(T-1) - k_1 - g_1 + 1]$, whenever 2SLS is performed on the

Within transformed equation (see Pliskin, 1991). Note also that the set of instruments is $\widetilde{X}$ and not X as emphasized in (7.6).

3. This is analogous to the result found in the single equation error component literature by Taylor (1980) and Baltagi (1981a).
4. Gardner (1998) shows how to modify the Hausman and Taylor (1981) instrumental variable estimator to allow for unbalanced panels. This utilizes the $\Omega^{-1/2}$ transformation derived for the unbalanced panel data model by Baltagi (1985), see (9.5), and the application of the IV interpretation of the HT estimator by Breusch, Mizon and Schmidt (1989) given above.
5. Im et al. (1999) point out that for panel data models, the exogeneity assumptions imply many more moment conditions than the standard random and fixed effects estimators use. Im et al. (1999) provide the assumptions under which the efficient GMM estimator based on the entire set of available moment conditions reduces to these simpler estimators. In other words, the efficiency of the simple estimators is established by showing the redundancy of the moment conditions that they do not use.

PROBLEMS

7.1 Verify that GLS on (7.7) yields (7.6) and GLS on (7.9) yields (7.8), the Within 2SLS and Between 2SLS estimators of δ_1, respectively.

7.2 Verify that GLS on (7.10) yields the EC2SLS estimator of δ_1 given in (7.11) (see Baltagi, 1981b).

7.3 Show that $A = [\widetilde{X}, \bar{X}]$, $B = [X^*, \widetilde{X}]$ and $C = [X^*, \bar{X}]$ yield the same projection, i.e. $P_A = P_B = P_C$ and hence the same EC2SLS estimator given by (7.11) (see Baltagi and Li, 1992d).

7.4 Verify that 3SLS on (7.21) with $(I_M \otimes \widetilde{X})$ as the set of instruments yields (7.22). Similarly, verify that 3SLS on (7.23) with $(I_M \otimes \bar{X})$ as the set of instruments yields (7.24). These are the Within 3SLS and Between 3SLS estimators of δ_1, respectively.

7.5 Verify that GLS on the stacked system (7.21) and (7.23) each premultiplied by $(I_M \otimes \widetilde{X}')$ and $(I_M \otimes \bar{X}')$, respectively yields the EC3SLS estimator of δ given in (7.25) (see Baltagi, 1981b).

7.6 (a) Prove that $A = (I_M \otimes \widetilde{X}, I_M \otimes \bar{X})$ yields the same projection as $B = (H \otimes \widetilde{X}, G \otimes \bar{X})$ or $C = [(H \otimes \widetilde{X} + G \otimes \bar{X}), H \otimes \widetilde{X}]$ or $D = [(H \otimes \widetilde{X} + G \otimes \bar{X}), G \otimes \bar{X}]$ where H and G are nonsingular $M \times M$ matrices (see Baltagi and Li, 1992d). Conclude that these sets of instruments yield the same EC3SLS estimator of δ given by (7.25).

(b) Let $H = \Sigma_\nu^{-1/2}$ and $G = \Sigma_1^{-1/2}$, and note that A is the set of instruments proposed by Baltagi (1981b) while B is the optimal set of instruments X^* defined below (7.30). Conclude that $H \otimes \widetilde{X}$ is redundant in C and $G \otimes \bar{X}$ is redundant in D with respect to the optimal set of instruments X^*.

7.7 (a) Consider a system of two structural equations with one-way error component disturbances. Show that if the disturbances between the two equations are uncorrelated, then EC3SLS is equivalent to EC2SLS (see Baltagi, 1981b).

(b) Show that if this system of two equations with one-way error component disturbances is just-identified, then EC3SLS does not necessarily reduce to EC2SLS (see Baltagi, 1981b).

7.8 (a) Using the partitioned inverse, show that GLS on (7.35) yields $\widehat{\beta}_{\mathrm{GLS}} = \widetilde{\beta}_{\mathrm{Within}}$ and $\widehat{\pi}_{\mathrm{GLS}} = \widehat{\beta}_{\mathrm{Between}} - \widetilde{\beta}_{\mathrm{Within}}$ as given in (7.37) and (7.38).

(b) Verify that $\mathrm{var}(\widehat{\pi}_{\mathrm{GLS}}) = \mathrm{var}(\widehat{\beta}_{\mathrm{Between}}) + \mathrm{var}(\widetilde{\beta}_{\mathrm{Within}})$ as given in (7.39).

7.9 For the two-way error component model given in (6.9) and the covariance matrix Ω_{jl} between the jth and lth equation disturbances given in (6.11):

(a) Derive the EC2SLS estimator for δ_1 in (7.1).

(b) Derive the EC3SLS estimator for δ in (7.20) (Hint: See Baltagi, 1981b).

(c) Repeat problem 7.7 parts (a) and (b) for the two-way error component EC2SLS and EC3SLS.

7.10 Using the Monte Carlo setup for a two-equation simultaneous model with error component disturbances, given in Baltagi (1984), compare EC2SLS and EC3SLS with the usual 2SLS and 3SLS estimators that ignore the error component structure.

7.11 Using the Cornwell and Rupert (1988) panel data set described in section 7.4 and given on the Wiley web site as Wage.xls, replicate Table 7.1 and the associated test statistics.

8 Dynamic Panel Data Models

8.1 INTRODUCTION

Many economic relationships are dynamic in nature and one of the advantages of panel data is that they allow the researcher to better understand the dynamics of adjustment. See, for example, Balestra and Nerlove (1966) on dynamic demand for natural gas, Houthakker, Verleger and Sheehan (1974) on dynamic demand for gasoline and residential electricity, Johnson and Oksanen (1977) on dynamic demand for alcoholic beverages, Baltagi and Levin (1986) on dynamic demand for an addictive commodity like cigarettes, Holtz-Eakin (1988) on a dynamic wage equation, Arellano and Bond (1991) on a dynamic model of employment, Blundell et al. (1992) on a dynamic model of company investment, Islam (1995) on a dynamic model for growth convergence, and Ziliak (1997) on a dynamic life-cycle labor supply model. These dynamic relationships are characterized by the presence of a lagged dependent variable among the regressors,[1] i.e.

$$y_{it} = \delta y_{i,t-1} + x_{it}'\beta + u_{it} \qquad i = 1, \ldots, N;\ t = 1, \ldots, T \tag{8.1}$$

where δ is a scalar, x_{it}' is $1 \times K$ and β is $K \times 1$. We will assume that the u_{it} follow a one-way error component model

$$u_{it} = \mu_i + \nu_{it} \tag{8.2}$$

where $\mu_i \sim \text{IID}(0, \sigma_\mu^2)$ and $\nu_{it} \sim \text{IID}(0, \sigma_\nu^2)$ independent of each other and among themselves. The dynamic panel data regressions described in (8.1) and (8.2) are characterized by two sources of persistence over time. Autocorrelation due to the presence of a lagged dependent variable among the regressors and individual effects characterizing the heterogeneity among the individuals. In this chapter, we review some of the recent econometric studies that propose new estimation and testing procedures for this model.

Let us start with some of the basic problems introduced by the inclusion of a lagged dependent variable. Since y_{it} is a function of μ_i, it immediately follows that $y_{i,t-1}$ is also a function of μ_i. Therefore, $y_{i,t-1}$, a right-hand regressor in (8.1), is correlated with the error term. This renders the OLS estimator biased and inconsistent even if the ν_{it} are not serially correlated. See Trognon (1978) and Sevestre and Trognon (1983, 1985) for the magnitude of this asymptotic bias in dynamic error component models. For the fixed effects (FE) estimator, the Within transformation wipes out the μ_i (see Chapter 2), but $(y_{i,t-1} - \bar{y}_{i.-1})$ where $\bar{y}_{i.-1} = \sum_{t=2}^{T} y_{i,t-1}/(T-1)$ will still be correlated with $(\nu_{it} - \bar{\nu}_{i.})$ even if the ν_{it} are not serially correlated. This is because $y_{i,t-1}$ is correlated with $\bar{\nu}_{i.}$ by construction. The latter average contains $\nu_{i,t-1}$ which is obviously correlated with $y_{i,t-1}$. In fact, the Within estimator will be biased of $O(1/T)$ and its consistency will depend upon T being large; see Nickell (1981).[2] More recently, Kiviet (1995) derived an approximation for the bias of the Within estimator in a dynamic panel data model with serially uncorrelated disturbances and strongly exogenous regressors. Kiviet (1995) proposed a corrected Within estimator that subtracts a consistent estimator of this bias from the original Within estimator.[3] Therefore, for the typical labor panel where N is large and T is fixed, the Within estimator is biased and inconsistent. It is worth emphasizing that only if $T \to \infty$ will the Within estimator of δ and β be consistent for the dynamic error component model. For macro panels, studying for example long-run growth, the data covers a large number of countries N over a moderate size T, see Islam (1995). In this case, T is not very small relative to N. Hence, some researchers may still favor the Within estimator arguing that its bias may not be large. Judson and Owen (1999) performed some Monte Carlo experiments for $N = 20$ or 100 and $T = 5, 10, 20$ and 30 and found that the bias in the Within estimator can be sizeable, even when $T = 30$. This bias increases with δ and decreases with T. But even for $T = 30$, this bias could be as much as 20% of the true value of the coefficient of interest.[4]

The random effects GLS estimator is also biased in a dynamic panel data model. In order to apply GLS, quasi-demeaning is performed (see Chapter 2), and $(y_{i,t-1} - \theta\bar{y}_{i.-1})$ will be correlated with $(u_{it} - \theta\bar{u}_{i.-1})$. An alternative transformation that wipes out the individual effects is the first difference (FD) transformation. In this case, correlation between the predetermined explanatory variables and the remainder error is easier to handle. In fact, Anderson and Hsiao (1981) suggested first differencing the model to get rid of the μ_i and then using $\Delta y_{i,t-2} = (y_{i,t-2} - y_{i,t-3})$ or simply $y_{i,t-2}$ as an instrument for $\Delta y_{i,t-1} = (y_{i,t-1} - y_{i,t-2})$. These instruments will not be correlated with $\Delta\nu_{it} = \nu_{it} - \nu_{i,t-1}$, as long as the ν_{it} themselves are not serially correlated. This instrumental variable (IV) estimation method leads to consistent but not necessarily efficient estimates of the parameters in the model because it does not make use of all the available moment conditions (see Ahn and Schmidt, 1995) and it does not take into account the differenced structure on the residual disturbances $(\Delta\nu_{it})$. Arellano (1989) finds that for simple dynamic error components models, the estimator that uses differences $\Delta y_{i,t-2}$ rather than levels $y_{i,t-2}$ for instruments has a singularity point and very large variances over a significant range of parameter values. In contrast, the estimator that uses instruments in levels, i.e. $y_{i,t-2}$, has no singularities and much smaller variances and is therefore recommended. Arellano and Bond (1991) proposed a generalized method of moments (GMM) procedure that is more efficient than the Anderson and Hsiao (1982) estimator. Meanwhile Ahn and Schmidt (1995) derived additional nonlinear moment restrictions not exploited by the Arellano and Bond (1991) GMM estimator. This literature is generalized and extended by Arellano and Bover (1995) and Blundell and Bond (1998) to mention a few. In addition, an alternative method of estimation of the dynamic panel data model is proposed by Keane and Runkle (1992). This is based on the forward filtering idea in time-series analysis. We focus on these studies and describe their respective contributions to the estimation and testing of dynamic panel data models. This chapter concludes with recent developments and some applications.

8.2 THE ARELLANO AND BOND STUDY

Arellano and Bond (1991) argue that additional instruments can be obtained in a dynamic panel data model if one utilizes the orthogonality conditions that exist between lagged values of y_{it} and the disturbances ν_{it}. Let us illustrate this with the simple autoregressive model with no regressors:

$$y_{it} = \delta y_{i,t-1} + u_{it} \quad i = 1, \ldots, N;\ t = 1, \ldots, T \tag{8.3}$$

where $u_{it} = \mu_i + \nu_{it}$ with $\mu_i \sim \text{IID}(0, \sigma_\mu^2)$ and $\nu_{it} \sim \text{IID}(0, \sigma_\nu^2)$, independent of each other and among themselves. In order to get a consistent estimate of δ as $N \to \infty$ with T fixed, we first difference (8.3) to eliminate the individual effects

$$y_{it} - y_{i,t-1} = \delta(y_{i,t-1} - y_{i,t-2}) + (\nu_{it} - \nu_{i,t-1}) \tag{8.4}$$

and note that $(\nu_{it} - \nu_{i,t-1})$ is MA(1) with unit root. For $t = 3$, the first period we observe this relationship, we have

$$y_{i3} - y_{i2} = \delta(y_{i2} - y_{i1}) + (\nu_{i3} - \nu_{i2})$$

In this case, y_{i1} is a valid instrument, since it is highly correlated with $(y_{i2} - y_{i1})$ and not correlated with $(\nu_{i3} - \nu_{i2})$ as long as the ν_{it} are not serially correlated. But note what happens for $t = 4$, the second period we observe (8.4):

$$y_{i4} - y_{i3} = \delta(y_{i3} - y_{i2}) + (\nu_{i4} - \nu_{i3})$$

In this case, y_{i2} as well as y_{i1} are valid instruments for $(y_{i3} - y_{i2})$, since both y_{i2} and y_{i1} are not correlated with $(\nu_{i4} - \nu_{i3})$. One can continue in this fashion, adding an extra valid instrument with each forward period, so that for period T, the set of valid instruments becomes $(y_{i1}, y_{i2}, \ldots, y_{i,T-2})$.

This instrumental variable procedure still does not account for the differenced error term in (8.4). In fact

$$E(\Delta\nu_i \Delta\nu_i') = \sigma_\nu^2(I_N \otimes G) \tag{8.5}$$

where $\Delta\nu_i' = (\nu_{i3} - \nu_{i2}, \ldots, \nu_{iT} - \nu_{i,T-1})$ and

$$G = \begin{pmatrix} 2 & -1 & 0 & \cdots & 0 & 0 & 0 \\ -1 & 2 & -1 & \cdots & 0 & 0 & 0 \\ \vdots & \vdots & \vdots & \ddots & \vdots & \vdots & \vdots \\ 0 & 0 & 0 & \cdots & -1 & 2 & -1 \\ 0 & 0 & 0 & \cdots & 0 & -1 & 2 \end{pmatrix}$$

is $(T-2) \times (T-2)$, since $\Delta\nu_i$ is MA(1) with unit root. Define

$$W_i = \begin{bmatrix} [y_{i1}] & & & 0 \\ & [y_{i1}, y_{i2}] & & \\ & & \ddots & \\ 0 & & & [y_{i1}, \ldots, y_{i,T-2}] \end{bmatrix} \tag{8.6}$$

Then, the matrix of instruments is $W = [W_1', \ldots, W_N']'$ and the moment equations described above are given by $E(W_i'\Delta\nu_i) = 0$. These moment conditions have also been pointed out by Holtz-Eakin (1988), Holtz-Eakin, Newey and Rosen (1988) and Ahn and Schmidt (1995). Premultiplying the differenced equation (8.4) in vector form by W', one gets

$$W'\Delta y = W'(\Delta y_{-1})\delta + W'\Delta\nu \tag{8.7}$$

Performing GLS on (8.7) one gets the Arellano and Bond (1991) preliminary one-step consistent estimator

$$\begin{aligned} \widehat{\delta}_1 = {} & [(\Delta y_{-1})'W(W'(I_N \otimes G)W)^{-1}W'(\Delta y_{-1})]^{-1} \\ & \times [(\Delta y_{-1})'W(W'(I_N \otimes G)W)^{-1}W'(\Delta y)] \end{aligned} \tag{8.8}$$

The optimal GMM estimator of δ_1 à la Hansen (1982) for $N \to \infty$ and T fixed using only the above moment restrictions yields the same expression as in (8.8) except that

$$W'(I_N \otimes G)W = \sum_{i=1}^{N} W_i'GW_i$$

is replaced by

$$V_N = \sum_{i=1}^{N} W_i'(\Delta\nu_i)(\Delta\nu_i)'W_i$$

This GMM estimator requires no knowledge concerning the initial conditions or the distributions of ν_i and μ_i. To operationalize this estimator, $\Delta\nu$ is replaced by differenced residuals obtained from the preliminary consistent estimator $\widehat{\delta}_1$. The resulting estimator is the two-step Arellano and Bond (1991) GMM estimator

$$\widehat{\delta}_2 = [(\Delta y_{-1})'W\widehat{V}_N^{-1}W'(\Delta y_{-1})]^{-1}[(\Delta y_{-1})'W\widehat{V}_N^{-1}W'(\Delta y)] \tag{8.9}$$

A consistent estimate of the asymptotic var($\widehat{\delta}_2$) is given by the first term in (8.9)

$$\widehat{\text{var}}(\widehat{\delta}_2) = [(\Delta y_{-1})'W\widehat{V}_N^{-1}W'(\Delta y_{-1})]^{-1} \tag{8.10}$$

Note that $\widehat{\delta}_1$ and $\widehat{\delta}_2$ are asymptotically equivalent if the ν_{it} are IID$(0, \sigma_\nu^2)$.

8.2.1 Testing for Individual Effects in Autoregressive Models

Holtz-Eakin (1988) derives a simple test for the presence of individual effects in dynamic panel data models. The basic idea of the test can be explained using the simple autoregressive model given in (8.3). Assume there are only three periods, i.e. $T = 3$. Then (8.3) can be estimated using the last two periods. Under the null hypothesis of no individual effects, the following orthogonality conditions hold:

$$E(y_{i2}u_{i3}) = 0 \quad E(y_{i1}u_{i3}) = 0 \quad E(y_{i1}u_{i2}) = 0$$

Three conditions to identify one parameter, the remaining two overidentifying restrictions can be used to test for individual effects. We can reformulate these orthogonality restrictions as follows:

$$E[y_{i1}(u_{i3} - u_{i2})] = 0 \tag{8.11a}$$

$$E(y_{i1}u_{i2}) = 0 \tag{8.11b}$$

$$E(y_{i2}u_{i3}) = 0 \tag{8.11c}$$

The first restriction can be used to identify δ even if there are individual effects in (8.3). The null hypothesis of no individual effects imposes only two additional restrictions (8.11b) and (8.11c) on the data. Intuitively, the test for individual effects is a test of whether the sample moments corresponding to these restrictions are sufficiently close to zero; contingent upon imposing (8.11a) to identify δ.

Stacking the following equations:

$$(y_3 - y_2) = (y_2 - y_1)\delta + (u_3 - u_2)$$

$$y_3 = y_2\delta + u_3$$

$$y_2 = y_1\delta + u_2$$

we can write

$$y^* = Y^*\delta + u^* \tag{8.12}$$

where $y^{*\prime} = (y_3' - y_2', y_3', y_2')$, $Y^{*\prime} = (y_2' - y_1', y_2', y_1')$ and $u^{*\prime} = (u_3' - u_2', u_3', u_2')$. Holtz-Eakin (1988) estimates this system of simultaneous equations with different instrumental variables for each equation. This is due to the dynamic nature of these equations. Variables which qualify for use as IVs in one period may not qualify in earlier periods. Let $W = \text{diag}[W_i]$ for $i = 1, 2, 3$ be the matrix of instruments such that $\text{plim}(W'u^*/N) = 0$ as $N \to \infty$. Perform GLS on (8.12) after premultiplying by W'. In this case, $\Omega = W'E(u^*u^{*\prime})W$ is estimated by $\widehat{\Omega} = (\sum_{i=1}^{N} \widehat{u}_{ir}^*\widehat{u}_{is}^* W_{ir}' W_{is})$ where $\widehat{u}_r^*$ denotes 2SLS residuals on each equation separately:

$$\widehat{\delta} = [Y^{*\prime}W\widehat{\Omega}^{-1}W'Y^*]^{-1}Y^{*\prime}W\widehat{\Omega}^{-1}W'y^*$$

Let SSQ be the weighted sum of the squared transformed residuals:

$$\text{SSQ} = (y^* - Y^*\widehat{\delta})'W\widehat{\Omega}^{-1}W'(y^* - Y^*\widehat{\delta})/N$$

This has a χ^2 distribution with degrees of freedom equal to the number of over-identifying restrictions as N grows. Compute $L = \text{SSQ}_\text{R} - \text{SSW}$ where SSQ_R is the sum of squared residuals when imposing the full set of orthogonality conditions implied by the null hypothesis, SSW is the sum of squared residuals that impose only those restrictions needed for the first-differenced version. The same estimate of Ω should be used in both computations, and Ω should be estimated under the null. Holtz-Eakin generalizes this to an AR(p) where p is unknown and applies this test to a dynamic wage equation based on a subsample of 898 males from the Panel Study of Income Dynamics (PSID) observed over the years 1968–81. He finds evidence of individual effects and thus support for controlling heterogeneity in estimating a dynamic wage equation.

Recently, Jimenez-Martin (1998) performed Monte Carlo experiments to study the performance of the Holtz-Eakin (1988) test for the presence of individual heterogeneity effects in dynamic small T unbalanced panel data models. The design of the experiment included both endogenous and time-invariant regressors in addition to the lagged dependent variable. The test behaved correctly for a moderate autoregressive coefficient. However, when this autoregressive coefficient approached unity, the presence of an additional regressor sharply affected the power and size of the test. The Monte Carlo results show that the power of this test is higher when the variance of the specific effects increases (they are easier to detect), when the sample size increases, when the data set is balanced (for a given number of cross-section units) and when the regressors are strictly exogenous.

8.2.2 Models with Exogenous Variables

If there are additional *strictly exogenous* regressors x_{it} as in (8.1) with $E(x_{it}\nu_{is}) = 0$ for all $t, s = 1, 2, \ldots, T$, but where all the x_{it} are correlated with μ_i, then all the x_{it} are valid instruments for the first-differenced equation of (8.1). Therefore, $[x'_{i1}, x'_{i2}, \ldots, x'_{iT}]$ should be added to each diagonal element of W_i in (8.6). In this case, (8.7) becomes

$$W'\Delta y = W'(\Delta y_{-1})\delta + W'(\Delta X)\beta + W'\Delta\nu$$

where ΔX is the stacked $N(T-2) \times K$ matrix of observations on Δx_{it}. One- and two-step estimators of (δ, β') can be obtained from

$$\begin{pmatrix} \widehat{\delta} \\ \widehat{\beta} \end{pmatrix} = ([\Delta y_{-1}, \Delta X]' W \widehat{V}_N^{-1} W'[\Delta y_{-1}, \Delta X])^{-1}([\Delta y_{-1}, \Delta X]' W \widehat{V}_N^{-1} W'\Delta y) \tag{8.13}$$

as in (8.8) and (8.9).

If x_{it} are *predetermined* rather than *strictly exogenous* with $E(x_{it}\nu_{is}) \neq 0$ for $s < t$ and zero otherwise, then only $[x'_{i1}, x'_{i2}, \ldots, x'_{i(s-1)}]$ are valid instruments for the differenced equation at period s. This can be illustrated as follows: for $t = 3$, the first-differenced equation of (8.1) becomes

$$y_{i3} - y_{i2} = \delta(y_{i2} - y_{i1}) + (x'_{i3} - x'_{i2})\beta + (\nu_{i3} - \nu_{i2})$$

For this equation, x'_{i1} and x'_{i2} are valid instruments, since both are not correlated with $(\nu_{i3} - \nu_{i2})$. For $t = 4$, the next period we observe this relationship

$$y_{i4} - y_{i3} = \delta(y_{i3} - y_{i2}) + (x'_{i4} - x'_{i3})\beta + (\nu_{i4} - \nu_{i3})$$

and we have additional instruments since now x'_{i1}, x'_{i2} and x'_{i3} are not correlated with $(\nu_{i4} - \nu_{i3})$. Continuing in this fashion, we get

$$W_i = \begin{bmatrix} [y_{i1}, x'_{i1}, x'_{i2}] & & & 0 \\ & [y_{i1}, y_{i2}, x'_{i1}, x'_{i2}, x'_{i3}] & & \\ & & \ddots & \\ 0 & & & [y_{i1}, \ldots, y_{i,T-2}, x'_{i1}, \ldots, x'_{i,T-1}] \end{bmatrix} \tag{8.14}$$

and one- and two-step estimators are again given by (8.13) with this choice of W_i.

In empirical studies, a combination of both *predetermined* and *strictly exogenous* variables may occur rather than the above two extreme cases, and the researcher can adjust the matrix of instruments W accordingly. Also, not all the x_{it} have to be correlated with μ_i. As in Hausman and Taylor (1981), we can separate $x_{it} = [x_{1it}, x_{2it}]$ where x_{1it} is uncorrelated with μ_i, while x_{2it} is correlated with μ_i. For the predetermined x_{it} case, Arellano and Bond (1991) count T additional restrictions from the level equations (8.1), i.e. $E(u_{i2}x_{1i1}) = 0$ and $E(u_{it}x_{1it}) = 0$ for $t = 2, \ldots, T$. All additional linear restrictions from the level equations are redundant given those already exploited from the first-differenced equations. Define $u_i = (u_{i2}, \ldots, u_{iT})'$ and $\nu_i^+ = (\Delta\nu'_i, u'_i)'$, where we stack the differenced disturbances from period $t = 3$ to $t = T$ on top of the undifferenced disturbances from period $t = 2$ to $t = T$. Now, let

$$\nu^+ = y^+ - y^+_{-1}\delta - X^+\beta \tag{8.15}$$

with $\nu^+ = (\nu_1^{+\prime}, \ldots, \nu_N^{+\prime})'$ and y^+, y^+_{-1} and X^+ defined similarly. The optimal matrix of instruments becomes

$$W_i^+ = \begin{bmatrix} W_i & & & & 0 \\ & [x'_{1i1}, x'_{1i2}] & & & \\ & & x'_{1i3} & & \\ & & & \ddots & \\ 0 & & & & x'_{1iT} \end{bmatrix} \tag{8.16}$$

where W_i is given by (8.14). The two-step estimator is of the same form as (8.13) with y^+, y^+_{-1}, X^+ and W^+ replacing Δy, Δy_{-1}, ΔX and W, respectively.

If x_{1it} is *strictly exogenous*, the observations for all periods become valid instruments in the level equations. However, given those previously exploited in first differences we only have T extra restrictions which Arellano and Bond (1991) express as $E(\sum_{s=1}^{T} x_{1it}u_{is}/T) = 0$ for $t = 1, \ldots, T$. Thus, the two-step estimator would just combine the $T - 1$ first-differenced equations and the average level equation.

Arellano and Bond (1991) propose a test for the hypothesis that there is no second-order serial correlation for the disturbances of the first-differenced equation. This test is important because the consistency of the GMM estimator relies upon the fact that $E[\Delta\nu_{it}\Delta\nu_{i,t-2}] = 0$. The test statistic is given in equation (8) of Arellano and Bond (1991, p. 282) and will not be reproduced here. This hypothesis is true if the ν_{it} are not serially correlated or follow a random walk. Under the latter situation, both OLS and GMM of the first-differenced version of (8.1) are consistent and Arellano and Bond (1991) suggest a Hausman-type test based on the difference between the two estimators.

Additionally, Arellano and Bond (1991) suggest Sargan's (1958) test of over-identifying restrictions given by[5]

$$m = \Delta\widehat{\nu}'W\left[\sum_{i=1}^{N} W_i'(\Delta\widehat{\nu}_i)(\Delta\widehat{\nu}_i)'W_i\right]^{-1} W'(\Delta\widehat{\nu}) \sim \chi^2_{p-K-1}$$

where p refers to the number of columns of W and $\Delta\widehat{\nu}$ denote the residuals from a two-step estimation given in (8.13).[6] Other tests suggested are Sargan's difference statistic to test nested hypotheses concerning serial correlation in a sequential way, or a Griliches and Hausman (1986) type test based on the difference between the two-step GMM estimators assuming the disturbances in levels are MA(0) and MA(1), respectively. These are described in more detail in Arellano and Bond (1991, p. 283).

A limited Monte Carlo study was performed based on 100 replications from a simple autoregressive model with one regressor and no constant, i.e. $y_{it} = \delta y_{i,t-1} + \beta x_{it} + \mu_i + \nu_{it}$ with $N = 100$ and $T = 7$. The results showed that the GMM estimators have negligible finite sample biases and substantially smaller variances than those associated with simpler IV estimators à la Anderson and Hsiao (1981). However, the estimated standard error of the two-step GMM estimator was found to be downward biased. The tests proposed above also performed reasonably well. These estimation and testing methods were applied to a model of employment using a panel of 140 quoted UK companies for the period 1979–84. For another application of a dynamic error component model dealing with the heterogeneity of workers and the dynamics of aggregate labor demand, see Bresson, Kramarz and Sevestre (1991) who used a panel of 586 French firms observed over the period 1975–83. Also, Blundell et al. (1992) used a panel of 532 UK manufacturing companies over the period 1975–86 to determine the importance of Tobin's q in the determination of investment decisions. Tobin's q was allowed to be endogenous and possibly correlated with the firm-specific effects. A GMM-type estimator was utilized using past variables as instruments, and Tobin's q effect was found to be small but significant. These results were sensitive to the choice of dynamic specification, exogeneity assumptions and measurement error in q. Similar findings using Tobin's q model are reported by Hayashi and Inoue (1991) based on a panel of 687 quoted Japanese manufacturing firms over the period 1977–86.

8.3 THE ARELLANO AND BOVER STUDY

Arellano and Bover (1995) developed a unifying GMM framework for looking at efficient IV estimators for dynamic panel data models. They did it in the context of the Hausman and Taylor (1981) model given in (7.40), which in static form is reproduced here for convenience:

$$y_{it} = x'_{it}\beta + Z'_i\gamma + u_{it} \tag{8.17}$$

where β is $K \times 1$ and γ is $g \times 1$. The Z_i are time-invariant variables whereas the x_{it} vary over individuals and time. In vector form, (8.17) can be written as

$$y_i = W_i\eta + u_i \tag{8.18}$$

with the disturbances following a one-way error component model

$$u_i = \mu_i\iota_T + \nu_i \tag{8.19}$$

where $y_i = (y_{i1}, \ldots, y_{iT})'$, $u_i = (u_{i1}, \ldots, u_{iT})'$, $\eta' = (\beta', \gamma')$, $W_i = [X_i, \iota_T Z'_i]$, $X_i = (x_{i1}, \ldots, x_{iT})'$ and ι_T is a vector of ones of dimension T. In general, $E(u_iu'_i/w_i)$ will be unrestricted depending on $w_i = (x'_i, Z'_i)'$ where $x_i = (x'_{i1}, \ldots, x'_{iT})'$. However, the literature emphasizes two cases with cross-sectional homoskedasticity.

Case 1: $E(u_iu'_i) = \Omega$ independent of w_i, but general to allow for arbitrary Ω as long as it is the same across individuals, i.e. Ω is the same for $i = 1, \ldots, N$.

Case 2: The traditional error component model where $\Omega = \sigma_\nu^2 I_T + \sigma_\mu^2\iota_T\iota'_T$.

Arellano and Bover transform the system of T equations in (8.18) using the nonsingular transformation

$$H = \begin{bmatrix} C \\ \iota'_T/T \end{bmatrix} \tag{8.20}$$

where C is any $(T-1) \times T$ matrix of rank $(T-1)$ such that $C\iota_T = 0$. For example, C could be the first $(T-1)$ rows of the Within group operator or the first difference operator.[7] Note that the transformed disturbances

$$u_i^+ = Hu_i = \begin{bmatrix} Cu_i \\ \bar{u}_i \end{bmatrix} \tag{8.21}$$

have the first $(T-1)$ transformed errors free of μ_i. Hence, all exogenous variables are valid instruments for these first $(T-1)$ equations. Let m_i denote the subset of variables of w_i assumed to be uncorrelated in levels with μ_i and such that the dimension of m_i is greater than or equal to the dimension of η. In the Hausman and Taylor study, $X = [X_1, X_2]$ and $Z = [Z_1, Z_2]$ where X_1 and Z_1 are exogenous of dimension $NT \times k_1$ and $N \times g_1$. X_2 and Z_2 are correlated with the individual effects and are of dimension $NT \times k_2$ and $N \times g_2$. In this case, m_i includes the set of X_1 and Z_1 variables and m_i would be based on

$(Z'_{1i}, x'_{1,i1}, \ldots, x'_{1,iT})'$. Therefore, a valid IV matrix for the complete transformed system is

$$M_i = \begin{bmatrix} w'_i & & & 0 \\ & \ddots & & \\ & & w'_i & \\ 0 & & & m'_i \end{bmatrix} \tag{8.22}$$

and the moment conditions are given by

$$E(M'_i H u_i) = 0 \tag{8.23}$$

Defining $W = (W'_1, \ldots, W'_N)'$, $y = (y'_1, \ldots, y'_N)'$, $M = (M'_1, \ldots, M'_N)'$, $\bar{H} = I_N \otimes H$ and $\bar{\Omega} = I_N \otimes \Omega$, and premultiplying (8.18) in vector form by $M'\bar{H}$ one gets

$$M'\bar{H}y = M'\bar{H}W\eta + M'\bar{H}u \tag{8.24}$$

Performing GLS on (8.24) one gets the Arellano and Bover (1995) estimator

$$\widehat{\eta} = [W'\bar{H}'M(M'\bar{H}\bar{\Omega}\bar{H}'M)^{-1}M'\bar{H}W]^{-1}W'\bar{H}'M(M'\bar{H}\bar{\Omega}\bar{H}'M)^{-1}M'\bar{H}y \tag{8.25}$$

In practice, the covariance matrix of the transformed system $\Omega^+ = H\Omega H'$ is replaced by a consistent estimator, usually

$$\widehat{\Omega}^+ = \sum_{i=1}^{N} \widehat{u}_i^+ \widehat{u}_i^{+\prime}/N \tag{8.26}$$

where $\widehat{u}_i^+$ are residuals based on consistent preliminary estimates. The resulting $\widehat{\eta}$ is the optimal GMM estimator of η with constant Ω based on the above moment restrictions. Further efficiency can be achieved using Chamberlain's (1982) or Hansen's (1982) GMM type estimator which replaces $(\sum_i M'_i \Omega^+ M_i)$ in (8.25) by $(\sum_i M'_i \widehat{u}_i^+ \widehat{u}_i^{+\prime} M_i)$. For the error component model, $\widetilde{\Omega}^+ = H\widetilde{\Omega}H'$ with $\widetilde{\Omega} = \widetilde{\sigma}_\nu^2 I_T + \widetilde{\sigma}_\mu^2 \iota_T \iota'_T$, where $\widetilde{\sigma}_\nu^2$ and $\widetilde{\sigma}_\mu^2$ denote consistent estimates σ_ν^2 and σ_μ^2.

The Hausman and Taylor (1981) (HT) estimator, given in section 7.3, is $\widehat{\eta}$ with $\widetilde{\Omega}^+$ and $m_i = (Z'_{1i}, \bar{x}'_{1i})'$ where $\bar{x}'_i = \iota'_T X_i/T = (\bar{x}'_{1i}, \bar{x}'_{2i})$. The Amemiya and MaCurdy (1986) (AM) estimator is $\widehat{\eta}$ with $\widetilde{\Omega}^+$ and $m_i = (Z'_{1i}, x'_{1,i1}, \ldots, x'_{1,iT})'$. The Breusch, Mizon and Schmidt (1989) (BMS) estimator exploits the additional moment restrictions that the correlation between $x_{2,it}$ and μ_i is constant over time. In this case, $\widetilde{x}_{2,it} = x_{2,it} - \bar{x}_{2i}$ are valid instruments for the last equation of the transformed system. Hence, BMS is $\widehat{\eta}$ with $\widetilde{\Omega}^+$ and $m_i = (Z'_{1i}, x'_{1,i1}, \ldots, x'_{1,iT}, \widetilde{x}'_{2,i1}, \ldots, \widetilde{x}'_{2,iT})'$.

Because the set of instruments M_i is block-diagonal, Arellano and Bover show that $\widehat{\eta}$ is invariant to the choice of C. Another advantage of their representation is that the form of $\Omega^{-1/2}$ need not be known. Hence, this approach generalizes the HT, AM, BMS type estimators to a more general form of Ω than that of error components, and it easily extends to the dynamic panel data case as can be seen next.[8]

Let us now introduce a lagged dependent variable into the right-hand side of (8.17):

$$y_{it} = \delta y_{i,t-1} + x'_{it}\beta + Z'_i\gamma + u_{it} \tag{8.27}$$

Assuming that $t = 0$ is observed, we redefine $\eta' = (\delta, \beta', \gamma')$ and $W_i = [y_{i(-1)}, X_i, \iota_T Z'_i]$ with $y_{i(-1)} = (y_{i0}, \ldots, y_{i,T-1})'$. Provided there are enough valid instruments to ensure identification, the GMM estimator defined in (8.25) remains consistent for this model. The matrix of instruments M_i is the same as before, adjusting for the fact that $t = 0$ is now the first period observed, so that $w_i = [x'_{i0}, ..., x'_{iT}, Z'_i]'$. In this case $y_{i(-1)}$ is excluded despite its presence in W_i. The same range of choices for m_i is available, for example, $m_i = (Z'_{1i}, x'_{1i}, \widetilde{x}'_{2,i1}, ..., \widetilde{x}'_{2,iT})$ is the BMS-type estimator. However, for this choice of m_i the rows of CX_i are linear combinations of m_i. This means that the same instrument set is valid for all equations and we can use $M_i = I_T \otimes m'_i$ without altering the estimator. The consequence is that the transformation is unnecessary and the estimator can be obtained by applying 3SLS to the original system of equations using m_i as the vector of instruments for all equations:

$$\begin{aligned}\widehat{\eta} = &\left[\sum_i (W_i \otimes m_i)' \left(\widehat{\Omega} \otimes \sum_i m_i m'_i\right)^{-1} \sum_i (W_i \otimes m_i)\right]^{-1} \sum_i (W_i \otimes m_i)' \\ &\times \left(\widehat{\Omega} \otimes \sum_i m_i m'_i\right)^{-1} \sum_i (y_i \otimes m_i)\end{aligned} \tag{8.28}$$

Arellano and Bover (1995) prove that this 3SLS estimator is asymptotically equivalent to the limited information maximum likelihood procedure with Ω unrestricted developed by Bhargava and Sargan (1983).

Regardless of the existence of individual effects, the previous model assumes *unrestricted* serial correlation in the ν_{it} implying that $y_{i,t-1}$ is an endogenous variable. If the ν_{it} are *not* serially correlated, additional orthogonality restrictions can easily be incorporated in estimating (8.27) provided that the transformation C is now upper triangular in addition to the previous requirements. In this case, the transformed error in the equation for period t is independent of μ_i and $(\nu_{i1}, \ldots, \nu_{i,t-1})$ so that $(y_{i0}, y_{i1}, \ldots, y_{i,t-1})$ are additional valid instruments for this equation (see section 8.2). Therefore, the matrix of instruments M_i becomes

$$M_i = \begin{bmatrix} (w'_i, y_{i0}) & & & & 0 \\ & (w'_i, y_{i0}, y_{i1}) & & & \\ & & \ddots & & \\ & & & (w'_i, y_{i0}, \ldots, y_{i,T-2}) & \\ 0 & & & & m'_i \end{bmatrix} \tag{8.29}$$

Once again, Arellano and Bover (1995) show that the GMM estimator (8.25) that uses (8.29) as the matrix of instruments is invariant to the choice of C provided C satisfies the above required conditions.

8.4 THE AHN AND SCHMIDT STUDY

Ahn and Schmidt (1995) show that under the standard assumptions used in a dynamic panel data model, there are additional moment conditions that are ignored by the IV estimators suggested by Anderson and Hsiao (1981), Holtz-Eakin, Newey and Rosen (1988) and Arellano and Bond (1991). In this section, we explain how these additional restrictions arise for the simple dynamic model and show how they can be utilized in a GMM framework.

Consider the simple dynamic model with no regressors given in (8.3) and assume that $y_{i0}, \ldots, y_{iT}$ are observable.[9] In vector form, this is given by

$$y_i = \delta y_{i-1} + u_i \tag{8.30}$$

where $y_i' = (y_{i1}, \ldots, y_{iT})$, $y_{i-1}' = (y_{i0}, \ldots, y_{i,T-1})$ and $u_i' = (u_{i1}, \ldots, u_{iT})$. The standard assumptions on the dynamic model (8.30) are that:

(A.1) For all i, ν_{it} is uncorrelated with y_{i0} for all t.
(A.2) For all i, ν_{it} is uncorrelated with μ_i for all t.
(A.3) For all i, the ν_{it} are mutually uncorrelated.

Ahn and Schmidt (1995) argue that these assumptions on the initial value y_{i0} are weaker than those often made in the literature (see Bhargava and Sargan, 1983; Hsiao, 1986; Blundell and Smith, 1991).

Under these assumptions, one obtains the following $T(T-1)/2$ moment conditions:

$$E(y_{is}\Delta u_{it}) = 0 \quad t = 2, \ldots, T;\ s = 0, \ldots, t-2 \tag{8.31}$$

These are the same moment restrictions given below (8.6) and exploited by Arellano and Bond (1991). However, Ahn and Schmidt (1995) find $T-2$ additional moment conditions not implied by (8.31). These are given by

$$E(u_{iT}\Delta u_{it}) = 0 \quad t = 2, \ldots, T-1 \tag{8.32}$$

Therefore, (8.31) and (8.32) imply a set of $T(T-1)/2+(T-2)$ moment conditions which represent all of the moment conditions implied by the assumptions that the ν_{it} are mutually uncorrelated among themselves and with μ_i and y_{i0}. More formally, the standard assumptions impose restrictions on the following covariance matrix:

$$\Sigma = \text{cov}\begin{bmatrix} \nu_{i1} \\ \nu_{i2} \\ \vdots \\ \nu_{iT} \\ y_{i0} \\ \mu_i \end{bmatrix} = \begin{bmatrix} \sigma_{11} & \sigma_{12} & \cdots & \sigma_{1T} & \sigma_{10} & \sigma_{1\mu} \\ \sigma_{21} & \sigma_{22} & \cdots & \sigma_{2T} & \sigma_{20} & \sigma_{2\mu} \\ \vdots & \vdots & & \vdots & \vdots & \vdots \\ \sigma_{T1} & \sigma_{T2} & \cdots & \sigma_{TT} & \sigma_{T0} & \sigma_{T\mu} \\ \sigma_{01} & \sigma_{02} & \cdots & \sigma_{0T} & \sigma_{00} & \sigma_{0\mu} \\ \sigma_{\mu 1} & \sigma_{\mu 2} & \cdots & \sigma_{\mu T} & \sigma_{\mu 0} & \sigma_{\mu\mu} \end{bmatrix} \tag{8.33}$$

But we do not observe μ_i and ν_{it}, only their sum $u_{it} = \mu_i + \nu_{it}$ which can be written in terms of the data and δ. Hence to get observable moment restrictions, we have to look at the following covariance matrix:

$$\Lambda = \text{cov}\begin{bmatrix} \mu_i + \nu_{i1} \\ \mu_i + \nu_{i2} \\ \vdots \\ \mu_i + \nu_{iT} \\ y_{i0} \end{bmatrix} = \begin{bmatrix} \lambda_{11} & \lambda_{12} & \dots & \lambda_{1T} & \lambda_{10} \\ \lambda_{21} & \lambda_{22} & \dots & \lambda_{2T} & \lambda_{20} \\ \vdots & \vdots & & \vdots & \vdots \\ \lambda_{T1} & \lambda_{T2} & \dots & \lambda_{TT} & \lambda_{T0} \\ \lambda_{01} & \lambda_{02} & \dots & \lambda_{0T} & \lambda_{00} \end{bmatrix}$$

$$= \begin{bmatrix} (\sigma_{\mu\mu} + \sigma_{11} + 2\sigma_{\mu 1}) & (\sigma_{\mu\mu} + \sigma_{12} + \sigma_{\mu 1} + \sigma_{\mu 2}) & \dots \\ (\sigma_{\mu\mu} + \sigma_{12} + \sigma_{\mu 1} + \sigma_{\mu 2}) & (\sigma_{\mu\mu} + \sigma_{22} + 2\sigma_{\mu 2}) & \dots \\ \vdots & \vdots & \dots \\ (\sigma_{\mu\mu} + \sigma_{1T} + \sigma_{\mu 1} + \sigma_{\mu T}) & (\sigma_{\mu\mu} + \sigma_{2T} + \sigma_{\mu 2} + \sigma_{\mu T}) & \dots \\ (\sigma_{0\mu} + \sigma_{01}) & (\sigma_{0\mu} + \mu_{02}) & \dots \end{bmatrix} \quad (8.34)$$

$$\begin{bmatrix} (\sigma_{\mu\mu} + \sigma_{1T} + \sigma_{\mu 1} + \sigma_{\mu T}) & (\sigma_{0\mu} + \sigma_{01}) \\ (\sigma_{\mu\mu} + \sigma_{2T} + \sigma_{\mu 2} + \sigma_{\mu T}) & (\sigma_{0\mu} + \sigma_{02}) \\ \vdots & \vdots \\ (\sigma_{\mu\mu} + \sigma_{TT} + 2\sigma_{\mu T}) & (\sigma_{0\mu} + \sigma_{0T}) \\ (\sigma_{0\mu} + \sigma_{0T}) & \sigma_{00} \end{bmatrix}$$

Under the standard assumptions (A.1)–(A.3), we have $\sigma_{ts} = 0$ for all $t \neq s$ and $\sigma_{\mu t} = \sigma_{0t} = 0$ for all t. Then Λ simplifies as follows:

$$\Lambda = \begin{bmatrix} (\sigma_{\mu\mu} + \sigma_{11}) & \sigma_{\mu\mu} & \dots & \sigma_{\mu\mu} & \sigma_{0\mu} \\ \sigma_{\mu\mu} & (\sigma_{\mu\mu} + \sigma_{22}) & \dots & \sigma_{\mu\mu} & \sigma_{0\mu} \\ \vdots & \vdots & & \vdots & \vdots \\ \sigma_{\mu\mu} & \sigma_{\mu\mu} & \dots & (\sigma_{\mu\mu} + \sigma_{TT}) & \sigma_{0\mu} \\ \sigma_{0\mu} & \sigma_{0\mu} & \dots & \sigma_{0\mu} & \sigma_{00} \end{bmatrix} \quad (8.35)$$

There are $T-1$ restrictions, that $\lambda_{0t} = E(y_{i0}u_{it})$ is the same for $t = 1, \dots, T$; and $[T(T-1)/2]-1$ restrictions, that $\lambda_{ts} = E(u_{is}u_{it})$ is the same for $t, s = 1, \dots, T$, $t \neq s$. Adding the number of restrictions, we get $T(T-1)/2 + (T-2)$.

In order to see how these additional moment restrictions are utilized, consider our simple dynamic model in differenced form along with the last period's observation in levels:

$$\Delta y_{it} = \delta \Delta y_{i,t-1} + \Delta u_{it} \quad t = 2, 3, \dots, T \quad (8.36)$$

$$y_{iT} = \delta y_{i,T-1} + u_{iT} \quad (8.37)$$

The usual IV estimator, utilizing the restrictions in (8.31), amounts to estimating the first-differenced equations (8.36) by three-stage least squares, imposing the restriction that δ is the same in every equation, where the instrument set is y_{i0} for $t = 2$; (y_{i0}, y_{i1}) for $t = 3$; $\dots (y_{i0}, \dots, y_{i,T-2})$ for $t = T$ (see section 8.2). Even though there are no legitimate observable instruments for the levels equation (8.37), Ahn and Schmidt argue that (8.37) is still useful in estimation because of the additional covariance restrictions implied by (8.32), i.e. that u_{iT}

are uncorrelated with Δu_{it} for $t = 2, ..., T-1$. Ahn and Schmidt show that any additional covariance restrictions besides (8.32) are redundant and implied by the basic moment conditions given by (8.31). Ahn and Schmidt also point out that the moment conditions (8.31) and (8.32) hold under weaker conditions than those implied by the standard assumptions (A.1)–(A.3). In fact, one only needs:

(B.1) $\text{cov}(\nu_{it}, y_{i0})$ is the same for all i and t instead of $\text{cov}(\nu_{it}, y_{i0}) = 0$, as in (A.1).
(B.2) $\text{cov}(\nu_{it}, \mu_i)$ is the same for all i and t instead of $\text{cov}(\nu_{it}, \mu_i) = 0$, as in (A.2).
(B.3) $\text{cov}(\nu_{it}, \nu_{is})$ is the same for all i and $t \neq s$, instead of $\text{cov}(\nu_{it}, \nu_{is}) = 0$, as in (A.3).

Problem 8.7 asks the reader to verify this claim in the same way as described above. Ahn and Schmidt (1995) show that GMM based on (8.31) and (8.32) is asymptotically equivalent to Chamberlain's (1982, 1984) optimal minimum distance estimator, and that it reaches the semiparametric efficiency bound. Ahn and Schmidt also explore additional moment restrictions obtained from assuming the ν_{it} homoskedastic for all i and t and the stationarity assumption of Arellano and Bover (1995) that $E(y_{it}\mu_i)$ is the same for all t. The reader is referred to their paper for more details. For specific parameter values, Ahn and Schmidt compute asymptotic covariance matrices and show that the extra moment conditions lead to substantial gains in asymptotic efficiency.

Ahn and Schmidt also consider the dynamic version of the Hausman and Taylor (1981) model studied in section 8.3 and show how one can make efficient use of exogenous variables as instruments. In particular, they show that the strong exogeneity assumption implies more orthogonality conditions which lie in the deviations from mean space. These are irrelevant in the static Hausman–Taylor model but are relevant for the dynamic version of that model. For more details on these conditions, see Schmidt, Ahn and Wyhowski (1992) and Ahn and Schmidt (1995).

8.5 THE BLUNDELL AND BOND STUDY

Blundell and Bond (1998) revisit the importance of exploiting the initial condition in generating efficient estimators of the dynamic panel data model when T is small. They consider a simple autoregressive panel data model with no exogenous regressors

$$y_{it} = \delta y_{i,t-1} + \mu_i + u_{it} \tag{8.38}$$

with $E(\mu_i) = 0$, $E(u_{it}) = 0$ and $E(\mu_i u_{it}) = 0$ for $i = 1, 2, \ldots, N$; $t = 1, 2, \ldots, T$. Blundell and Bond (1998) focus on the case where $T = 3$ and therefore there is only one orthogonality condition given by $E(y_{i1}\Delta u_{i3}) = 0$, so that δ is just-identified. In this case, the first stage IV regression is obtained by running Δy_{i2} on y_{i1}. Note that this regression can be obtained from (8.38) evaluated at $t = 2$ by subtracting y_{i1} from both sides of this equation, i.e.

$$\Delta y_{i2} = (\delta - 1)y_{i1} + \mu_i + u_{i2} \tag{8.39}$$

Since we expect $E(y_{i1}\mu_i) > 0$, $(\delta - 1)$ will be biased upwards with

$$\text{plim}(\widehat{\delta} - 1) = (\delta - 1)\frac{c}{c + (\sigma_\mu^2/\sigma_u^2)} \tag{8.40}$$

where $c = (1 - \delta)/(1 + \delta)$. The bias term effectively scales the estimated coefficient on the instrumental variable y_{i1} towards zero. They also find that the F-statistic of the first stage IV regression converges to χ_1^2 with noncentrality parameter

$$\tau = \frac{(\sigma_u^2 c)^2}{\sigma_\mu^2 + \sigma_u^2 c} \to 0 \quad \text{as } \delta \to 1 \tag{8.41}$$

As $\tau \to 0$, the instrumental variable estimator performs poorly. Hence, Blundell and Bond attribute the bias and the poor precision of the first-difference GMM estimator to the problem of weak instruments described in Nelson and Startz (1990) and Staiger and Stock (1997) and characterize this weak IV by its concentration parameter τ.

Next, Blundell and Bond (1998) show that an additional mild stationarity restriction on the initial conditions process allows the use of an extended system GMM estimator that uses lagged differences of y_{it} as instruments for equations in levels, in addition to lagged levels of y_{it} as instruments for equations in first differences, see Arellano and Bover (1995). The system GMM estimator is shown to have dramatic efficiency gains over the basic first-difference GMM as $\delta \to 1$ and $(\sigma_\mu^2/\sigma_u^2)$ increases. In fact, for $T = 4$ and $(\sigma_\mu^2/\sigma_u^2) = 1$, the asymptotic variance ratio of the first-difference GMM estimator to this system GMM estimator is 1.75 for $\delta = 0$ and increases to 3.26 for $\delta = 0.5$ and 55.4 for $\delta = 0.9$. This clearly demonstrates that the levels restrictions suggested by Arellano and Bover (1995) remain informative in cases where first-differenced instruments become weak. Things improve for first-difference GMM as T increases. However, with short T and persistent series, the Blundell and Bond findings support the use of the extra moment conditions. These results are reviewed and corroborated in Blundell and Bond (2000) and Blundell, Bond and Windmeijer (2000). Using Monte Carlo experiments, Blundell, Bond and Windmeijer (2000) find that simulations that include the weakly exogenous covariates exhibit large finite sample bias and very low precision for the standard first-differenced estimator. However, the system GMM estimator not only improves the precision but also reduces the finite sample bias. Blundell and Bond (2000) revisit the estimates of the capital and labor coefficients in a Cobb–Douglas production function considered by Griliches and Mairesse (1998). Using data on 509 R&D performing US manufacturing companies observed over 8 years (1982–89), the standard GMM estimator that uses moment conditions on the first-differenced model finds a low estimate of the capital coefficient and low precision for all coefficients estimated. However, the system GMM estimator gives reasonable and more precise estimates of the capital coefficient and constant returns to scale are not rejected. Blundell, Bond and Windmeijer conclude that "a careful examination of the original series and consideration of the system GMM estimator can usefully overcome many of the disappointing features of the standard GMM estimator for dynamic panel models".

Recently, Hahn (1999) examined the role of the initial condition imposed by the Blundell and Bond (1998) estimator. This was done by numerically comparing the semiparametric information bounds for the case that incorporates the stationarity of the initial condition and the case that does not. Hahn (1999) finds that the efficiency gain can be substantial.

8.6 THE KEANE AND RUNKLE STUDY

Let $y = X\beta + u$ be our panel data model with X containing a lagged dependent variable. We consider the case where $E(u_{it}/X_{it}) \neq 0$, and there exists a set of predetermined instruments W such that $E(u_{it}/W_{is}) = 0$ for $s \leqslant t$, but $E(u_{it}/W_{is}) \neq 0$ for $s > t$. In other words, W may contain lagged values of y_{it}. For this model, the 2SLS estimator will provide a consistent estimator for β. Now consider the random effects model or any other kind of serial correlation which is invariant across individuals, $\Omega_{TS} = E(uu') = I_N \otimes \Sigma_{TS}$. In this case, 2SLS will not be efficient. Keane and Runkle (1992), henceforth KR, suggest an alternative more efficient algorithm that takes into account this more general variance–covariance structure for the disturbances based on the forward filtering idea from the time-series literature. This method of estimation eliminates the general serial correlation pattern in the data, while preserving the use of predetermined instruments in obtaining consistent parameter estimates. First, one gets a consistent estimate of Σ_{TS}^{-1} and its corresponding Cholesky decomposition $\widehat{P}_{TS}$. Next, one premultiplies the model by $\widehat{Q}_{TS} = (I_N \otimes \widehat{P}_{TS})$ and estimates the model by 2SLS using the original instruments. In this case

$$\widehat{\beta}_{\text{KR}} = [X'\widehat{Q}'_{TS}P_W\widehat{Q}_{TS}X]^{-1}X'\widehat{Q}'_{TS}P_W\widehat{Q}_{TS}y \tag{8.42}$$

where $P_W = W(W'W)^{-1}W'$ is the projection matrix for the set of instruments W. Note that this allows for a general covariance matrix Σ_{TS} and its distinct elements $T(T+1)/2$ have to be much smaller than N. This is usually the case for large consumer or labor panels where N is very large and T is very small. Using the consistent 2SLS residuals, say $\widehat{u}_i$ for the ith individual, where $\widehat{u}_i$ is of dimension $(T \times 1)$, one can form

$$\widehat{\Sigma}_{TS} = \widehat{U}'\widehat{U}/N = \sum_{i=1}^{N} \widehat{u}_i\widehat{u}'_i/N$$

where $\widehat{U}' = [\widehat{u}_1, \widehat{u}_2, \ldots, \widehat{u}_N]$ is of dimension $(T \times N)$.[10]

First differencing is also used in dynamic panel data models to get rid of individual specific effects. The resulting first-differenced errors are serially correlated of an MA(1) type with unit root if the original ν_{it} are classical errors. In this case, there will be a gain in efficiency in performing the KR procedure on the first-differenced (FD) model. Get $\widehat{\Sigma}_{\text{FD}}$ from FD-2SLS residuals and obtain $\widehat{Q}_{\text{FD}} = I_N \otimes \widehat{P}_{\text{FD}}$, then estimate the transformed equation by 2SLS using the original instruments.

Underlying this estimation procedure are two important hypotheses that are testable. The first is H_A: the set of instruments W are *strictly exogenous*. In order to test H_A, KR propose a test based on the difference between fixed effects 2SLS (FE-2SLS) and first-difference 2SLS (FD-2SLS). FE-2SLS is consistent only if H_A is true. In fact if the W are predetermined rather than strictly exogenous, then $E(W_{it}\bar{\nu}_{i.}) \neq 0$ and our estimator would not be consistent. In contrast, FD-2SLS is consistent whether H_A is true or not, i.e. $E(W_{it}\Delta\nu_{it}) = 0$ rain or shine. An example of this is when $y_{i,t-2}$ is a member of W_{it}, then $y_{i,t-2}$ is predetermined and not correlated with $\Delta\nu_{it}$ as long as the ν_{it} are not serially correlated. However, $y_{i,t-2}$ is correlated with $\bar{\nu}_{i.}$ because this last average contains $\nu_{i,t-2}$. If H_A is not rejected, one should check whether the individual effects are correlated with the set of instruments. In this case, the usual Hausman and Taylor (1981) test applies. This is based on the difference between the FE and GLS estimator of the regression model. The FE estimator would be consistent rain or shine since it wipes out the individual effects. However, the GLS estimator would be consistent and efficient only if $E(\mu_i/W_{it}) = 0$, and inconsistent otherwise. If H_A is rejected, the instruments are predetermined and the Hausman–Taylor test is inappropriate. The test for H_B: $E(\mu_i/W_{it}) = 0$ will now be based on the difference between FD-2SLS and 2SLS. Under H_B, both estimators are consistent, but if H_B is not true, FD-2SLS remains consistent while 2SLS does not.

These tests are Hausman (1978) type tests except that

$$\begin{aligned}
\text{var}(\widehat{\beta}_{\text{FE-2SLS}} - \widehat{\beta}_{\text{FD-2SLS}}) = & (\widetilde{X}' P_W \widetilde{X})^{-1} (\widetilde{X}' P_W \widetilde{\Omega}_{\text{FE-2SLS}} P_W \widetilde{X}) (\widetilde{X}' P_W \widetilde{X})^{-1} \\
& - (\widetilde{X}' P_W \widetilde{X})^{-1} (\widetilde{X}' P_W \widetilde{\Omega}_{\text{FEFD}} P_W X_{\text{FD}}) (X'_{\text{FD}} P_W X_{\text{FD}})^{-1} \\
& - (X'_{\text{FD}} P_W X_{\text{FD}})^{-1} (X'_{\text{FD}} P_W \widetilde{\Omega}_{\text{FEFD}} P_W \widetilde{X}) (\widetilde{X}' P_W \widetilde{X})^{-1} \\
& + (X'_{\text{FD}} P_W X_{\text{FD}})^{-1} (X'_{\text{FD}} P_W \widehat{\Omega}_{\text{FD-2SLS}} P_W X_{\text{FD}}) \\
& \times (X'_{\text{FD}} P_W X_{\text{FD}})^{-1}
\end{aligned} \tag{8.43}$$

where $\widetilde{\Sigma}_{\text{FE-2SLS}} = \widetilde{U}'_{\text{FE}} \widetilde{U}_{\text{FE}}/N$, $\widehat{\Sigma}_{\text{FD-2SLS}} = \widehat{U}'_{\text{FD}} \widehat{U}_{\text{FD}}/N$ and $\widehat{\Sigma}_{\text{FEFD}} = \widetilde{U}'_{\text{FE}} \widehat{U}_{\text{FD}}/N$. As described above, $\widetilde{U}'_{\text{FE}} = [\widetilde{u}_1, \ldots, \widetilde{u}_N]_{\text{FE}}$ denotes the FE-2SLS residuals and $\widetilde{U}'_{\text{FD}} = [\widetilde{u}_1, \ldots, \widetilde{u}_N]_{\text{FD}}$ denotes the FD-2SLS residuals. Recall that for the Keane–Runkle approach, $\Omega = I_N \otimes \Sigma$.

Similarly, the $\text{var}(\widehat{\beta}_{\text{2SLS}} - \widehat{\beta}_{\text{FD}-\text{2SLS}})$ is computed as above with $\widetilde{X}$ being replaced by X, $\widetilde{\Omega}_{\text{FE-2SLS}}$ by $\widehat{\Omega}_{\text{2SLS}}$ and $\widetilde{\Omega}_{\text{FEFD}}$ by $\widehat{\Omega}_{\text{2SLSFD}}$. Also, $\widehat{\Sigma}_{\text{2SLS}} = \widehat{U}'_{\text{2SLS}} \widehat{U}_{\text{2SLS}}/N$ and $\widehat{\Sigma}_{\text{2SLSFD}} = \widehat{U}'_{\text{2SLS}} \widehat{U}_{\text{FD}}/N$.

The variances are complicated because KR do not use the efficient estimator under the null as required by a Hausman-type test (see Schmidt, Ahn and Wyhowski, 1992). Keane and Runkle (1992) apply their testing and estimation procedures to a simple version of the rational expectations life-cycle consumption model. Based on a sample of 627 households surveyed between 1972 and 1982 by the Michigan Panel Study on Income Dynamics (PSID), KR reject the strong exogeneity of the instruments. This means that the Within estimator is inconsistent and the standard Hausman–Taylor (1981) test based on the difference between the standard Within and GLS estimators is inappropriate. In fact, for this consumption example the Hausman–Taylor test leads to the wrong conclusion that the Within estimator is appropriate. KR also fail to reject the null hypothesis of no correlation between the individual effects and the instruments. This means that there is no need to first difference to get rid of the individual effects. Based on the KR-2SLS estimates, the authors cannot reject the simple life-cycle model. However, they show that if one uses the inconsistent Within estimates for inference one would get misleading evidence against the life-cycle model.

8.7 RECENT DEVELOPMENTS

The literature on dynamic panel data models continues to exhibit phenomenal growth. This is understandable given that most of our economic models are implicitly or explicitly dynamic in nature. This section summarizes some of the findings of these recent studies. In section 8.4, we pointed out that Ahn and Schmidt (1995) gave a complete count of the set of orthogonality conditions corresponding to a variety of assumptions imposed on the disturbances and the initial conditions of the dynamic panel data model. Many of these moment conditions were nonlinear in the parameters. More recently, Ahn and Schmidt (1997) proposed a linearized GMM estimator that is asymptotically as efficient as the nonlinear GMM estimator. They also provided simple moment tests of the validity of these nonlinear restrictions. In addition, they investigated the circumstances under which the optimal GMM estimator is equivalent to a linear instrumental variable estimator. They find that these circumstances are quite restrictive and go beyond uncorrelatedness and homoskedasticity of the errors. Ahn and Schmidt (1995) provide some evidence on the efficiency gains from the nonlinear moment conditions which in turn provide support for their use in practice. By employing all these conditions, the resulting GMM estimator is asymptotically efficient and has the same asymptotic variance as the MLE under normality. In fact, Hahn (1997) showed that GMM based on an increasing set of instruments as $N \to \infty$ would achieve the semiparametric efficiency bound.

Hahn (1997) considered the asymptotic efficient estimation of the dynamic panel data model with sequential moment restrictions in an environment with IID observations. Hahn shows that the GMM estimator with an increasing set of instruments as the sample size grows attains the semiparametric efficiency bound of the model. He also explains how Fourier series or polynomials may be used as the set of instruments for efficient estimation. In a limited Monte Carlo comparison, Hahn finds that this estimator has similar finite sample properties as the Keane and Runkle (1992) and/or Schmidt, Ahn and Wyhowski (1992) estimators when the latter estimators are efficient. In cases where the latter estimators are not efficient, the Hahn efficient estimator outperforms both estimators in finite samples.

Recently, Wansbeek and Bekker (1996) considered a simple dynamic panel data model with no exogenous regressors and disturbances u_{it} and random effects μ_i that are independent and normally distributed. They derived an expression for the optimal instrumental variable estimator, i.e. one with minimal asymptotic variance. A striking result is the difference in efficiency between the IV and ML estimators. They found that for regions of the autoregressive parameter δ which are likely in practice, ML is superior. The gap between IV (or GMM) and ML can be narrowed down by adding moment restrictions of the type considered by Ahn and Schmidt (1995). Hence, Wansbeek and Bekker (1996) find support for adding these nonlinear moment restrictions and warn against the loss in efficiency as compared with MLE by ignoring them.

Ziliak (1997) asks the question whether the bias/efficiency trade-off for the GMM estimator considered by Tauchen (1986) for the time-series case is still binding in panel data where the sample size is normally larger than 500. For time-series data, Tauchen (1986) shows that even for $T = 50$ or 75 there is a bias/efficiency trade-off as the number of moment conditions increases. Therefore, Tauchen recommends the use of suboptimal instruments in small samples. This result was also corroborated by Andersen and Sørensen (1996) who argue that GMM using too few moment conditions is just as bad as GMM using too many moment conditions. This problem becomes more pronounced with panel data since the number of moment conditions increases dramatically as the number of strictly exogenous variables and the number of time-series observations increase. Even though it is desirable from an asymptotic efficiency point of view to include as many moment conditions as possible, it may be infeasible or impractical to do so in many cases. For example, for $T = 10$ and five strictly exogenous regressors, this generates 500 moment conditions for GMM. Ziliak (1997) performs an extensive set of Monte Carlo experiments for a dynamic panel data model and finds that the same trade-off between bias and efficiency exists for GMM as the number of moment conditions increases, and that one is better off with suboptimal instruments. In fact, Ziliak finds that GMM performs well with suboptimal instruments, but is not recommended for panel data applications when all the moments are exploited for estimation. Ziliak estimates a life-cycle labor supply model under uncertainty based on 532 men observed over 10 years of data (1978–87) from the panel study of income dynamics. The sample was restricted to continuously married, continuously working prime age men aged 22–51 in 1978. These men were paid an hourly wage or salaried and could not be piece-rate workers or self-employed. Ziliak finds that the downward bias of

GMM is quite severe as the number of moment conditions expands, outweighing the gains in efficiency. Ziliak reports estimates of the intertemporal substitution elasticity which is the focal point of interest in the labor supply literature. This measures the intertemporal changes in hours of work due to an anticipated change in the real wage. For GMM, this estimate changes from 0.519 to 0.093 when the number of moment conditions used in GMM is increased from 9 to 212. The standard error of this estimate drops from 0.36 to 0.07. Ziliak attributes this bias to the correlation between the sample moments used in estimation and the estimated weight matrix. Interestingly, Ziliak finds that the forward filter 2SLS estimator proposed by Keane and Runkle (1992) performs best in terms of the bias/efficiency trade-off and is recommended. Forward filtering eliminates all forms of serial correlation while still maintaining orthogonality with the initial instrument set. Schmidt, Ahn and Wyhowski (1992) argued that filtering is irrelevant if one exploits all sample moments during estimation. However, in practice, the number of moment conditions increases with the number of time periods T and the number of regressors K and can become computationally intractable. In fact for $T = 15$ and $K = 10$, the number of moment conditions for Schmidt, Ahn and Wyhowski (1992) is $T(T-1)K/2$ which is 1040 restrictions, highlighting the computational burden of this approach. In addition, Ziliak argues that the overidentifying restrictions are less likely to be satisfied, possibly due to the weak correlation between the instruments and the endogenous regressors.[11] In this case, the forward filter 2SLS estimator is desirable, yielding less bias than GMM and sizeable gains in efficiency. In fact, for the life-cycle labor example, the forward filter 2SLS estimate of the intertemporal substitution elasticity was 0.135 for 9 moment conditions compared to 0.296 for 212 moment conditions. The standard error of these estimates dropped from 0.32 to 0.09.

The practical problem of not being able to use more moment conditions as well as the statistical problem of the trade-off between small sample bias and efficiency prompted Ahn and Schmidt (1999a) to pose the following questions. "Under what conditions can we use a smaller set of moment conditions without incurring any loss of asymptotic efficiency?". In other words "Under what conditions are some moment conditions redundant in the sense that utilizing them does not improve efficiency?". These questions were first dealt with by Im et al. (1999) who considered panel data models with strictly exogenous explanatory variables. They argued that, for example, with 10 strictly exogenous time-varying variables and six time periods, the moment conditions available for the random effects (RE) model is 360 and this reduces to 300 moment conditions for the FE model. GMM utilizing all these moment conditions leads to an efficient estimator. However, these moment conditions exceed what the simple RE and FE estimators use. Im et al. (1999) provide the assumptions under which this efficient GMM estimator reduces to the simpler FE or RE estimator. In other words, Im et al. (1999) show the redundancy of the moment conditions that these simple estimators do not use. Ahn and Schmidt (1999a) provide a more systematic method by which redundant instruments can be found and generalize this result to models with time-varying individual effects. However, both papers deal only with strictly exogenous regressors. In a related paper, Ahn and Schmidt (1999b) consider the cases of strictly and weakly exogenous regressors. They show that the GMM estimator takes the form of an instrumental variables estimator if the assumption of no conditional heteroskedasticity (NCH) holds. Under this assumption, the efficiency of standard estimators can often be established showing that the moment conditions not utilized by these estimators are redundant. However, Ahn and Schmidt (1999b) conclude that the NCH assumption necessarily fails if the full set of moment conditions for the dynamic panel data model is used. In this case, there is clearly a need to find modified versions of GMM, with reduced sets of moment conditions that lead to estimates with reasonable finite sample properties.

Crépon, Kramarz and Trognon (1997) argue that for the dynamic panel data model, when one considers a set of orthogonal conditions, the parameters can be divided into parameters of interest (like δ) and nuisance parameters (like the second-order terms in the autoregressive error component model). They show that the elimination of such nuisance parameters using their empirical counterparts does not entail an efficiency loss when only the parameters of interest are estimated. In fact, Sevestre and Trognon in Chapter 6 of Mátyás and Sevestre (1996) argue that if one is only interested in δ, then one can reduce the number of orthogonality restrictions without loss in efficiency as far as δ is concerned. However, the estimates of the other nuisance parameters are not generally as efficient as those obtained from the full set of orthogonality conditions.

The Alonso-Borrego and Arellano (1999) paper is also motivated by the finite sample bias in panel data instrumental variable estimators when the instruments are weak. The dynamic panel model generates many overidentifying restrictions even for moderate values of T. Also, the number of instruments increases with T, but the quality of these instruments is often poor because they tend to be only weakly correlated with first-differenced endogenous variables that appear in the equation. Limited information maximum likelihood (LIML) is strongly preferred to 2SLS if the number of instruments gets large as the sample size tends to infinity. Hillier (1990) showed that the alternative normalization rules adopted by LIML and 2SLS are at the root of their different sampling behavior. Hillier (1990) also showed that a symmetrically normalized 2SLS estimator has properties similar to those of LIML. Following Hillier (1990), Alonso-Borrego and Arellano (1999) derived a symmetrically normalized GMM (SNM) and compared it with ordinary GMM and LIML analogues by means of simulations. Monte Carlo and empirical results show that GMM can exhibit large biases when the instruments are poor, while LIML and SNM remain essentially unbiased. However, LIML and SNM always had a larger interquartile range than GMM. For $T = 4$, $N = 100$, $\sigma_{\mu}^2 = 0.2$ and $\sigma_{\nu}^2 = 1$, the bias for $\delta = 0.5$ was 6.9% for GMM, 1.7% for SNM and 1.7% for LIML. This bias increased to 17.8% for GMM, 3.7% for SNM and 4.1% for LIML for $\delta = 0.8$.

Alvarez and Arellano (1997) studied the asymptotic properties of FE, one-step GMM and nonrobust LIML for a first-order autoregressive model when both N and T tend to infinity with $N/T \rightarrow c$ for $0 \leqslant c < 2$. For this autoregressive model, the FE estimator is inconsistent for T fixed and N large, but becomes consistent as T gets large. GMM is consistent for fixed T, but the number of orthogonality conditions increases with T. The common conclusion among the studies cited above is that GMM estimators that use the full set of moments available can be severely biased, especially when the instruments are weak and the number of moment conditions is large relative to N. Alvarez and Arellano show that for $T < N$, GMM bias is always smaller than FE bias and LIML bias is smaller than the other two. In a fixed T framework, GMM and LIML are asymptotically equivalent, but as T increases, LIML has a smaller asymptotic bias than GMM. These results provide some theoretical support for LIML over GMM.[12]

Wansbeek and Knaap (1999) consider a simple dynamic panel data model with heterogeneous coefficients on the lagged dependent variable and the time trend, i.e.

$$y_{it} = \delta_i y_{i,t-1} + \xi_i t + \mu_i + u_{it} \tag{8.44}$$

This model results from Islam's (1995) version of Solow's model on growth convergence among countries. Wansbeek and Knaap (1999) show that double differencing gets rid of the individual country effects (μ_i) on the first round of differencing and the heterogeneous coefficient on the time trend (ξ_i) on the second round of differencing. Modified OLS, IV and GMM methods are adapted to this model and LIML is suggested as a viable alternative to GMM to guard against the small sample bias of GMM. Simulations show that LIML is the superior estimator for $T \geqslant 10$ and $N \geqslant 50$. Macroeconomic data are subject to measurement error and Wansbeek and Knaap (1999) show how these estimators can be modified to account for measurement error that is white noise. For example, GMM is modified so that it discards the orthogonality conditions that rely on the absence of measurement error.

Andrews and Lu (2001) develop consistent model and moment selection criteria and downward testing procedures for GMM estimation that are able to select the correct model and moments with probability that goes to one as the sample size goes to infinity. This is applied to dynamic panel data models with unobserved individual effects. The selection criteria can be used to select the lag length for the lagged dependent variables, to determine the exogeneity of the regressors, and/or to determine the existence of correlation between some regressors and the individual effects. Monte Carlo experiments are performed to study the small sample performance of the selection criteria and the testing procedures and their impact on parameter estimation.

8.8 EMPIRICAL ILLUSTRATION

Baltagi and Levin (1992) estimate a dynamic demand model for cigarettes based on panel data from 46 American states over the period 1963–88. The estimated equation is

$$\ln C_{it} = \alpha + \beta_1 \ln C_{i,t-1} + \beta_2 \ln P_{it} + \beta_3 \ln Y_{it} + \beta_4 \ln Pn_{it} + u_{it} \tag{8.45}$$

where the subscript i denotes the ith state ($i = 1, \ldots, 46$), and the subscript t denotes the tth year ($t = 1, \ldots, 26$). C_{it} is real per capita sales of cigarettes by persons of smoking age (14 years and older). This is measured in packs of cigarettes per head. P_{it} is the average retail price of a pack of cigarettes measured in real terms. Y_{it} is real per capita disposable income. Pn_{it} denotes the minimum real price of cigarettes in any neighboring state. This last variable is a proxy for the casual smuggling effect across state borders. It acts as a substitute price attracting consumers from high-tax states like Massachusetts with 26¢ per pack to cross over to New Hampshire where the tax is only 12¢ per pack. The disturbance term is specified as a two-way error component model

$$u_{it} = \mu_i + \lambda_t + \nu_{it} \quad i = 1, \ldots, 46;\ t = 1, \ldots, 26 \tag{8.46}$$

where μ_i denotes a state-specific effect and λ_t denotes a year-specific effect. The time-period effects (the λ_t) are assumed fixed parameters to be estimated as coefficients of time dummies for each year in the sample. This can be justified given the numerous policy interventions as well as health warnings and Surgeon General's reports. For example:

(1) The imposition of warning labels by the Federal Trade Commission effective January 1965.
(2) The application of the Fairness Doctrine Act to cigarette advertising in June 1967, which subsidized antismoking messages from 1968 to 1970.
(3) The Congressional ban on broadcast advertising of cigarettes effective January 1971.

The μ_i are state-specific effects which can represent any state-specific characteristic including the following:

(1) States with Indian reservations like Montana, New Mexico and Arizona are among the biggest losers in tax revenues from non-Indians purchasing tax-exempt cigarettes from the reservations.
(2) Florida, Texas, Washington and Georgia are among the biggest losers of revenues due to the purchasing of cigarettes from tax-exempt military bases in these states.
(3) Utah, which has a high percentage of Mormon population (a religion which forbids smoking), has a per capita sales of cigarettes in 1988 of 55 packs, a little less than half the national average of 113 packs.
(4) Nevada, which is a highly touristic state, has a per capita sales of cigarettes of 142 packs in 1988, 29 more packs than the national average.

These state-specific effects may be assumed fixed, in which case one includes state dummy variables in (8.45). The resulting estimator is the Within estimator reported in Table 8.1. Alternatively, one can assume the μ_i are random IID(0, σ_μ^2). In fact, if these state effects are hopelessly correlated with all the regressors, i.e. $E(\mu_i/X_{it}) \neq 0$, then the Within estimator is the appropriate one. On the other hand, if $E(\mu_i/X_{it}) = 0$ and the state effects are uncorrelated with the regressors, then one can apply the Anderson and Hsiao (1981) method to estimate the dynamic demand for cigarettes given in (8.45). Specifically, one first-differences (8.45) and uses $\ln C_{i,t-2}$ as an instrumental variable for $(\ln C_{i,t-1} - \ln C_{i,t-2})$ (see Anderson and Hsiao, 1981; Arellano, 1989). The result is reported as the Anderson–Hsiao estimator in Table 8.1. All coefficients are statistically significant with the lagged coefficient of consumption estimated at 0.60 for the Anderson–Hsiao estimator, indicating a significant habit-persistence effect for this addictive commodity. The price elasticity is inelastic and ranges from −0.48 for the Anderson–Hsiao estimator to −0.14 for the OLS estimator. The OLS and Within estimators do not take into account the endogeneity of the lagged dependent variable, and therefore 2SLS and Within-2SLS are performed. These give lower estimates of lagged consumption and higher own price elasticities. The test for H_A: that the set of instruments is strictly exogenous is based on Within-2SLS and FD-2SLS and yields a χ_4^2 statistic of 46.8. This rejects H_A and argues against the use of the Within estimator. The test for H_B: that the individual effects are uncorrelated with the set of instruments is based on 2SLS and FD-2SLS and yields a χ_4^2 statistic of 172.0. This rejects H_B, giving support to first-differencing the data. The last row of Table 8.1 gives the FD-2SLS-KR estimator. Note the lower coefficient estimate of lagged consumption (0.37). This implies a much lower long-run multiplier of $1.6 = 1/(1 - 0.37)$. The own price elasticity is −0.43 and significant. The income effect is very small but significant and the bootlegging effect is small and significant.

Table 8.1 Pooled Estimation Results.* Cigarette Demand Equation 1963–88

	$\ln C_{i,t-1}$	$\ln P_{it}$	$\ln Y_{it}$	$\ln Pn_{it}$	Constant	$\bar{R}^2$
OLS	0.953	−0.142	0.0005	0.048	0.121	0.97
	(145)	(8.6)	(0.06)	(3.5)	(3.2)	
Within	0.792	−0.350	0.144	0.064	0.189	0.97
	(59)	(14)	(5.7)	(2.3)	(1.9)	
Anderson–Hsiao	0.602	−0.476	0.134	0.085	—	0.77
	(2.7)	(13)	(2.5)	(1.8)		
2SLS	0.614	−0.553	0.176	0.105	0.881	0.79
	(11.4)	(7.8)	(5.6)	(3.9)	(6.3)	
Within-2SLS	0.607	−0.508	0.212	0.036	—	0.97
	(18.9)	(13.9)	(7.2)	(1.2)		
FD-2SLS-KR	0.371	−0.430	0.0001	0.051	—	0.70
	(9.8)	(20.9)	(4.1)	(2.0)		

*Numbers in parentheses are t-statistics. All regressions include time dummies
Source: First three rows in this table are from Baltagi and Levin (1992)

8.9 FURTHER READING

Hsiao (1986) has an excellent treatment of the dynamic panel data model under the various assumptions on the initial values; see also Anderson and Hsiao (1981, 1982), Lee (1981), Bhargava and Sargan (1983) and Ridder and Wansbeek (1990). In particular, Hsiao (1986) shows that for the random effects dynamic model the consistency property of MLE and GLS depends upon various assumptions on the initial observations and on the way in which N and T tend to infinity. Read also the Arellano and Honoré (2000) chapter in the *Handbook of Econometrics*. The latter chapter pays careful attention to the implications of strict exogeneity for identification of the regression parameters controlling for unobserved heterogeneity and contrasts those with the case of predetermined regressors.

For applications of the dynamic error component model, see Bhargava (1991a) who estimates short- and long-run income elasticities of foods and nutrients in south India. Using data on 240 households in six south Indian villages, surveyed twice a year for two years (1976–77), Bhargava estimates expenditure–income elasticities of six categories of foods. The results support the view that increases in household incomes will in turn improve the intake of nutrients. Becker, Grossman and Murphy (1994) estimate a rational addiction model for cigarettes using a panel of 50 states (and the District of Columbia) over the period 1955–85. They apply fixed effects 2SLS to estimate a second-order difference equation in consumption of cigarettes, finding support for forward looking consumers and rejecting myopic behavior. Their long-run price elasticity estimate is -0.78 compared to -0.44 for the short-run. Baltagi and Griffin (2001) apply the FD-2SLS, FE-2SLS and GMM dynamic panel estimation methods studied in this chapter to the Becker, Grossman and Murphy rational addiction model for cigarettes. Although the results are in general supportive of rational addiction, the estimates of the implied discount rate are not precise. Baltagi and Griffin (1995) estimate a dynamic demand for liquor across 43 states over the period 1960–82. Fixed effects 2SLS as well as FD-2SLS-KR are performed. A short-run price elasticity of -0.20 and a long-run price elasticity of -0.69 are reported. Their findings support strong habit persistence, a small positive income elasticity and weak evidence of bootlegging from adjoining states.

Alternative estimation methods of a static and dynamic panel data model with arbitrary error structure are considered by Chamberlain (1982, 1984). Chamberlain (1984) considers the panel data model as a multivariate regression of T equations subject to restrictions and derives an efficient minimum distance estimator that is robust to residual autocorrelation of arbitrary form. Chamberlain (1984) also first-differences these equations to get rid of the individual effects and derives an asymptotically equivalent estimator to his efficient minimum distance estimator based on 3SLS of the $(T-2)$ differenced equations. Building on Chamberlain's work, Arellano (1990) develops minimum chi-square tests for various covariance restrictions. These tests are based on 3SLS residuals of the dynamic error component model and can be calculated from a generalized linear regression involving the sample autocovariance and dummy variables. The asymptotic distribution of the unrestricted autocovariance estimates is derived without imposing the normality assumption. In particular, Arellano (1990) considers testing covariance restrictions for error components or first-difference structures with white noise, moving average or autoregressive schemes. If these covariance restrictions are true, 3SLS is inefficient and Arellano (1990) proposes a GLS estimator which achieves asymptotic efficiency in the sense that it has the same limiting distribution as the optimal minimum distance estimator. Meghir and Windmeijer (1999) argue that it is important to model the higher order moments of the dynamic process using panel data. For example, in a model for income dynamics and uncertainty, it is likely that persons at different levels of the income distribution face a different variance of their time–income profile. Meghir and Windmeijer model the dynamic variance process as an ARCH type variance with multiplicative individual effects. They derive orthogonality conditions for estimating the coefficients of the conditional variance using GMM. This is done for nonautocorrelated errors, moving average errors and for models allowing for time-varying individual effects. Monte Carlo results show that large sample sizes are needed for estimating this conditional variance function with precision.

Li and Stengos (1992) propose a Hausman specification test based on $\sqrt{N}$-consistent semiparametric estimators. They apply it in the context of a dynamic panel data model of the form

$$y_{it} = \delta y_{i,t-1} + g(x_{it}) + u_{it} \quad i = 1, \ldots, N;\ t = 1, \ldots, T \tag{8.47}$$

where the function $g(\cdot)$ is unknown, but satisfies certain moment and differentiability conditions. The x_{it} observations are IID with finite fourth moments and the disturbances u_{it} are IID$(0, \sigma^2)$ under the null hypothesis. Under the alternative, the disturbances u_{it} are IID in the i subscript but are serially correlated in the t subscript. Li and Stengos base the Hausman test for H_0: $E(u_{it}|y_{i,t-1}) = 0$ on the difference between two $\sqrt{N}$-consistent instrumental variables estimators for δ, under the null and the alternative respectively. More recently, Li and Stengos (1996) derived a $\sqrt{N}$-consistent instrumental variable estimator for a semiparametric dynamic panel data model, while Li and Stengos (1995) proposed a non-nested test for parametric vs semiparametric dynamic panel data models. Berg, Li and Ullah (2000) consider the problem of estimating a semiparametric partially linear dynamic panel data model with disturbances that follow a one-way error component structure. Two new semiparametric instrumental variable (IV) estimators are proposed for the coefficient of the parametric component. These are shown to be more efficient than the ones suggested by Li and Stengos (1996) and Li and Ullah (1998) because they make full use of the error component structure. This is confirmed using Monte Carlo experiments.

Kniesner and Li (2001) considered a semiparametric dynamic panel data model

$$y_{it} = \gamma z_{it} + f(y_{i,t-1}, x_{it}) + u_{it}$$

where the functional form of $f(\cdot)$ is unknown to the researcher. They considered the common case of N large and T small, and proposed a two-step semiparametric $\sqrt{N}$-consistent estimation procedure for this model. Kniesner and Li (2001) also used labor panel data to illustrate the advantages of their semiparametric approach, vs OLS or IV approaches, which treat the parameters as constants. They argued that when the regression function is unknown, imposing a false parametric functional form may not only lead to inconsistent parameter estimation, but may aggravate the problem of individual heterogeneity. For a survey of nonparametric and semiparametric panel data models, see Ullah and Roy (1998).

Holtz-Eakin, Newey and Rosen (1988) formulated a coherent set of procedures for estimating and testing vector autoregressions (VAR) with panel data. The model builds upon Chamberlain's (1984) study and allows for nonstationary individual effects. It is applied to the study of dynamic relationships between wages and hours worked in two samples of American males. The data are based on a sample of 898 males from the PSID covering the period 1968–81. Two variables are considered for each individual, log of annual average hourly earnings and log of annual hours of work. Some of the results are checked using data from the National Longitudinal Survey of Men 45–59. Tests for parameter stationarity, minimum lag length and causality are performed. Holtz-Eakin, Newey and Rosen (1988) emphasize the importance of testing for the appropriate lag length before testing for causality, especially in short panels. Otherwise, misleading results on causality can be obtained. They suggest a simple method of estimating VAR equations with panel data that has a straightforward GLS interpretation. This is based on applying instrumental variables to the quasi-differenced autoregressive equations. They demonstrate how inappropriate methods that deal with individual effects in a VAR context can yield misleading results. Another application of these VAR methods with panel data is Holtz-Eakin, Newey and Rosen (1989) who study the dynamic relationships between local government revenues and expenditures. The data are based on 171 municipal governments over the period 1972–80. It is drawn from the Annual Survey of Governments between 1973 and 1980 and the Census of Governments conducted in 1972 and 1977. The main findings include the following:

(1) Lags of one or two years are sufficient to summarize the dynamic interrelationships in local public finance.
(2) There are important intertemporal linkages among expenditures, taxes and grants.
(3) Results of the stationarity test cast doubt over the stability of parameters over time.
(4) Contrary to previous studies, this study finds that past revenues help predict current expenditures, but past expenditures do not alter the future path of revenues.

NOTES

1. For the identification and estimation of the related literature on distributed lags with short panels, see Pakes and Griliches (1984).

2. Other derivations of this bias include Beggs and Nerlove (1988) and Ridder and Wansbeek (1990).
3. This corrected Within estimator performed well in simulations when compared with eight other consistent instrumental variable or GMM estimators discussed later in this chapter. Kiviet (1999) later extends this derivation of the bias to the case of weakly exogenous variables and examines to what degree this order of approximation is determined by the initial conditions of the dynamic panel data model.
4. Judson and Owen (1999) recommended the corrected Within estimator proposed by Kiviet (1995) as the best choice, followed by GMM as the second best choice. For long panels, they recommended the computationally simpler Anderson and Hsiao (1982) estimator.
5. Bhargava (1991b) also provides sufficient conditions for the identification of both static and dynamic panel data models containing endogenous regressors.
6. Arellano and Bond (1991) warn about circumstances where their proposed serial correlation test is not defined, but where Sargan's overidentification test can still be computed. This is evident for $T = 4$ where no differenced residuals two periods apart are available to compute the serial correlation test. However, for the simple autoregressive model given in (8.3), Sargan's statistic tests two linear combinations of the three moment restrictions available, i.e. $E[(\nu_{i3}-\nu_{i2})y_{i1}] = E[(\nu_{i4}-\nu_{i3})y_{i1}] = E[(\nu_{i4}-\nu_{i3})y_{i2}] = 0$.
7. Arellano and Bover (1995) also discuss a forward orthogonal deviations operator as another example of C which is useful in the context of models with predetermined variables. This transformation essentially subtracts the mean of future observations available in the sample from the first $(T-1)$ observations, see problem 8.4.
8. Arellano and Bover (1995) derive the Fisher information bound for η in order to assess the efficiency of the GMM estimators proposed in this section.
9. Note that one observation for each individual will be lost due to the presence of $y_{i,t-1}$ in (8.3).
10. It may be worth emphasizing that if $T > N$, this procedure will fail since Σ_{TS} will be singular with rank N. Also, the estimation of an unrestricted P_{TS} matrix will be difficult with missing data.
11. See the growing literature on weak instruments by Nelson and Startz (1990), Angrist and Kreuger (1995), Bound, Jaeger and Baker (1995) and Staiger and Stock (1997) to mention a few.
12. An alternative one-step method that achieves the same asymptotic efficiency as robust GMM or LIML estimators is the maximum empirical likelihood estimation method, see Imbens (1997). This maximizes a multinomial pseudo-likelihood function subject to the orthogonality restrictions. These are invariant to normalization because they are maximum likelihood estimators.

PROBLEMS

8.1 For the simple autoregressive model with no regressors given in (8.3):
   (a) Write the first-differenced form of this equation for $t = 5$ and $t = 6$ and list the set of valid instruments for these two periods.
   (b) Show that the variance–covariance matrix of the first-difference disturbances is given by (8.5).
   (c) Verify that (8.8) is the GLS estimator of (8.7).

8.2 Consider the Monte Carlo setup given in Arellano and Bond (1991, p. 283) for a simple autoregressive equation with one regressor with $N = 100$ and $T = 7$.

(a) Compute the bias and mean squared error based on 100 replications of the following estimators: OLS, Within, one-step and two-step Arellano and Bond GMM estimators, two Anderson and Hsiao type estimators that use $\Delta y_{i,t-2}$ and $y_{i,t-2}$ as an instrument for $\Delta y_{i,t-1}$, respectively. Compare with Table 1, p. 284 of Arellano and Bond (1991).

(b) Compute Sargan's (1958) test of overidentifying restrictions given below (8.16) and count the number of rejections out of 100 replications. Compare with Table 2 of Arellano and Bond (1991).

8.3 For $T = 5$, list the moment restrictions available for the simple autoregressive model given in (8.3). What overidentifying restrictions are being tested by Sargan's statistic given below (8.16)?

8.4 Consider three $(T-1) \times T$ matrices defined in (8.20) as follows: $C_1 =$ the first $(T-1)$ rows of $(I_T - \bar{J}_T)$, $C_2 =$ the first-difference operator, $C_3 =$ the forward orthogonal deviations operator which subtracts the mean of future observations from the first $(T-1)$ observations. This last matrix is given by Arellano and Bover (1995) as

$$C_3 = \text{diag}\left[\frac{T-1}{T}, \ldots, \frac{1}{2}\right]^{1/2}$$

$$\times \begin{bmatrix} 1 & -\frac{1}{(T-1)} & -\frac{1}{(T-1)} & \cdots & -\frac{1}{(T-1)} & -\frac{1}{(T-1)} & -\frac{1}{(T-1)} \\ 0 & 1 & -\frac{1}{(T-2)} & \cdots & -\frac{1}{(T-2)} & -\frac{1}{(T-2)} & -\frac{1}{(T-2)} \\ \vdots & \vdots & \vdots & & \vdots & \vdots & \vdots \\ 0 & 0 & 0 & \cdots & 1 & -\frac{1}{2} & -\frac{1}{2} \\ 0 & 0 & 0 & \cdots & 0 & 1 & -1 \end{bmatrix}$$

Verify that each one of these C matrices satisfies:

(a) $C_j \iota_T = 0$ for $j = 1, 2, 3$.

(b) $C_j'(C_j C_j')^{-1} C_j = I_T - \bar{J}_T$, the Within transformation, for $j = 1, 2, 3$.

(c) For C_3, show that $C_3 C_3' = I_{T-1}$ and $C_3' C_3 = I_T - \bar{J}_T$. Hence $C_3 = (C'C)^{-1/2} C$ for any upper triangular C such that $C\iota_T = 0$.

8.5 (a) Verify that GLS on (8.24) yields (8.25).

(b) For the error component model with $\widetilde{\Omega} = \widetilde{\sigma}_\nu^2 I_T + \widetilde{\sigma}_\mu^2 J_T$ and $\widetilde{\sigma}_\nu^2$ and $\widetilde{\sigma}_\mu^2$ denoting consistent estimates of σ_ν^2 and σ_μ^2, respectively, show that $\widehat{\eta}$ in (8.25) can be written as

$$\widehat{\eta} = \left[\sum_{i=1}^N W_i'(I_T - \bar{J}_T)W_i + \widetilde{\theta}^2 T \sum_{i=1}^N \bar{w}_i m_i' \left(\sum_{i=1}^N m_i m_i'\right)^{-1} \sum_{i=1}^N m_i \bar{w}_i'\right]^{-1}$$

$$\times \left[\sum_{i=1}^N W_i'(I_T - \bar{J}_T)y_i + \widetilde{\theta}^2 T \sum_{i=1}^N \bar{w}_i m_i' \left(\sum_{i=1}^N m_i m_i'\right)^{-1} \sum_{i=1}^N m_i \bar{y}_i\right]$$

where $\bar{w}_i = W_i' \iota_T / T$ and $\widetilde{\theta}^2 = \widetilde{\sigma}_\nu^2 / (T\widetilde{\sigma}_\mu^2 + \widetilde{\sigma}_\nu^2)$. These are the familiar expressions for the HT, AM and BMS estimators for the corresponding choices of m_i. (Hint: See the proof in the Appendix of Arellano and Bover (1995)).

8.6 For $T = 4$ and the simple autoregressive model considered in (8.3):
  (a) What are the moment restrictions given by (8.31)? Compare with problem 8.3.
  (b) What are the additional moment restrictions given by (8.32)?
  (c) Write down the system of equations to be estimated by 3SLS using these additional restrictions and list the matrix of instruments for each equation.

8.7 Using the notation in (8.33)–(8.35), show that (8.31) and (8.32) hold under the weaker conditions (B.1)–(B.3) than those implied by assumptions (A.1)–(A.3).

8.8 Consider the Baltagi and Levin (1992) cigarette demand example for 46 states described in section 8.8. This data, updated from 1963–92, is available on the Wiley web site as cigar.txt.
  (a) Estimate (8.45) using 2SLS, FD-2SLS and the Keane and Runkle (1992) version. (Assume only $\ln C_{i,t-1}$ is endogenous.)
  (b) Estimate (8.45) using the Within and FE-2SLS and perform the Hausman-type test based on FE-2SLS vs FD-2SLS.
  (c) Perform the Hausman-type test based on 2SLS vs FD-2SLS.
  (d) Perform the Anderson and Hsiao (1981) estimator for (8.45).
  (e) Perform the Arellano and Bond (1991) GMM estimator for (8.45).
  Hint: Some of the results are available in Table 1 of Baltagi, Griffin and Xiong (2000).

9 Unbalanced Panel Data Models

9.1 INTRODUCTION

So far we have dealt only with "complete panels" or "balanced panels", i.e. cases where the individuals are observed over the entire sample period. Incomplete panels are more likely to be the norm in typical economic empirical settings. For example, in collecting data on US airlines over time, a researcher may find that some firms have dropped out of the market while new entrants emerged over the sample period observed. Similarly, while using labor or consumer panels on households, one may find that some households moved and can no longer be included in the panel. Additionally, if one is collecting data on a set of countries over time, a researcher may find some countries can be traced back longer than others. These typical scenarios lead to "unbalanced" or "incomplete" panels. This chapter deals with the econometric problems associated with these incomplete panels and how they differ from the complete panel data case. Throughout this chapter the panel data are assumed to be incomplete due to randomly missing observations. Nonrandomly missing data and rotating panels will be considered in Chapter 10.[1] Section 9.2 starts with the simple one-way error component model case with unbalanced data and surveys the estimation methods proposed in the literature. Section 9.3 treats the more complicated two-way error component model with unbalanced data. Section 9.4 looks at how some of the tests introduced earlier in the book are affected by the unbalanced panel, while section 9.5 gives some extensions of these unbalanced panel data methods to the nested error component model.

9.2 THE UNBALANCED ONE-WAY ERROR COMPONENT MODEL

To simplify the presentation, we analyze the case of two cross-sections with an unequal number of time-series observations and then generalize the analysis to the case of N cross-sections. Let n_1 be the shorter time series observed for the first cross-section ($i = 1$), and n_2 be the extra time-series observations available for the second cross-section ($i = 2$).[2] Stacking the n_1 observations for the first individual on top of the $(n_1 + n_2)$ observations on the second individual, we get

$$\begin{pmatrix} y_1 \\ y_2 \end{pmatrix} = \begin{pmatrix} X_1 \\ X_2 \end{pmatrix} \beta + \begin{pmatrix} u_1 \\ u_2 \end{pmatrix} \tag{9.1}$$

where y_1 and y_2 are vectors of dimensions n_1 and $n_1 + n_2$, respectively. X_1 and X_2 are matrices of dimensions $n_1 \times K$ and $(n_1 + n_2) \times K$, respectively. In this case, $u_1' = (u_{11}, \ldots, u_{1,n_1})$, $u_2' = (u_{21}, \ldots, u_{2,n_1}, \ldots, u_{2,n_1+n_2})$ and the variance–covariance matrix is given by

$$\Omega = \begin{bmatrix} \sigma_\nu^2 I_{n_1} + \sigma_\mu^2 J_{n_1 n_1} & 0 & 0 \\ 0 & \sigma_\nu^2 I_{n_1} + \sigma_\mu^2 J_{n_1 n_1} & \sigma_\mu^2 J_{n_1 n_2} \\ 0 & \sigma_\mu^2 J_{n_2 n_1} & \sigma_\nu^2 I_{n_2} + \sigma_\mu^2 J_{n_2 n_2} \end{bmatrix} \tag{9.2}$$

where $u' = (u_1', u_2')$, I_{n_i} denotes an identity matrix of order n_i and $J_{n_i n_j}$ denotes a matrix of ones of dimension $n_i \times n_j$. Note that all the nonzero off-diagonal elements of Ω are equal to σ_μ^2. Therefore, if we let $T_j = \sum_{i=1}^{j} n_i$ for $j = 1, 2$, then Ω is clearly block-diagonal with the jth block

$$\Omega_j = (T_j \sigma_\mu^2 + \sigma_\nu^2) \bar{J}_{T_j} + \sigma_\nu^2 E_{T_j} \tag{9.3}$$

where $\bar{J}_{T_j} = J_{T_j}/T_j$, $E_{T_j} = I_{T_j} - \bar{J}_{T_j}$ and there is no need for the double subscript anymore. Using the Wansbeek and Kapteyn trick (1982b) extended to the unbalanced case, Baltagi (1985) derived

$$\Omega_j^r = (T_j \sigma_\mu^2 + \sigma_\nu^2)^r \bar{J}_{T_j} + (\sigma_\nu^2)^r E_{T_j} \tag{9.4}$$

where r is any scalar. Let $w_j^2 = T_j \sigma_\mu^2 + \sigma_\nu^2$, then the Fuller and Battese (1974) transformation for the unbalanced case is the following:

$$\sigma_\nu \Omega_j^{-1/2} = (\sigma_\nu / w_j) \bar{J}_{T_j} + E_{T_j} = I_{T_j} - \theta_j \bar{J}_{T_j} \tag{9.5}$$

where $\theta_j = 1 - \sigma_\nu / w_j$ and $\sigma_\nu \Omega_j^{-1/2} y_j$ has a typical element $(y_{jt} - \theta_j \bar{y}_{j.})$ with $\bar{y}_{j.} = \sum_{t=1}^{T_j} y_{jt}/T_j$. Note that θ_j varies for each cross-sectional unit j depending on T_j. Hence GLS can be obtained as a simple weighted least squares (WLS) as in the complete panel data case. The basic difference, however, is that in the incomplete panel data case the weights are crucially dependent on the lengths of the time series available for each cross-section.

The above results generalize in two directions: (i) the same analysis applies no matter how the observations for the two firms overlap; (ii) the results extend from the two cross-sections to the N cross-sections case. The proof is simple. Since the off-diagonal elements of the covariance matrix are zero for observations belonging to different firms, Ω remains block-diagonal as long as the observations are ordered by firms. Also, the nonzero off-diagonal elements are all equal to σ_μ^2. Hence $\Omega_j^{-1/2}$ can be derived along the same lines shown above.

In general, the regression model with unbalanced one-way error component disturbances is given by

$$y_{it} = \alpha + X'_{it}\beta + u_{it} \quad i = 1, \ldots, N; \; t = 1, \ldots, T_i \tag{9.6}$$

$$u_{it} = \mu_i + \nu_{it}$$

where X_{it} is a $(K-1) \times 1$ vector of regressors, $\mu_i \sim \text{IIN}(0, \sigma_\mu^2)$ and independent of $\nu_{it} \sim \text{IIN}(0, \sigma_\nu^2)$. This model is unbalanced in the sense that there are N individuals observed over varying time-period length (T_i for $i = 1, \ldots, N$). Writing this equation in vector form, we have

$$y = \alpha\iota_n + X\beta + u = Z\delta + u \tag{9.7}$$

$$u = Z_\mu \mu + \nu$$

where y and Z are of dimensions $n \times 1$ and $n \times K$, respectively, $Z = (\iota_n, X)$, $\delta' = (\alpha', \beta')$, $n = \sum T_i$, $Z_\mu = \text{diag}(\iota_{T_i})$ and ι_{T_i} is a vector of ones of dimension T_i. $\mu = (\mu_1, \mu_2, \ldots, \mu_N)'$ and $\nu = (\nu_{11}, \ldots, \nu_{1T_1}, \ldots, \nu_{N1}, \ldots, \nu_{NT_N})'$.

The ordinary least squares (OLS) on the unbalanced data is given by

$$\widehat{\delta}_{\text{OLS}} = (Z'Z)^{-1}Z'y \tag{9.8}$$

OLS is the best linear unbiased estimator when the variance component σ_μ^2 is equal to zero. Even when σ_μ^2 is positive, OLS is still unbiased and consistent, but its standard errors are biased (see Moulton, 1986). The OLS residuals are denoted by $\widehat{u}_{\text{OLS}} = y - Z\widehat{\delta}_{\text{OLS}}$.

The Within estimator can be obtained by first transforming the dependent variables y and X, the exogenous regressors excluding the intercept, using the matrix $Q = \text{diag}(E_{T_i})$, and then applying OLS to the transformed data:

$$\widetilde{\beta} = (\widetilde{X}'\widetilde{X})^{-1}\widetilde{X}'\widetilde{y} \tag{9.9}$$

where $\widetilde{X} = QX$, $\widetilde{y} = Qy$. The estimate of the intercept can be retrieved as follows: $\widetilde{\alpha} = (\bar{y}_{..} - \bar{X}_{..}\widetilde{\beta})$ where the dot indicates summation and the bar indicates averaging, for example, $\bar{y}_{..} = \sum\sum y_{it}/n$. Following Amemiya (1971), the Within residuals $\widetilde{u}$ for the unbalanced panel are given by

$$\widetilde{u} = y - \widetilde{\alpha}\iota_n - X\widetilde{\beta} \tag{9.10}$$

The Between estimator $\widehat{\delta}_{\text{Between}}$ is obtained as follows:

$$\widehat{\delta}_{\text{Between}} = (Z'PZ)^{-1}Z'Py \tag{9.11}$$

where $P = \text{diag}[\bar{J}_{T_i}]$ and the Between residuals are denoted by $\hat{u}^b = y - Z\widehat{\delta}_{\text{Between}}$.

GLS using the true variance components is obtained as follows:

$$\widehat{\delta}_{\text{GLS}} = (Z'\Omega^{-1}Z)^{-1}Z'\Omega^{-1}y \tag{9.12}$$

where $\Omega = \sigma_\nu^2\Sigma = E(uu')$ with

$$\Sigma = I_n + \rho Z_\mu Z'_\mu = \text{diag}(E_{T_i}) + \text{diag}[(1 + \rho T_i)\bar{J}_{T_i}] \tag{9.13}$$

and $\rho = \sigma_\mu^2/\sigma_\nu^2$. Note that $(1 + \rho T_i) = (w_i^2/\sigma_\nu^2)$ where $w_i^2 = (T_i\sigma_\mu^2 + \sigma_\nu^2)$ was defined in (9.4). Therefore, GLS can be obtained by applying OLS on the transformed variables y^* and Z^*, i.e.

$$\widehat{\delta} = (Z^{*\prime}Z^*)^{-1}Z^{*\prime}y^*$$

where $Z^* = \sigma_\nu\Omega^{-1/2}Z$, $y^* = \sigma_\nu\Omega^{-1/2}y$ and

$$\sigma_\nu\Omega^{-1/2} = \text{diag}(E_{T_i}) + \text{diag}[(\sigma_\nu/w_i)\bar{J}_{T_i}] \tag{9.14}$$

as described in (9.5).

We now focus on methods of estimating the variance components, which are described in more detail in Baltagi and Chang (1994).

9.2.1 ANOVA Methods

The ANOVA method is one of the most popular methods in the estimation of variance components. The ANOVA estimators are method of moments type estimators, which equate quadratic sums of squares to their expectations and solve the resulting linear system of equations. For the balanced model, ANOVA estimators are best quadratic unbiased (BQU) estimators of the variance components (see Searle, 1971). Under normality of the disturbances, these ANOVA estimators are minimum variance unbiased. For the unbalanced one-way model, BQU estimators of the variance components are a function of the variance components themselves (see Townsend and Searle, 1971). Still, unbalanced ANOVA methods are available (see Searle, 1987), but optimal properties beyond unbiasedness are lost. In what follows, we generalize some of the ANOVA methods described in Chapter 2 to the unbalanced case. In particular, we consider the two quadratic forms defining the Within and Between sums of squares:

$$q_1 = u'Qu \quad \text{and} \quad q_2 = u'Pu \tag{9.15}$$

where $Q = \text{diag}[E_{T_i}]$ and $P = \text{diag}[\bar{J}_{T_i}]$. Since the true disturbances are not known, we follow the Wallace and Hussain (1969) suggestion by substituting OLS residuals $\widehat{u}_{\text{OLS}}$ for u in (9.15). Upon taking expectations, we get

$$\begin{aligned} E(\widehat{q}_1) &= E(\hat{u}_{\text{OLS}}'Q\hat{u}_{\text{OLS}}) = \delta_{11}\sigma_\mu^2 + \delta_{12}\sigma_\nu^2 \\ E(\widehat{q}_2) &= E(\hat{u}_{\text{OLS}}'P\hat{u}_{\text{OLS}}) = \delta_{21}\sigma_\mu^2 + \delta_{22}\sigma_\nu^2 \end{aligned} \tag{9.16}$$

where $\delta_{11}, \delta_{12}, \delta_{21}, \delta_{22}$ are given by

$$\begin{aligned} \delta_{11} &= \text{tr}((Z'Z)^{-1}Z'Z_\mu Z_\mu'Z) - \text{tr}((Z'Z)^{-1}Z'PZ(Z'Z)^{-1}Z'Z_\mu Z_\mu'Z) \\ \delta_{12} &= n - N - K + \text{tr}((Z'Z)^{-1}Z'PZ) \\ \delta_{21} &= n - 2\,\text{tr}((Z'Z)^{-1}Z'Z_\mu Z_\mu'Z) + \text{tr}((Z'Z)^{-1}Z'PZ(Z'Z)^{-1}Z'Z_\mu Z_\mu'Z) \\ \delta_{22} &= N - \text{tr}((Z'Z)^{-1}Z'PZ) \end{aligned}$$

Equating $\widehat{q}_i$ to its expected value $E(\widehat{q}_i)$ in (9.16) and solving the system of equations, we get the Wallace and Hussain (WH) type estimators of the variance components.

Alternatively, we can substitute Within residuals in the quadratic forms given in (9.15) to get $\widetilde{q}_1 = \widetilde{u}'Q\widetilde{u}$ and $\widetilde{q}_2 = \widetilde{u}'P\widetilde{u}$ as suggested by Amemiya (1971) for the balanced case. The expected values of $\widetilde{q}_1$ and $\widetilde{q}_2$ are given by

$$E(\widetilde{q}_1) = (n - N - K + 1)\sigma_\nu^2 \tag{9.17}$$

$$E(\widetilde{q}_2) = (N - 1 + \text{tr}[(X'QX)^{-1}X'PX] - \text{tr}[(X'QX)^{-1}X'\bar{J}_nX])\sigma_\nu^2 + \left[n - \left(\sum_{i=1}^{N} T_i^2/n\right)\right]\sigma_\mu^2$$

Equating $\widetilde{q}_i$ to its expected value $E(\widetilde{q}_i)$ in (9.17), we get the Amemiya-type estimators of the variance components

$$\widehat{\sigma}_\nu^2 = \widetilde{u}'Q\widetilde{u}/(n - N - K + 1) \tag{9.18}$$

$$\widehat{\sigma}_\mu^2 = \frac{\widetilde{u}'P\widetilde{u} - \{N - 1 + \text{tr}[(X'QX)^{-1}X'PX] - \text{tr}[(X'QX)^{-1}X'\bar{J}_nX]\}\widehat{\sigma}_\nu^2}{n - \sum_{i=1}^{N} T_i^2/n}$$

Next, we follow the Swamy and Arora (1972) suggestion of using the Between and Within regression mean square errors to estimate the variance components. In fact, their method amounts to substituting Within residuals in q_1 and Between residuals in q_2, to get $\widetilde{q}_1 = \widetilde{u}'Q\widetilde{u}$ and $\hat{q}_2^b = \hat{u}^{b\prime}P\hat{u}^b$. Since $\widetilde{q}_1$ is exactly the same as that for the Amemiya method, the Swamy and Arora (SA) type estimator of $\widehat{\sigma}_\nu^2$ is the same as that given in (9.18). The expected value of $\hat{q}_2^b$ is given by

$$E(\hat{q}_2^b) = [n - \text{tr}((Z'PZ)^{-1}Z'Z_\mu Z_\mu'Z)]\sigma_\mu^2 + (N - K)\sigma_\nu^2 \tag{9.19}$$

Equating $E(\hat{q}_2^b)$ to $\hat{q}_2^b$ one gets the following estimator of σ_μ^2:

$$\widehat{\sigma}_\mu^2 = \frac{\hat{u}^{b\prime}P\hat{u}^b - (N - K)\widehat{\sigma}_\nu^2}{n - \text{tr}((Z'PZ)^{-1}Z'Z_\mu Z_\mu'Z)} \tag{9.20}$$

Note that $\hat{u}^{b\prime}P\hat{u}^b$ can be obtained as the OLS residual sum of squares from the regression involving $\sqrt{T_i}\bar{y}_{i.}$ on $\sqrt{T_i}\bar{Z}_{i.}$.

Finally, we consider Henderson's method III (see Fuller and Battese, 1974) which will be denoted by HFB. This method utilizes the fitting constants method described in Searle (1971, p. 489). Let

$$R(\mu) = y'Z_\mu(Z_\mu'Z_\mu)^{-1}Z_\mu'y = \sum_{i=1}^{N}(y_{i.}^2/T_i) \qquad R(\delta \mid \mu) = \tilde{y}'\widetilde{X}(\widetilde{X}'\widetilde{X})^{-1}\widetilde{X}'\tilde{y}$$

$$R(\delta) = y'Z(Z'Z)^{-1}Z'y \qquad R(\mu \mid \delta) = R(\delta \mid \mu) + R(\mu) - R(\delta)$$

Then Henderson's (1953) method III estimators are given by

$$\widehat{\sigma}_\nu^2 = \frac{y'y - R(\delta \mid \mu) - R(\mu)}{n - K - N + 1}$$

$$\widehat{\sigma}_\mu^2 = \frac{R(\mu \mid \delta) - (N-1)\widehat{\sigma}_\nu^2}{n - \mathrm{tr}(Z_\mu' Z(Z'Z)^{-1}Z'Z_\mu)} \tag{9.21}$$

9.2.2 Maximum Likelihood Estimators

Maximum likelihood (ML) estimates of the variance components and regression coefficients are obtained by maximizing the following log-likelihood function:

$$\log L = -(n/2)\log(2\pi) - (n/2)\log\sigma_\nu^2 - \tfrac{1}{2}\log|\Sigma|$$
$$-(y - Z\delta)'\Sigma^{-1}(y - Z\delta)/2\sigma_\nu^2 \tag{9.22}$$

where ρ and Σ are given in (9.13). The first-order conditions give closed form solutions for $\widehat{\delta}$ and $\widehat{\sigma}_\nu^2$ conditional on $\widehat{\rho}$:

$$\widehat{\delta} = (Z'\widehat{\Sigma}^{-1}Z)^{-1}Z'\widehat{\Sigma}^{-1}y$$
$$\widehat{\sigma}_\nu^2 = (y - Z\delta)'\widehat{\Sigma}^{-1}(y - Z\delta)/n \tag{9.23}$$

However, the first-order condition based on ρ is nonlinear in ρ even for known values of δ and σ_ν^2:

$$0 = \frac{\partial \log L}{\partial \rho} = \frac{1}{2}\mathrm{tr}(Z'\Sigma^{-1}Z) + \frac{1}{2\sigma_\nu^2}(y - Z\delta)'\Sigma^{-1}Z_\mu Z_\mu'\Sigma^{-1}(y - Z\delta) \tag{9.24}$$

A numerical solution by means of iteration is necessary for $\widehat{\rho}$. The second derivative of $\log L$ with respect to ρ is given by

$$\frac{\partial^2 \log L}{\partial\rho\partial\rho} = \frac{1}{2}\mathrm{tr}\{(Z_\mu'\Sigma^{-1}Z_\mu)(Z_\mu'\Sigma^{-1}Z_\mu)\}$$
$$-\frac{1}{\sigma_\nu^2}\{(y - Z\delta)'\Sigma^{-1}Z_\mu(Z_\mu'\Sigma^{-1}Z_\mu)Z_\mu'\Sigma^{-1}(y - Z\delta)\} \tag{9.25}$$

Starting with an initial value of ρ_0, one obtains $\widehat{\Sigma}_0$ from (9.13) and $\widehat{\delta}_0$ and $\widehat{\sigma}_{\nu 0}^2$ from (9.23). The updated value ρ_1 is given from the following formula:

$$\rho_1 = \rho_0 - s\left[\frac{\partial^2 \log L}{\partial\rho\partial\rho}\right]_0^{-1}\left[\frac{\partial \log L}{\partial \rho}\right]_0 \tag{9.26}$$

where the subscript zero means evaluated at $\widehat{\Sigma}_0$, $\widehat{\delta}_0$ and $\widehat{\sigma}_{\nu 0}^2$ and s is a step size which is adjusted by step halving.[3] For the computational advantage of this algorithm as well as other algorithms like the Fisher scoring algorithm, see Jennrich and Sampson (1976) and Harville (1977). Maximum likelihood estimators are functions of sufficient statistics and are consistent and asymptotically efficient; see Harville (1977) for a review of the properties, advantages and disadvantages of ML estimators.

The ML approach has been criticized on grounds that it does not take into account the loss of degrees of freedom due to the regression coefficients in estimating the variance components. Patterson and Thompson (1971) remedy this by partitioning the likelihood function into two parts. One part depends only on the variance components and is free of the regression coefficients. Maximizing this part yields the restricted maximum likelihood estimator (REML). REML estimators of the variance components are asymptotically equivalent to the ML estimators (see Das, 1979); however, little is known about their finite sample properties, and they reduce to the ANOVA estimators under several balanced data cases. For details, see Corbeil and Searle (1976a, b) and Hocking (1985).

9.2.3 Minimum Norm and Minimum Variance Quadratic Unbiased Estimators (MINQUE and MIVQUE)

Under normality of the disturbances, Rao's (1971a) MINQUE and MIVQUE procedures for estimating the variance components are identical. Since we assume normality, we will focus on MIVQUE. Basically, the MIVQUE of a linear combination of the variance components, $p_\mu\sigma_\mu^2 + p_\nu\sigma_\nu^2$, is obtained by finding a symmetric matrix G such that $\text{var}(y'Gy) = 2\ \text{tr}\{\sigma_\mu^2(GZ_\mu Z_\mu') + \sigma_\nu^2 G\}^2$ is minimized subject to the conditions that $y'Gy$ is an unbiased estimator of $(p_\mu\sigma_\mu^2 + p_\nu\sigma_\nu^2)$ and is invariant to any translation of the δ parameter. These yield the following constraints:

(1) GZ = 0;
(2) $\text{tr}(GZ_\mu Z_\mu') = p_\mu$ and $\text{tr}(G) = p_\nu$.

Rao (1971b) showed that the MIVQUE estimates of the variance components are given by

$$\begin{bmatrix} \hat{\sigma}_\mu^2 \\ \hat{\sigma}_\nu^2 \end{bmatrix} = \begin{bmatrix} \gamma_{11} & \gamma_{12} \\ \gamma_{12} & \gamma_{22} \end{bmatrix}^{-1} \begin{bmatrix} \delta_1 \\ \delta_2 \end{bmatrix}$$

where $\gamma_{11} = \text{tr}(Z_\mu Z_\mu' R Z_\mu Z_\mu' R)$, $\gamma_{12} = \text{tr}(Z_\mu Z_\mu' RR)$, $\gamma_{22} = \text{tr}(RR)$, $\delta_1 = y'RZ_\mu Z_\mu' Ry$, $\delta_2 = y'RRy$ and $R = (\Sigma^{-1} - \Sigma^{-1}Z(Z'\Sigma^{-1}Z)^{-1}Z'\Sigma^{-1})/\sigma_\nu^2$. It is clear that MIVQUE requires a priori values of the variance components, and the resulting estimators possess the minimum variance property only if these a priori values coincide with the true values. Therefore MIVQUE are only "locally best" (see Harville, 1969) and "locally minimum variance" (see LaMotte, 1973a, b). If one iterates on the initial values of the variance components, the iterative estimators (IMIVQUE) become biased after the first iteration and MINQUE properties are not preserved. Two priors for the MINQUE estimator used in practice are: (i) the identity matrix, denoted by MQ0 and (ii) the ANOVA estimator of Swamy and Arora denoted by MQA. Under normality, if one iterates until convergence, IMINQUE, IMIVQUE and REML will be identical (see Hocking and Kutner, 1975; Swallow and Monahan, 1984).[4]

9.2.4 Monte Carlo Results

Baltagi and Chang (1994) performed an extensive Monte Carlo study using a simple as well as a multiple regression with unbalanced one-way error component disturbances. The degree of unbalance in the sample as well as the variance component ratio ρ were varied across the experiments. The total number of observations as well as the total variance were fixed across the experiments to allow comparison of MSE for the various estimators considered. Some of the basic results of the Monte Carlo study suggest the following:

(1) As far as the estimation of regression coefficients is concerned, the simple ANOVA type feasible GLS estimators compare well with the more complicated estimators such as ML, REML and MQA and are never more than 4% above the MSE of true GLS. However, MQ0 is not recommended for large ρ and unbalanced designs.
(2) For the estimation of the remainder variance component σ_ν^2 the ANOVA, MIVQUE(A), ML and REML estimators show little difference in relative MSE performance. However, for the individual specific variance component estimation, σ_μ^2, the ANOVA type estimators perform poorly relative to ML, REML and MQA when the variance component ratio $\rho > 1$ and the pattern is severely unbalanced. MQ0 gives an extremely poor performance for severely unbalanced patterns and large ρ and is not recommended for these cases.
(3) Better estimates of the variance components, in the MSE sense, do not necessarily imply better estimates of the regression coefficients. This echoes similar findings for the balanced panel data case.
(4) Negative estimates of the variance components occurred when the true value of σ_μ^2 was zero or close to zero. In these cases, replacing these negative estimates by zero did not lead to much loss in efficiency.
(5) Extracting a balanced panel out of an unbalanced panel by either maximizing the number of households observed or the total number of observations in the balanced panel leads in both cases to an enormous loss in efficiency and is not recommended.[5]

9.2.5 Empirical Applications

Example 1

Baltagi and Chang (1994) apply the various unbalanced variance components methods to the data set collected by Harrison and Rubinfeld (1978) for a study of hedonic housing prices and the willingness to pay for clean air. This data is available on the Wiley web site as Hedonic.xls. The total number of observations is 506 census tracts in the Boston area in 1970 and the number of variables is 14. Belsley, Kuh and Welsch (1980) identify 92 towns, consisting of 15 within Boston and 77 in its surrounding area. Thus, it is possible to group these data and analyze them as an unbalanced one-way model with random group effects. The group sizes range from one to 30 observations. The dependent variable is the median value (MV) of owner-occupied homes. The regressors include two structural variables, RM the average number of rooms, and AGE representing the proportion of owner units built prior to 1940. In addition there are eight neighborhood variables: B, the proportion of blacks in the population; LSTAT, the proportion of population that is lower status; CRIM, the crime rate; ZN, the proportion of 25 000 square feet residential lots; INDUS, the proportion of non-retail business acres; TAX, the full value property tax rate ($/$10 000); PTRATIO, the pupil–teacher ratio; and CHAS, the dummy variable for Charles River (= 1 if a tract bounds the Charles). There are also two accessibility variables: DIS, the weighted distances to five employment centers in the Boston region and RAD, the index of accessibility to radial highways. One more regressor is an air pollution variable NOX, the annual average nitrogen oxide concentration in parts per hundred million.[6] Moulton (1987) performed the Breusch and Pagan (1980) Lagrange multiplier (LM) test on this data set and found compelling evidence against the exclusion of random group effects.[7]

Table 9.1 shows the OLS, Within, ANOVA, ML, REML and MIVQUE type estimates using the entire data set of 506 observations for 92 towns. Unlike the drastic difference between OLS and the Within estimators which were analyzed in Moulton (1987), the various ANOVA, MLE and MIVQUE type estimators, reported in Table 9.1, give similar estimates. Exceptions are ZN, INDUS and CHAS estimates which vary across methods, but are all statistically insignificant. For the statistically significant variables, AGE varies from −0.86 for SA to −0.97 for REML, and DIS varies from −1.25 for REML to −1.44 for SA.[8]

In conclusion, for the regression coefficients, both the Monte Carlo and the empirical illustration indicate that the computationally simple ANOVA estimates compare favorably with the computationally demanding ML, REML and MQA type estimators. For the variance components, the ANOVA methods are recommended except when ρ is large and the unbalancedness of the data is severe. For these cases, ML, REML or MQA are recommended. As a check for misspecification, one should perform at least one of the ANOVA methods and one of the ML methods to see if the estimates differ widely. This is the Maddala and Mount (1973) suggestion for the balanced data case and applies as well for the unbalanced data case.

Example 2

In studying the damage associated with proximity to a hazardous waste site, Mendelsohn et al. (1992) use panel data on repeated single family home sales in the harbor area surrounding New Bedford, Massachusetts over the period 1969–88. Note that one observes the dependent variable, in this case the value of the house, only when an actual sale occurs. Therefore, these data are "unbalanced" with different time-period intervals between sales, and different numbers of repeated sales for each single family house over the period observed. These comprised 780 properties and 1916 sales. Mendelsohn et al. (1992) used first-differenced and fixed effects estimation methods to control for specific individual housing characteristics. Information

Table 9.1 One-way Unbalanced Variance Components Estimates for the Harrison–Rubinfeld Hedonic Housing Equation. Dependent Variable: MV

	OLS	Within	SA	WH	HFB	ML	REML	MQ0	MQA
Intercept	9.76	—	9.69	9.68	9.67	9.68	9.67	9.68	9.67
	(0.15)	—	(0.19)	(0.21)	(0.21)	(0.21)	(0.21)	(0.21)	(0.21)
CRIM	−1.19	−0.63	−0.74	−0.74	−0.72	−0.72	−0.71	−0.73	−0.71
	(0.12)	(0.10)	(0.10)	(0.11)	(0.10)	(0.10)	(0.10)	(0.11)	(0.10)
ZN	0.08	—	0.08	0.07	0.02	0.03	0.01	0.06	0.01
	(0.51)	—	(0.63)	(0.68)	(0.70)	(0.69)	(0.71)	(0.69)	(0.71)
INDUS	0.02	—	0.16	0.16	0.24	0.22	0.24	0.18	0.24
	(0.24)	—	(0.39)	(0.43)	(0.45)	(0.44)	(0.46)	(0.43)	(0.45)
CHAS	0.94	−0.46	−0.04	−0.06	−0.13	−0.12	−0.14	−0.08	−0.14
	(0.34)	(0.31)	(0.28)	(0.30)	(0.29)	(0.28)	(0.29)	(0.30)	(0.29)
NOX	−0.64	−0.56	−0.58	−0.58	−0.59	−0.59	−0.59	−0.59	−0.59
	(0.11)	(0.14)	(0.12)	(0.13)	(0.12)	(0.12)	(0.12)	(0.13)	(0.12)
RM	0.63	0.93	0.91	0.91	0.92	0.92	0.92	0.91	0.92
	(0.13)	(0.12)	(0.11)	(0.12)	(0.12)	(0.12)	(0.12)	(0.12)	(0.12)
AGE	0.09	−1.41	−0.86	−0.87	−0.96	−0.94	−0.97	−0.90	−0.96
	(0.53)	(0.49)	(0.45)	(0.49)	(0.46)	(0.46)	(0.46)	(0.48)	(0.46)
DIS	−1.91	0.80	−1.44	−1.42	−1.27	−1.30	−1.25	−1.38	−1.26
	(0.33)	(0.71)	(0.42)	(0.46)	(0.46)	(0.45)	(0.47)	(0.46)	(0.47)
RAD	0.96	—	0.96	0.96	0.97	0.97	0.98	0.96	0.97
	(0.19)	—	(0.26)	(0.28)	(0.29)	(0.28)	(0.30)	(0.28)	(0.29)
TAX	−0.42	—	−0.38	−0.38	−0.37	−0.37	−0.37	−0.38	−0.37
	(0.12)	—	(0.17)	(0.19)	(0.19)	(0.19)	(0.20)	(0.19)	(0.20)
PTRATIO	−3.11	—	−2.95	−2.95	−2.99	−2.98	−2.99	−2.96	−2.99
	(0.50)	—	(0.87)	(0.96)	(1.01)	(0.98)	(1.02)	(0.97)	(1.02)
B	0.36	0.66	0.56	0.57	0.58	0.58	0.58	0.57	0.58
	(0.10)	(0.10)	(0.10)	(0.11)	(0.10)	(0.10)	(0.10)	(0.10)	(0.10)
LSTAT	−3.71	−2.45	−2.91	−2.90	−2.82	−2.84	−2.82	−2.88	−2.82
	(0.25)	(0.26)	(0.23)	(0.25)	(0.24)	(0.24)	(0.24)	(0.25)	(0.24)
$\hat{\sigma}_\nu^2$	—	—	0.017	0.020	0.017	0.017	0.017	0.019	0.017
$\hat{\sigma}_\mu^2$	—	—	0.013	0.016	0.019	0.018	0.020	0.017	0.020

*Approximate standard errors are given in parentheses. $n = 506$ observations for $N = 92$ towns
Source: Baltagi and Chang (1994). Reproduced by permission of Elsevier Science Publishers B.V. (North-Holland)

on the latter variables is rarely available or complete. They find a significant reduction in housing values, between 7000 and 10 000 (1989 dollars), as a result of these houses' proximity to hazardous waste sites.[9]

9.3 THE UNBALANCED TWO-WAY ERROR COMPONENT MODEL

Wansbeek and Kapteyn (1989), henceforth WK, consider the regression model with unbalanced two-way error component disturbances

$$y_{it} = X_{it}'\beta + u_{it} \quad i = 1, \ldots, N_t;\ t = 1, \ldots, T \tag{9.27}$$

$$u_{it} = \mu_i + \lambda_t + \nu_{it}$$

where N_t ($N_t \leqslant N$) denotes the number of individuals observed in year t, with $n = \sum_t N_t$. Let D_t be the ($N_t \times N$) matrix obtained from I_N by omitting the rows corresponding to individuals not observed in year t. Define

$$\Delta = (\Delta_1, \Delta_2) \equiv \begin{bmatrix} D_1 & D_1\iota_N & & \\ \vdots & & \ddots & \\ D_T & & & D_T\iota_N \end{bmatrix} \tag{9.28}$$

where $\Delta_1 = (D_1', \ldots, D_T')'$ is $n \times N$ and $\Delta_2 = \text{diag}[D_t\iota_N] = \text{diag}[\iota_{N_t}]$ is $n \times T$. The matrix Δ gives the dummy variable structure for the incomplete data model. Note that WK order the data on the N individuals in T consecutive sets, so that t runs slowly and i runs fast. This is exactly the opposite ordering that has been used so far in the text. For complete panels, $\Delta_1 = (\iota_T \otimes I_N)$ and $\Delta_2 = I_T \otimes \iota_N$.

9.3.1 The Fixed Effects Model

If the μ_i and λ_t are fixed, one has to run the regression given in (9.27) with the matrix of dummies given in (9.28). Most likely, this will be infeasible for large panels with many households or individuals and we need the familiar Within transformation. This was easy for the balanced case and extended easily to the unbalanced one-way case. However, for the unbalanced two-way case, WK showed that this transformation is a little complicated but nevertheless manageable. To see this, we need some more matrix results.

Note that $\Delta_N \equiv \Delta_1'\Delta_1 = \text{diag}[T_i]$ where T_i is the number of years individual i is observed in the panel. Also, $\Delta_T \equiv \Delta_2'\Delta_2 = \text{diag}[N_t]$ and $\Delta_{TN} \equiv \Delta_2'\Delta_1$ is the ($T \times N$) matrix of zeros and ones indicating the absence or presence of a household in a certain year. For complete panels, $\Delta_N = TI_N$, $\Delta_T = NI_T$ and $\Delta_{TN} = \iota_T\iota_N' = J_{TN}$. Define $P_{[\Delta]} = \Delta(\Delta'\Delta)^-\Delta'$, then the Within transformation is $Q_{[\Delta]} = I_n - P_{[\Delta]}$. For the two-way unbalanced model with $\Delta = (\Delta_1, \Delta_2)$ given by (9.28), WK show that

$$P_{[\Delta]} = P_{\Delta_1} + P_{[Q_{[\Delta_1]}\Delta_2]} \tag{9.29}$$

The proof is sketched out in problem 9.6. Therefore

$$Q_{[\Delta]} = Q_{[\Delta_1]} - Q_{[\Delta_1]}\Delta_2(\Delta_2'Q_{[\Delta_1]}\Delta_2)^-\Delta_2'Q_{[\Delta_1]} \tag{9.30}$$

Davis (2001) generalizes the WK Within transformation to the three-way, four-way and higher order error component models. Davis shows that the Within transformation can be applied in stages to the variables in the regression, just like in (9.30). This reduces the computational burden considerably. For example, consider a three-way error component model, representing products sold at certain locations and observed over some time period. These fixed effects are captured by three dummy variables matrices $\Delta = [\Delta_1, \Delta_2, \Delta_3]$. In order to get the Within transformation, Davis (2001) applies (9.29) twice and obtains $Q_{[\Delta]} = Q_{[A]} - P_{[B]} - P_{[C]}$ where $A = \Delta_1$, $B = Q_{[A]}\Delta_2$ and $C = Q_{[B]}Q_{[A]}\Delta_3$, see problem

9.27. This idea generalizes readily to higher order fixed effects error components models.

9.3.2 The Random Effects Model

In vector form, the incomplete two-way random effects model can be written as

$$u = \Delta_1\mu + \Delta_2\lambda + \nu \tag{9.31}$$

where $\mu' = (\mu_1, \ldots, \mu_N)$, $\lambda' = (\lambda_1, \ldots, \lambda_T)$ and ν are random variables described exactly as in the two-way error component model considered in Chapter 3. μ, λ and ν are independent of each other and among themselves with zero means and variances σ_μ^2, σ_λ^2 and σ_ν^2, respectively. In this case

$$\begin{aligned}\Omega = E(uu') &= \sigma_\nu^2 I_n + \sigma_\mu^2\Delta_1\Delta_1' + \sigma_\lambda^2\Delta_2\Delta_2' \\ &= \sigma_\nu^2(I_n + \phi_1\Delta_1\Delta_1' + \phi_2\Delta_2\Delta_2') = \sigma_\nu^2\Sigma \end{aligned}\tag{9.32}$$

with $\phi_1 = \sigma_\mu^2/\sigma_\nu^2$ and $\phi_2 = \sigma_\lambda^2/\sigma_\nu^2$. Using the general expression for the inverse of $(I + XX')$, see problem 9.8, Wansbeek and Kapteyn (1989) obtain the inverse of Σ as

$$\Sigma^{-1} = V - V\Delta_2\widetilde{P}^{-1}\Delta_2'V \tag{9.33}$$

where

$$\begin{aligned} V &= I_n - \Delta_1\widetilde{\Delta}_N^{-1}\Delta_1' && (n \times n) \\ \widetilde{P} &= \widetilde{\Delta}_T - \Delta_{TN}\widetilde{\Delta}_N^{-1}\Delta_{TN}' && (T \times T) \\ \widetilde{\Delta}_N &= \Delta_N + (\sigma_\nu^2/\sigma_\mu^2)I_N && (N \times N) \\ \widetilde{\Delta}_T &= \Delta_T + (\sigma_\nu^2/\sigma_\lambda^2)I_T && (T \times T) \end{aligned}$$

Note that we can no longer obtain the simple Fuller and Battese (1973) transformation for the unbalanced two-way model. The expression for Σ^{-1} is messy and asymmetric in individuals and time, but it reduces computational time considerably relative to inverting Σ numerically. Davis (2001) shows that the WK results can be generalized to an arbitrary number of random error components. In fact, for a three-way random error component, like the one considered in problem 9.7, the added random error component η adds an extra $\sigma_\eta^2\Delta_3\Delta_3'$ term to the variance–covariance given in (9.32). Therefore, Σ remains of the $(I + XX')$ form and its inverse can be obtained by repeated application of this inversion formula. This idea generalizes readily to higher order unbalanced random error component models. WK suggest an ANOVA type quadratic unbiased estimator (QUE) of the variance components based on the Within residuals. In fact, the MSE of the Within regression is unbiased for σ_ν^2 even under the random effects specification. Let $e = y - X\widetilde{\beta}$ where $\widetilde{\beta}$ denote the Within estimates and define

$$q_W = e'Q_{[\Delta]}e \tag{9.34}$$

$$q_N = e'\Delta_2\Delta_T^{-1}\Delta_2'e = e'P_{[\Delta_2]}e \tag{9.35}$$

$$q_T = e'\Delta_1\Delta_N^{-1}\Delta_1'e = e'P_{[\Delta_1]}e \tag{9.36}$$

By equating q_W, q_N and q_T to their expected values and solving these three equations one gets QUE of σ_ν^2, σ_μ^2 and σ_λ^2. WK also derive the ML iterative first-order conditions as well as the information matrix under normality of the disturbances. These will not be reproduced here and the reader is referred to the WK article for details. A limited Monte Carlo experiment was performed using 50 replications and three kinds of data designs: complete panel data, 20% random attrition and a rotating panel. This was done using a simple regression with a Nerlove-type X for fixed $\sigma_\mu^2 = 400$, $\sigma_\lambda^2 = 25$ and $\sigma_\nu^2 = 25$. The regression coefficients were fixed at $\alpha = 25$ and $\beta = 2$, and the number of individuals and time periods were $N = 100$ and $T = 5$, respectively. The results imply that the QUE of the variance components are in all cases at least as close to the true value as the MLE, so that iteration on these values does not seem to pay off. Also, GLS gives nearly identical results to MLE as far as the regression coefficient estimates are concerned. Therefore, WK recommend GLS over MLE in view of the large difference in computational cost.

Baltagi, Song and Jung (2000) reconsider the unbalanced two-way error component given in (9.27) and (9.28) and provide alternative analysis of variance (ANOVA), minimum norm quadratic unbiased (MINQUE) and restricted maximum likelihood (REML) estimation procedures. These are similar to the methods studied in section 9.2 for the unbalanced one-way error component model. The mean squared error performance of these estimators are compared using Monte Carlo experiments. Focusing on the estimates of the variance components, the computationally more demanding MLE, REML and MIVQUE estimators are recommended especially if the unbalanced pattern is severe. However, focusing on the regression coefficients estimates, the simple ANOVA methods perform just as well as the computationally demanding MLE, REML and MIVQUE methods and are recommended.

9.4 TESTING FOR INDIVIDUAL AND TIME EFFECTS USING UNBALANCED PANEL DATA

In Chapter 4, we derived the Breusch and Pagan (1980) LM test for H_0: $\sigma_\mu^2 = \sigma_\lambda^2 = 0$ in a complete panel data model with two-way error component disturbances. Baltagi and Li (1990b) derived the corresponding LM test for the unbalanced two-way error component model. This model is given by (9.27) and the variance–covariance matrix of the disturbances is given by (9.32). Following the same derivations as given in section 4.2 (see problem 9.8), one can show that under normality of the disturbances

$$\partial\Omega/\partial\sigma_\mu^2 = \Delta_1\Delta_1' \quad \partial\Omega/\partial\sigma_\lambda^2 = \Delta_2\Delta_2' \quad \text{and} \quad \partial\Omega/\partial\sigma_\nu^2 = I_n \tag{9.37}$$

with

$$\operatorname{tr}(\Delta_2\Delta_2') = \operatorname{tr}(\Delta_2'\Delta_2) = \operatorname{tr}(\operatorname{diag}[N_t]) = \sum_{t=1}^{T} N_t = n \tag{9.38}$$

and

$$\operatorname{tr}(\Delta_1'\Delta_1) = \operatorname{tr}(\operatorname{diag}[T_i]) = \sum_{i=1}^{N} T_i = n \tag{9.39}$$

Substituting these results in (4.17) and noting that under H_0, $\widetilde{\Omega}^{-1} = (1/\widetilde{\sigma}_\nu^2)I_n$, where $\widehat{\sigma}_\nu^2 = \widetilde{u}'\widetilde{u}/NT$ and $\widetilde{u}$ denote the OLS residuals, one gets

$$\widetilde{D} = (\partial L/\partial\theta)|_{\theta=\widetilde{\theta}} = (n/2\widetilde{\sigma}_\nu^2)\begin{bmatrix} A_1 \\ A_2 \\ 0 \end{bmatrix} \tag{9.40}$$

where $\theta' = (\sigma_\mu^2, \sigma_\lambda^2, \sigma_\nu^2)$ and $\widetilde{\theta}$ denotes the restricted MLE of θ under H_0. Also, $A_r = [(\widetilde{u}'\Delta_r\Delta_r'\widetilde{u}/\widetilde{u}'\widetilde{u}) - 1]$ for $r = 1, 2$. Similarly, one can use (4.19) to obtain the information matrix

$$\widetilde{J} = (n/2\widetilde{\sigma}_\nu^4)\begin{bmatrix} M_{11}/n & 1 & 1 \\ 1 & M_{22}/n & 1 \\ 1 & 1 & 1 \end{bmatrix} \tag{9.41}$$

where $M_{11} = \sum_{i=1}^{N} T_i^2$ and $M_{22} = \sum_{t=1}^{T} N_t^2$. This makes use of the fact that

$$\operatorname{tr}(\Delta_2\Delta_2')^2 = \sum_{t=1}^{T} N_t^2 \quad \operatorname{tr}(\Delta_1\Delta_1')^2 = \sum_{i=1}^{N} T_i^2 \tag{9.42}$$

and

$$\operatorname{tr}[(\Delta_1\Delta_1')(\Delta_2\Delta_2')] = \sum_{t=1}^{T} \operatorname{tr}[(D_t D_t')J_{N_t}] = \sum_{t=1}^{T} \operatorname{tr}(J_{N_t}) = \sum_{t=1}^{T} N_t = n$$

Using (9.40) and (9.41) one gets the LM statistic

$$\text{LM} = \widetilde{D}'\widetilde{J}^{-1}\widetilde{D} = (\tfrac{1}{2})n^2[A_1^2/(M_{11} - n) + A_2^2/(M_{22} - n)] \tag{9.43}$$

which is asymptotically distributed as χ_2^2 under the null hypothesis. For computational purposes, one need not form the Δ_r matrices to compute A_r $(r = 1, 2)$. In fact

$$\widetilde{u}\Delta_1\Delta_1'\widetilde{u} = \sum_{i=1}^{N} \widetilde{u}_{i.}^2 \quad \text{where} \quad \widetilde{u}_{i.} = \sum_{t=1}^{T_i} \widetilde{u}_{it} \tag{9.44}$$

and

$$\widetilde{u}'\Delta_2\Delta_2'\widetilde{u} = \sum_{t=1}^{T} \widetilde{u}_{.t}^2 \quad \text{where} \quad \widetilde{u}_{.t} = \sum_{i=1}^{N_t} \widetilde{u}_{it} \tag{9.45}$$

(9.45) is obvious, since $\Delta_2 = \operatorname{diag}[\iota_{N_t}]$, and (9.44) can be similarly obtained, by restacking the residuals such that the faster index is t. The LM statistic given in (9.43) is easily computed using least squares residuals, and retains a similar form to that of the complete panel data case. In fact, when $N_t = N$, (9.43) reverts back to the LM statistic derived in Breusch and Pagan (1980). Also, (9.43) retains the additive property exhibited in the complete panel data case, i.e. if H_0: $\sigma_\mu^2 = 0$, the LM test reduces to the first term of (9.43), whereas if H_0: $\sigma_\lambda^2 = 0$, the LM test reduces to the second term of (9.43). Both test statistics are asymptotically distributed as χ_1^2 under the respective null hypotheses.

These variance components cannot be negative and therefore H_0: $\sigma_\mu^2 = 0$ has to be against a one-sided alternative H_1: $\sigma_\mu^2 > 0$. Moulton and Randolph (1989) derived the one-sided LM_1 statistic

$$\text{LM}_1 = n[2(M_{11} - n)]^{-1/2} A_1 \tag{9.46}$$

which is the square root of the first term in (9.43). Under weak conditions as $n \to \infty$ and $N \to \infty$ the LM_1 statistic has an asymptotic standard normal distribution under H_0. However, Moulton and Randolph (1989) showed that this asymptotic $N(0, 1)$ approximation can be poor even in large samples. This occurs when the number of regressors is large or the intraclass correlation of some of the regressors is high. They suggest an alternative standardized Lagrange multiplier SLM given by

$$\text{SLM} = \frac{\text{LM}_1 - E(\text{LM}_1)}{\sqrt{\text{var}(\text{LM}_1)}} = \frac{d - E(d)}{\sqrt{\text{var}(d)}} \tag{9.47}$$

where $d = (\tilde{u}' D \tilde{u})/\tilde{u}'\tilde{u}$ and $D = \Delta_1 \Delta_1'$. Using the results on moments of quadratic forms in regression residuals (see, for example, Evans and King, 1985), we get

$$E(d) = \text{tr}(D\bar{P}_Z)/p$$

where $p = [n - (K + 1)]$ and

$$\text{var}(d) = 2\{p \ \text{tr}(D\bar{P}_Z)^2 - [\text{tr}(D\bar{P}_Z)]^2\}/p^2(p + 2)$$

Under H_0, this SLM has the same asymptotic $N(0, 1)$ distribution as the LM_1 statistic. However, the asymptotic critical values for the SLM are generally closer to the exact critical values than those of the LM_1 statistic. Similarly, for H_0: $\sigma_\lambda^2 = 0$, the one-sided LM test statistic is the square root of the second term in (9.43), i.e.

$$\text{LM}_2 = n[2(M_{22} - n)]^{-1/2} A_2 \tag{9.48}$$

Honda's (1985) "handy" one-sided test for the two-way model with unbalanced data is simply

$$\text{HO} = (\text{LM}_1 + \text{LM}_2)/\sqrt{2}$$

It is also easy to show, see Baltagi, Chang and Li (1998), that the locally mean most powerful (LMMP) one-sided test suggested by King and Wu (1997) for the unbalanced two-way error component model is given by

$$\text{KW} = \frac{\sqrt{M_{11} - n}}{\sqrt{M_{11} + M_{22} - 2n}} \text{LM}_1 + \frac{\sqrt{M_{22} - n}}{\sqrt{M_{11} + M_{22} - 2n}} \text{LM}_2 \tag{9.49}$$

where LM_1 and LM_2 are given by (9.46) and (9.48), respectively. Both HO and KW are asymptotically distributed as $N(0, 1)$ under H_0. These test statistics can be standardized and the resulting SLM given by $\{d - E(d)\}/\sqrt{\text{var}(d)}$ where $d = \tilde{u}'D\tilde{u}/\tilde{u}'\tilde{u}$ with

$$D = \frac{1}{2}\frac{n}{\sqrt{M_{11} - n}}(\Delta_1\Delta_1') + \frac{1}{2}\frac{n}{\sqrt{M_{22} - n}}(\Delta_2\Delta_2') \tag{9.50}$$

for Honda's (1985) version and

$$D = \frac{n}{\sqrt{2}\sqrt{M_{11} + M_{22} - 2n}}[(\Delta_1\Delta_1') + (\Delta_2\Delta_2')] \tag{9.51}$$

for the King and Wu (1997) version of this test. $E(d)$ and $\text{var}(d)$ are obtained from the same formulae shown below (9.47) using the appropriate D matrices.

Since LM_1 and LM_2 can be negative for a specific application, especially when one or both variance components are small and close to zero, one can use the Gourieroux, Holly and Monfort (1982) (GHM) test which is given by

$$\chi_m^2 = \begin{cases} \text{LM}_1^2 + \text{LM}_2^2 & \text{if } \text{LM}_1 > 0,\ \text{LM}_2 > 0 \\ \text{LM}_1^2 & \text{if } \text{LM}_1 > 0,\ \text{LM}_2 \leqslant 0 \\ \text{LM}_2^2 & \text{if } \text{LM}_1 \leqslant 0,\ \text{LM}_2 > 0 \\ 0 & \text{if } \text{LM}_1 \leqslant 0,\ \text{LM}_2 \leqslant 0 \end{cases} \tag{9.52}$$

where χ_m^2 denotes the mixed χ^2 distribution. Under the null hypothesis

$$\chi_m^2 \sim \left(\tfrac{1}{4}\right)\chi^2(0) + \left(\tfrac{1}{2}\right)\chi^2(1) + \left(\tfrac{1}{4}\right)\chi^2(2)$$

where $\chi^2(0)$ equals zero with probability one.[11] The weights $(\frac{1}{4})$, $(\frac{1}{2})$ and $(\frac{1}{4})$ follow from the fact that LM_1 and LM_2 are asymptotically independent of each other and the results in Gourieroux, Holly and Monfort (1982). This proposed test has the advantage over the Honda and KW tests in that it is immune to the possible negative values of LM_1 and LM_2.

Baltagi, Chang and Li (1998) compare the performance of these tests using Monte Carlo experiments for an unbalanced two-way error component model. The results of the Monte Carlo experiments show that the nominal size of the Honda and King–Wu tests based on asymptotic critical values is inaccurate for all unbalanced patterns considered. However, the nominal size of the standardized version of these tests is closer to the true significance value and is recommended. This confirms similar results for the unbalanced one-way error component model by Moulton and Randolph (1989). In cases where at least one of the variance components is close to zero, the Gourieroux, Holly and Monfort (1982) test is found to perform well in Monte Carlo experiments and is recommended. All the tests considered have larger power as the number of individuals N in the panel and/or the variance components increase. In fact, for typical labor or consumer panels with large N, the Monte Carlo results show that the power of these tests is one except for cases where the variance components comprise less than 10% of the total variance.[12]

9.5 THE UNBALANCED NESTED ERROR COMPONENT MODEL

Baltagi, Song and Jung (2001) extend the ANOVA, MINQUE and MLE estimation procedures described in section 9.2 to the unbalanced nested error component regression model. For this model, the incomplete panel data exhibits a natural nested grouping. For example, data on firms may be grouped by industry, data on states by region, data on individuals by profession and data on students by schools.[13] The unbalanced panel data regression model is given by

$$y_{ijt} = x'_{ijt}\beta + u_{ijt} \quad i = 1, \ldots, M; \; j = 1, \ldots, N_i; \; t = 1, \ldots, T_i \tag{9.53}$$

where y_{ijt} could denote the output of the jth firm in the ith industry for the tth time period. x_{ijt} denotes a vector of k nonstochastic inputs. The disturbances are given by

$$u_{ijt} = \mu_i + \nu_{ij} + \varepsilon_{ijt} \quad i = 1, \ldots, M; \; j = 1, \ldots, N_i; \; t = 1, \ldots, T_i \tag{9.54}$$

where μ_i denotes the ith unobservable industry-specific effect which is assumed to be IID$(0, \sigma_\mu^2)$, ν_{ij} denotes the nested effect of the jth firm within the ith industry which is assumed to be IID$(0, \sigma_\nu^2)$ and ε_{ijt} denotes the remainder disturbance which is also assumed to be IID$(0, \sigma_\varepsilon^2)$. The μ_i's, ν_{ij}'s and ε_{ijt}'s are independent of each other and among themselves. This is a nested classification in that each successive component of the error term is imbedded or "nested" within the preceding component, see Graybill (1961, p. 350). This model allows for unequal number of firms in each industry as well as different number of observed time periods across industries. Detailed derivation of the variance–covariance matrix Ω, the Fuller and Battese (1973) transformation, as well as ANOVA, MINQUE and MLE methods are given in Baltagi, Song and Jung (2001) and will not be reproduced here. Baltagi, Song and Jung (2001) compared the performance of these estimators using Monte Carlo experiments. While the MLE and MIVQUE methods perform the best in estimating the variance components and the standard errors of the regression coefficients, the simple ANOVA methods perform just as well in estimating the regression coefficients. These estimation methods are also used to investigate the productivity of public capital in private production. In a companion paper, Baltagi, Song and Jung (1999) extend the Lagrange multiplier tests described in section 9.4 to this unbalanced nested error component model.

9.5.1 Empirical Example

In Chapter 2, example 3, we estimated a Cobb–Douglas production function investigating the productivity of public capital in each state's private output. This was based on a panel of 48 states over the period 1970–86. The data was provided by Munnell (1990). Here we group these states into nine geographical regions with the Middle Atlantic region for example containing three states: New York,

New Jersey and Pennsylvania and the Mountain region containing eight states: Montana, Idaho, Wyoming, Colorado, New Mexico, Arizona, Utah and Nevada. In this case, the primary group would be the regions, the nested group would be the states and these are observed over 17 years. The dependent variable y is the gross state product and the regressors include the private capital stock (K) computed by apportioning the Bureau of Economic Analysis (BEA) national estimates. The public capital stock is measured by its components: highways and streets (KH), water and sewer facilities (KW), and other public buildings and structures (KO), all based on the BEA national series. Labor (L) is measured by the employment in nonagricultural payrolls. The state unemployment rate is included to capture the business cycle in a given state. All variables except the unemployment rate are expressed in natural logarithm

$$y_{ijt} = \alpha + \beta_1 \mathrm{K}_{ijt} + \beta_2 \mathrm{KH}_{ijt} + \beta_3 \mathrm{KW}_{ijt} + \beta_4 \mathrm{KO}_{ijt} + \beta_5 \mathrm{L}_{ijt} + \beta_6 \text{ Unemp}_{ijt} + u_{it} \tag{9.55}$$

where $i = 1, 2, \ldots, 9$ regions, $j = 1, \ldots, N_i$ with N_i equaling three for the Middle Atlantic region and eight for the Mountain region and $t = 1, 2, \ldots, 17$. The data is unbalanced only in the differing number of states in each region. The disturbances follow the nested error component specification given by (9.54).

Table 9.2 gives the OLS, Within, ANOVA, MLE, REML and MIVQUE type estimates using this unbalanced nested error component model. The OLS estimates show that the highways and streets and water and sewer components of public capital have a positive and significant effect upon private output, whereas that of other public buildings and structures is not significant. Because OLS ignores the state and region effects, the corresponding standard errors and t-statistics are biased, see Moulton (1986). The Within estimator shows that the effect of KH and KW is insignificant, whereas that of KO is negative and significant. The primary region and nested state effects are significant using several LM tests developed in Baltagi, Song and Jung (1999). This justifies the application of the feasible GLS, MLE and MIVQUE methods. For the variance components estimates, there are no differences in the estimate of σ_ε^2. But estimates of σ_μ^2 and σ_ν^2 vary. $\widehat{\sigma}_\mu^2$ is as low as 0.0015 for SA and MLE and as high as 0.0029 for HFB. Similarly, $\widehat{\sigma}_\nu^2$ is as low as 0.0043 for SA and as high as 0.0069 for WK. This variation had little effect on estimates of the regression coefficients or their standard errors. For all estimators of the random effects model, the highways and streets and water and sewer components of public capital had a positive and significant effect, while the other public buildings and structures had a negative and significant effect upon private output.

Other empirical applications of the nested error component model include Montemarquette and Mahseredjian (1989) who studied whether schooling matters in educational achievements in Montreal's Francophone public elementary schools. Also, Antweiler (2001) who derived the maximum likelihood estimator for an unbalanced nested three-way error component model. This is applied to the problem of explaining the determinants of pollution concentration (measured by the log of atmospheric sulfuric dioxide) at 293 observation stations located

Table 9.2 Cobb–Douglas Production Function Estimates with Unbalanced Nested Error Components 1970–86: Nine Regions, 48 States*

Variable	OLS	Within	WH	WK	SA	HFB	MLE	REML	MV1	MV2	MV3
Intercept	1.926	—	2.082	2.131	2.089	2.084	2.129	2.127	2.083	2.114	2.127
	(0.053)	—	(0.152)	(0.160)	(0.144)	(0.150)	(0.154)	(0.157)	(0.152)	(0.154)	(0.156)
K	0.312	0.235	0.273	0.264	0.274	0.272	0.267	0.266	0.272	0.269	0.267
	(0.011)	(0.026)	(0.021)	(0.022)	(0.020)	(0.021)	(0.021)	(0.022)	(0.021)	(0.021)	(0.021)
L	0.550	0.801	0.742	0.758	0.740	0.743	0.754	0.756	0.742	0.750	0.755
	(0.016)	(0.030)	(0.026)	(0.027)	(0.025)	(0.026)	(0.026)	(0.026)	(0.026)	(0.026)	(0.026)
KH	0.059	0.077	0.075	0.072	0.073	0.075	0.071	0.072	0.075	0.072	0.072
	(0.015)	(0.031)	(0.023)	(0.024)	(0.022)	(0.022)	(0.023)	(0.023)	(0.023)	(0.023)	(0.023)
KW	0.119	0.079	0.076	0.076	0.076	0.076	0.076	0.076	0.076	0.076	0.076
	(0.012)	(0.015)	(0.014)	(0.014)	(0.014)	(0.014)	(0.014)	(0.014)	(0.014)	(0.014)	(0.014)
KO	0.009	−0.115	−0.095	−0.102	−0.094	−0.096	−0.100	−0.101	−0.095	−0.098	−0.100
	(0.012)	(0.018)	(0.017)	(0.017)	(0.017)	(0.017)	(0.017)	(0.017)	(0.017)	(0.017)	(0.017)
Unemp	−0.007	−0.005	−0.006	−0.006	−0.006	−0.006	−0.006	−0.006	−0.006	−0.006	−0.006
	(0.001)	(0.001)	(0.001)	(0.001)	(0.001)	(0.001)	(0.001)	(0.001)	(0.001)	(0.001)	(0.001)
σ_ε^2	0.0073	0.0013	0.0014	0.0014	0.0014	0.0014	0.0013	0.0014	0.0014	0.0014	0.0014
σ_μ^2	—	—	0.0027	0.0022	0.0015	0.0029	0.0015	0.0019	0.0027	0.0017	0.0017
σ_ν^2	—	—	0.0045	0.0069	0.0043	0.0044	0.0063	0.0064	0.0046	0.0056	0.0063

*The dependent variable is log of gross state product. Standard errors are given in parentheses
Source: Baltagi, Song and Jung (2001). Reproduced by permission of Elsevier Science Publishers B.V. (North-Holland)

in 44 countries over the time period 1971–96. This data is highly unbalanced in that out of a total of 2621 observations, about a third of these are from stations in one country, the United States. Also, the time period of observation is not necessarily continuous. Comparing the results of maximum likelihood for a nested vs a simple (non-nested) unbalanced error component model, Antweiler (2001) found that the scale elasticity coefficient estimate for the nested model is less than half that for the non-nested model. Scale elasticity is the coefficient of log of economic intensity as measured by GDP per square kilometer. This is also true for the estimate of the income effect which is negative and much lower in absolute value for the nested model than the non-nested model. Finally, the estimate of the composition effect which is the coefficient of the log of the country's capital abundance is higher for the nested model than for the non-nested model.

Davis (2001) applies OLS, Within, MIVQUE and MLE procedures to a three-way unbalanced error component model using data on film revenues for six movie theaters near New Haven, Connecticut observed over a six week period in 1998. Some of the reasons for unbalancedness in the data occur because (i) not all films are shown at all locations, (ii) films start and stop being shown at theaters during the observation period, and (iii) data on revenues are missing due to nonresponse. The estimates obtained reveal a complex set of asymmetric cross-theater price elasticities of demand. These estimates are useful for the analysis of the impact of mergers on pricing, and for determining the appropriate extent of geographic market definition in these markets.

NOTES

1. Other methods of dealing with missing data include: (i) imputing the missing values and analyzing the filled-in data by complete panel data methods; (ii) discarding the nonrespondents and weighting the respondents to compensate for the loss of cases; see Little (1988) and the section on nonresponse adjustments in Kasprzyk et al. (1989).
2. This analysis assumes that the observations of the individual with the shortest time series are nested in a specific manner within the observations of the other individuals. However, the same derivations apply for different types of overlapping observations.
3. Note that if the updated value is negative, it is replaced by zero and the iteration continues until the convergence criterion is satisfied.
4. It is important to note that ML and restricted ML estimates of the variance components are by definition non-negative. However, ANOVA and MINQUE methods can produce negative estimates of the variance component σ_μ^2. In these cases, the negative variance estimates are replaced by zero. This means that the resulting variance component estimator is $\widetilde{\sigma}_\mu^2 = \max(\widehat{\sigma}_\mu^2, 0)$ which is no longer unbiased.
5. Baltagi and Li (1990a) demonstrated analytically that for a random error component model, one can construct a simple unbiased estimator of the variance components using the entire unbalanced panel that is more efficient than the BQU estimator using only the sub-balanced pattern (see problem 9.5). Also, Chowdhury (1991) showed that for the fixed effects error component model, the Within estimator based on the entire unbalanced panel is efficient relative to any Within estimator based on a sub-balanced pattern. Mátyás and Lovrics (1991) performed some Monte Carlo

experiments to compare the loss in efficiency of Within and GLS based on the entire incomplete panel data and complete subpanel. They found the loss in efficiency is negligible if $NT > 250$, but serious for $NT < 150$.

6. The variable descriptions are from Table IV of Harrison and Rubinfeld (1978). See Belsley, Kuh and Welsch (1980) for a listing of the data and further diagnostic analysis of these data. Moulton (1986) used these data to show the inappropriate use of OLS in the presence of random group effects and Moulton (1987) applied a battery of diagnostic tools to this data set.
7. Later, Moulton and Randolph (1989) found that asymptotic critical values of the one-sided LM test can be very poor, and suggested a standardized LM test whose asymptotic critical value approximations are likely to be much better than those of the LM statistic. They applied it to this data set and rejected the null hypothesis of no random group effect using an exact critical value.
8. Note that the Amemiya-type estimator is not calculated for this data set since there are some regressors without Within variation.
9. Another application of unbalanced panels includes the construction of a number of quality adjusted price indexes for personal computers in the USA over the period 1989–92, see Berndt, Griliches and Rappaport (1995).
10. If the data were arranged differently, one would get the generalized inverse of an $(N \times N)$ matrix rather than that of a $(T \times T)$ one such as P. Since $N > T$ in most cases, this choice is most favorable from the point of view of computations.
11. Critical values for the mixed $\chi^2_{\rm m}$ are $7.289, 4.321$ and 2.952 for $\alpha = 0.01, 0.05$ and 0.1, respectively.
12. A GAUSS program for testing individual and time effects using unbalanced panel data is given in the Appendix of Baltagi, Chang and Li (1998, pp. 16–19).
13. See problem 3.14 for an introduction to the balanced nested error component model.

PROBLEMS

9.1 (a) Show that the variance–covariance matrix of the disturbances in (9.1) is given by (9.2).

(b) Show that the two nonzero block matrices in (9.2) can be written as in (9.3).

(c) Show that $\sigma_\nu \Omega_j^{-1/2} y_j$ has a typical element $(y_{jt} - \theta_j \bar{y}_{j.})$, where $\theta_j = 1 - \sigma_\nu/\omega_j$ and $\omega_j^2 = T_j\sigma_\mu^2 + \sigma_\nu^2$.

9.2 (a) Verify the $E(\widehat{q}_1)$ and $E(\widehat{q}_2)$ equations given in (9.16).

(b) Verify $E(\widetilde{q}_1)$ and $E(\widetilde{q}_2)$ given in (9.17).

(c) Verify $E(\hat{q}_2^b)$ given in (9.19).

9.3 Using the Monte Carlo setup for the unbalanced one-way error component model considered by Baltagi and Chang (1994), compare the various estimators of the variance components and the regression coefficients considered in section 9.2.4.

9.4 Using the Harrison and Rubinfeld (1978) data published in Belsley, Kuh and Welsch (1980) and provided on the Wiley web site as Hedonic.xls, reproduce Table 9.1.

9.5 This exercise is based on problem 90.2.3 in *Econometric Theory* by Baltagi and Li (1990a). Consider the following unbalanced one-way analysis of variance model:

$$y_{it} = \mu_i + \nu_{it} \quad i = 1, \ldots, N;\ t = 1, 2, \ldots, T_i$$

where for simplicity's sake no explanatory variables are included. y_{it} could be the output of firm i at time period t and μ_i could be the managerial ability of firm i, whereas ν_{it} is a remainder disturbance term. Assume that $\mu_i \sim \text{IIN}(0, \sigma_\mu^2)$ and $\nu_{it} \sim \text{IIN}(0, \sigma_\nu^2)$ independent of each other. Let T be the maximum overlapping period over which a complete panel could be established ($T \leqslant T_i$ for all i). In this case the corresponding vector of balanced observations on y_{it} is denoted by y_b and is of dimension NT. One could estimate the variance components using this complete panel as follows:

$$\widehat{\sigma}_\nu^2 = y_b'(I_N \otimes E_T)y_b/N(T-1)$$

and

$$\sigma_\mu^2 = [y_b'(I_N \otimes \bar{J}_T)y_b/NT] - (\widehat{\sigma}_\nu^2/T)$$

where $E_T = I_T - \bar{J}_T$, $\bar{J}_T = J_T/T$ and J_T is a matrix of ones of dimension T. $\widehat{\sigma}_\nu^2$ and $\widehat{\sigma}_\mu^2$ are the best quadratic unbiased estimators (BQUE) of the variance components based on the complete panel (see Balestra, 1973). Alternatively, one could estimate the variance components from the entire unbalanced panel as follows:

$$\widetilde{\sigma}_\nu^2 = y' \operatorname{diag}(E_{T_i})y/(n-N)$$

where $n = \sum_{i=1}^N T_i$ and $E_{T_i} = I_{T_i} - \bar{J}_{T_i}$. Also, $\sigma_i^2 = (T_i\sigma_\mu^2 + \sigma_\nu^2)$ can be estimated by $\widetilde{\sigma}_i^2 = y_i'\bar{J}_{T_i}y_i$, where y_i denotes the vector of T_i observations on the ith individual. Therefore, there are N estimators of σ_μ^2 obtained from $(\widetilde{\sigma}_i^2 - \widetilde{\sigma}_\nu^2)/T_i$ for $i = 1, \ldots, N$. One simple way of combining them is to take the average

$$\widetilde{\sigma}_\mu^2 = \sum_{i=1}^N [(\widetilde{\sigma}_i^2 - \widetilde{\sigma}_\nu^2)/T_i]/N = \left\{ y' \operatorname{diag}[\bar{J}_{T_i}/T_i]y - \sum_{i=1}^N \widetilde{\sigma}_\nu^2/T_i \right\}/N$$

(a) Show that $\widetilde{\sigma}_\nu^2$ and $\widetilde{\sigma}_\mu^2$ are unbiased estimators of σ_ν^2 and σ_μ^2.
(b) Show that $\text{var}(\widetilde{\sigma}_\nu^2) \leqslant \text{var}(\widehat{\sigma}_\nu^2)$ and $\text{var}(\widetilde{\sigma}_\mu^2) \leqslant \text{var}(\widehat{\sigma}_\mu^2)$. (Hint: See solution 90.2.3 in *Econometric Theory* by Koning (1991).)

9.6 For $X = (X_1, X_2)$, the generalized inverse of $(X'X)$ is given by

$$(X'X)^- = \begin{bmatrix} (X_1'X_1)^- & 0 \\ 0 & 0 \end{bmatrix} + \begin{bmatrix} -(X_1'X_1)^- X_1'X_2 \\ I \end{bmatrix} \times (X_2'Q_{[X_1]}X_2)^-[-X_2'X_1(X_1'X_1)^- \ \ I]$$

see Davis (2001, Appendix A). Use this result to show that $P_{[X]} = P_{[X_1]} + P_{[Q_{[X_1]}X_2]}$. (Hint: Premultiply this expression by X, and postmultiply by X'.) This verifies (9.29).

9.7 Consider the three-way error component model described in problem 3.15. The panel data can be unbalanced and the matrices of dummy variables are $\Delta = [\Delta_1, \Delta_2, \Delta_3]$ with

$$u = \Delta_1\mu + \Delta_2\lambda + \Delta_3\eta + \nu$$

where μ, λ and ν are random variables defined below (9.31) and the added random error η has mean zero and variance σ_η^2. All random errors are independent among themselves and with each other. Show that $P_{[\Delta]} = P_{[A]} + P_{[B]} + P_{[C]}$ where $A = \Delta_1$, $B = Q_{[A]}\Delta_2$ and $C = Q_{[B]}Q_{[A]}\Delta_3$. This is Corollary 1 of Davis (2001). (Hint: Apply (9.29) twice. Let $X_1 = \Delta_1$ and $X_2 = (\Delta_2, \Delta_3)$. Using problem 9.6, we get $P_{[X]} = P_{[\Delta_1]} + P_{[Q_{[\Delta_1]}X_2]}$. Now, $Q_{[\Delta_1]}X_2 = Q_{[\Delta_1]}(\Delta_2, \Delta_3) = [B, Q_{[A]}\Delta_3]$. Applying (9.29) again we get $P_{[B, Q_{[A]}\Delta_3]} = P_{[B]} + P_{[Q_{[B]}Q_{[A]}\Delta_3]}$.)

9.8 (a) For Δ_1 and Δ_2 defined in (9.28), verify that $\Delta_N \equiv \Delta_1'\Delta_1 = \text{diag}[T_i]$ and $\Delta_T \equiv \Delta_2'\Delta_2 = \text{diag}[N_t]$. Show that for the complete panel data case $\Delta_1 = \iota_T \otimes I_N$, $\Delta_2 = I_T \otimes \iota_N$, $\Delta_N = TI_N$ and $\Delta_T = NI_T$.
(b) Under the complete panel data case, verify that $\Delta_{TN} \equiv \Delta_2'\Delta_1$ is J_{TN} and $Q = E_T \otimes E_N$, see Chapter 3, (3.3) and problem 3.1.
(c) Let $X = (X_1, X_2)$ with $|I + XX'| \neq 0$. Using the result that $[I_n + XX']^{-1} = I_n - X(I + X'X)^{-1}X'$, apply the partitioned inverse formula for matrices to show that $(I + XX')^{-1} =, \widetilde{Q}_{[X_2]} - \widetilde{Q}_{[X_2]}X_1S^{-1}X_1'\widetilde{Q}_{[X_2]}$ where $\widetilde{Q}_{[X_2]} = I - X_2(I + X_2'X_2)^{-1}X_2' = (I + X_2X_2')^{-1}$ and $S = I + X_1'\widetilde{Q}_{[X_2]}X_1$. This is lemma 2 of Davis (2001).
(d) Apply the results in part (c) using $X = (\frac{\sigma_\mu}{\sigma_\nu}\Delta_1, \frac{\sigma_\lambda}{\sigma_\nu}\Delta_2)$ to verify Σ^{-1} given in (9.33). Hint: Show that $V = \widetilde{Q}_{\Delta_1}$ and $S = \phi_2 P^*$.
(e) Derive $E(q_W)$, $E(q_N)$ and $E(q_T)$ given in (9.34), (9.35) and (9.36).

9.9 Using the Monte Carlo setup for the unbalanced two-way error component model considered by Wansbeek and Kapteyn (1989), compare the MSE performance of the variance components and the regression coefficients estimates.

9.10 Assuming normality on the disturbances, verify (9.37), (9.40) and (9.41).

9.11 Verify that the King and Wu (1997) test for the unbalanced two-way error component model is given by (9.49).

9.12 Verify that the SLM version of the KW and HO tests is given by (9.47) with D defined in (9.50) and (9.51).

10
Special Topics

10.1 MEASUREMENT ERROR AND PANEL DATA

Micro panel data on households, individuals and firms are highly likely to exhibit measurement error. In Chapter 1, we cited Duncan and Hill (1985) who found serious measurement error in average hourly earnings in the Panel Study of Income Dynamics (PSID). This got worse for a two-year recall as compared to a one-year recall. Bound et al. (1990) use two validation data sets to study the extent of measurement error in labor market variables. The first data set is the Panel Study of Income Dynamics Validation Study (PSIDVS) which uses a two-wave panel survey taken in 1983 and 1987 from a single large manufacturing company. The second data set matches panel data on earnings from the 1977 and 1978 waves of the US Current Population Survey (CPS) to Social Security earnings records for those same individuals. They find that biases from measurement errors could be very serious for hourly wages and unemployment spells, but not severe for annual earnings.[1] In analyzing data from household budget surveys, total expenditure and income are known to contain measurement error. Aasness, Biorn and Skjerpen (1993) estimate a system of consumer expenditure functions from a Norwegian panel of households over the years 1975–77. The hypothesis of no measurement error in total expenditure is soundly rejected and substantial biases in Engle function elasticities are found when measurement error in total expenditure is ignored. Altonji and Siow (1987) find that measurement error in micro panel data sets has a strong influence on the relationship between consumption and income. Based on data from the 1968–81 PSID individuals tape, they show that ignoring the measurement error in the income process, a Keynesian model of consumption cannot be rejected. However, when one accounts for this measurement error, the results are supportive of the rational expectations life-cycle model of consumption and reject the Keynesian model.

Econometric textbooks emphasize that measurement error in the explanatory variables results in bias and inconsistency of the OLS estimates, and the solution typically involves the existence of *extraneous* instrumental variables or additional assumptions to identify the model parameters (see Maddala, 1977). Using panel data, Griliches and Hausman (1986) showed that one can identify and estimate a variety of errors in variables models *without* the use of external instruments. Let us illustrate their approach with a simple regression with random individual effects:

$$y_{it} = \alpha + \beta x_{it}^* + u_{it} \quad i = 1, \ldots, N;\ t = 1, \ldots, T \tag{10.1}$$

where the error follows a one-way error component model

$$u_{it} = \mu_i + \nu_{it} \tag{10.2}$$

and the x_{it}^* are observed only with error

$$x_{it} + x_{it}^* = \eta_{it} \tag{10.3}$$

In this case, $\mu_i \sim \text{IID}(0, \sigma_\mu^2)$, $\nu_{it} \sim \text{IID}(0, \sigma_\nu^2)$ and $\eta_{it} \sim \text{IID}(0, \sigma_\eta^2)$ are all independent of each other. Additionally, x_{it}^* is independent of u_{it} and η_{it}. In terms of observable variables, the model becomes

$$y_{it} = \alpha + \beta x_{it} + \epsilon_{it} \tag{10.4}$$

where

$$\epsilon_{it} = \mu_i + \nu_{it} - \beta \eta_{it} \tag{10.5}$$

It is clear that OLS on (10.4) is inconsistent, since x_{it} is correlated with η_{it} and therefore ϵ_{it}. We follow Wansbeek and Koning (1989) by assuming that the variance–covariance matrix of x denoted by $\Sigma_x(T \times T)$ is the same across individuals, but otherwise of general form over time. In vector form, the model becomes

$$y = \alpha \iota_{NT} + x\beta + \epsilon \tag{10.6}$$

with

$$\epsilon = (\iota_T \otimes \mu) + \nu - \beta\eta \quad \mu' = (\mu_1, \ldots, \mu_N)$$

$$\nu = (\nu_{11}, \ldots, \nu_{N1}, \ldots, \nu_{1T}, \ldots, \nu_{NT})$$

and

$$\eta' = (\eta_{11}, \ldots, \eta_{N1}, \ldots, \eta_{1T}, \ldots, \eta_{NT})$$

Note that the data are ordered such that the faster index is over individuals. Now consider any matrix P that wipes out the individual effects. P must satisfy $P\iota_T = 0$ and let $Q = P'P$. For example, $P = I_T - (\iota_T\iota_T'/T)$ is one such matrix, and the resulting estimator is the Within estimator. In general, for any Q, the estimator of β is given by

$$\begin{aligned}\widehat{\beta} &= x'(Q \otimes I_N)y/x'(Q \otimes I_N)x \\ &= \beta + x'(Q \otimes I_N)(\nu - \beta\eta)/x'(Q \otimes I_N)x \end{aligned} \tag{10.7}$$

For a fixed T, taking probability limits as the limit of expectations of the numerator and denominator as $N \to \infty$, we get

$$\frac{1}{N}E[x'(Q \otimes I_N)(\nu - \beta\eta)] = -\frac{1}{N}\beta \operatorname{tr}[(Q \otimes I_N)E(\eta\eta')] = -\beta\sigma_\eta^2 \operatorname{tr} Q$$

$$\frac{1}{N}E[x'(Q \otimes I_N)x] = \frac{1}{N} \operatorname{tr}[(Q \otimes I_N)(\Sigma_x \otimes I_N)] = \operatorname{tr} Q\Sigma_x$$

and

$$\begin{aligned}\text{plim}\,\widehat{\beta} &= \beta - \beta\sigma_\eta^2(\text{tr}\,Q/\text{tr}\,Q\Sigma_x) \\ &= \beta(1-\sigma_\eta^2\phi)\end{aligned} \tag{10.8}$$

where $\phi \equiv (\text{tr}\,Q/\text{tr}\,Q\Sigma_x) > 0$. Griliches and Hausman (1986) used various Q transformations like the Within estimator and difference estimators to show that although these transformations wipe out the individual effect, they may aggravate the measurement error bias. Also, consistent estimators of β and σ_η^2 can be obtained by combining these inconsistent estimators. There are actually $\frac{1}{2}T(T-1)-1$ linearly independent Q transformations. Let Q_1 and Q_2 be two choices for Q and $\phi_i = \text{tr}(Q_i)/\text{tr}(Q_i\Sigma_x)$ be the corresponding choices for ϕ, for $i=1,2$. Then $\text{plim}\,\widehat{\beta}_i = \beta(1-\sigma_\eta^2\phi_i)$, and by replacing $\text{plim}\,\widehat{\beta}_i$ by $\widehat{\beta}_i$ itself, one can solve these two equations in two unknowns to get

$$\widehat{\beta} = \frac{\phi_1\widehat{\beta}_2 - \phi_2\widehat{\beta}_1}{\phi_1-\phi_2} \tag{10.9}$$

and

$$\widehat{\sigma}_\eta^2 = \frac{\widehat{\beta}_2 - \widehat{\beta}_1}{\phi_1\widehat{\beta}_2 - \phi_2\widehat{\beta}_1} \tag{10.10}$$

In order to make these estimators operational, ϕ_i is replaced by $\widehat{\phi}_i$, where $\widehat{\phi}_i = \text{tr}(Q_i)/\text{tr}(Q_i\widehat{\Sigma}_x)$. Note that $P = I_T - (\iota_T\iota_T')/T$ yields the Within estimator, while $P = L'$, where L' is the $(T-1)\times T$ matrix defined in Chapter 8, yields the first-difference estimator. Other P matrices suggested by Griliches and Hausman (1986) are based on differencing the data j periods apart, $(y_{it} - y_{i,t-j})$, thus generating "different length" difference estimators. The remaining question is how to combine these consistent estimators of β into an efficient estimator of β. The generalized method of moments (GMM) approach can be used and this is based upon fourth-order moments of the data. Alternatively, under normality one can derive the asymptotic covariance matrix of the $\widehat{\beta}_i$ which can be consistently estimated by second-order moments of the data. Using the latter approach, Wansbeek and Koning (1989) showed that for m different consistent estimators of β given by $b = (\widehat{\beta}_1,\ldots,\widehat{\beta}_m)'$ based on m different Q_i

$$\sqrt{N}[b - \beta(\iota_m - \sigma_\eta^2\phi)] \sim N(0,V)$$

where

$$\begin{aligned}\phi &= (\phi_1,\ldots,\phi_m)' \\ V &= F'\{\sigma_\nu^2\Sigma_x \otimes I_T + \beta^2\sigma_\eta^2(\Sigma_x + \sigma_\eta^2 I_N)\otimes I_T\}F\end{aligned} \tag{10.11}$$

and F is the $(T^2\times m)$ matrix with ith column $f_i = \text{vec}\,Q_i/(\text{tr}\,Q_i\Sigma_x)$. By minimizing $[b-\beta(\iota_m - \sigma_\eta^2\phi)]'V^{-1}[b-\beta(\iota_m-\sigma_\eta^2\phi)]$ one gets the asymptotically efficient estimators (as far as they are based on b) of β and σ_v^2 given by

$$\widehat{\beta} = \left\{ \frac{\phi'\widehat{V}^{-1}b}{\phi'\widehat{V}^{-1}\phi} - \frac{\iota'\widehat{V}^{-1}b}{\iota'\widehat{V}^{-1}\phi} \right\} \Big/ \left\{ \frac{\phi'\widehat{V}^{-1}\iota}{\phi'\widehat{V}^{-1}\phi} - \frac{\iota'\widehat{V}^{-1}\iota}{\iota'\widehat{V}^{-1}\phi} \right\} \tag{10.12}$$

and

$$\widehat{\sigma}_v^2 = \left\{ \frac{\phi'\widehat{V}^{-1}\iota}{\phi'\widehat{V}^{-1}b} - \frac{\iota'\widehat{V}^{-1}\iota}{\iota'\widehat{V}^{-1}b} \right\} \Big/ \left\{ \frac{\phi'\widehat{V}^{-1}\phi}{\phi'\widehat{V}^{-1}b} - \frac{\iota'\widehat{V}^{-1}\phi}{\iota'\widehat{V}^{-1}b} \right\} \tag{10.13}$$

with $\sqrt{N}(\widehat{\beta} - \beta, \widehat{\sigma}_v^2 - \sigma_v^2)$ asymptotically distributed as $N(0, W)$ and

$$W = \frac{1}{\Delta} \begin{bmatrix} \beta^2\phi'V^{-1}\phi & \beta(\iota_m - \sigma_\eta^2\phi)'V^{-1}\phi \\ & (\iota_m - \sigma_\eta^2\phi)'V^{-1}(\iota_m - \sigma_\eta^2\phi) \end{bmatrix} \tag{10.14}$$

where

$$\Delta = \beta^2(\iota_m - \sigma_\eta^2\phi)'V^{-1}(\iota_m - \sigma_\eta^2\phi)(\phi'V^{-1}\phi) - \beta^2[\phi'V^{-1}(\iota_m - \sigma_\eta^2\phi)]^2 \tag{10.15}$$

Griliches and Hausman (1986) argue that their results can be extended to the case of several independent variables provided that the measurement errors in the explanatory variables are mutually uncorrelated, or correlated with a known correlation structure. Under some stringent assumptions these results can be extended to the case of serially correlated η_{it}. Griliches and Hausman (1986) illustrate their approach by estimating a labor demand relationship using data on $N = 1242$ US manufacturing firms over six years (1972–77) drawn from the National Bureau of Economic Research R&D panel. Chowdhury and Nickell (1985) is another early panel data application taking into account omitted individual effects and measurement error in the context of an earnings equation. For some recent applications of measurement error in panel data, see Hamermesh (1989) for the case of academic salaries in the USA, Björklund (1989) for the case of job mobility in Sweden and Abowd and Card (1989) on the covariance structure of earnings and hours changes. Extensions of this model to the case where the measurement error itself follows an error component structure are given by Biorn (1992). Biorn (1996) also gives an extensive treatment for the case where the model disturbances u_{it} in (10.1) are white noise, i.e. without any error component, and the case where η_{it}, the measurement error, is autocorrelated over time. For all cases considered, Biorn derives the asymptotic bias of the Within, Between, various difference estimators and the GLS estimator as either N or T tend to ∞. Biorn shows how the different panel data transformations implied by these estimators affect measurement error differently. Biorn and Klette (1998) consider GMM estimation of a simple static panel data regression with errors in variables, as described in (10.4). Assuming μ_i to be fixed effects and the measurement error to be not autocorrelated, Biorn and Klette show that only the one-period and a few two-period differences are essential, i.e. relevant for GMM estimation. The total number of orthogonality conditions is $T(T-1)(T-2)/2$ while the essential set of orthogonality conditions is only a fraction $2/(T-1)$ of the complete set, i.e. $T(T-2)$. Among these essential conditions, $(T-1)(T-2)$ are based on one-period differences, and $(T-2)$ on two-period differences. Exploiting only the nonredundant moment conditions reduces the computational burden considerably. For a moderate size panel with $T = 9$, the essential moment conditions are one-fourth of the complete set of orthogonality conditions and involve inverting a 63×63 matrix rather than a 252×252 matrix to compute GMM. Biorn (2000) proposes GMM estimators that use either (A) equations in differences with level values as instruments, or (B) equations in levels with differenced values as instruments. The conditions needed for the consistency of the (B) procedures under individual heterogeneity are stronger than for the (A) procedures. These procedures are illustrated for a simple regression of log of gross production on log of material input for the manufacture of textiles. The data uses $N = 215$ firms observed over $T = 8$ years (1983–90) and obtained from the annual Norwegian manufacturing census. For this empirical illustration, Biorn shows that adding the essential two-period difference orthogonality conditions to the one-period conditions in the GMM algorithm may significantly increase estimation efficiency. However, redundant orthogonality conditions are of little practical use. Overall, the GMM estimates based on the level equations are more precise than those based on differenced equations. Wansbeek and Kapteyn (1992) consider simple estimators for *dynamic* panel data models with measurement error; Kao and Schnell (1987a, b) study the fixed effects logit model and the random effects probit model for panel data with measurement error; and Hsiao (1991) provides identification conditions for binary choice errors in variables models as well as conditions for consistency and asymptotic normality of the maximum likelihood estimators when the explanatory variables are unbounded.

10.2 ROTATING PANELS

Biorn (1981) considers the case of rotating panels, where in order to keep the *same* number of households in the survey, the fraction of households that drops from the sample in the second period is replaced by an equal number of new households that are freshly surveyed. This is a necessity in survey panels where the same household may not want to be interviewed again and again. In the study by Biorn and Jansen (1983) based on data from the Norwegian household budget surveys, half the sample is rotated in each period. In other words, half the households surveyed drop from the sample each period and are replaced by new households.[2] To illustrate the basics of rotating panels, let us assume that $T = 2$ and that half the sample is being rotated each period. In this case, without loss of generality, households $1, 2, \ldots, N/2$ are replaced by households $N + 1, N + 2, \ldots, N + N/2$ in period 2. It is clear that only households $N/2 + 1, N/2 + 2, \ldots, N$ are observed over two periods.[3] In this case there are $3N/2$ distinct households, only $N/2$ households of which are observed for two periods. In our case, the first and last $N/2$ households surveyed are only observed for one period. Now consider the usual one-way error component model

$$u_{it} = \mu_i + \nu_{it}$$

with $\mu_i \sim \text{IID}(0, \sigma_\mu^2)$ and $\nu_{it} \sim \text{IID}(0, \sigma_\nu^2)$ independent of each other and the x_{it}. Order the observations such that the faster index is that of households and the slower index is that of time. This is different from the ordering we used in Chapter 2. In this case, $u' = (u_{11}, u_{21}, \ldots, u_{N1}, u_{N/2+1,2}, \ldots, u_{3N/2,2})$ and

$$E(uu') = \Omega = \begin{bmatrix} \sigma^2 I_{N/2} & 0 & 0 & 0 \\ 0 & \sigma^2 I_{N/2} & \sigma_\mu^2 I_{N/2} & 0 \\ 0 & \sigma_\mu^2 I_{N/2} & \sigma^2 I_{N/2} & 0 \\ 0 & 0 & 0 & \sigma^2 I_{N/2} \end{bmatrix} \tag{10.16}$$

where $\sigma^2 = \sigma_\mu^2 + \sigma_\nu^2$. It is easy to see that Ω is block-diagonal and that the middle block has the usual error component model form $\sigma_\mu^2(J_2 \otimes I_{N/2}) + \sigma_\nu^2(I_2 \otimes I_{N/2})$. Therefore

$$\Omega^{-1/2} = \begin{bmatrix} \frac{1}{\sigma} I_{N/2} & 0 & 0 \\ 0 & \left(\frac{1}{\sigma_1^*}\bar{J}_2 + \frac{1}{\sigma_\nu}E_2\right) \otimes I_{N/2} & 0 \\ 0 & 0 & \frac{1}{\sigma} I_{N/2} \end{bmatrix} \tag{10.17}$$

where $E_2 = I_2 - \bar{J}_2$, $\bar{J}_2 = J_2/2$ and $\sigma_1^{*2} = 2\sigma_\mu^2 + \sigma_\nu^2$. By premultiplying the regression model by $\Omega^{-1/2}$ and performing OLS one gets the GLS estimator of the rotating panel. In this case, one divides the first and last $N/2$ observations by σ. For the middle N observations, with $i = (N/2) + 1, \ldots, N$ and $t = 1, 2$, quasi-demeaning similar to the usual error component transformation is performed, i.e. $(y_{it} - \theta^* \bar{y}_{i.})/\sigma_\nu$ with $\theta^* = 1 - (\sigma_\nu/\sigma_1^*)$ and $\bar{y}_{i.} = (y_{i1} + y_{i2})/2$. A similar transformation is also performed on the regressors. In order to make this GLS estimator feasible, we need estimates of σ_μ^2 and σ_ν^2. One consistent estimator of σ_ν^2 can be obtained from the middle N observations or simply the households that are observed over two periods. For these observations, σ_ν^2 is estimated consistently from the Within residuals

$$\widetilde{\sigma}_\nu^2 = \sum_{t=1}^{2} \sum_{i=N/2+1}^{N} [(y_{it} - \bar{y}_{i.}) - (x_{it} - \bar{x}_{i.})'\widetilde{\beta}_{\text{Within}}]^2/N \tag{10.18}$$

whereas the total variance can be estimated consistently from the least squares mean square error over the entire sample

$$\widetilde{\sigma}^2 = \widetilde{\sigma}_\nu^2 + \widetilde{\sigma}_\mu^2 = \sum_{t=1}^{2} \sum_{i=1}^{3N/2} (y_{it} - x_{it}'\widehat{\beta}_{\text{OLS}})^2/(3N/2) \tag{10.19}$$

Note that we could have reordered the data such that households observed over one period are stacked on top of households observed over two time periods. This way the rotating panel problem becomes an unbalanced panel problem with N households observed over one period and $N/2$ households observed for two periods. In fact, except for this different way of ordering the observations, one can handle the estimation as in Chapter 9.

This feasible GLS estimation can easily be derived for other rotating schemes. In fact, the reader is asked to do that for $T = 3$ with $N/2$ households rotated every period, and $T = 3$ with $N/3$ households rotated every period (see problem 10.2). For the estimation of more general rotation schemes as well as maximum likelihood estimation under normality, see Biorn (1981). The analysis of rotating panels can also easily be extended to a set of seemingly unrelated regressions, simultaneous equations or a dynamic model. Biorn and Jansen (1983) consider a rotating panel of 418 Norwegian households, one half of which are observed in 1975 and 1976 and the other half in 1976 and 1977. They estimate a complete system of consumer demand functions using maximum likelihood procedures. Nijman, Verbeek and van Soest (1991) consider the optimal choice of the rotation period for the estimation of linear combinations of period means.

Rotating panels allow the researcher to test for the existence of "time-in-sample" bias effects mentioned in Chapter 1. These correspond to a significant change in response between the initial interview and a subsequent interview when one would expect the same response.[4] With rotating panels, the fresh group of individuals added to the panel with each wave provides a means of testing for time-in-sample bias effects. Provided that all other survey conditions remain constant for all rotation groups at a particular wave, one can compare these various rotation groups (for that wave) to measure the extent of rotation group bias. This has been done for various labor force characteristics in the Current Population Survey. For example, several studies have found that the first rotation reported an unemployment rate that is 10% higher than that of the full sample (see Bailar, 1975; Solon, 1986). While the findings indicate a pervasive effect of rotation group bias in panel surveys, the survey conditions do not remain the same in practice and hence it is hard to disentangle the effects of time-in-sample bias from other effects.

10.3 PSEUDO-PANELS

For some countries, panel data may not exist. Instead the researcher may find annual household surveys based on a large random sample of the population. Examples of some of these cross-sectional consumer expenditure surveys include: the British Family Expenditure Survey which surveys about 7000 households annually, and also a number of household surveys from less developed countries like the World Bank's poverty net inventory of household surveys. This is available at http://www.world.bank.org/poverty/data/index.htm. Examples of repeated surveys in the USA include the Current Population Survey, the National Health Interview Survey, the Consumer Expenditure Survey, the National Crime Survey, the Monthly Retail Trade Survey and the Survey of Manufacturers' Shipments, Inventories and Orders. See Bailar (1989) for the corresponding data sources. Also, the adult education and lifelong learning surveys and the early childhood program participation surveys available from the National Center for Education Statistics at http://nces.ed.gov/surveys/. The general social survey available from the National Opinion Research Center at http://www.norc.uchicago.edu/gss/homepage.htm and the survey of small business finances from the Federal Reserve Board at http://www.federalreserve.gov/ssbf/, to mention a few. For these repeated cross-section surveys, it may be impossible to track the same household over time as required in a genuine panel. Instead, Deaton (1985) suggests tracking cohorts and estimating economic relationships based on cohort means rather than individual observations. One cohort could be the set of all males born between 1945 and 1950. This age cohort is well defined, and can easily be identified from the data. Deaton (1985) argued that these pseudo-panels do not suffer the attrition problem that plagues genuine panels, and may be available over longer time periods compared to genuine panels.[5] In order to illustrate the basic ideas involved in constructing a pseudo-panel, we start with the set of T independent cross-sections given by

$$y_{it} = x_{it}'\beta + \mu_i + \nu_{it} \quad t = 1, \ldots, T \tag{10.20}$$

Note that the individual subscript i corresponds to a new and most likely different set of N individuals in each period. For ease of exposition, we assume the same number of households N is randomly surveyed each period. Define a set of C cohorts, each with a fixed membership that remains the same throughout the entire period of observation. Each individual observed in the survey belongs to exactly one cohort. Averaging the observations over individuals in each cohort, one gets

$$\bar{y}_{ct} = \bar{x}_{ct}'\beta + \bar{\mu}_{ct} + \bar{\nu}_{ct} \quad c = 1, \ldots, C;\ t = 1, \ldots, T \tag{10.21}$$

where $\bar{y}_{ct}$ is the average of y_{it} over all individuals belonging to cohort c at time t. Since the economic relationship for the individual includes an individual fixed effect, the corresponding relationship for the cohort will also include a fixed cohort effect. However, $\bar{\mu}_{ct}$ now varies with t, because it is averaged over a different number of individuals belonging to cohort c at time t. These $\bar{\mu}_{ct}$ are most likely correlated with the x_{it} and a random effect specification will lead to inconsistent estimates. On the other hand, treating the $\bar{\mu}_{ct}$ as fixed effects leads to an identification problem, unless $\bar{\mu}_{ct} = \bar{\mu}_c$ and is invariant over time. The latter assumption is plausible if the number of observations in each cohort is very large. In this case

$$\bar{y}_{ct} = \bar{x}_{ct}'\beta + \bar{\mu}_c + \bar{\nu}_{ct} \quad c = 1, \ldots, C;\ t = 1, \ldots, T \tag{10.22}$$

For this pseudo-panel with T observations on C cohorts, the fixed effects estimator $\widetilde{\beta}_W$, based on the Within cohort transformation $\widetilde{y}_{ct} = \bar{y}_{ct} - \bar{y}_c$, is a natural candidate for estimating β. Note that the cohort population means are genuine panels in that, at the population level, the groups contain the same individuals over time. However, as Deaton (1985) argued, the sample-based averages of the cohort means, $\bar{y}_{ct}$, can only estimate the unobserved population cohort means with measurement error. Therefore, one has to correct the Within estimator for measurement error using estimates of the errors in measurement variance–covariance matrix obtained from the individual survey data. Details are given in

Deaton (1985), Verbeek (1996) and Verbeek and Nijman (1993). Deaton (1985) shows that his proposed measurement error corrected within-groups estimator for the static model with individual effects is consistent for a fixed number of observations per cohort. Verbeek and Nijman (1993) modify Deaton's estimator to achieve consistency for a fixed number of time periods and a fixed number of individuals per cohort. If the number of individuals in each cohort is large, so that the average cohort size $n_c = N/C$ tends to infinity, then the measurement errors as well as their estimates tend to zero and the Within cohort estimator of β is asymptotically identical to Deaton's (1985) estimator of β, denoted by $\widetilde{\beta}_{\mathrm{D}}$. In fact, when n_c is large, most applied researchers ignore the measurement error problem and compute the Within cohort estimator of β (see Browning, Deaton and Irish, 1985).

There is an obvious trade-off in the construction of a pseudo-panel. The larger the number of cohorts, the smaller the number of individuals per cohort. In this case, C is large and the pseudo-panel is based on a large number of observations. However, the fact that n_c is not large implies that the sample cohort averages are not precise estimates of the population cohort means. In this case, we have a large number C of imprecise observations. In contrast, a pseudo-panel constructed with a smaller number of cohorts (C) and therefore more individuals per cohort (n_c) is trading a large pseudo-panel with imprecise observations for a smaller pseudo-panel with more precise observations. Verbeek and Nijman (1992b) study the consistency properties of the above two estimators as the number of cohorts C, the number of individuals per cohort n_c, and N and T are fixed or tend to infinity. They find that $n_c \to \infty$ is a crucial condition for the consistency of the Within estimator. On the other hand, Deaton's estimator is consistent for β, for finite n_c when either C or T tend to infinity. Verbeek and Nijman (1992b) also find that the bias in the Within estimator may be substantial even for large n_c. They also emphasize the importance of choosing the cohorts under study very carefully. For example, in order to minimize the measurement error variance, the individuals in each cohort should be as homogeneous as possible. Additionally, to maximize the variation in the pseudo-panel and get precise estimates the different cohorts should be as heterogeneous as possible.

Moffitt (1993) extends Deaton's (1985) analysis to the estimation of dynamic models with repeated cross-sections. By imposing certain restrictions, Moffitt shows that linear and nonlinear models, with and without fixed effects, can be identified and consistently estimated with pseudo-panels.[6] Moffitt (1993) gives an instrumental variable interpretation for the Within estimator based on the pseudo-panel using cohort dummies, and a set of time dummies interacted with the cohort dummies. Since n_c is assumed to tend to ∞, the measurement error problem is ignored. Moffitt (1993) illustrates his estimation method for the linear fixed effects life-cycle model of labor supply using repeated cross-sections from the US Current Population Survey (CPS). The sample included white males, ages 20–59, drawn from 21 waves over the period 1968–88. In order to keep the estimation problem manageable, the data were randomly subsampled to include a total of 15 500 observations. Moffitt concludes that there is a considerable amount of parsimony achieved in the specification of age and cohort effects. Also, individual characteristics are considerably more important than either age, cohort or year effects. Blundell, Meghir and Neves (1993) use the annual UK Family Expenditure Survey covering the period 1970–84 to study the intertemporal labor supply and consumption of married women. The total number of households considered was 43 671. These were allocated to 10 different cohorts depending on the year of birth. The average number of observations per cohort was 364. Their findings indicate reasonably sized intertemporal labor supply elasticities.

Collado (1997) proposes measurement error corrected estimators for dynamic models with individual effects using time series of independent cross-sections. A GMM estimator corrected for measurement error is proposed that is consistent as the number of cohorts tends to infinity for a fixed T and a fixed number of individuals per cohort. In addition, a measurement error corrected within-groups estimator is proposed which is consistent as T tends to infinity. Monte Carlo simulations are performed to study the small sample properties of the estimators proposed. Some of the main results indicate that the measurement error correction is important, and that corrected estimators reduce the bias obtained. Also, for small T, GMM estimators are better than within-groups estimators. Recently, McKenzie (2000a) allowed for parameter heterogeneity amongst cohorts, and showed that consistency of least squares depends on $n_c \rightarrow \infty$, $(T/n_c) \rightarrow 0$, and that instrumental variables estimators are consistent under weaker conditions. McKenzie (2000b) also considered the problem of estimating dynamic models with unequally spaced pseudo-panel data. Surveys in developing countries are often taken at unequally spaced intervals and this unequal spacing, in turn, imposes nonlinear restrictions on the parameters.[7] Nonlinear least squares, minimum distance and one-step estimators are suggested that are consistent and asymptotically normal for finite T as the number of individuals per cohort is allowed to pass to infinity. Verbeek and Vella (2000) review the identification conditions for consistent estimation of a linear dynamic model from repeated cross-sections. They show that Moffitt's (1993) estimator is inconsistent, unless the exogenous variables are either time-invariant or exhibit no autocorrelation. They propose an alternative instrumental variable estimator, corresponding to the Within estimator applied to the pseudo-panel of cohort averages. This estimator is consistent under the same conditions as those suggested by Collado (1997). However, Verbeek and Vella argue that those conditions are not trivially satisfied in applied work.

Girma (2000) suggests an alternative GMM method of estimating linear dynamic models from a time series of independent cross-sections. Unlike the Deaton (1985) approach of averaging across individuals in a cohort, Girma suggests a quasi-differencing transformation across pairs of individuals that belong to the same group. The asymptotic properties of the proposed GMM estimators are based upon having a large number of individuals per group/time cell. This is in contrast to the Deaton-type estimator which requires the number of group/time periods to grow without limit. Some of the other advantages of this method include the fact that no aggregation is involved, the dynamic response parameters can freely vary across groups, and the presence of unobserved individual specific heterogeneity is explicitly allowed for.

10.4 ALTERNATIVE METHODS OF POOLING TIME SERIES OF CROSS-SECTION DATA

This book has focused on the error component model as a popular method in economics for pooling time series of cross-section data. Another alternative method for pooling these data is described in Kmenta (1986) using timewise autocorrelated and cross-sectionally heteroskedastic disturbances.[8] The basic idea is to allow for first-order autoregressive disturbances

$$u_{it} = \rho_i u_{i,t-1} + \epsilon_{it} \quad i = 1, \ldots, N;\ t = 1, \ldots, T \tag{10.23}$$

where the autoregressive parameter can vary across cross-sections with $|\rho_i| < 1$. Also, the remainder error ϵ_{it} is assumed to be normal with zero mean and a general variance–covariance matrix that allows for possible heteroskedasticity as well as correlation across cross-sections, i.e.

$$E(\epsilon\epsilon') = \Sigma \otimes I_T \quad \text{where} \quad \epsilon' = (\epsilon_{11}, \ldots, \epsilon_{1T}, \ldots, \epsilon_{N1}, \ldots, \epsilon_{NT}) \tag{10.24}$$

and Σ is $N \times N$. The initial values are assumed to have the following properties:

$$u_{i0} \sim N\left(0, \frac{\sigma_{ii}}{1-\rho_i^2}\right) \quad \text{and} \quad E(u_{i0}u_{j0}) = \frac{\sigma_{ij}}{1-\rho_i\rho_j} \qquad i, j = 1, 2, \ldots, N$$

Kmenta (1986) describes how to obtain feasible GLS estimators of the regression coefficients.[9] In the first step, OLS residuals are used to get consistent estimates of the ρ_i. Next, a Prais–Winsten transformation is applied using the estimated $\widehat{\rho}_i$ to get a consistent estimate of Σ from the resulting residuals. In the last step, GLS is applied to the Prais–Winsten transformed model using the consistent estimate of Σ. This may be a suitable pooling method for N small and T very large, but for typical labor or consumer panels where N is large and T is small it may be infeasible. In fact, for $N > T$, the estimate of Σ will be singular. Note that the number of extra parameters to be estimated for this model is $N(N+1)/2$, corresponding to the elements of Σ plus N distinct ρ_i. This is in contrast to the simple one-way error component model with N extra parameters to estimate for the fixed effects model or two extra variance components to estimate for the random effects model. For example, even for a small $N = 50$, the number of extra parameters to estimate for the Kmenta technique is 1325 compared to 50 for fixed effects and two for the random effects model. Baltagi (1986) discusses the advantages and disadvantages of the Kmenta and the error components methods and compares their performance using Monte Carlo experiments. For typical panels with N large and T small, the error component model is parsimonious in its estimation of variance–covariance parameters compared to the timewise autocorrelated, cross-sectionally heteroskedastic specification and is found to be more robust to misspecification.

Some economic applications of the Kmenta method include: (1) van der Gaag et al. (1977) who applied the timewise autocorrelated cross-sectionally heteroskedastic technique to estimate a dynamic model of demand for specialist medical care in the Netherlands. The panel data covered 11 provinces ($N = 11$) in the Netherlands collected over the period 1960–72 ($T = 13$). The disturbances were allowed to be timewise autocorrelated with differing ρ_i cross-sectionally heteroskedastic and correlated across regions. (2) Wolpin (1980) who used annual observations on robberies covering the period 1955–71 for three countries: Japan, England and the USA (represented by California). Per capita robbery rate in country i at time t was modeled as a log-linear function of a set of deterrence variables, a set of environment variables and a time-invariant "culture" variable which is related to the propensity to commit robbery. Country-specific dummy variables were used to capture these cultural effects. The remainder error was assumed cross-sectionally heteroskedastic and timewise autocorrelated with a different ρ_i for each country. In addition, the disturbances were allowed to be correlated across countries. (3) Griffin (1982) who applied the Kmenta technique to estimate the demand for long-distance telephone service. The panel data consisted of seasonally adjusted quarterly data for the period 1964–78, for five southwestern states. Per capita intrastate long-distance messages were modeled as a distributed lag of real per capita income, advertising exposure and the real price of message telecommunication service. Additionally, population and population squared were used to measure the effect of market size, since the quantity of long-distance service depends on the number of possible calling combinations. A dummy variable was included for each state with the remainder error assumed to be first-order autocorrelated with a different ρ for each state, heteroskedastic, and not correlated across states. Griffin (1982) found a long-run price elasticity of -0.6 and a statistically significant effect of advertising. This price elasticity, coupled with marginal costs between one-fourth and one-half price indicated a large welfare loss in the long-distance market.

Recently, Baltagi, Chang and Li (1992a) considered the case where all cross-sections in (10.23) have the same autoregressive parameter ρ, with $|\rho| < 1$ and $\epsilon_{it} \sim \text{IIN}(0, \sigma_\epsilon^2)$, but where the initial disturbance $u_{i1} \sim \text{IIN}(0, \sigma_\epsilon^2/\tau)$ where τ is an arbitrary positive number. They show that the resulting disturbances are heteroskedastic unless $\tau = (1 - \rho^2)$ or the process started a long time ago. With panel data, no matter when the process started, one can translate this starting date into an "effective" initial variance assumption. This initial variance can be estimated and tested for departures from homoskedasticity. Using Monte Carlo experiments, the authors show that for short time series ($T = 10, 20$), if $\tau \neq (1 - \rho^2)$, the conventional MLE which assumes $\tau = 1 - \rho^2$ performs poorly relative to the MLE that estimates the arbitrary τ.

Finally, Larson and Watters (1993) suggested a joint test of functional form and nonspherical disturbances for the Kmenta model with fixed effects using the Box–Cox transformation and an artificial linear regression approach. They apply this test to a model of intrastate long-distance demand for Southwestern Bell's five-state region observed quarterly over the period 1979–88. Their results reject the logarithmic transformation on both the dependent and independent variables and are in favor of correcting for serial correlation and heteroskedasticity.

10.5 SPATIAL PANELS

In randomly drawn samples at the individual level, one does not usually worry about cross-section correlation. However, when one starts looking at a cross-section of countries, regions, states, counties, etc. these aggregate units are likely to exhibit cross-sectional correlation that has to be dealt with. There is an extensive literature using spatial statistics that deals with this type of correlation. These spatial dependence models are popular in regional science and urban economics. More specifically, these models deal with spatial interaction (spatial autocorrelation) and spatial structure (spatial heterogeneity) primarily in cross-section data, see Anselin (1988, 2001) for a nice introduction to this literature. Spatial dependence models may use a metric of economic distance which provides cross-sectional data with a structure similar to that provided by the time index in time series. With the increasing availability of micro as well as macro level panel data, spatial panel data models are becoming increasingly attractive in empirical economic research. See Case (1991), Holtz-Eakin (1994), Driscoll and Kraay (1998), Bell and Bockstael (2000) and Baltagi and Li (2001) for a few applications. For example, in explaining per capita R&D expenditures and spillover effects across countries, one can model the spatial correlation as well as the heterogeneity across countries using a spatial error component regression model:

$$y_{ti} = X'_{ti}\beta + u_{ti} \quad i = 1, \ldots, N; \; t = 1, \ldots, T \tag{10.25}$$

where y_{ti} is the observation on the ith country for the tth time period, X_{ti} denotes the $k \times 1$ vector of observations on the nonstochastic regressors and u_{ti} is the regression disturbance. In vector form, the disturbance vector of (10.25) is assumed to have random country effects as well as spatially autocorrelated remainder disturbances, see Anselin (1988):

$$u_t = \mu + \epsilon_t \tag{10.26}$$

with

$$\epsilon_t = \lambda W \epsilon_t + \nu_t \tag{10.27}$$

where $\mu' = (\mu_1, \cdots, \mu_N)$ denotes the vector of random country effects which are assumed to be $\text{IIN}(0, \sigma_\mu^2)$. λ is the scalar spatial autoregressive coefficient with $|\lambda| < 1$. W is a known $N \times N$ spatial weight matrix whose diagonal elements are zero. W also satisfies the condition that $(I_N - \lambda W)$ is nonsingular. $\nu'_t = (\nu_{t1}, \cdots, \nu_{tN})$, where ν_{ti} is assumed to be $\text{IIN}(0, \sigma_\nu^2)$ and also independent of μ_i. One can rewrite (10.27) as

$$\epsilon_t = (I_N - \lambda W)^{-1}\nu_t = B^{-1}\nu_t \tag{10.28}$$

where $B = I_N - \lambda W$ and I_N is an identity matrix of dimension N. The model (10.25) can be rewritten in matrix notation as

$$y = X\beta + u \tag{10.29}$$

where y is now of dimension $NT \times 1$, X is $NT \times k$, β is $k \times 1$ and u is $NT \times 1$. X is assumed to be of full column rank and its elements are assumed to be bounded in absolute value. Equation (10.26) can be written in vector form as

$$u = (\iota_T \otimes I_N)\mu + (I_T \otimes B^{-1})\nu \tag{10.30}$$

where $\nu' = (\nu_1', \cdots, \nu_T')$. Under these assumptions, the variance–covariance matrix for u is given by

$$\Omega = \sigma_\mu^2 (J_T \otimes I_N) + \sigma_\nu^2 (I_T \otimes (B'B)^{-1}) \tag{10.31}$$

This matrix can be rewritten as

$$\Omega = \sigma_\nu^2 \left[\bar{J}_T \otimes (T\phi I_N + (B'B)^{-1}) + E_T \otimes (B'B)^{-1} \right] = \sigma_\nu^2 \Sigma \tag{10.32}$$

where $\phi = \sigma_\mu^2/\sigma_\nu^2$, $\bar{J}_T = J_T/T$ and $E_T = I_T - \bar{J}_T$. Using results in Wansbeek and Kapteyn (1983), Σ^{-1} is given by

$$\Sigma^{-1} = \bar{J}_T \otimes (T\phi I_N + (B'B)^{-1})^{-1} + E_T \otimes B'B \tag{10.33}$$

Also, $|\Sigma| = |T\phi I_N + (B'B)^{-1}| \cdot |(B'B)^{-1}|^{T-1}$. Under the assumption of normality, the log-likelihood function for this model was derived by Anselin (1988, p. 154) as

$$\begin{aligned} L &= -\frac{NT}{2} \ln 2\pi\sigma_\nu^2 - \frac{1}{2} \ln |\Sigma| - \frac{1}{2\sigma_\nu^2} u'\Sigma^{-1}u \\ &= -\frac{NT}{2} \ln 2\pi\sigma_\nu^2 - \frac{1}{2} \ln[|T\phi I_N + (B'B)^{-1}|] + \frac{(T-1)}{2} \ln |B'B| \\ &\quad - \frac{1}{2\sigma_\nu^2} u'\Sigma^{-1}u \end{aligned} \tag{10.34}$$

with $u = y - X\beta$. For a derivation of the first-order conditions of MLE as well as the LM test for $\lambda = 0$ for this model, see Anselin (1988). As an extension to this work, Baltagi, Song and Koh (1999) derived the joint LM test for spatial error correlation as well as random country effects. Additionally, they derived conditional LM tests, which test for random country effects given the presence of spatial error correlation. Also, spatial error correlation given the presence of random country effects. These conditional LM tests are an alternative to the one-directional LM tests that test for random country effects ignoring the presence of spatial error correlation or the one-directional LM tests for spatial error correlation ignoring the presence of random country effects. Extensive Monte Carlo experiments are conducted to study the performance of these LM tests as well as the corresponding likelihood ratio tests.

More recently, generalized methods of moments have been proposed for spatial cross-section models by Kelejian and Prucha (1999) and Conley (1999) and these have been applied to spatial panels by Bell and Bockstael (2000). Frees (1995) derives a distribution-free test for spatial correlation in panels. This is based on Spearman rank correlation across pairs of cross-section disturbances. Driscoll and Kraay (1998) show through Monte Carlo simulations that the presence of even modest spatial dependence can impart large bias to OLS standard errors when N is large. They present conditions under which a simple modification of the standard nonparametric time series covariance matrix estimator yields estimates of the standard errors that are robust to general forms of spatial and temporal dependence as $T \to \infty$. However, if T is small, they conclude that the problem of consistent nonparametric covariance matrix estimation is much less tractable. Parametric corrections for spatial correlation are possible only if one places strong restrictions on their form, i.e. knowing W. For typical micro panels with N much larger than T, estimating this correlation is impossible without imposing restrictions, since the number of spatial correlations increases at the rate N^2, while the number of observations grows at the rate N. Examples of some parametric structures imposed on spatial correlations include Keane and Runkle (1992) and Case (1991). Even for macro panels where $N = 100$ countries observed over $T = 20$ to 30 years, N is still larger than T and prior restrictions on the form of spatial correlation are still needed.

Baltagi and Li (2001) derive the best linear unbiased predictor for the random error component model with spatial correlation using a simple demand equation for cigarettes based on a panel of 46 states over the period 1963–92. They compare the performance of several predictors of the states' demand for cigarettes for one year and five years ahead. The estimators whose predictions are compared include OLS, fixed effects ignoring spatial correlation, fixed effects with spatial correlation, random effects GLS estimator ignoring spatial correlation and random effects estimator accounting for the spatial correlation. Based on the RMSE criteria, the fixed effects and the random effects spatial estimators gave the best out-of-sample forecast performance. For the estimation and testing of spatial autoregressive panel models as well as an extensive set of references on spatial studies, read Anselin (1988, 2001).

10.6 SHORT-RUN VS LONG-RUN ESTIMATES IN POOLED MODELS

Applied studies using panel data find that the Between estimator (which is based on the cross-sectional component of the data) tends to give long-run estimates while the Within estimator (which is based on the time-series component of the data) tends to give short-run estimates. This agrees with the folk wisdom that cross-sectional studies tend to yield long-run responses while time-series studies tend to yield short-run responses (see Kuh, 1959; Houthakker, 1965). Both are consistent estimates of the same regression coefficients as long as the disturbances are uncorrelated with the explanatory variables. In fact, Hausman's specification test is based on the difference between these estimators (see Chapter 4).

Rejection of the null implies that the random individual effects are correlated with the explanatory variables. This means that the Between estimator is inconsistent while the Within estimator is consistent since it sweeps away the individual effects. In these cases, the applied researcher settles on the Within estimator rather than the Between or GLS estimators. (See Mundlak, 1978 for additional support of the Within estimator.) Baltagi and Griffin (1984) argue that in panel data models, the difference between the Within and Between estimators is due to dynamic misspecification. The basic idea is that even with a rich panel data set, long-lived lag effects coupled with the shortness of the time series is a recipe for dynamic underspecification. This is illustrated using Monte Carlo experiments.[10,11] Griliches and Hausman (1986) attribute the difference between these estimators to measurement error in panel data (see section 10.1). Mairesse (1990) tries to explain why these two estimators differ in economic applications using three samples of large manufacturing firms in France, Japan and the USA over the period 1967–79, and a Cobb–Douglas production function. Mairesse (1990) compares OLS, Between and Within estimators using levels and first-differenced regressions with and without constant returns to scale. Assuming constant returns to scale, he finds that the Between estimates of the elasticity of capital are of the order of 0.31 for France, 0.47 for Japan and 0.22 for the USA, whereas the Within estimates are lower, varying from 0.20 for France to 0.28 for Japan and 0.21 for the USA. Mairesse (1990) argues that if the remainder error ν_{it} is correlated with the explanatory variables, then the Within estimator will be inconsistent, while the Between estimator is much less affected by these correlations because the ν_{it} are averaged and practically wiped out for large enough T. This is also the case when measurement error in the explanatory variables is present. In fact, if these measurement errors are not serially correlated from one year to the next, the Between estimator tends to minimize their importance by averaging. In contrast, the Within estimator magnifies the variability of these measurement errors and increases the resulting bias. (For additional arguments in favor of the Between estimator, see Griliches and Mairesse, 1984.)

10.7 HETEROGENEOUS PANELS

Robertson and Symons (1992) studied the properties of some panel data estimators when the regression coefficients vary across individuals, i.e. they are heterogeneous but are assumed homogeneous in estimation. This is done for both stationary and nonstationary regressors. The basic conclusion is that severe biases can occur in dynamic estimation even for relatively small parameter variation.

In order to illustrate the basic idea, they consider the case of say two countries ($N = 2$), where the asymptotics depend on $T \to \infty$. Their true model is a simple heterogeneous static regression model with one regressor

$$y_{it} = \beta_i x_{it} + \nu_{it} \quad i = 1, 2;\ t = 1, \ldots, T \tag{10.35}$$

where ν_{it} is independent for $i = 1, 2$ and β_i varies across $i = 1, 2$. However, their estimated model is dynamic and homogeneous with $\beta_1 = \beta_2 = \beta$ and assumes an identity covariance matrix for the disturbances:

$$y_{it} = \lambda y_{i,t-1} + \beta x_{it} + w_{it} \quad i = 1, 2 \tag{10.36}$$

The regressors are assumed to follow a stationary process $x_{it} = \rho x_{i,t-1} + \epsilon_{it}$ with $|\rho| < 1$ but different variances σ_i^2 for $i = 1, 2$. Seemingly unrelated regression estimation with the equality restriction imposed and an identity covariance matrix reduces to OLS on this system of two equations. Robertson and Symons (1992) obtain the probability limits of the resulting $\widehat{\lambda}$ and $\widehat{\beta}$ as $T \to \infty$. They find that the coefficient λ of $y_{i,t-1}$ is overstated, while the mean effect of the regressors (the x_{it}) is underestimated. In case the regressors are random walks ($\rho = 1$), then $\text{plim}\,\widehat{\lambda} = 1$ and $\text{plim}\,\widehat{\beta} = 0$. Therefore, false imposition of parameter homogeneity and dynamic estimation of a static model when the regressors follow a random walk lead to perverse results. Using Monte Carlo experiments they show that the dynamics become misleading even for T as small as 40, which corresponds to the annual postwar data period. Even though these results are derived for $N = 2$, one regressor and no lagged dependent variable in the true model, Robertson and Symons (1992) show that the same phenomenon occurs for an empirical example of a real wage equation for a panel of 13 OECD countries observed over the period 1958–86. Parameter homogeneity across countries is rejected and the true relationship appears dynamic. Imposing false equality restriction biases the coefficient of the lagged wage upwards and the coefficient of the capital–labor ratio downwards.

For typical labor or consumer panels where N is large but T is fixed, Robertson and Symons (1992) assume that the true model is given by (10.35) with $\beta_i \sim \text{IID}(\beta, \sigma_\beta^2)$ for $i = 1, \ldots, N$, and $\nu_{it} \sim \text{IID}(0, 1)$. In addition, x_{it} is AR(1) with innovations $\epsilon_{it} \sim \text{IID}(0, 1)$ and $x_{i0} = \nu_{i0} = 0$. The estimated model is dynamic as given by (10.36), with known variance covariance matrix I, and $\beta_i = \beta$ imposed for $i = 1, \ldots, N$. For fixed T and random walk regressors, $\text{plim}\,\widehat{\lambda} > 0$ and $\text{plim}\,\widehat{\beta} < \beta$ as $N \to \infty$, so that the coefficient of $y_{i,t-1}$ is overestimated and the mean effect of the β_i is underestimated. As $T \to \infty$, one gets the same result obtained previously, $\text{plim}\,\widehat{\lambda} = 1$ and $\text{plim}\,\widehat{\beta} = 0$. If the regressor x_{it} is white noise, no biases arise. These results are confirmed with Monte Carlo experiments for $T = 5$ and $N = 50$, 100 and 200. The dynamics are overstated even for $N = 50$ and $T = 5$, but they disappear as the regressor approaches white noise, and remain important for autoregressive regressors with $\rho = 0.5$. Finally, Robertson and Symons (1992) reconsider the Anderson and Hsiao (1982) estimator of a dynamic panel data model that gets rid of the individual effects by first-differencing and uses lagged first-differences of the regressors as instruments. Imposing false equality restrictions renders these instruments invalid unless x_{it} is white noise or follows a random walk. Only the second case is potentially important because many economic variables are well approximated by random walks. However, Robertson and Symons (1992) show that if x_{it} is a random walk, the instrument is orthogonal to the instrumented variable and the resulting estimator has infinite asymptotic variance, a result obtained in the stationary case by Arellano (1989). Using levels $(y_{i,t-2})$ as instruments as suggested by Arellano (1989) will not help when x_{it} is a random walk, since the correlation between the stationary variable $(y_{i,t-1} - y_{i,t-2})$ and the $I(1)$ variable y_{it} will be asymptotically zero. Using Monte Carlo experiments, with $T = 5$ and $N = 50$, Robertson and Symons (1992) conclude that the Anderson and Hsiao (1982) estimator is useful only when x_{it} is white noise or a random walk. Otherwise, severe biases occur when x_{it} is stationary and autocorrelated.

Pesaran and Smith (1995) consider the problem of estimating a dynamic panel data model when the parameters are individually heterogeneous and illustrate their results by estimating industry-specific UK labor demand functions. In this case the model is given by

$$y_{it} = \lambda_i y_{i,t-1} + \beta_i x_{it} + u_{it} \quad i = 1, \ldots, N;\ t = 1, \ldots, T \tag{10.37}$$

where λ_i is IID$(\lambda, \sigma_\lambda^2)$ and β_i is IID(β, σ_β^2). Further, λ_i and β_i are independent of y_{is}, x_{is} and u_{is} for all s. The objective in this case is to obtain consistent estimates of the mean values of λ_i and β_i. Pesaran and Smith (1995) present four different estimation procedures:

(1) Aggregate time-series regressions of group averages.
(2) Cross-section regressions of averages over time.
(3) Pooled regressions allowing for fixed or random intercepts.
(4) Separate regressions for each group, where coefficients estimates are averaged over these groups.

They show that when T is small (even if N is large), all the procedures yield inconsistent estimators. The difficulty in obtaining consistent estimates for λ and β can be explained by rewriting (10.37) as

$$y_{it} = \lambda y_{i,t-1} + \beta x_{it} + \nu_{it} \tag{10.38}$$

where $\nu_{it} = u_{it} + (\lambda_i - \lambda) y_{i,t-1} + (\beta_i - \beta) x_{it}$. By continuous substitution of $y_{i,t-s}$ it is easy to see that ν_{it} is correlated with all present and past values of $y_{i,t-1-s}$ and $x_{i,t-s}$ for $s \geqslant 0$. The fact that ν_{it} is correlated with the regressors of (10.38) renders the OLS estimator inconsistent, and the fact that ν_{it} is correlated with $(y_{i,t-1-s}, x_{i,t-s})$ for $s > 0$ rules out the possibility of choosing any lagged value of y_{it} and x_{it} as legitimate instruments. When both N and T are large, Pesaran and Smith (1995) show that the cross-section regression procedure will yield consistent estimates of the mean values of λ and β. Intuitively, when T is large, the individual parameters λ_i and β_i can be consistently estimated using T observations of each individual i, say $\widehat{\lambda}_i$ and $\widehat{\beta}_i$, then averaging these individual estimators, $\sum_{i=1}^N \widehat{\lambda}_i/N$ and $\sum_{i=1}^N \widehat{\beta}_i/N$, will lead to consistent estimators of the mean values of λ and β. Maddala, Srivastava and Li (1994) argued that shrinkage estimators are superior to either heterogeneous or homogeneous parameter estimates, especially for prediction purposes. In fact, Maddala et al. (1997) considered the problem of estimating short-run and long-run elasticities of residential demand for electricity and natural gas for each of 49 states over the period 1970–90.[12] They conclude that individual heterogeneous state estimates were hard to interpret and had the wrong signs. Pooled data regressions were not valid because the hypothesis of homogeneity of the coefficients was rejected. They recommend shrinkage estimators if one is interested in obtaining elasticity estimates for each state since these give more reliable results. Baltagi and Griffin (1997) compare short-run and long-run estimates as well as forecasts for pooled homogeneous, individual heterogeneous and shrinkage estimators of a dynamic demand model for gasoline across 18 OECD countries over the period 1960–90. Based on one-, five- and 10-year forecasts and plausibility of the short-run and long-run elasticity estimates, the results are in favor of pooling. Similar results were obtained for a dynamic model for cigarette demand across 46 states over the period 1963–92, see Baltagi, Griffin and Xiong (2000).

Hsiao and Tahmiscioglu (1997) use a panel of 561 US firms over the period 1971–92 to study the influence of financial constraints on company investment. They find substantial differences across firms in terms of their investment behavior. When a homogeneous pooled model is assumed, the impact of liquidity on firm investment is seriously underestimated. The authors recommend a mixed fixed and random coefficients framework based on the recursive predictive density criteria.

Pesaran, Smith and Im (1996) investigated the small sample properties of various estimators of the long-run coefficients for a dynamic heterogeneous panel data model using Monte Carlo experiments. Their findings indicate that the mean group estimator performs reasonably well for large T. However, when T is small, the mean group estimator could be seriously biased, particularly when N is large relative to T. Pesaran and Zhao (1999) examined the effectiveness of alternative bias-correction procedures in reducing the small sample bias of these estimators using Monte Carlo experiments. An interesting finding is that when the coefficient of the lagged dependent variable is greater than or equal to 0.8, none of the bias correction procedures seem to work. Hsiao, Pesaran and Tahmiscioglu (1999) suggest a Bayesian approach for estimating the mean parameters of a dynamic heterogeneous panel data model. The coefficients are assumed to be normally distributed across cross-sectional units and the Bayes estimator is implemented using Markov Chain Monte Carlo methods. Hsiao, Pesaran and Tahmiscioglu (1999) argue that Bayesian methods can be a viable alternative in the estimation of mean coefficients in dynamic panel data models even when the initial observations are treated as fixed constants. They establish the asymptotic equivalence of this Bayes estimator and the mean group estimator proposed by Pesaran and Smith (1995). The asymptotics are carried out for both N and $T \to \infty$ with $\sqrt{N}/T \to 0$. Monte Carlo experiments show that this Bayes estimator has better sampling properties than other estimators for both small and moderate size T. Hsiao, Pesaran and Tahmiscioglu also caution against the use of the mean group estimator unless T is sufficiently large relative to N. The bias in the mean coefficient of the lagged dependent variable appears to be serious when T is small and the true value of this coefficient is larger than 0.6. Hsiao, Pesaran and Tahmiscioglu apply their methods to estimate the q-investment model using a panel of 273 US firms over the period 1972–93.

NOTES

1. Peracchi and Welch (1995) use the Current Population Survey (CPS) to illustrate some problems that arise from analyzing panel data constructed by matching person records across files of rotating cross-section surveys. In particular, the matched CPS is studied to understand the process of attrition from the sample and the nature of measurement error.
2. Estimation of the consumer price index in the USA is based on a complex rotating panel survey, with 20% of the sample being replaced by rotation each year (see Valliant, 1991).
3. In general, for any T, as long as the fraction of the sample being rotated is greater or equal to half, then no individual will be observed more than twice.
4. The terms "panel conditioning", "reinterview effect" and "rotation group bias" are also used in the literature synonymously with "time-in-sample bias" effects.
5. Blundell and Meghir (1990) also argue that pseudo-panels allow the estimation of life-cycle models which are free from aggregation bias. In addition, Moffitt (1993) explains that many researchers in the USA prefer to use pseudo-panels like the CPS because it has larger, more representative samples and the questions asked are more consistently defined over time than the available US panels.
6. Moffitt (1993) also considers dynamic discrete dependent variable models estimated using pseudo-panels.
7. Table 1 of McKenzie (2000b) provides examples of unequally spaced surveys and their sources.
8. Another alternative method for pooling is suggested by Beggs (1986) who recommends the use of spectral methods to pool cross-sectional replication of time series.
9. Two special cases of this general specification are also considered. The first assumes that Σ is diagonal, with no correlation across different cross-sections but allowing for heteroskedasticity. The second special case uses the additional restriction that all the ρ_i are equal for $i = 1, 2, \ldots, N$.
10. For other studies dealing with the consequences of dynamic misspecification on panel data estimators, see Ridder and Wansbeek (1990) for the case of a partial adjustment model and van den Doel and Kiviet (1994) for the case of a covariance stationary and the case of a nonstationary regressor.
11. Recently, Pirotte (1999) showed that the probability limit of the Between estimator for a *static* panel data regression converges to the long-run effect. This occurs despite the fact that the true model is a *dynamic* error components model. The only requirements are that the number of individuals tend to infinity with the time periods held fixed and the coefficients of the model are homogeneous among individual units.
12. Maddala and Hu (1996) and Maddala et al. (1997) provide a unified treatment of classical, Bayes and empirical Bayes procedures for estimating this model.

PROBLEMS

10.1 This problem is based upon Griliches and Hausman (1986). Using the simple regression given in (10.1)–(10.3):

(a) Show that for the first-difference (FD) estimator of β, the expression in (10.8) reduces to

$$\operatorname{plim} \widehat{\beta}_{\mathrm{FD}} = \beta \left(1 - \frac{2\sigma_\eta^2}{\operatorname{var}(\Delta x)}\right)$$

where $\Delta x_{it} = x_{it} - x_{i,t-1}$.

(b) Also show that (10.8) reduces to

$$\text{plim}\ \widetilde{\beta}_{\text{W}} = \beta\left(1 - \frac{T-1}{T}\frac{\sigma_\eta^2}{\text{var}(\widetilde{x})}\right)$$

where $\widetilde{\beta}_{\text{W}}$ denotes the Within estimator and $\widetilde{x}_{it} = x_{it} - \bar{x}_{i.}$

(c) For most economic series, the x_{it}^* are positively serially correlated exhibiting a declining correlogram, with

$$\text{var}(\Delta x) < \frac{2T}{T-1}\text{var}(\widetilde{x}) \quad \text{for } T > 2$$

Using this result, conclude that

$$|\ \text{bias}\ \widehat{\beta}_{\text{FD}}\ | > |\ \text{bias}\ \widetilde{\beta}_{\text{W}}\ |$$

(d) Solve the expressions in parts (a) and (b) for β and σ_η^2 and verify that the expressions in (10.9) and (10.10) reduce to

$$\widehat{\beta} = \frac{[2\widetilde{\beta}_{\text{W}}/\text{var}(\Delta x) - (T-1)\widehat{\beta}_{\text{FD}}/T\ \text{var}(\widetilde{x})]}{[2/\text{var}(\Delta x) - (T-1)/T\ \text{var}(\widetilde{x})]}$$

$$\sigma_\eta^2 = (\widehat{\beta} - \widehat{\beta}_{\text{FD}})\text{var}(\Delta x)/2\widehat{\beta}$$

(e) For $T = 2$, the Within estimator is the same as the first-difference estimator since $(1/2)\Delta x_{it} = \widetilde{x}_{it}$. Verify that the expressions in parts (a) and (b) are also the same.

10.2 For the rotating panel considered in section 10.2, assume that $T = 3$ and that the number of households being replaced each period is equal to $N/2$.
(a) Derive the variance–covariance of the disturbances Ω.
(b) Derive $\Omega^{-1/2}$ and describe the transformation needed to make GLS a weighted least squares regression.
(c) How would you consistently estimate the variance components σ_μ^2 and σ_ν^2?
(d) Repeat this exercise for the case where the number of households being replaced each period is $N/3$. How about $2N/3$?

10.3 Using the Grunfeld data, perform
(a) the common ρ and
(b) the varying ρ estimation methods, described in Baltagi (1986). Compare with the error component estimates obtained in Chapter 2.

10.4 Using the gasoline data, perform
(a) the common ρ and
(b) the varying ρ estimation methods, described in Baltagi (1986). Compare with the error component estimates obtained in Chapter 2.

10.5 Using the Monte Carlo setup of Baltagi (1986), compare the timewise autocorrelated, cross-sectionally heteroskedastic estimation method with the error component method and observe which method is more robust to misspecification.

10.6 *Prediction in the spatially autocorrelated error component model.* This is based on problem 99.2.4 in *Econometric Theory* by Baltagi and Li (1999). Consider the panel data regression model described in (10.25) with random country effects and spatially autocorrelated remainder disturbances described by (10.26) and (10.27). Using the Goldberger (1962) best linear unbiased prediction results discussed in section 2.5, equation (2.37), derive the BLUP of $y_{i,T+S}$ for the ith country at period $T + S$ for this spatial panel model. Hint: See solution 99.2.4 in *Econometric Theory* by Song and Jung (2000).

10.7 Download the Maddala et al. (1997) data set on residential natural gas and electricity consumption for 49 states over 21 years (1970–90) from the *Journal of Business and Economic Statistics* web site www.amstat.org/publications/jbes/ftp.html.

(a) Using this data set, replicate the individual OLS state regressions for electricity, given in Table 6 and natural gas, given in Table 8 of Maddala et al. (1997).

(b) Replicate the shrinkage estimates for electricity and natural gas given in Tables 7 and 9, respectively.

(c) Replicate the fixed effects estimator given in column 1 of Table 2 and the pooled OLS model given in column 2 of the table.

(d) Replicate the average OLS, the average shrinkage estimator and the average Stein rule estimator in Table 2.

(e) Redo parts (c) and (d) for the natural gas equation as given in Table 4 in that paper.

11
Limited Dependent Variables and Panel Data

In many economic studies, the dependent variable is discrete, indicating for example that a household purchased a car or that an individual is unemployed or that he or she joined the union. This dependent variable is usually represented by a binary choice variable $y_{it} = 1$ if the event happens and 0 if it does not for individual i at time t. In fact, if p_{it} is the probability that household i purchases a car at time t, then $E(y_{it}) = 1 \cdot p_{it} + 0 \cdot (1 - p_{it}) = p_{it}$, and this is usually modeled as a function of some explanatory variables

$$p_{it} = \Pr[y_{it} = 1] = E(y_{it}/x_{it}) = F(x'_{it}\beta) \tag{11.1}$$

For the linear probability model, $F(x'_{it}\beta) = x'_{it}\beta$ and the usual panel data methods apply except that $\widehat{y}_{it}$ is not guaranteed to lie in the unit interval. The standard solution has been to use the logistic or normal cumulative distribution functions that constrain $F(x'_{it}\beta)$ to be between zero and one. These probability functions are known in the literature as logit and probit, corresponding to the logistic and normal distributions, respectively.[1] For example, a worker participates in the labor force if his offered wage exceeds his unobserved reservation wage. This threshold can be described as

$$\begin{aligned} y_{it} &= 1 \quad \text{if } y^*_{it} > 0 \\ &= 0 \quad \text{if } y^*_{it} \leqslant 0 \end{aligned} \tag{11.2}$$

where $y^*_{it} = x'_{it}\beta + u_{it}$. So that

$$\Pr[y_{it} = 1] = \Pr[y^*_{it} > 0] = \Pr[u_{it} > -x'_{it}\beta] = F(x'_{it}\beta) \tag{11.3}$$

where the last equality holds as long as the density function describing F is symmetric around zero. This is true for the logistic and normal density functions.

11.1 FIXED AND RANDOM LOGIT AND PROBIT MODELS

For panel data, the presence of individual effects complicates matters significantly. To see this, consider the random effects model, $u_{it} = \mu_i + \nu_{it}$ where $\mu_i \sim \text{IID}(0, \sigma_\mu^2)$ and $\nu_{it} \sim \text{IID}(0, \sigma_\nu^2)$ independent of each other and the x_{it}. In this case, $E(u_{it}u_{is}) = \sigma_\mu^2$ and the joint likelihood of $(y_{1t}, \ldots, y_{Nt})$ can no longer be written as the product of the marginal likelihoods of the y_{it}. This complicates the derivation of maximum likelihood and will now involve bivariate numerical integration. On the other hand, if there are no random individual effects, the joint likelihood will be the product of the marginals and one can proceed as in the usual cross-sectional limited dependent variable case (see Maddala, 1983; McFadden, 1984).

For the fixed effects panel data model, $y_{it}^* = x_{it}'\beta + \mu_i + \nu_{it}$ and

$$\Pr[y_{it} = 1] = \Pr[y_{it}^* > 0] = \Pr[\nu_{it} > -x_{it}'\beta - \mu_i] = F(x_{it}'\beta + \mu_i) \tag{11.4}$$

where the last equality holds as long as the density function describing F is symmetric around zero. In this case, μ_i and β are unknown parameters and as $N \to \infty$, for a fixed T, the number of parameters μ_i increases with N. This means that μ_i cannot be consistently estimated for a fixed T. This is known as the incidental parameters problem in statistics discussed by Neyman and Scott (1948) and reviewed more recently by Lancaster (2000). For the linear panel data regression model, when T is fixed, only β was estimated consistently by first getting rid of the μ_i using the Within transformation.[2] This was possible for the linear case because the MLE of β and μ_i are asymptotically independent (see Hsiao, 1986). This is no longer the case for a qualitative limited dependent variable model with fixed T as demonstrated by Chamberlain (1980). For a simple illustration of how the inconsistency of the MLE of μ_i is transmitted into inconsistency for $\widehat{\beta}_{\text{MLE}}$, see Hsiao (1986). This is done in the context of a logit model with one regressor that is observed over two periods.

The usual solution around this incidental parameters (μ_i) problem is to find a minimal sufficient statistic for μ_i. For the logit model, Chamberlain (1980) finds that $\sum_{t=1}^T y_{it}$ is a minimum sufficient statistic for μ_i. Therefore, Chamberlain suggests maximizing the *conditional* likelihood function

$$L_c = \prod_{i=1}^N \Pr\left(y_{i1}, \ldots, y_{iT} / \sum_{t=1}^T y_{it}\right) \tag{11.5}$$

to obtain the conditional logit estimates for β.[3] By definition of a sufficient statistic, the distribution of the data given this sufficient statistic will not depend on μ_i. For the fixed effects logit model, this approach results in a computationally convenient estimator and the basic idea can be illustrated for $T = 2$. The observations over the two periods and for all individuals are independent and the *unconditional* likelihood is given by

$$L = \prod_{i=1}^{N} \Pr(y_{i1})\Pr(y_{i2}) \tag{11.6}$$

The sum $(y_{i1} + y_{i2})$ can be 0, 1 or 2. If it is 0, both y_{i1} and y_{i2} are 0 and

$$\Pr[y_{i1} = 0, y_{i2} = 0 / y_{i1} + y_{i2} = 0] = 1 \tag{11.7}$$

Similarly, if the sum is 2 both y_{i1} and y_{i2} are 1 and

$$\Pr[y_{i1} = 1, y_{i2} = 1 / y_{i1} + y_{i2} = 2] = 1 \tag{11.8}$$

These terms add nothing to the conditional log-likelihood since $\log 1 = 0$. Only the observations for which $y_{i1} + y_{i2} = 1$ matter in $\log L_c$ and these are given by

$$\Pr[y_{i1} = 0, y_{i2} = 1 / y_{i1} + y_{i2} = 1] \quad \text{and} \quad \Pr[y_{i1} = 1, y_{i2} = 0 / y_{i1} + y_{i2} = 1]$$

The latter can be calculated as $\Pr[y_{i1} = 1, y_{i2} = 0]/\Pr[y_{i1} + y_{i2} = 1]$ with

$$\Pr[y_{i1} + y_{i2} = 1] = \Pr[y_{i1} = 0, y_{i2} = 1] + \Pr[y_{i1} = 1, y_{i2} = 0]$$

since the latter two events are mutually exclusive. For the logit model see (11.4)

$$\Pr[y_{it} = 1] = \frac{e^{\mu_i + x'_{it}\beta}}{1 + e^{\mu_i + x'_{it}\beta}} \tag{11.9}$$

Therefore

$$\Pr[y_{i1} = 1, y_{i2} = 0 / y_{i1} + y_{i2} = 1] = \frac{e^{x'_{i1}\beta}}{e^{x'_{i1}\beta} + e^{x'_{i2}\beta}} = \frac{1}{1 + e^{(x_{i2} - x_{i1})'\beta}} \tag{11.10}$$

Similarly

$$\Pr[y_{i1} = 0, y_{i2} = 1 / y_{i1} + y_{i2} = 1] = \frac{e^{x'_{i2}\beta}}{e^{x'_{i1}\beta} + e^{x'_{i2}\beta}} = \frac{e^{(x_{i2} - x_{i1})'\beta}}{1 + e^{(x_{i2} - x_{i1})'\beta}} \tag{11.11}$$

and neither probability involves the μ_i. Therefore, by conditioning on $y_{i1} + y_{i2}$, we swept away the μ_i. The product of terms such as these with $y_{i1} + y_{i2} = 1$ gives the conditional likelihood function which can be maximized with respect to β using conventional maximum likelihood logit programs. In this case, only the observations for individuals who switched status are used in the estimation. A standard logit package can be used with $x'_{i2} - x'_{i1}$ as explanatory variables and the dependent variable taking the value one if y_{it} switches from 0 to 1, and zero if y_{it} switches from 1 to 0. This procedure can easily be generalized for $T > 2$ (see problem 10.3). However, the computations become excessive for large T (see Greene, 2000).

In order to test for fixed individual effects one can perform a Hausman-type test based on the difference between Chamberlain's conditional MLE and the usual logit MLE ignoring the individual effects. The latter estimator is consistent and efficient only under the null of no individual effects and inconsistent under the alternative. Chamberlain's estimator is consistent whether H_0 is true or not, but it is inefficient under H_0 because it may not use all the data. Both estimators can easily be obtained from the usual logit ML routines. The constant is dropped and estimates of the asymptotic variances are used to form Hausman's χ^2 statistic. This will be distributed as χ^2_K under H_0. For an application of Chamberlain's conditional MLE to a study of newsstand prices of 38 magazines observed over a 27-year period, see Cecchetti (1986). Björklund (1985) also applies this approach to study the linkage between unemployment and mental health problems in Sweden using the Swedish Level of Living Surveys. The data are based on a random sample of 6500 individuals between the ages of 15 and 75 surveyed in 1968, 1974 and 1981. More recently, Winkelmann and Winkelmann (1998) applied the conditional logit approach to study the effect of unemployment on the level of satisfaction. Using data from the first six waves of the GSOEP over the period 1984–89, the authors show that unemployment has a large detrimental effect on satisfaction. This effect becomes even larger after controlling for individual specific effects. The dependent variable is based on the response to the question "How satisfied are you at present with your life as a whole?". An ordinal scale from 0 to 10 is recorded, where 0 means "completely dissatisfied" and 10 means "completely satisfied". Winkelmann and Winkelmann constructed a binary variable taking the value 1 if this score is above 7 and 0 otherwise. Since average satisfaction is between 7 and 8, this is equivalent to classifying individuals into those who report above and those who report below average satisfaction. The explanatory variables include a set of dummy variables indicating current labor market status (unemployed out of the labor force) with employed as the reference category. A good health variable defined as the absence of any chronic condition or handicap. Age, age-squared, marital status and the duration of unemployment and its square. Since unemployment reduces income which in turn may reduce satisfaction, household income is included as a control variable to measure the nonpecuniary effect of unemployment holding income constant. Of particular concern with the measurement of life satisfaction is that individuals "anchor" their scale at different levels, rendering interpersonal comparisons of responses meaningless. This problem bears a close resemblance to the issue of cardinal vs ordinal utility. Any statistic that is calculated from a cross-section of individuals, for instance an average satisfaction, requires cardinality of the measurement scale. This problem is closely related to the unobserved individual specific effects. Hence anchoring causes the estimator to be biased as long as it is not random but correlated with the explanatory variables. Panel data help if the metric used by individuals is time-invariant. Fixed effects make inference based on intra- rather than interpersonal comparisons of satisfaction. This avoids not only the potential bias caused by anchoring, but also bias caused by other unobserved individual specific factors. Hausman's test based on the difference between a standard logit and a fixed effects logit yields a significant χ^2 variable. After controlling for individual specific effects, this study finds that unemployment has a significant and substantial negative impact on satisfaction. The nonpecuniary costs of unemployment by far exceed the pecuniary costs associated with loss of income while unemployed.

In contrast to the fixed effects logit model, the conditional likelihood approach does not yield computational simplifications for the fixed effects *probit* model. In particular, the fixed effects cannot be swept away and maximizing the likelihood over all the parameters including the fixed effects will in general lead to inconsistent estimates for large N and fixed T. Heckman (1981b) performed some limited Monte Carlo experiments on a probit model with a single regressor and a Nerlove (1971a) type x_{it}. For $N = 100$, $T = 8$, $\sigma_\nu^2 = 1$ and $\sigma_\mu^2 = 0.5$, 1 and 3, Heckman computed the bias of the fixed effects MLE of β using 25 replications. He found at most 10% bias for $\beta = 1$ which was always towards zero.

In cases where the conditional likelihood function is not feasible, Manski (1987) shows that it is possible to relax the logistic assumption in (11.9) above. Manski allows for a strictly increasing distribution function which differs across individuals, but not over time for a given individual. For $T = 2$, the identification of β is based on the fact that, under certain regularity conditions on the distribution of the exogenous variables

$$\operatorname{sgn}[\Pr(y_{i2} = 1/x_{i1}, x_{i2}, \mu_i) - \Pr(y_{i1} = 1/x_{i1}, x_{i2}, \mu_i)] = \operatorname{sgn}[(x_{i2} - x_{i1})'\beta]$$

This prompted Manski (1987) to suggest a conditional version of his maximum score estimator which can be applied to the first differences of the data in the subsample for which $y_{i1} \neq y_{i2}$. This estimator leaves the distribution of the errors unspecified but it requires these disturbances to be stationary conditional on the sequence of explanatory variables. Unlike the conditional logit approach, Manski's estimator is not root-N consistent or asymptotically normal.[4] In fact, Chamberlain (1993) showed that even if the distribution of the disturbances is known, the logit model is the only version of (11.4) for which β can be estimated at rate root-N. Honoré and Lewbel (2000) show that Chamberlain's negative result can be overturned as long as there is one explanatory variable which is independent of the fixed effects and the ν_{it}'s, conditional on the other explanatory variables and on a set of instruments. This strong assumption allows the root-N consistent estimation of the parameters of the binary choice model with individual specific effects which are valid even when the explanatory variables are predetermined as opposed to strictly exogenous.

Although the probit model does not lend itself to a fixed effects treatment, it has been common to use it for the random effects specification. For the random effects probit model, MLE yields a consistent and efficient estimator of β. However, MLE is computationally more involved. Essentially, one has to compute the joint probabilities of a T-variate normal distribution which involves T-dimensional integrals (see Hsiao, 1986). This gets to be infeasible if T is big. However, by conditioning on the individual effects, this T-dimensional integral problem reduces to a single integral involving the product of a standard normal density and the difference of two normal cumulative density functions. This can be evaluated using the Gaussian quadrature procedure suggested by Butler and Moffitt (1982). This approach has the advantage of being computationally feasible even for fairly large T. For one of the early applications of the random effects probit model, see Heckman and Willis (1975). Another application is given by

Sickles and Taubman (1986) who estimate a two-equation structural model of the health and retirement decisions of the elderly using five biennial panels of males drawn from the Retirement History Survey. Both the health and retirement variables are limited dependent variables and MLE using the Butler and Moffitt (1982) Gaussian quadrature procedure is implemented. Sickles and Taubman find that retirement decisions are strongly affected by health status, and that workers not yet eligible for social security are less likely to retire. Recently, Guilkey and Murphy (1993) performed a Monte Carlo study using a random effects probit model. They showed that ignoring the random effects and performing a standard probit analysis can lead to very misleading inference since the coefficient standard errors are badly biased. However, a probit estimator with a corrected asymptotic covariance matrix performed as well as MLE for almost all parametric configurations and is recommended. LIMDEP and STATA provide basic routines for the random effects probit model.

Underlying the random effects probit model is the equicorrelation assumption between successive disturbances belonging to the same individual. Avery, Hansen and Hotz (1983) suggest a method of moments estimator that allows for a general type of serial correlation among the disturbances. They apply their "orthogonality condition" estimators to the study of labor force participation of married women. They reject the hypothesis of equicorrelation across the disturbances. These random effects probit methods assume that the μ_i and x_{it} are uncorrelated and this may be a serious limitation, as emphasized in Chapter 7. Avery, Hansen and Hotz (1983) suggest an exogeneity test that can be implemented with their HOTZTRAN program. If exogeneity is not rejected, then one should apply the above method of moments estimator. If exogeneity is rejected, then one needs to put more structure on the type of correlation between μ_i and the x_{it} to estimate this model. This is what we will turn to next.

If the μ_i are correlated with the x_{it}, Chamberlain (1980, 1984) assumes that

$$\mu_i = x_i'a + \epsilon_i \qquad (11.12)$$

where $a' = (a_1', \ldots, a_T')$, $x_i' = (x_{i1}', \ldots, x_{iT}')$ and $\epsilon_i \sim \text{IID}(0, \sigma_\epsilon^2)$ independent of ν_{it}. In this case

$$y_{it} = 1 \quad \text{if } (x_{it}'\beta + x_i'a + \epsilon_i + \nu_{it}) > 0 \qquad (11.13)$$

and the distribution of y_{it} conditional on x_{it} but marginal on μ_i has the probit form

$$\Pr[y_{it} = 1] = \Phi[(1 + \sigma_\epsilon^2)^{-1/2}(x_{it}'\beta + x_i'a)] \qquad (11.14)$$

where Φ denotes the cumulative normal distribution function. Once again, MLE involves numerical integration, but a computationally simpler approach suggested by Chamberlain is to run simple probit on this equation to get $\widehat{\Pi}$. In this case, Π satisfies the restriction

$$\Pi = (1 + \sigma_\epsilon^2)^{-1/2}(I_T \otimes \beta' + \iota_T a') \qquad (11.15)$$

Therefore, Chamberlain suggests a minimum distance estimator based on $(\widehat{\pi}-\pi)$, where $\pi = \text{vec}(\Pi')$, that imposes this restriction. For details, see Chamberlain (1984).

Chamberlain (1984) applies both his fixed effects logit estimator and his minimum distance random effects probit estimator to a study of the labor force participation of 924 married women drawn from the PSID. These estimation methods give different results, especially with regard to the effect of the presence of young children on labor force participation. These different results could be attributed to the misspecification of the relationship between μ_i and the x_{it} in the random effects specification or a misspecification of the fixed effects logit model in its omission of leads and lags of the x_{it} from the structural equation.

For another application of Chamberlain's (1984) approach to panel data probit estimation, see Laisney, Lechner and Pohlmeier (1992) who studied the process innovation behavior of 1325 West German exporting firms observed over the 1984–88 period. Also, Lechner (1995) who suggests several specification tests for the panel data probit model. These are generalized score and Wald tests employed to detect omitted variables, neglected dynamics, heteroskedasticity, non-normality and random-coefficient variations. The performance of these tests in small samples is investigated using Monte Carlo experiments. In addition, an empirical example is given on the probability of self-employment in West Germany using a random sample of 1926 working men selected from the German Socio-Economic Panel and observed over the period 1984–89. Extensive Monte Carlo simulations comparing the performance of several simple GMM estimators for the panel data probit model are given by Lechner and Breitung (1996), Bertschek and Lechner (1998) and Breitung and Lechner (1999). Their results show that the efficiency loss for GMM when compared to maximum likelihood is small. In addition, these GMM estimators are easy to compute and are robust to serial correlation in the error. Asymptotically optimal GMM estimators based on the conditional mean function are obtained by using both parametric and nonparametric methods. The Monte Carlo results indicate that the nonparametric method is superior in small samples. Bertschek and Lechner (1998) apply these GMM procedures to the product innovation decisions of 1270 German firms observed over the period 1984–88.

Bover and Arellano (1997) provide extensions of the random effects probit model of Chamberlain (1984) which has applications in the analysis of binary choice, linear regression subject to censoring and other models with endogenous selectivity. They propose a simple two-step Within estimator for limited dependent variable models, which may include lags of the dependent variable, other exogenous variables and unobservable individual effects. This estimator is based on reduced form predictions of the latent endogenous variables. It can be regarded as a member of Chamberlain's class of random effects minimum distance estimators, and as such it is consistent and asymptotically normal for fixed T. However, this Within estimator is not asymptotically efficient within the minimum distance class, since it uses a nonoptimal weighting matrix. Therefore, Bover and Arellano

(1997) show how one can obtain in one more step a chi-squared test statistic for overidentifying restrictions and linear GMM estimators that are asymptotically efficient. The drawbacks of this approach are the same as those for the Chamberlain probit model. Both require the availability of strictly exogenous variables, and the specification of the conditional distribution of the effects. Labeaga (1999) applies the Bover and Arellano (1997) method to estimate a double-hurdle rational addiction model for tobacco consumption using an unbalanced panel of households drawn from the Spanish Permanent Survey of Consumption (SPSC). This is a panel collected by the Spanish Statistical Office for approximately 2000 households between 1977 and 1983.

11.2 FIXED AND RANDOM TOBIT MODELS

So far, we have studied economic relationships, say labor supply, based on a random sample of individuals where the dependent variable is one if the individual is employed and zero if the individual is unemployed. However, for these random samples, one may observe the number of hours worked if the individual is employed. This sample is censored in that the hours worked are reported as zero if the individual does not work and the regression model is known as the Tobit model (see Maddala, 1983).[5] Heckman and MaCurdy (1980) consider a fixed effects Tobit model to estimate a life-cycle model of female labor supply. They argue that the individual effects have a specific meaning in a life-cycle model and therefore cannot be assumed independent of the x_{it}. Hence, a fixed effects rather than a random effects specification is appropriate. For this fixed effects Tobit model

$$y_{it}^* = x_{it}'\beta + \mu_i + \nu_{it} \tag{11.16}$$

with $\nu_{it} \sim \text{IIN}(0, \sigma_\nu^2)$ and

$$\begin{aligned} y_{it} &= y_{it}^* \quad && \text{if } y_{it}^* > 0 \\ &= 0 && \text{otherwise} \end{aligned} \tag{11.17}$$

where y_{it} could be the expenditures on a car or a house, or the number of hours worked. This will be zero if the individual does not buy a car or a house or if the individual is unemployed.[6] As in the fixed effects probit model, the μ_i cannot be swept away and as a result β and σ_ν^2 cannot be estimated consistently for T fixed, since the inconsistency in the μ_i is transmitted to β and σ_ν^2. Heckman and MaCurdy (1980) suggest estimating the log-likelihood using iterative methods. In contrast, Honoré (1992) suggested trimmed least absolute deviations and trimmed least squares estimators for truncated and censored regression models with fixed effects defined in (11.16). These are semiparametric estimators with no distributional assumptions necessary on the error term. The main assumption is that the remainder error ν_{it} is independent and identically distributed conditional on the x_{it} and the μ_i for $t = 1, \ldots, T$. Honoré (1992) exploits the symmetry in the distribution of the latent variables and finds that when the true values of the parameters are known, trimming can transmit the same symmetry in distribution to the observed variables. This generates orthogonality conditions which must hold at the true value of the parameters. Therefore, the resulting GMM estimator is consistent provided the orthogonality conditions are satisfied at a unique point in the parameter space. Honoré (1992) shows that these estimators are consistent and asymptotically normal. Monte Carlo results show that as long as $N \geqslant 200$, the asymptotic distribution is a good approximation of the small sample distribution. However, if N is small, the small sample distribution of these estimators is skewed.[7]

Honoré and Kyriazidou (2000a) review recent estimators for censored regression and sample selection panel data models with unobserved individual specific effects and show how they can easily be extended to other Tobit-type models. The proposed estimators are semiparametric and do not require the parametrization of the distribution of the unobservables. However, they do require that the explanatory variables be strictly exogenous. This rules out lags of the dependent variables among the regressors. The general approach exploits stationarity and exchangeability assumptions on the models' transistory error terms in order to construct moment conditions that do not depend on the individual specific effects.

Kyriazidou (1997) studies the panel data sample selection model, also known as the Type 2 Tobit model with

$$y_{1it}^* = x_{1it}'\beta_1 + \mu_{1i} + \nu_{1it} \tag{11.18}$$

$$y_{2it}^* = x_{2it}'\beta_2 + \mu_{2i} + \nu_{2it} \tag{11.19}$$

where

$$\begin{aligned} y_{1it} &= 1 \quad \text{if } y_{1it}^* > 0 \\ &= 0 \quad \text{otherwise} \end{aligned}$$

and

$$\begin{aligned} y_{2it} &= y_{2it}^* \quad \text{if } y_{1it} = 1 \\ &= 0 \quad \text{otherwise} \end{aligned}$$

Kyriazidou suggests estimating β_1 by one of the estimation methods for discrete choice models with individual effects that were discussed in section 11.1. Next, μ_{2i} is eliminated by first-differencing the data for which y_{2it}^* is observed. With this sample selection, Kyriazidou (1997) focuses on individuals for whom $x_{1it}'\beta_1 = x_{1is}'\beta_1$. For these individuals, the same first-differencing that will eliminate the fixed effects will also eliminate the sample selection. This suggests a two-step Heckman procedure where β_1 is estimated in the first step and then β_2 is estimated by applying OLS to the first differences but giving more weight to observations for which $(x_{1it} - x_{1is})'\widehat{\beta}_1$ is close to zero. This weighting can be done using a kernel whose bandwidth h_N shrinks to zero as the sample size increases. The resulting estimator is $\sqrt{Nh_N}$-consistent and asymptotically normal. Monte Carlo results for $N = 250$, 1000 and 4000 and $T = 2$ indicate that this estimator works well for sufficiently large data sets. However, it is quite sensitive to the choice of the bandwidth parameters.

Kim and Maddala (1992) analyze dividend behavior using panel data on 649 US manufacturing firms observed for 12 years (1976–87). A censored Tobit model is used which allows for firm-specific and time effects. Unlike the usual error component model, the error is assumed heteroskedastic and free of autocorrelation. Based on specification tests, the authors argue that it is important to allow for zero observations, industry, firm-specific and time effects in the estimation of models of dividend behavior.

Charlier, Melenberg and van Soest (2001) apply the methods proposed by Kyriazidou (1997) to a model of expenditure on housing for owners and renters using an endogenous switching regression. The data is based on three waves of the Dutch Socio-Economic Panel from 1987–89. The share of housing in total expenditure is modeled using a household-specific effect, family characteristics, constant-quality prices and total expenditure, where the latter is allowed to be endogenous. Estimates from a random effects model are compared to estimates from a linear panel data model in which selection only enters through the fixed effects, and a Kyriazidou-type estimator allowing for fixed effects and a more general type of selectivity. Hausman-type tests reject the random effects and linear panel data models as too restrictive. However, the overidentification restrictions of the more general semiparametric fixed effects model of Kyriazidou (1997) were rejected, suggesting possible misspecification.

11.3 SIMULATION ESTIMATION OF LIMITED DEPENDENT VARIABLE MODELS WITH PANEL DATA

Recently, Keane (1994) derived a computationally practical simulation estimator for the panel data probit model. Simulation estimation methods were developed by McFadden (1989) and Pakes and Pollard (1989) and the basic idea is to replace intractable integrals by unbiased Monte Carlo probability simulators. This is ideal for limited dependent variable models, whereas for a multinominal probit model the choice probabilities involve multivariate integrals.[8] In fact, for cross-section data, McFadden's method of simulated moments (MSM) involves an $M - 1$ integration problem, where M is the number of possible choices facing the individual. For panel data, things get more complicated, because there are M choices facing any individual at each period. This means that there are M^T possible choice sequences facing each individual over the panel. Hence the MSM estimator becomes infeasible as T gets large. Keane (1994) sidesteps this problem of having to simulate M^T possible choice sequences by factorizing the method of simulated moments first-order conditions into transition probabilities. The latter are simulated using highly accurate importance sampling techniques (see Keane, 1993, 1994 for details). This method of simulating probabilities is referred to as the Geweke, Hajivassiliou and Keane (GHK) simulator because it was independently developed by these authors. Keane (1994) performs Monte Carlo experiments and finds that even for large T and small simulation sizes, the bias in the MSM estimator is negligible. When maximum likelihood methods are feasible, Keane (1994) finds that the MSM estimator performs well relative to quadrature-based maximum likelihood methods even where the latter are based on a large number of quadrature points. When maximum likelihood is not feasible, the MSM estimator outperforms the simulated MLE even when the highly accurate GHK probability simulator is used. Keane (1994) argues that MSM has three advantages over the other practical nonmaximum likelihood estimators considered above, i.e. Chamberlain's (1984) minimum distance estimator and the Avery, Hansen and Hotz (1983) orthogonality condition estimator. First, MSM is asymptotically as efficient as maximum likelihood (in simulation size) while the other estimators are not. Second, MSM can easily be extended to handle multinominal probit situations whereas the extension of the other estimators is computationally burdensome. Third, MSM can be extended to handle nonlinear systems of equations which are intractable with maximum likelihood. Keane (1994) also finds that MSM can estimate random effects models with autoregressive moving average error in about the same time necessary for estimating a simple random effects model using maximum likelihood quadrature. The extension of limited dependent variable models to allow for a general pattern of serial correlation is now possible using MSM and could prove useful for out-of-sample predictions. An example of the MSM estimator is given by Keane (1993) who estimates probit employment equations using data from the National Longitudinal Survey of Young Men (NLS). This is a sample of 5225 males aged 14–24 and interviewed 12 times over the period 1966–81. For this example, Keane (1993) concludes that relaxing the equicorrelation assumption by including an MA(1) or AR(1) component to the error term had little effect on the parameter estimates. Keane (1993) discusses simulation estimation of models more complex than probit models. He argues that it is difficult to put panel data selection models and Tobit models in an MSM framework and that the method of simulated scores (MSS) may be a preferable way to go. Keane (1993) applies the MSS estimator to the same data set used by Keane, Moffitt and Runkle (1988) to study the cyclical behavior of real wages. He finds that the Keane, Moffitt and Runkle conclusion of a weakly procyclical movement in the real wage appears to be robust to relaxation of the equicorrelation assumption. Finally, Hajivassiliou (1994) reconsiders the problem of external debt crisis of 93 developing countries observed over the period 1970–88. Using several simulation estimation methods, Hajivassiliou concludes that allowing for flexible correlation patterns changes the estimates substantially and raises doubts over previous studies that assumed restrictive correlation structures.

11.4 STATE DEPENDENCE AND HETEROGENEITY

So far the model is static implying that, for example, the probability of buying a car is independent of the individual's past history of car purchases. If the probability of buying a car is more likely if the individual has bought a car in the past than if he or she has not, then a dynamic model that takes into account the individual's past experience is more appropriate. Heckman (1981a, b, c) gives an extensive treatment of these dynamic models and the consequences of various assumptions on the initial values on the resulting estimators. (See also the literature on autoregressive logit and probit models surveyed in Maddala, 1987b.) Heckman (1981c) also emphasizes the importance of distinguishing between "true state dependence" and "spurious state dependence". In the "true" case, once an individual experiences an event like unemployment, his preferences change and he or she will behave differently in the future as compared with an identical individual who has not experienced this event in the past. In fact, it is observed that individuals with a long history of unemployment are less likely to leave unemployment. They may be less attractive for employers to hire or may become discouraged in looking for a job. In the "spurious" case, past experience has no effect on the probability of experiencing the event in the future. It is the individual's characteristics that make him or her less likely to leave unemployment. However, one cannot properly control for all the variables that distinguish one individual's decision from another's. In this case, past experience which is a good proxy for these omitted variables shows up as a significant determinant of the future probability of occurrence of this event. Testing for true vs spurious state dependence is therefore important in these studies, but it is complicated by the presence of the individual effects or heterogeneity. In fact, even if there is no state dependence, $\Pr[y_{it}/x_{it}, y_{i,t-l}] \neq \Pr[y_{it}/x_{it}]$ as long as there are random individual effects present in the model. If in addition to the absence of the state dependence, there is also no heterogeneity, then $\Pr[y_{it}/x_{it}, y_{i,t-l}] = \Pr[y_{it}/x_{it}]$. A test for this equality can be based on a test for $\gamma = 0$ in the model

$$\Pr[y_{it} = 1/x_{it}, y_{it-1}] = F'(x_{it}'\beta + \gamma y_{i,t-1})$$

using standard maximum likelihood techniques. If $\gamma = 0$ is not rejected, we ignore the heterogeneity issue and proceed as in conventional limited dependent variable models not worrying about the panel data nature of the data. However, rejecting the null does not necessarily imply that there is heterogeneity since γ can be different from zero due to serial correlation in the remainder error or due to state dependence. In order to test for time dependence one has to condition on the individual effects, i.e. test $\Pr[y_{it}/y_{i,t-l}, x_{it}, \mu_i] = \Pr[y_{it}/x_{it}, \mu_i]$. This can be implemented following the work of Lee (1987). In fact, if $\gamma = 0$ is rejected, Hsiao (1996) suggests testing for time dependence against heterogeneity. If heterogeneity is rejected, the model is misspecified. If heterogeneity is not rejected then one estimates the model correcting for heterogeneity. See Heckman (1981c) for an application to married women's employment decisions based on a three-year sample from the PSID. One of the main findings of this study is that neglecting heterogeneity in dynamic models overstates the effect of past experience on labor market participation. Other applications dealing with heterogeneity and state dependence include Heckman and Willis (1977), Heckman and Borjas (1980) and more recently Vella and Verbeek (1999).

Chamberlain's fixed effects conditional logit approach can be generalized to include lags of the dependent variable, provided there are *no* explanatory variables and $T \geqslant 4$, see Chamberlain (1985). Assuming the initial period y_{i0} is observed but its probability is unspecified, the model is given by

$$\Pr[y_{i0} = 1/\mu_i] = p_0(\mu_i)$$

$$\Pr[y_{it} = 1/\mu_i, y_{i0}, y_{i1}, \ldots, y_{i,t-1}] = \frac{e^{\gamma y_{i,t-1}+\mu_i}}{1 + e^{\gamma y_{i,t-1}+\mu_i}} \quad t = 1, \ldots, T \tag{11.20}$$

where $p_0(\mu_i)$ is unknown but the logit specification is imposed from period one to T. Consider the two events

$$A = \{y_{i0} = d_0, y_{i1} = 0, y_{i2} = 1, y_{i3} = d_3\} \tag{11.21}$$

$$B = \{y_{i0} = d_0, y_{i1} = 1, y_{i2} = 0, y_{i3} = d_3\} \tag{11.22}$$

where d_0 and d_3 are either 0 or 1. If $T = 3$, inference on γ is based upon the observation that $\Pr[A/y_{i1} + y_{i2} = 1, \mu_i]$ and $\Pr[B/y_{i1} + y_{i2} = 1, \mu_i]$ do not depend upon μ_i, see problem 11.2. Honoré and Kyriazidou (2000b) consider the identification and estimation of panel data discrete choice models with lags of the dependent variable and strictly exogenous variables that allow for unobservable heterogeneity. In particular, they extend Chamberlain's (1985) fixed effects logit model in (11.20) to include strictly exogenous variables $x_i' = (x_{i1}, \ldots, x_{iT})$, i.e.

$$\Pr[y_{i0} = 1/x_i', \mu_i] = p_0(x_i', \mu_i) \tag{11.23}$$

$$\Pr[y_{it} = 1/x_i', \mu_i, y_{i0}, \ldots, y_{i,t-1}] = \frac{e^{x_{it}'\beta+\gamma y_{i,t-1}+\mu_i}}{1 + e^{x_{it}'\beta+\gamma y_{i,t-1}+\mu_i}} \quad t = 1, \ldots, T$$

The crucial assumption is that the errors in the threshold-crossing model leading to (11.23) are IID over time with logistic distributions and independent of (x_i', μ_i, y_{i0}) at all time periods. Honoré and Kyriazidou (2000b) show that $\Pr(A/x_i', \mu_i, A{\cup}B)$ and $\Pr(B/x_i', \mu_i, A{\cup}B)$ will still depend upon μ_i. This means that a conditional likelihood approach will not eliminate the fixed effects. However, if $x_{i2}' = x_{i3}'$, then the conditional probabilities

$$\Pr(A/x_i', \mu_i, A{\cup}B, x_{i2}' = x_{i3}') = \frac{1}{1 + e^{(x_{i1}-x_{i2})'\beta+\gamma(d_0-d_3)}} \tag{11.24}$$

$$\Pr(B/x_i', \mu_i, A{\cup}B, x_{i2}' = x_{i3}') = \frac{e^{(x_{i1}-x_{i2})'\beta+\gamma(d_0-d_3)}}{1 + e^{(x_{i1}-x_{i2})'\beta+\gamma(d_0-d_3)}}$$

do *not* depend on μ_i, see problem 11.3. If all the explanatory variables are discrete and $\Pr[x_{i2}' = x_{i3}'] > 0$, Honoré and Kyriazidou (2000b) suggest maximizing a weighted likelihood function based upon (11.24) for observations that satisfy $x_{i2}' = x_{i3}'$ and $y_{i1} + y_{i2} = 1$. The weakness of this approach is its reliance on observations for which $x_{i2}' = x_{i3}'$ which may not be useful for many economic applications. However, Honoré and Kyriazidou suggest weighting the likelihood function with weights that depend inversely on $x_{i2}' - x_{i3}'$, giving more weight to observations for which x_{i2}' is close to x_{i3}'. This is done using a kernel density $K[(x_{i2}' - x_{i3}')/h_N]$ where h_N is a bandwidth that shrinks as N increases.

The resulting estimators are consistent and asymptotically normal under standard assumptions. However, their rate of convergence will be slower than $\sqrt{N}$ and will depend upon the number of continuous covariates in x'_{it}. The results of a small Monte Carlo study suggest that this estimator performs well and that the asymptotics provide a reasonable approximation to the finite sample behavior of the estimator. Honoré and Kyriazidou also consider identification in the semi-parametric case where the logit assumption is relaxed. A conditional maximum score estimator à la Manski (1987) is proposed which is shown to be consistent.[9] In addition, Honoré and Kyriazidou discuss an extension of the identification result to multinomial discrete choice models and to the case where the dependent variable is lagged twice.

Honoré (1993) also considers the dynamic Tobit model with fixed effects, i.e.

$$y^*_{it} = x'_{it}\beta + \lambda y_{i,t-1} + \mu_i + \nu_{it} \tag{11.25}$$

with $y_{it} = \max\{0, y^*_{it}\}$ for $i = 1, \ldots, N$; $t = 1, \ldots, T$. The basic assumption is that ν_{it} is IID$(0, \sigma^2_\nu)$ for $t = 1, \ldots, T$, conditional on y_{i0}, x_{it} and μ_i. Honoré (1993) shows how to trim the observations from a dynamic Tobit model so that the symmetry conditions are preserved for the observed variables at the true values of the parameters. These symmetry restrictions are free of the individual effects and no assumption is needed on the distribution of the μ_i or their relationship with the explanatory variables. These restrictions generate orthogonality conditions which are satisfied at the true value of the parameters. The orthogonality conditions can be used in turn to construct method of moments estimators. Honoré (1993) does not prove that the true values of the parameters are the only values in the parameter space where the orthogonality conditions are satisfied. This means that the resulting GMM estimator is not necessarily consistent. Using Monte Carlo experiments, Honoré (1993) shows that MLE for a dynamic Tobit model with fixed effects performs poorly, whereas the GMM estimator performs quite well, when λ is the only parameter of interest.[10] The assumption that the ν_{it} are IID is too restrictive, especially for a dynamic model. Honoré (1993) relaxes this assumption to the case of stationary ν_{it} for $t = 1, \ldots, T$ conditional on the x_{it} and the μ_i. Still, this assumption is likely to be violated by many interesting economic models.

Arellano, Bover and Labeaga (1999) consider a linear autoregressive model for a latent variable which is only partly observed due to a selection mechanism:

$$y^*_{it} = \alpha y^*_{i,t-1} + \mu_i + \nu_{it} \tag{11.26}$$

with $|\alpha| < 1$ and $E(\nu_{it}/y^*_{i1}, \ldots, y^*_{i,t-1}) = 0$. The variable y^*_{it} is observed subject to endogenous selection. Arellano, Bover and Labeaga (1999) show that the intractability of this dynamic model subject to censoring using a single time series can be successfully handled using panel data by noting that individuals without censored past observations are exogenously selected. They propose an asymptotic least squares method to estimate features of the distribution of the censored endogenous variable conditional on its past. They apply these methods to a study of female labor supply and wages using two different samples from the PSID covering the periods 1970–76 and 1978–84.

11.5 SELECTION BIAS IN PANEL DATA

In Chapter 9, we studied incomplete panels that had randomly missing data. In section 10.2 we studied rotating panels where, by the design of the survey, households that drop from the sample in one period are intentionally replaced in the next period. However, in many surveys, nonrandomly missing data may occur due to a variety of self-selection rules. One such self-selection rule is the problem of nonresponse of the economic agent. Nonresponse occurs, for example, when the individual refuses to participate in the survey, or refuses to answer particular questions. This problem occurs in cross-section studies, but it becomes aggravated in panel surveys. After all, panel surveys are repeated cross-sectional interviews. So, in addition to the above kinds of nonresponse, one may encounter individuals who refuse to participate in subsequent interviews or simply move or die. Individuals leaving the survey cause attrition in the panel. This distorts the random design of the survey and questions the representativeness of the observed sample in drawing inference about the population we are studying. Inference based on the balanced subpanel is inefficient even in randomly missing data since it is throwing away data. In nonrandomly missing data, this inference is misleading because it is no longer representative of the population. Verbeek and Nijman (1996) survey the reasons for nonresponse and distinguish between "ignorable" and "nonignorable" selection rules. This is important because, if the selection rule is ignorable for the parameters of interest, one can use the standard panel data methods for consistent estimation. If the selection rule is nonignorable, then one has to take into account the mechanism that causes the missing observations in order to obtain consistent estimates of the parameters of interest.

For the one-way error component regression model

$$y_{it} = x'_{it}\beta + \mu_i + \nu_{it} \tag{11.27}$$

where $\mu_i \sim \text{IID}(0, \sigma_\mu^2)$ and $\nu_{it} \sim \text{IIN}(0, \sigma_\nu^2)$ independent of each other and the x_{it}. Observations on y_{it} (and possibly x_{it}) are missing if a selection variable $r_{it} = 0$ and not missing if $r_{it} = 1$. The missing data mechanism is ignorable of order one for β if $E(\mu + \nu_i/r_i) = 0$ for $i = 1, \ldots, N$, where $\mu' = (\mu_1, \ldots, \mu_N)$, $\nu'_i = (\nu_{i1}, \ldots, \nu_{iT})$ and $r'_i = (r_{i1}, \ldots, r_{iT})$. In this case, both GLS on the unbalanced panel and the balanced subpanel are consistent if $N \to \infty$. The Within estimator is consistent for both the unbalanced and balanced subpanel as $N \to \infty$ if $E(\widetilde{\nu}_i/r_i) = 0$ where $\widetilde{\nu}'_i = (\widetilde{\nu}_{i1}, \ldots, \widetilde{\nu}_{iT})$ and $\widetilde{\nu}_{it} = \nu_{it} - \overline{\nu}_i$.[11]

We now consider a simple model of nonresponse in panel data. Following the work of Hausman and Wise (1979), Ridder (1990, 1992) and Verbeek and Nijman (1996), we assume that y_{it} is observed, i.e. $r_{it} = 1$, if a latent variable

$r_{it}^* \geqslant 0$. This latent variable is given by

$$r_{it}^* = z_{it}'\gamma + \epsilon_i + \eta_{it} \quad (11.28)$$

where z_{it} is a set of explanatory variables possibly including some of the x_{it}.[12] The one-way error component structure allows for heterogeneity in the selection process. The errors are assumed to be normally distributed $\epsilon_i \sim \text{IIN}(0, \sigma_\epsilon^2)$ and $\eta_{it} \sim \text{IIN}(0, \sigma_\eta^2)$ with the only nonzero covariances being $\text{cov}(\epsilon_i, \mu_i) = \sigma_{\mu\epsilon}$ and $\text{cov}(\eta_{it}, \nu_{it}) = \sigma_{\eta\nu}$. In order to get a consistent estimator for β, a generalization of Heckman's (1979) selectivity bias correction procedure from the cross-sectional to the panel data case can be employed. The conditional expectation of u_{it} given selection now involves two terms. Therefore, instead of one selectivity bias correction term, there are now two terms corresponding to the two covariances $\sigma_{\mu\epsilon}$ and $\sigma_{\eta\nu}$. However, unlike the cross-sectional case, these correction terms cannot be computed from simple probit regressions and require numerical integration. Fortunately, this is only a one-dimensional integration problem because of the error component structure. Once the correction terms are estimated, they are included in the regression equation as in the cross-sectional case and OLS or GLS can be run on the resulting augmented model. For details, see Verbeek and Nijman (1996) who also warn about heteroskedasticity and serial correlation in the second step regression if the selection rule is nonignorable. Verbeek and Nijman (1996) also discuss MLE for this random effect probit model with selection bias. The computations require two-dimensional numerical integration for all individuals with $r_{it} = 0$ for at least one t. Verbeek (1990) also considers the estimation of a fixed effects model with selection bias using the marginal maximum likelihood principle. As in the random effects case, the computation is reduced to a two-dimensional numerical integration problem but it is simpler in this case because the two variables over which we are integrating are independent. Verbeek's (1990) model is a hybrid of a fixed individual effect (μ_i) in the behavioral equation, and a random individual effect (ϵ_i) in the selectivity equation. Zabel (1992) argues that if μ_i and x_{it} are correlated then it is highly likely (though not necessary) that ϵ_i and z_{it} are correlated. If the latter is true, the estimates of γ and β will be inconsistent. Zabel suggests modeling the ϵ_i as a function of the $\bar{z}_i$, arguing that this will reduce the inconsistency. Zabel also criticizes Verbeek's specification because it excludes economic models that have the same individual effect in both the behavioral and selectivity equation. For these models both effects should be either fixed or random.

Before one embarks on these complicated estimation procedures one should first test whether the selection rule is ignorable. Verbeek and Nijman (1992a) consider a Lagrange multiplier (LM) test for H_0: $\sigma_{\nu\eta} = \sigma_{\mu\epsilon} = 0$. The null hypothesis is a sufficient condition for the selection rule to be ignorable for the random effects model. Unfortunately, this also requires numerical integration over a maximum of two dimensions and is cumbersome to use in applied work. In addition, the LM test is highly dependent on the specification of the selectivity equation and the distributional assumptions. Alternatively, Verbeek and Nijman (1992a) suggest some simple Hausman-type tests based on GLS and

Within estimators for the unbalanced panel and the balanced subpanel.[13] All four estimators are consistent under the null hypothesis that the selection rule is ignorable and all four estimators are inconsistent under the alternative. This is different from the usual Hausman-type test where one estimator is consistent under both the null and alternative hypotheses, whereas the other estimator is efficient under the null but inconsistent under the alternative. As a consequence, these tests may have low power, especially if under the alternative these estimators have close asymptotic biases. On the other hand, the advantages of these tests are that they are computationally simple and do not require the specification of a selection rule to derive these tests. Let $\widehat{\delta} = (\widetilde{\beta}_W(B), \widetilde{\beta}_W(U), \widehat{\beta}_{GLS}(B), \widehat{\beta}_{GLS}(U))$ where $\widetilde{\beta}_W$ denotes the Within estimator and $\widehat{\beta}_{GLS}$ denotes the GLS estimator, $\beta(B)$ corresponds to an estimator of β from the balanced subpanel and $\widehat{\beta}(U)$ corresponds to an estimator of β from the unbalanced panel. Verbeek and Nijman (1992a) show that the variance–covariance matrix of $\widehat{\delta}$ is given by

$$\text{var}(\widehat{\delta}) = \begin{bmatrix} V_{11} & V_{22} & V_{33} & V_{44} \\ & V_{22} & V_{22}V_{11}^{-1}V_{13} & V_{44} \\ & & V_{33} & V_{44} \\ & & & V_{44} \end{bmatrix} \tag{11.29}$$

where $V_{11} = \text{var}(\widetilde{\beta}_W(B))$, $V_{22} = \text{var}(\widetilde{\beta}_W(U))$, $V_{33} = \text{var}(\widehat{\beta}_{GLS}(B))$ and $V_{44} = \text{var}(\widehat{\beta}_{GLS}(U))$. Therefore an estimate of $\text{var}(\widehat{\delta})$ can be obtained from the estimated variance–covariance matrices of the four estimation procedures. Hausman-type tests can now be performed on say H_0: $R\delta = 0$, where R is a known matrix, as follows:

$$m = N\widehat{\delta}'R'[R\ \text{var}(\widehat{\delta})R']^{-}R\widehat{\delta} \tag{11.30}$$

and this is distributed as χ^2 under the null with degrees of freedom equal to the rank of $[R\ \text{var}(\widehat{\delta})R']$. Natural candidates for R are $R_1 = [I, 0, -I, 0]$, $R_2 = [0, I, 0, -I]$, $R_3 = [I, -I, 0, 0]$ and $R_4 = [0, 0, I, -I]$. The first two are the standard Hausman tests based on the difference between the Within and GLS estimators for the balanced subpanel (R_1) and the unbalanced panel (R_2). The third is based on the difference between the Within estimators from the balanced and unbalanced panels (R_3), while the last is based on the difference between the GLS estimators from the balanced and unbalanced panels (R_4). For all four cases considered, the variance of the difference is the difference between the two variances and hence it is easy to compute. Verbeek and Nijman (1992a) perform some Monte Carlo experiments verifying the poor power of these tests in some cases, but also illustrating their usefulness in other cases. In practice, they recommend performing the tests based on R_2 and R_4.

Wooldridge (1995) derives some simple variable addition tests of selection bias as well as easy-to-apply estimation techniques that correct for selection bias in linear fixed effects panel data models. The auxiliary regressors are either Tobit residuals or inverse Mill's ratios and the disturbances are allowed to be arbitrarily serially correlated and unconditionally heteroskedastic. Wooldridge (1995) considers the fixed effects model where the μ_i's are correlated with x_{it}. However, the remainder disturbances ν_{it} are allowed to display arbitrary serial correlation and unconditional heteroskedasticity. The panel is unbalanced with the selection indicator vector for each individual i denoted by $s_i' = (s_{i1}, s_{i2}, \ldots, s_{it})$. When $s_{it} = 1$, it is assumed that (x_{it}', y_{it}) is observed. The fixed effects estimator is given by

$$\widetilde{\beta} = \left(\sum_{i=1}^{N}\sum_{t=1}^{T} s_{it}\widetilde{x}_{it}\widetilde{x}_{it}'\right)^{-1}\left(\sum_{i=1}^{N}\sum_{t=1}^{T} s_{it}\widetilde{x}_{it}\widetilde{y}_{it}\right) \tag{11.31}$$

where $\widetilde{x}_{it}' = x_{it}' - \left(\sum_{r=1}^{T} s_{ir}x_{ir}'/T_i\right)$, $\widetilde{y}_{it} = y_{it} - \left(\sum_{r=1}^{T} s_{ir}y_{ir}/T_i\right)$ and $T_i = \sum_{i=1}^{T} s_{it}$. A sufficient condition for the fixed estimator to be consistent and asymptotically normal, as $N \to \infty$, is that $E(\nu_{it}/\mu_i,\ x_i',\ s_i') = 0$ for $t = 1, 2, \ldots, T$. Recall, that $x_i' = (x_{i1}', \ldots, x_{iT}')$. Under this assumption, the selection process is strictly exogenous conditional on μ_i and x_i'.

Wooldridge (1995) considers two cases. The first is when the latent variable determining selection is partially observed. Define a latent variable

$$h_{it}^* = \delta_{t0} + x_{i1}'\delta_{t1} + \ldots + x_{iT}'\delta_{tT} + \epsilon_{it} \tag{11.32}$$

where ϵ_{it} is independent of (μ_i, x_i'), δ_{tr} is a $K \times 1$ vector of unknown parameters for $r = 1, 2, \ldots, T$ and $\epsilon_{it} \sim N(0, \sigma_t^2)$.

The binary selection indicator is defined as $s_{it} = 1$ if $h_{it}^* > 0$. For this case, the censored variable $h_{it} = \max(0, h_{it}^*)$ is observed. For example, this could be a wage equation, and selection depends on whether or not individuals are working. If a person is working, the working hours h_{it} are recorded, and selection is determined by nonzero hours worked. This is what is meant by partial observability of the selection variable.

Because s_i is a function of (x_i', ϵ_i') where $\epsilon_i' = (\epsilon_{i1}, \ldots, \epsilon_{iT})$, a sufficient condition for the fixed effects estimator to be consistent and asymptotically normal as $N \to \infty$ is $E(\nu_{it}/\mu_i, x_i', \epsilon_i') = 0$ for $t = 1, 2, \ldots, T$. The simplest alternative that implies selectivity bias is $E(\nu_{it}/\mu_i, x_i', \epsilon_i') = E(\nu_{it}/\epsilon_{it}) = \gamma\epsilon_{it}$ for $t = 1, 2, \ldots, T$, with γ being an unknown scalar. Therefore

$$E(y_{it}/\mu_i, x_i', \epsilon_i', s_i') = E(y_{it}/\mu_i, x_i', \epsilon_i') = \mu_i + x_{it}'\beta + \gamma\epsilon_{it} \tag{11.33}$$

It follows that, if we could observe ϵ_{it} when $s_{it} = 1$, then we could test for selectivity bias by including the ϵ_{it} as an additional regressor in fixed effects estimation and testing H_0: $\gamma = 0$ using standard methods. While ϵ_{it} cannot be observed, it can be estimated whenever $s_{it} = 1$ because ϵ_{it} is simply the error of a Tobit model.

When h_{it} is observed, Wooldridge's (1995) test for selection bias is as follows:

Step 1: For each $t = 1, 2, \ldots, T$, estimate the equation

$$h_{it} = \max(0, x_i'\delta_t + \epsilon_{it}) \tag{11.34}$$

by standard Tobit, where $\delta_t' = (\delta_{t0}, \delta_{t1}', \ldots, \delta_{tT}')$ and x_i now has unity as its first element. For $s_{it} = 1$, let $\widehat{\epsilon}_{it} = h_{it} - x_i'\widehat{\delta}_t$ denote the Tobit residuals.

Step 2: Estimate the equation

$$\widetilde{y}_{it} = \widetilde{x}'_{it}\beta + \gamma\widetilde{\epsilon}_{it} + \text{residuals} \tag{11.35}$$

by pooled OLS using those observations for which $s_{it} = 1$. $\widetilde{x}_{it}$ and $\widetilde{y}_{it}$ were defined above, and

$$\widetilde{\epsilon}_{it} = \widehat{\epsilon}_{it} - \left(\sum_{r=1}^{T} s_{ir}\widehat{\epsilon}_{ir}/T\right) \tag{11.36}$$

Step 3: Test H_0: $\gamma = 0$ using the t-statistic for $\widehat{\gamma}$. A serial correlation and heteroskedasticity-robust standard error should be used unless $E[\nu_i\nu'_i/\mu_i, x'_i, s_i] = \sigma^2_\nu I_T$. This robust standard error is given in the Appendix to Wooldridge's (1995) paper.

The second case considered by Wooldridge is when h_{it} is not observed. In this case, one conditions on s_i rather than ϵ_i. Using iterated expectations, this gives

$$\begin{aligned} E(y_{it}/\mu_i, x'_i, s'_i) &= \mu_i + x'_{it}\beta + \gamma E(\epsilon_{it}/\mu_i, x'_i, s'_i) \\ &= \mu_i + x'_{it}\beta + \gamma E(\epsilon_{it}/x'_i, s'_i) \end{aligned} \tag{11.37}$$

If the ϵ_{it} were independent across t, then $E(\epsilon_{it}/x'_i, s'_i) = E(\epsilon_{it}/x'_i, s_{it})$. The conditional expectation we need to estimate is $E[\epsilon_{it}/x'_i, s_{it} = 1] = E[\epsilon_{it}/x'_i, \epsilon_{it} > -x'_i\delta_t]$. Assuming that $\text{var}(\epsilon_{it}) = 1$, we get $E[\epsilon_{it}/x'_i, \epsilon_{it} > -x'_i\delta_t] = \lambda(x'_i\delta_t)$ where $\lambda(\cdot)$ denotes the inverse Mill's ratio.

When h_{it} is not observed, Wooldridge's (1995) test for selection bias is as follows:

Step 1: For each $t = 1, 2, \ldots, T$, estimate the equation

$$\Pr[s_{it} = 1/x'_i] = \Phi(x'_i\delta_t) \tag{11.38}$$

using standard probit. For $s_{it} = 1$, compute $\widehat{\lambda}_{it} = \lambda(x'_i\widehat{\delta}_t)$.

Step 2: Estimate the equation

$$\widetilde{y}_{it} = \widetilde{x}'_{it}\beta + \gamma\widetilde{\lambda}_{it} + \text{residuals} \tag{11.39}$$

by pooled OLS using those observations for which $s_{it} = 1$. $\widetilde{x}_{it}$ and $\widetilde{y}_{it}$ were defined above, and

$$\widetilde{\lambda}_{it} = \widehat{\lambda}_{it} - \left(\sum_{r=1}^{T} s_{ir}\widehat{\lambda}_{ir}/T_i\right) \tag{11.40}$$

Step 3: Test H_0: $\gamma = 0$ using the t-statistic for $\gamma = 0$. Again, a serial correlation and heteroskedasticity-robust standard error is warranted unless

$$E(\nu_i\nu'_i/\mu_i, x'_i, s_i) = \sigma^2 I_T \qquad \text{under } H_0$$

Both tests proposed by Wooldridge (1995) are computationally simple involving variable addition tests. These require either Tobit residuals or inverse Mill's ratios obtained from probit estimation for each time period. This is followed by fixed effects estimation.

For the random effects model, Verbeek and Nijman (1992a) suggest including three simple variables in the regression to check for the presence of selection bias. These are (i) the number of waves the ith individual participates in the panel, T_i, (ii) a binary variable taking the value 1 if and only if the ith individual is observed over the entire sample, $\prod_{r=1}^{T} s_{ir}$, and (iii) $s_{i,t-1}$ indicating whether the individual was present in the last period. Intuitively, testing the significance of these variables checks whether the pattern of missing observations affects the underlying regression. Wooldridge (1995) argues that the first two variables have no time variation and cannot be implemented in a fixed effects model. He suggested other variables to be used in place of $\widehat{\lambda}_{it}$ in a variable addition test during fixed effects estimation. These are $\sum_{r\neq t}^{T} s_{ir}$ and $\prod_{r\neq t}^{T} s_{ir}$. Such tests have the computational simplicity advantage and the need to only observe x_{it} when $s_{it} = 1$.[14]

Vella and Verbeek (1999) suggest two-step estimators for a wide range of parametric panel data models with censored endogenous variables and sample selection bias. This generalizes the treatment of sample selection models by Ridder (1990) and Nijman and Verbeek (1992a) to a wide range of selection rules. This also generalizes the panel data dummy endogenous regressor model in Vella and Verbeek (1998) by allowing for other forms of censored endogenous regressors. In addition, this analysis shows how Wooldridge's (1995) estimation procedures for sample selection can be applied to more general specifications. The two-step procedure derives estimates of the unobserved heterogeneity responsible for the endogeneity/selection bias in the first step. These in turn are included as additional regressors in the primary equation. This is computationally simple compared to maximum likelihood procedures, since it requires only one-dimensional numerical integration. The panel nature of the data allows adjustment and testing for two forms of endogeneity and/or sample selection bias. Furthermore, it allows for dynamics and state dependence in the reduced form. This procedure is applied to the problem of estimating the impact of weekly hours worked on the offered hourly wage rate:

$$\begin{aligned} w_{it} &= x'_{1,it}\beta_1 + x'_{2,it}\beta_2 + m(\text{hours}_{it};\beta_3) + \mu_i + \eta_{it} \qquad (11.41) \\ \text{hours}^*_{it} &= x'_{3,it}\theta_1 + \text{hours}_{i,t-1}\theta_2 + \alpha_i + \nu_{it} \\ \text{hours}_{it} &= \text{hours}^*_{it} \qquad \text{if hours}^*_{it} > 0 \\ \text{hours}_{it} &= 0, \quad w_{it} \text{ not observed if hours}^*_{it} \leqslant 0 \end{aligned}$$

Here, w_{it} represents log of the hourly wage for individual i at time t; $x_{1,it}$ and $x_{3,it}$ are variables representing individual characteristics; $x_{2,it}$ are work place characteristics for individual i; hours^*_{it} and hours_{it} represent desired and observed number of hours worked; m denotes a polynomial of known length with unknown coefficients β_3. This is estimated using data for young females from the NLSY for the period 1980–87. This included a total of 18 400 observations of which 12 039 observations report positive hours of work in a given period.

Lee (2001) proposes a semiparametric first-difference estimator for panel censored-selection models where the selection equation is of the Tobit type. This estimator minimizes a convex function and does not require any smoothing. This estimator is compared with that of Wooldridge (1995) and Honoré and Kyriazidou (2000a) using Monte Carlo experiments. The results show that all three estimators are quite robust to model assumption violation.

11.6 EMPIRICAL APPLICATIONS

There are many empirical applications illustrating the effects of attrition bias; see Hausman and Wise (1979) for a study of the Gary Income Maintenance Experiment. For this experimental panel study of labor supply response, the treatment effect is an income guarantee/tax rate combination. People who benefit from this experiment are more likely to remain in the sample. Therefore, the selection rule is nonignorable, and attrition can overestimate the treatment effect on labor supply. For the Gary Income Maintenance Experiment, Hausman and Wise (1979) found little effect of attrition bias on the experimental labor supply response. Similar results were obtained by Robins and West (1986) for the Seattle and Denver Income Maintenance Experiments. For the latter sample, attrition was modest (11% for married men and 7% for married women and single heads during the period studied) and its effect was not serious enough to warrant extensive correction procedures.

Ridder (1992) studied the determinants of the total number of trips using the first seven waves of the Dutch Transportation Panel (DTP). This panel was commissioned by the Department of Transportation in the Netherlands to evaluate the effect of price increases on the use of public transportation. The first wave of interviews was conducted in March 1984. There is heavy attrition in the DTP with only 38% of the original sample participating in all seven waves of the panel. Ridder (1992) found that nonrandom attrition from the DTP did not bias time-constant regression coefficients. However, it did bias the time-varying coefficients. Ridder (1992) also found that the restrictions imposed by the standard Hausman and Wise (1979) model for nonrandom attrition on the correlations between individual effects and random shocks may even prevent the detection of nonrandom attrition.

Keane, Moffitt and Runkle (1988) studied the movement of real wages over the business cycle for a panel data drawn from the National Longitudinal Survey of Young Men (NLS) over the period 1966–81. They showed that failure to account for self-selection biased the behavior of real wages in a procyclical direction.

Nijman and Verbeek (1992a) studied the effects of nonresponse on the estimates of a simple life-cycle consumption function using a Dutch panel of households interviewed over the period April 1984–March 1987. Several tests for attrition bias were performed, and the model was estimated using (i) one wave of the panel, (ii) the balanced subpanel, and (iii) the unbalanced panel. For this application, attrition bias was not serious. The balanced subpanel estimates had implausible signs, while the one-wave estimates and the unbalanced panel estimates gave reasonably close estimates with the latter having lower standard errors.

Dionne, Gagne′ and Vanasse (1998) estimate a cost model based on an incomplete panel of Ontario trucking firms. The data consists of 445 yearly observations of general freight carriers in Ontario observed over the period 1981–88. It includes 163 firms for which information is available for 2.7 years on average. The cost-input demand system is jointly estimated with a bivariate probit selection model of entry and exit from the sample. A test for selectivity bias reveals potential bias related to exit but not entry from the sample.

Vella and Verbeek (1998) estimate the union premium for young men over a period of declining unionization (1980–87). The panel data is taken from the NLSY and includes 545 full-time working males who completed their schooling by 1980. The probability of union membership is estimated using a dynamic random effects probit model. The coefficient of lagged union status is estimated at 0.61 with a standard error of 0.07 indicating a positive and statistically significant estimate of state dependence. OLS estimates of the wage equation yield a union wage effect of 15% to 18% depending on whether occupational status dummies are included or not. These estimates are contaminated by endogeneity. The corresponding fixed effects estimates are much lower yielding 7.9% to 8.0%. These estimates eliminate only the endogeneity operating through the individual-specific effects. Thus, any time-varying endogeneity continues to contaminate these estimates. Including correction terms based on the estimated union model yields negative significant coefficients and reveals selection bias. This indicates that workers who receive lower wages, after conditioning on their characteristics and in the absence of unions, are most likely to be in the union. This is consistent with the findings that minority groups who are lower paid for discriminatory reasons have a greater tendency to seek union employment than whites. Vella and Verbeek conclude that the union effect is approximately 21% over the period studied. However, the return to unobserved heterogeneity operating through union status is substantial, making the union premium highly variable among individuals. Moreover, this union premium is sensitive to the pattern of sorting into union employment allowed in the estimation.

11.7 FURTHER READING

One should read the related nonlinear panel data model literature, see for example Abrevaya (1999) who proposes a leapfrog estimator for the monotonic transformation panel data model of the type

$$h_t(y_{it}) = x'_{it}\beta + \mu_i + \nu_{it}$$

where $h_t(\cdot)$ is assumed to be strictly increasing. The trick here is to difference across pairs of individuals at a given time period, rather than across time periods. This semiparametric estimator is shown to be $\sqrt{N}$-consistent and asymptotically normal. Examples of this model include the multiple-spell proportional hazards model and dependent variable transformation models with fixed effects. Abrevaya (2000) introduces a class of rank estimators that consistently estimate the coefficients of a generalized fixed effects regression model. This model allows for censoring, places no parametric assumptions on the error disturbances and allows the fixed effects to be correlated with the covariates. The maximum score estimator for the binary choice fixed effects model proposed by Manski (1987) is a member of this class of estimators. The class of rank estimators converge at less than $\sqrt{N}$ rate, while smoothed versions of these estimators converge at rates approaching the $\sqrt{N}$ rate. Some of the limitations of this approach are that the estimation relies on a strict exogeneity assumption and does not deal with the inclusion of lagged dependent variables. Also, the coefficients of time-invariant covariates are not identified by this class of estimators.

Wooldridge (1997) considers the estimation of multiplicative, unobserved components panel data models without imposing a strict exogeneity assumption on the conditioning variables. A robust method of moments estimator is proposed which requires only a conditional mean assumption. This applies to binary choice models with multiplicative unobserved effects, and models containing parametric nonlinear transformations of the endogenous variables. This model is particularly suited to non-negative explained variables, including count variables. In addition, it can also be applied to certain nonlinear Euler equations. Wooldridge (1999) offers some distribution-free estimators for multiplicative unobserved components panel data models. Requiring only the correct specification of the conditional mean, the multinomial quasi-conditional MLE is shown to be consistent and asymptotically normal. This estimation method is popular for estimating fixed effects count models, see Hausman, Hall and Griliches (1984). Wooldridge's results show that it can be used to obtain consistent estimates even when the dependent variable y_{it} is not a vector of counts. In fact, y_{it} can be a binary response variable, a proportion, a non-negative continuously distributed random variable, or it can have discrete and continuous characteristics. Neither the distribution of y_{it} nor its temporal dependence are restricted. Additional orthogonality conditions can be used in a GMM framework to improve the efficiency of the estimator. Finally, Wooldridge (2000) proposes a method of estimating very general, nonlinear, dynamic, unobserved effects panel data models with feedback. Wooldridge shows how to construct the likelihood function for the conditional maximum likelihood estimator in dynamic, unobserved effects models where not all conditioning variables are strictly exogenous. A useful innovation is the treatment of the initial conditions which offers a flexible, relatively simple alternative to existing methods.

Hansen (1999) considers the estimation of threshold panel regressions with individual specific effects. This is useful for situations where the regression function is not identical across all observations in the sample. In fact, the observations are divided into two regimes depending on whether a threshold variable q_{it} is smaller or larger than the threshold γ:

$$y_{it} = \mu_i + \beta_1' x_{it} 1(q_{it} \leqslant \gamma) + \beta_2' x_{it} 1(q_{it} > \gamma) + \nu_{it}$$

where $1(\cdot)$ is the indicator function. The regimes are distinguished by differing slopes β_1 and β_2. Hansen (1999) proposes a least squares procedure to estimate the threshold and regression slopes using fixed effects transformations. Nonstandard asymptotic theory with T fixed and $N \to \infty$ is developed to allow the construction of confidence intervals and test of hypotheses. This method is applied to a panel of 565 US firms observed over the period 1973–87 to test whether financial constraints affect investment decisions. Hansen finds overwhelming evidence of a double threshold effect which separates the firms based on their debt to asset ratio. The weakness of this approach is that it does not allow for heteroskedasticity, lagged dependent variables, endogenous variables and random effects.

NOTES

1. For the probit model

$$F(x_{it}'\beta) = \Phi(x_{it}'\beta) = \int_{-\infty}^{x_{it}'\beta} \frac{1}{\sqrt{2\pi}} \mathrm{e}^{-u^2/2} \mathrm{d}u$$

and for the logit model

$$F(x_{it}'\beta) = \frac{\mathrm{e}^{x_{it}'\beta}}{1 + \mathrm{e}^{x_{it}'\beta}}$$

2. Note that for this nonlinear panel data model, it is not possible to get rid of the μ_i by taking differences or performing the Within transformation as in Chapter 2.
3. Cornwell and Schmidt (1992) prove that the unconditional MLE and the conditional MLE coincide in a linear regression model with fixed individual effects and investigate whether this property holds for SUR and simultaneous equation models.
4. Charlier, Melenberg and van Soest (1995) provide a smoothed maximum score estimator for the binary choice panel data model which has an asymptotic normal distribution but a convergence rate that is slower than root-N. Lee (1999) proposes a $\sqrt{N}$-consistent semiparametric estimator which does not depend on a smoothing parameter and is asymptotically normal.
5. Alternatively, one could condition on the set of continuously working individuals, i.e. use only the sample with positive hours of work. In this case the sample is considered truncated (see Maddala, 1983).
6. Researchers may also be interested in panel data economic relationships where the dependent variable is a count of some individual actions or events. For example, the number of patents filed, the number of drugs introduced, the number of hospital visits or the number of jobs held. These models can be estimated using Poisson panel data regressions (see Hausman, Hall and Griliches, 1984) and the recent monographs on count data by Cameron and Trivedi (1998) and Winkelmann (2000).
7. For the special case of only one regressor and two panels ($T = 2$), Campbell and Honoré (1993) show that the semiparametric estimator derived by Honoré (1992) is

median unbiased in finite samples under (basically) the same conditions that are used to derive its asymptotic distribution.

8. For good surveys of simulation methods, see Hajivassiliou and Ruud (1994) for limited dependent variable models and Gourieroux and Monfort (1993) with special reference to panel data. The methods surveyed include simulation of the likelihood, simulation of the moment functions and simulation of the score. For the use of the Gibbs sampling method to estimate panel data models, see Chib (1996).
9. In both the logistic and semiparametric case, the main limitations of the Honoré and Kyriazidou (2000b) approach are (i) the assumption that the errors in the underlying threshold-crossing model are independent over time and (ii) the assumption that $x'_{i2} - x'_{i3}$ has support in a neighborhood of 0. The latter restriction rules out time dummies.
10. This agrees with the Monte Carlo results obtained by Heckman (1981b) who found that for a probit model with fixed effects and lagged dependent variable, the inconsistency of the maximum likelihood estimator can be "disturbingly large" when the coefficient of the lagged dependent variable $\lambda \neq 0$.
11. Other sufficient conditions for consistency of these estimators are given by Verbeek and Nijman (1996). These are derived for specific selection rules. One interesting and practical sufficient condition that emerges is that the Within estimator is consistent and free of selectivity bias if the probability of being in the sample is constant over time. In this case, the correction for selectivity bias is time-invariant and hence is absorbed in the individual effect term.
12. If the selection rule is unknown, identification problems arise regarding the parameters of interest (see Verbeek and Nijman, 1996). Also, for a more comprehensive analysis of the attrition problem in panel data studies with an arbitrary number of waves, see Ridder (1990).
13. Verbeek and Nijman (1992a) show that under nonresponse, the conditions for consistency of the Within estimator are weaker than those for the random effects GLS estimator. This means that the Within estimator is more robust to nonresponse bias than GLS.
14. It is important to point out that both Verbeek and Nijman (1992a) as well as Wooldridge (1995) assume that the unobservable effects and the idiosyncratic errors in the selection process are normally distributed. Kyriazidou's (1997) treatment of sample selection, discussed in section 11.2, leaves the distributions of all unobservables unspecified.

PROBLEMS

11.1 In section 11.1 we considered the fixed effects logit model with $T = 2$.

(a) In this problem, we look at $T = 3$ and ask the reader to compute the conditional probabilities that would get rid of the individual effects by conditioning on $\sum_{t=1}^{3} = y_{it}$. Note that this sum can now be 0, 1, 2 or 3. (Hint: First show that terms in the conditional likelihood function, which are conditioned upon $\sum_{t=1}^{3} y_{it} = 0$ or 3, add nothing to the likelihood. Then focus on terms that condition on $\sum_{t=1}^{3} y_{it} = 1$ or 2.)

(b) Show that for $T = 10$, one has to condition on the sum being $1, 2, \ldots, 9$. One can see that for this case the computations are excessive. To convince yourself, write down the probabilities conditioning on $\sum_{t=1}^{10} y_{it} = 1$.

11.2 Consider the Chamberlain (1985) fixed effects conditional logit model with a lagged dependent variable given in (11.20). Show that for $T = 3$,

$\Pr[A/y_{i1}+y_{i2}=1,\mu_i]$ and therefore $\Pr[B/y_{i1}+y_{i2}=1,\mu_i]$ do not depend on μ_i. Note that A and B are defined in (11.21) and (11.22), respectively.

11.3 Consider the Honoré and Kyriazidou (2000b) fixed effects logit model given in (11.23).

(a) Show that for $T=3$, $\Pr[A/x_i',\mu_i,A\cup B]$ and $\Pr[B/x_i',\mu_i,A\cup B]$ both depend on μ_i. This means that the conditional likelihood approach will *not* eliminate the fixed effect μ_i.

(b) If $x_{i2}'=x_{i3}'$, show that $\Pr[A/x_i',\mu_i,A\cup B,x_{i2}'=x_{i3}']$ and $\Pr[B/x_i',\mu_i,A\cup B,x_{i2}'=x_{i3}']$ do *not* depend on μ_i.

11.4 *Fixed effects logit model.* This is based on Abrevaya (1997). Consider the fixed effects logit model given in (11.4) with $T=2$. In (11.10) and (11.11) we showed the conditional maximum likelihood of β, call it $\widehat{\beta}_{\mathrm{CML}}$, can be obtained by running a logit estimator of the dependent variable $1(\Delta y=1)$ on the independent variables Δx for the subsample of observations satisfying $y_{i1}+y_{i2}=1$. Here $1(\Delta y=1)$ is an indicator function taking the value one if $\Delta y=1$. Therefore, $\widehat{\beta}_{\mathrm{CML}}$ maximizes the log-likelihood

$$\ln L_c(\beta)=\sum_{i\epsilon\vartheta}[1(\Delta y=1)\ln F(\Delta x\beta)+1(\Delta y=-1)\ln(1-F(\Delta x\beta))]$$

where $\vartheta=\{i:y_{i1}+y_{i2}=1\}$.

(a) Maximize the unconditional log-likelihood for (11.4) given by

$$\ln L(\beta,\alpha_i)=\sum_{i=1}^{n}\sum_{t=1}^{2}[y_{it}\ln F(x_{it}\beta+\alpha_i)+(1-y_{it})\times\ln(1-F(x_{it}\beta+\alpha_i))]$$

with respect to α_i and show that

$$\widehat{\alpha}_i=\begin{cases}-\infty & \text{if } y_{i1}+y_{i2}=0\\ -(x_{i1}+x_{i2})\beta/2 & \text{if } y_{i1}+y_{i2}=1\\ +\infty & \text{if } y_{i1}+y_{i2}=2\end{cases}$$

(b) Concentrate the likelihood by plugging $\widehat{\alpha}_i$ in the unconditional likelihood and show that

$$\ln L(\beta,\widehat{\alpha}_i)=\sum_{i\epsilon\vartheta}2[1(\Delta y=1)\ln F(\Delta x\beta/2)+1(\Delta y=-1)\times\ln(1-F(\Delta x\beta/2))]$$

Hint: Use the symmetry of F and the fact that

$$1(\Delta y=1)=y_{i2}=1-y_{i1}\quad\text{and}$$
$$1(\Delta y=-1)=y_{i1}=1-y_{i2}\quad\text{for } i\epsilon\vartheta$$

(c) Conclude that $\ln L(\beta,\widehat{\alpha}_i)=2\ln L_c(\beta/2)$. This shows that a scale adjusted maximum likelihood estimator is equivalent to the conditional maximum likelihood estimator, i.e. $\widehat{\beta}_{\mathrm{ML}}=2\widehat{\beta}_{\mathrm{CML}}$. Whether a similar result holds for $T>2$ remains an open question.

11.5 *Binary response model regression* (BRMR). This is based on problem 95.5.4 in *Econometric Theory* by Baltagi (1995d). Davidson and MacKinnon (1993) derive an artificial regression for testing hypotheses in a binary response model. For the fixed effects model described in (11.4), the reader is asked to derive the BRMR to test H_0: $\mu_i = 0$, for $i = 1, 2, \ldots, N$. Show that if $F(\cdot)$ is the logistic (or normal) cumulative distribution function, this BRMR is simply a weighted least squares regression of logit (or probit) residuals, ignoring the fixed effects, on the matrix of regressors X and the matrix of individual dummies. The test statistic in this case is the explained sum of squares from this BRMR. See Baltagi (1999a) or solution 95.5.4 in *Econometric Theory* by Gurmu (1996).

11.6 Using the Vella and Verbeek (1998) data set posted on the *Journal of Applied Econometrics* web site:
(a) Replicate their descriptive statistics given in Table I and confirm that the unconditional union premium is around 15%.
(b) Replicate their random effects probit estimates of union membership given in Table II.
(c) Replicate the wage regressions with union effects given in Table III.
(d) Replicate the wage regressions under unrestricted sorting given in Table V.

12 Nonstationary Panels

12.1 INTRODUCTION

With the growing use of cross-country data over time to study purchasing power parity, growth convergence and international R&D spillovers, the focus of panel data econometrics has shifted towards studying the asymptotics of macro panels with large N (number of countries) and large T (length of time series) rather than the usual asymptotics of micro panels with large N and small T. The limiting distribution of double indexed integrated processes has been extensively studied by Phillips and Moon (1999, 2000). The fact that T is allowed to increase to infinity in macro panel data generated two strands of ideas. The first rejected the homogeneity of the regression parameters implicit in the use of a pooled regression model in favor of heterogeneous regressions, i.e. one for each country, see Pesaran and Smith (1995), Im, Pesaran and Shin (1997), Lee, Pesaran and Smith (1997), Pesaran, Shin and Smith (1999) and Pesaran and Zhao (1999) to mention a few. This literature critically relies on T being large to estimate each country's regression separately. This literature warns against the use of standard pooled estimators such as FE to estimate the dynamic panel data model, arguing that they are subject to large potential bias when the parameters are heterogeneous across countries and the regressors are serially correlated. Another strand of literature applied time-series procedures to panels, worrying about nonstationarity, spurious regressions and cointegration.[1,2] Consider, for example, the Penn World Tables which have been used to study growth convergence among various countries, see /www.nber.org/. Phillips and Moon (2000) argue that the time-series components of the variables used in these tables, like per capita GDP growth, have strong nonstationarity, a feature which we have paid no attention to in the previous chapters. This is understandable given that micro panels deal with large N and small T. With large N, large T macro panels, nonstationarity deserves more attention. In particular, time-series fully modified estimation techniques that account for endogeneity of the regressors and correlation and heteroskedasticity of the residuals can now be combined with fixed and random effects panel estimation methods. Some of the distinctive results that are obtained with nonstationary panels are that many test statistics and estimators of interest have normal limiting distributions. This is in contrast to the nonstationary time-series literature where the limiting distributions are complicated functionals of Weiner processes. Several unit root tests applied in the time-series literature have been extended to panel data. When the panel data are both heterogeneous and nonstationary, issues of combining individual unit root tests applied on each time series are tackled by Im, Pesaran and Shin (1997), Maddala and Wu (1999) and Choi (1999a). Using panel data, one can avoid the problem of spurious regression, see Kao (1999) and Phillips and Moon (1999). Unlike the single time-series spurious regression literature, the panel data spurious regression estimates give a consistent estimate of the true value of the parameter as both N and T tend to ∞. This is because the panel estimator averages across individuals and the information in the independent cross-section data in the panel leads to a stronger overall signal than the pure time-series case. Of course letting both N and T tend to ∞ brings in a new host of issues dealing with how to do asymptotic analysis. This is studied by Phillips and Moon (1999, 2000) and Kauppi (2000).

One can find numerous applications of time-series methods applied to panels in recent years, especially panel unit root tests, panel cointegration tests and the estimation of long-run average relations. Examples from the purchasing power parity literature and real exchange rate stationarity include Frankel and Rose (1996), Jorion and Sweeney (1996), MacDonald (1996), Oh (1996), Wu (1996), Coakley and Fuertes (1997), Papell (1997), O'Connell (1998), Groen and Kleibergen (1999), Choi (1999a), Canzoneri, Cumby and Diba (1999), Groen (2000) and Pedroni (2001), to mention a few. On real wage stationarity, see Fleissig and Strauss (1997). On the inflation rate, see Culver and Papell (1997); on the current account balance, see Wu (2000); on the consumption–income ratio stationarity, see Sarantis and Stewart (1999). On health care expenditures, see McCoskey and Selden (1998); on growth and convergence, see Islam (1995), Bernard and Jones (1996), Evans and Karras (1996), Sala-i-Martin (1996), Lee, Pesaran and Smith (1997) and Nerlove (2000a). On international R&D spillovers, see Kao, Chiang and Chen (1999). On savings and investment models, see Coakely, Kulasi and Smith (1996) and Moon and Phillips (1998).

However, the use of such panel data methods is not without critics, see Maddala, Wu and Liu (2000) who argue that panel data unit root tests do not rescue purchasing power parity (PPP). In fact, the results on PPP with panels are mixed depending on the group of countries studied, the period of study and the type of unit root test used. More damaging is the argument by Maddala, Wu and Liu (2000) that for PPP, panel data tests are the wrong answer to the low power of unit root tests in single time series. After all, the null hypothesis of a single unit root is different from the null hypothesis of a panel unit root for the PPP hypothesis. Using the same line of criticism, Maddala (1999) argued that panel unit root tests did not help settle the question of growth convergence among countries. However, it was useful in spurring much needed research into dynamic panel data models. Also, Quah (1996) argued that the basic issues of whether poor countries catch up with the rich can never be answered by the use of traditional panels.

Instead, Quah suggested formulating and estimating models of income dynamics. Recently, Smith (2000) warned about the mechanical application of panel unit root or cointegration tests, arguing that the application of these tests requires that the hypotheses involved be interesting in the context of the substantive application. The latter is a question of theory rather than statistical technique.

Recent surveys on nonstationary panels include Phillips and Moon (2000) on multi-indexed processes, Banerjee (1999), Baltagi and Kao (2000) and Smith (2000) on panel unit roots and cointegration tests. This chapter studies panel unit root tests in section 12.2, while section 12.3 discusses the panel spurious models. Section 12.4 considers the panel cointegration tests, while section 12.5 discusses panel cointegration models.

12.2 PANEL UNIT ROOT TESTS

Testing for unit roots in time-series studies is now common practice among applied researchers and has become an integral part of econometric courses. However, testing for unit roots in panels is recent, see Levin and Lin (1992), Im, Pesaran and Shin (1997), Harris and Tzavalis (1999), Maddala and Wu (1999), Choi (1999a) and Hadri (1999). Exceptions are Bhargava, Franzini and Narendranathan (1982), Boumahdi and Thomas (1991), Breitung and Meyer (1994) and Quah (1994). Bharagava, Franzini and Narendranathan (1982) proposed a test for random walk residuals in a dynamic model with fixed effects. They suggested a modified Durbin–Watson (DW) statistic based on fixed effects residuals and two other test statistics based on differenced OLS residuals. In typical micro panels with $N \to \infty$, they recommended their modified DW statistic. Boumahdi and Thomas (1991) proposed a generalization of the Dickey–Fuller (DF) test for unit roots in panel data to assess the efficiency of the French capital market using 140 French stock prices over the period January 1973 to February 1986. Breitung and Meyer (1994) applied various modified DF test statistics to test for unit roots in a panel of contracted wages negotiated at the firm and industry level for Western Germany over the period 1972–87. Quah (1994) suggested a test for unit root in a panel data model without fixed effects where both N and T go to infinity at the same rate such that N/T is constant. Levin and Lin (1992) generalized this model to allow for fixed effects, individual deterministic trends and heterogeneous serially correlated errors. They assumed that both N and T tend to infinity. However, T increases at a faster rate than N with $N/T \to 0$. Even though this literature grew from time-series and panel data, the way in which N, the number of cross-section units, and T, the length of the time series, tend to infinity is crucial for determining asymptotic properties of estimators and tests proposed for nonstationary panels, see Phillips and Moon (1999). Several approaches are possible including (i) sequential limits where one index, say N, is fixed and T is allowed to increase to infinity, giving an intermediate limit. Then by letting N tend to infinity subsequently, a sequential limit theory is obtained. Phillips and Moon (2000) argued that these sequential limits are easy to derive and are helpful in extracting quick asymptotics. However, Phillips and Moon provided a simple example that illustrates how sequential limits can sometimes give misleading asymptotic results. (ii) A second approach, used by Quah (1994) and Levin and Lin (1992) is to allow the two indexes, N and T to pass to infinity along a specific diagonal path in the two-dimensional array. This path can be determined by a monotonically increasing functional relation of the type $T = T(N)$ which applies as the index $N \to \infty$. Phillips and Moon (2000) showed that the limit theory obtained by this approach is dependent on the specific functional relation $T = T(N)$ and the assumed expansion path may not provide an appropriate approximation for a given (T, N) situation. (iii) A third approach is a joint limit theory allowing both N and T to pass to infinity simultaneously without placing specific diagonal path restrictions on the divergence. Some control over the relative rate of expansion may have to be exercised in order to get definitive results. Phillips and Moon argued that, in general, joint limit theory is more robust than either the sequential limit or diagonal path limit. However, it is usually more difficult to derive and requires stronger conditions such as the existence of higher moments that will allow for uniformity in the convergence arguments. The multi-index asymptotic theory in Phillips and Moon (1999, 2000) is applied to joint limits in which $T, N \to \infty$ and $(T/N) \to \infty$, i.e. to situations where the time-series sample is large relative to the cross-section sample. However, the general approach given there is also applicable to situations in which $(T/N) \to 0$ although different limit results will generally obtain in that case.

12.2.1 Levin and Lin Tests

Consider the model

$$y_{it} = \rho_i y_{i,t-1} + z_{it}^{'}\gamma + u_{it} \qquad i = 1, ..., N;\ t = 1, ..., T \tag{12.1}$$

where z_{it} is the deterministic component and u_{it} is a stationary process. z_{it} could be zero, one, the fixed effects, μ_i, or fixed effect as well as a time trend, t. The Levin and Lin (1992) (LL) tests assume that u_{it} are IID$(0, \sigma_u^2)$ and $\rho_i = \rho$ for all i. This means that the coefficient of the lagged dependent variable is assumed to be homogeneous across all cross-section units of the panel. Also, the individual processes are cross-sectionally independent. The null hypothesis is that each series in the panel contains a unit root, i.e. $H_0: \rho = 1$ against the alternative hypothesis that *all* individual series in the panel are stationary, i.e. $H_1: \rho < 1$.

Let $\widehat{\rho}$ be the OLS estimator of ρ in (12.1) and define $z_t = (z_{1t}, \ldots, z_{Nt})'$, $h(t, s) = z_t' \left(\sum_{t=1}^{T} z_t z_t'\right)^{-1} z_s$, $\widetilde{u}_{it} = u_{it} - \sum_{s=1}^{T} h(t, s) u_{is}$ and $\widetilde{y}_{it} = y_{it} - \sum_{s=1}^{T} h(t, s) y_{is}$. Then we have

$$\sqrt{N}T\,(\widehat{\rho} - 1) = \frac{\dfrac{1}{\sqrt{N}} \sum_{i=1}^{N} \dfrac{1}{T} \sum_{t=1}^{T} \widetilde{y}_{i,t-1}\widetilde{u}_{it}}{\dfrac{1}{N} \sum_{i=1}^{N} \dfrac{1}{T^2} \sum_{t=1}^{T} \widetilde{y}_{i,t-1}^2} \tag{12.2}$$

and the corresponding t-statistic, under the null hypothesis is given by

$$t_\rho = \frac{(\widehat{\rho}-1)\sqrt{\sum_{i=1}^{N}\sum_{t=1}^{T}\widetilde{y}_{i,t-1}^2}}{s_e} \tag{12.3}$$

where $s_e^2 = (1/NT)\sum_{i=1}^{N}\sum_{t=1}^{T}\widetilde{u}_{it}^2$.

Levin and Lin (1992) obtained the following limiting distributions of $\sqrt{N}T$ $(\widehat{\rho}-1)$ and t_ρ:

z_{it}	$\widehat{\rho}$	$t_\rho \Rightarrow$
0	$\sqrt{N}T\,(\widehat{\rho}-1) \Rightarrow N\,(0,2)$	$t_\rho \Rightarrow N\,(0,1)$
1	$\sqrt{N}T\,(\widehat{\rho}-1) \Rightarrow N\,(0,2)$	$t_\rho \Rightarrow N\,(0,1)$
μ_i	$\sqrt{N}T\,(\widehat{\rho}-1)+3\sqrt{N} \Rightarrow N\left(0,\frac{51}{5}\right)$	$\sqrt{1.25}t_\rho+\sqrt{1.875N} \Rightarrow N\,(0,1)$
$(\mu_i,t)'$	$\sqrt{N}\,(T\,(\widehat{\rho}-1)+7.5) \Rightarrow N\left(0,\frac{2895}{112}\right)$	$\sqrt{\frac{448}{277}}\left(t_\rho+\sqrt{3.75N}\right) \Rightarrow N\,(0,1)$

(12.4)

Sequential limit theory, i.e. $T \to \infty$ followed by $N \to \infty$, is used to derive the limiting distributions in (12.4) and $\Rightarrow$ denotes weak convergence of the underlying probability measures. Levin and Lin (1992) therefore provided correction and standardization factors required for the unit root estimators to have a normal distribution in the limit. They also extended their work to more general correlated and heteroskedastic structures. When serial correlation is allowed, this introduces correlation between the lagged dependent variable and the disturbances. Levin and Lin (1993) show how an augmented Dickey–Fuller test statistic for each individual time series can be used to construct a test for $\rho = 0$.

Harris and Tzavalis (1999) also derived unit root tests for (12.1) with $z_{it} = \{0\}, \{\mu_i\}$ or $\{(\mu_i,t)'\}$ when the time dimension of the panel T is *fixed*. This is the typical case for micro panel studies. The main results are:

z_{it}	$\widehat{\rho}$
0	$\sqrt{N}\,(\widehat{\rho}-1) \Rightarrow N\left(0,\frac{2}{T(T-1)}\right)$
μ_i	$\sqrt{N}\left(\widehat{\rho}-1+\frac{3}{T+1}\right) \Rightarrow N\left(0,\frac{3(17T^2-20T+17)}{5(T-1)(T+1)^3}\right)$
$(\mu_i,t)'$	$\sqrt{N}\left(\widehat{\rho}-1+\frac{15}{2(T+2)}\right) \Rightarrow N\left(0,\frac{15(193T^2-728T+1147)}{112(T+2)^3(T-2)}\right)$

(12.5)

Harris and Tzavalis (1999) also showed that the assumption that T tends to infinity at a faster rate than N as in Levin and Lin rather than T fixed as in the case of micro panels yields tests which are substantially undersized and have low power especially when T is small.

Recently, Frankel and Rose (1996), Oh (1996) and Lothian (1996) tested the PPP hypothesis using panel data. All of these articles use Levin and Lin tests and some of them report evidence supporting the PPP hypothesis. O'Connell (1998), however, showed that the Levin and Lin tests suffered from significant size distortion in the presence of correlation among contemporaneous cross-sectional error terms. O'Connell highlighted the importance of controlling for cross-sectional dependence when testing for a unit root in panels of real exchange rates. He showed that, controlling for cross-sectional dependence, no evidence against the null of a random walk can be found in panels of up to 64 real exchange rates.

Virtually all the existing nonstationary panel literature assume cross-sectional independence. It is true that the assumption of independence across i is rather strong, but it is needed in order to satisfy the requirement of the Lindeberg–Lévy central limit theorem. Moreover, as pointed out by Quah (1994), modeling cross-sectional dependence is involved because individual observations in a cross-section have no natural ordering. Driscoll and Kraay (1998) presented a simple extension of common nonparametric covariance matrix estimation techniques which yields standard errors that are robust to very general forms of spatial and temporal dependence as the time dimension becomes large. In a recent paper, Conley (1999) presented a spatial model of dependence among agents using a metric of economic distance that provides cross-sectional data with a structure similar to time-series data. Conley proposed a generalized method of moments (GMM) using such dependent data and a class of nonparametric covariance matrix estimators that allow for a general form of dependence characterized by economic distance.

12.2.2 Im, Pesaran and Shin Tests

The Levin and Lin test is restrictive in the sense that it requires ρ to be homogeneous across i. As Maddala (1999) pointed out, the null may be fine for testing convergence in growth among countries, but the alternative restricts every country to converge at the same rate. Im, Pesaran and Shin (1997) (IPS) allow for a heterogeneous coefficient of $y_{i,t-1}$ and propose an alternative testing procedure based on averaging individual unit root test statistics. IPS suggest an average of the augmented DF (ADF) tests when u_{it} is serially correlated with different serial correlation properties across cross-sectional units, i.e. $u_{it} = \sum_{j=1}^{p_i} \varphi_{ij} u_{i,t-j} + \varepsilon_{it}$. Substituting this u_{it} in (12.1) we get

$$y_{it} = \rho_i y_{i,t-1} + \sum_{j=1}^{p_i} \varphi_{ij} \Delta y_{i,t-j} + z_{it}'\gamma + \varepsilon_{it} \tag{12.6}$$

The null hypothesis is that each series in the panel contains a unit root, i.e. H_0: $\rho_i = 1$ for all i and the alternative hypothesis is that at least one of the individual series in the panel is stationary, i.e. H_1: $\rho_i < 1$ for at least one i. The IPS t-bar statistic is defined as the average of the individual ADF statistic as

$$\bar{t} = \frac{1}{N}\sum_{i=1}^{N} t_{\rho_i} \tag{12.7}$$

where t_{ρ_i} is the individual t-statistic for testing H_0: $\rho_i = 1$ for all i in (12.6). It is known that for a fixed N

$$t_{\rho_i} \Rightarrow \frac{\int_0^1 W_{iZ} \mathrm{d}W_{iZ}}{\left[\int_0^1 W_{iZ}^2\right]^{1/2}} = t_{iT} \tag{12.8}$$

as $T \to \infty$, where $\int W(r)\mathrm{d}r$ denotes a Weiner integral with the argument r suppressed in (12.8). IPS assume that t_{iT} are IID and have finite mean and variance. Then

$$\frac{\sqrt{N}\left(\frac{1}{N}\sum_{i=1}^{N} t_{iT} - \frac{1}{N}\sum_{i=1}^{N} E\left[t_{iT}|\rho_i = 1\right]\right)}{\sqrt{\frac{1}{N}\sum_{i=1}^{N} \operatorname{var}\left[t_{iT}|\rho_i = 1\right]}} \Rightarrow N(0, 1) \qquad (12.9)$$

as $N \to \infty$ by the Lindeberg–Lévy central limit theorem. Hence

$$t_{\mathrm{IPS}} = \frac{\sqrt{N}\left(\bar{t} - \frac{1}{N}\sum_{i=1}^{N} E\left[t_{iT}|\rho_i = 1\right]\right)}{\sqrt{\frac{1}{N}\sum_{i=1}^{N} \operatorname{var}\left[t_{iT}|\rho_i = 1\right]}} \Rightarrow N(0, 1) \qquad (12.10)$$

as $T \to \infty$ followed by $N \to \infty$ sequentially. The values of $E\left[t_{iT}|\rho_i = 1\right]$ and $\operatorname{var}[t_{iT}|\rho_i = 1]$ have been computed by IPS via simulations for different values of T and p_i's. IPS also suggested a group mean Lagrange multiplier test for testing $\rho_i = 1$. In Monte Carlo experiments, they show that the average LM and t-statistics have better finite sample properties than the LL test.

The LL and IPS tests require $N \to \infty$ such that $N/T \to 0$, i.e. N should be small enough relative to T. This means that both tests may not keep nominal size well when either N is small or N is large relative to T. In fact, the simulation results of Im, Pesaran and Shin (1997) show that both IPS and LL have size distortions as N gets large relative to T. Breitung (2000) studies the local power of LL and IPS test statistics against a sequence of local alternatives. Breitung finds that the LL and IPS tests suffer from a dramatic loss of power if individual specific trends are included. This is due to the bias correction that also removes the mean under the sequence of local alternatives. Breitung suggests a test statistic that does not employ a bias adjustment whose power is substantially higher than that of LL or the IPS tests using Monte Carlo experiments. The simulation results indicate that the power of LL and IPS tests is very sensitive to the specification of the deterministic terms.

McCoskey and Selden (1998) applied the IPS test for testing unit roots for per capita national health care expenditures (HE) and gross domestic product (GDP) for a panel of 20 OECD countries. McCoskey and Selden rejected the null hypothesis that these two series contain unit roots. Gerdtham and Löthgren (2000) claimed that the stationarity found by McCoskey and Selden is driven by the omission of time trends in their ADF regression in (12.6). Using the IPS test with a time trend, Gerdtham and Löthgren found that both HE and GDP are nonstationary. They concluded that HE and GDP are cointegrated around linear trends. Wu (2000) applied the IPS test to the current account balances for 10 OECD countries over the period 1977Q1 to 1997Q4. Current account balances measure changes in national net indebtedness. Persistent deficits could have serious effects. Wu does not reject current account stationarity which in turn is consistent with the sustainability of external debts among the industrial countries considered.

12.2.3 Combining p-Value Tests

Let G_{iT_i} be a unit root test statistic for the ith group in (12.1) and assume that as the time-series observations for the ith group $T_i \to \infty$, $G_{iT_i} \Rightarrow G_i$ where G_i is a nondegenerate random variable. Let p_i be the asymptotic p-value of a unit root test for cross-section i, i.e. $p_i = F\left(G_{iT_i}\right)$, where $F(\cdot)$ is the distribution function of the random variable G_i. Maddala and Wu (1999) and Choi (1999a) proposed a Fisher-type test

$$P = -2\sum_{i=1}^{N} \ln p_i \tag{12.11}$$

which combines the p-values from unit root tests for each cross-section i to test for unit roots in panel data. Note that $-2\ln p_i$ has a χ^2 distribution with two degrees of freedom. This means that P is distributed as χ^2 with $2N$ degrees of freedom as $T_i \to \infty$ for finite N. Maddala and Wu (1999) argued that the IPS and Fisher tests relax the restrictive assumption of the LL test that ρ_i is the same under the alternative. Both the IPS and Fisher tests combine information based on individual unit root tests. However, the Fisher test has the advantage over the IPS test in that it does not require a balanced panel. Also, the Fisher test can use different lag lengths in the individual ADF regressions and can be applied to any other unit root tests. The disadvantage is that the p-values have to be derived by Monte Carlo simulations. Maddala and Wu (1999) find that the Fisher test with bootstrap-based critical values performed the best and is the preferred choice for testing nonstationarity as the null and also in testing for cointegration in panels. Choi (1999a) proposes two other test statistics besides Fisher's inverse chi-square test statistic P. The first is the inverse normal test $Z = (1/\sqrt{N})\sum_{i=1}^{N}\Phi^{-1}(p_i)$ where Φ is the standard normal cumulative distribution function. Since $0 \leqslant p_i \leqslant 1$, $\Phi^{-1}(p_i)$ is an $N(0,1)$ random variable and as $T_i \to \infty$ for all i, $Z \Rightarrow N(0,1)$. The second is the logit test $L = \sum_{i=1}^{N}\ln(p_i/1 - p_i)$ where $\ln(p_i/1 - p_i)$ has the logistic distribution with mean 0 and variance $\pi^2/3$. As $T_i \to \infty$ for all i, $\sqrt{m}L \Rightarrow t_{5N+4}$ where $m = 3(5N+4)/\pi^2 N(5N+2)$. Choi (1999a) echoes similar advantages for these three combining p-value tests: (1) the cross-sectional dimension, N, can be either finite or infinite; (2) each group can have different types of nonstochastic and stochastic components; (3) the time-series dimension, T, can be different for each i; and (4) the alternative hypothesis would allow some groups to have unit roots while others may not.

When N is large, Choi (1999a) proposed a modified P test

$$P_{\mathrm{m}} = \frac{1}{2\sqrt{N}}\sum_{i=1}^{N}(-2\ln p_i - 2) \tag{12.12}$$

since $E\left[-2\ln p_i\right] = 2$ and $\mathrm{var}\left[-2\ln p_i\right] = 4$. Applying the Lindeberg–Lévy central limit theorem to (12.12) we get $P_{\mathrm{m}} \Rightarrow N(0,1)$ as $T_i \to \infty$ followed by $N \to \infty$.[3] The distribution of the Z-statistic is invariant to infinite N, and $Z \Rightarrow N(0,1)$ as $T_i \to \infty$ and then $N \to \infty$. Also, the distribution of $\sqrt{m}L \approx (1/\sqrt{\pi^2 N/3})\sum_{i=1}^{N}\ln(p_i/1-p_i) \Rightarrow N(0,1)$ by the Lindeberg–Lévy central limit theorem as $T_i \to \infty$ and then $N \to \infty$. Therefore, Z and $\sqrt{m}L$ can be used without modification for infinite N. Simulation results for $N = 5, 10, 25, 50$ and 100, and $T = 50$ and 100 show that the empirical size of all the tests is reasonably close to the 0.05 nominal size when N is small. P and P_{m} show mild size distortions at $N = 100$, while Z and IPS show the most stable size. All tests become more powerful as N increases. The combined p-value tests have superior size adjusted power to the IPS test. In fact, the power of the Z-test is in some cases more than three times that of the IPS test. Overall, the Z-test seems to outperform the other tests and is recommended.

Choi (1999a) applied the combining p-value tests and the IPS test given in (12.7) to panel data of monthly US real exchange rates sampled from 1973:3 to 1996:3. The combining p-value tests provided evidence in favor of the PPP hypothesis while the IPS test did not. Choi claimed that this is due to the improved finite sample power of the combination tests. Maddala and Wu (1999) and Maddala, Wu and Liu (2000) find that the Fisher test is superior to the IPS test which in turn is more powerful than the LL test. They argue that these panel unit root tests still do not rescue the PPP hypothesis. When allowance is made for the deficiency in the panel data unit root tests and panel estimation methods, support for PPP turns out to be weak.

Choi (2000) considers four instrumental variable estimators of an error component model with stationary and nearly nonstationary regressors. The remainder disturbances follow an autoregressive process whose order as well as parameters vary across individuals. The IV estimators considered include the Within-IV, Within-IV-OLS, Within-IV-GLS and IV-GLS estimators. Using sequential and joint limit theories, Choi shows that, under proper conditions, all the estimators have normal distributions in the limit as N and $T \to \infty$. Simulation results show that the efficiency rankings of the estimators crucially depend on the type of regressor and the number of instruments. The Wald test for coefficient restrictions keeps reasonable nominal size as $N \to \infty$ and its power depends upon the number of instruments and the degree of serial correlation and heterogeneity in the errors.

12.2.4 Residual-based LM Test

Hadri (1999) proposed a residual-based Lagrange multiplier (LM) test for the null that the time series for each i are stationary around a deterministic trend against the alternative of a unit root in panel data. Consider the following model:

$$y_{it} = z'_{it}\gamma + r_{it} + \varepsilon_{it} \tag{12.13}$$

where z_{it} is the deterministic component, r_{it} is a random walk

$$r_{it} = r_{i,t-1} + u_{it}$$

$u_{it} \sim \mathrm{IID}(0, \sigma_u^2)$ and ε_{it} is a stationary process. (12.13) can be written as

$$y_{it} = z'_{it}\gamma + e_{it} \tag{12.14}$$

where

$$e_{it} = \sum_{j=1}^{t} u_{ij} + \varepsilon_{it}$$

Let $\widehat{e}_{it}$ be the residuals from the regression in (12.14) and $\widehat{\sigma}_e^2$ be the estimate of the error variance. Also, let S_{it} be the partial sum process of the residuals, $S_{it} = \sum_{j=1}^{t} \widehat{e}_{ij}$. Then the LM statistic is

$$\text{LM} = \frac{\frac{1}{N}\sum_{i=1}^{N} \frac{1}{T^2} \sum_{t=1}^{T} S_{it}^2}{\widehat{\sigma}_e^2}$$

It can be shown that

$$\text{LM} \xrightarrow{p} E\left[\int W_{iZ}^2\right]$$

as $T \to \infty$ followed by $N \to \infty$ provided $E\left[\int W_{iZ}^2\right] < \infty$. Also

$$\frac{\sqrt{N}\left(\text{LM} - E\left[\int W_{iZ}^2\right]\right)}{\sqrt{\text{var}\left[\int W_{iZ}^2\right]}} \Rightarrow N(0, 1)$$

as $T \to \infty$ followed by $N \to \infty$.

Consider the nonstationary dynamic panel data model

$$y_{it} = \alpha_{i0} + \alpha_{i1}t + y_{it}^0$$
$$y_{it}^0 = \beta y_{i,t-1}^0 + u_{it}$$

with $\beta = \exp(c/T)$. Moon and Phillips (2000) focused on estimating the localizing parameter c in β which characterizes the local behavior of the unit root process. Information about c is useful for the analysis of the power properties of unit root tests, cointegration tests, the construction of confidence intervals for the long-run autoregressive coefficient, the development of efficient detrending methods and the construction of point optimal invariant tests for a unit root and cointegrating rank. Moon and Phillips (2000) show that when $c \leqslant 0$, it is possible to estimate this local parameter consistently using panel data. In turn, they show how to extract the deterministic trend efficiently using this consistent estimate of c.

Extensive simulations have been conducted to explore the finite sample performance of panel unit root tests, e.g. Karlsson and Löthgren (2000), Im, Pesaran and Shin (1997), Maddala and Wu (1999) and Choi (1999a). Choi (1999a) studied the small sample properties of the IPS t-bar test in (12.7) and Fisher's test in (12.11). Choi's major findings are the following:

(1) The empirical size of the IPS and the Fisher test are reasonably close to their nominal size 0.05 when N is small. But the Fisher test shows mild size distortions at $N = 100$, which is expected from the asymptotic theory. Overall, the IPS t-bar test has the most stable size.

(2) In terms of the size-adjusted power, the Fisher test seems to be superior to the IPS t-bar test.
(3) When a linear time trend is included in the model, the power of all tests decreases considerably.

Karlsson and Löthgren (2000) compare the LL and IPS tests for various size panels. They warn that for large T, panel unit root tests have high power and there is the potential risk of concluding that the whole panel is stationary even when there is only a small proportion of stationary series in the panel. For small T, panel unit root tests have low power and there is the potential risk of concluding that the whole panel is nonstationary even when there is a large proportion of stationary series in the panel. They suggest careful analysis of both the individual and panel unit root test results to fully assess the stationarity properties of the panel.

12.3 SPURIOUS REGRESSION IN PANEL DATA

Entorf (1997) studied spurious fixed effects regressions when the true model involves independent random walks with and without drifts. Entorf found that for $T \to \infty$ and N finite, the nonsense regression phenomenon holds for spurious fixed effects models and inference based on t-values can be highly misleading. Kao (1999) and Phillips and Moon (1999) derived the asymptotic distributions of the least squares dummy variable estimator and various conventional statistics from the spurious regression in panel data.

Suppose that y_t and X_t are unit root nonstationary time-series variables with long-run variance matrix

$$\Omega = \begin{pmatrix} \Omega_{yy} & \Omega_{yx} \\ \Omega_{xy} & \Omega_{xx} \end{pmatrix}$$

Then $\beta = \Omega_{yx}\Omega_{xx}^{-1}$ can be interpreted as a classical long-run regression coefficient relating the two nonstationary variables y_t and X_t. When Ω has deficient rank, β is a cointegrating coefficient because $y_t - \beta X_t$ is stationary. Even in the absence of time-series cointegration, β is a measure of a statistical long-run correlation between y_t and X_t. Phillips and Moon (1999) extend this concept to panel regressions with nonstationary data. In this case, heterogeneity across individuals i can be characterized by heterogeneous long-run covariance matrices Ω_i. Then Ω_i are randomly drawn from a population with mean $\Omega = E(\Omega_i)$. In this case

$$\beta = E(\Omega_{y_i x_i})E(\Omega_{x_i x_i})^{-1} = \Omega_{yx}\Omega_{xx}^{-1}$$

is the regression coefficient corresponding to the average long-run covariance matrix Ω.

Phillips and Moon (1999) studied various regressions between two panel vectors that may or may not have cointegrating relations, and presented a fundamental framework for studying sequential and joint limit theories in nonstationary panel data. The panel models considered allow for four cases: (i) panel spurious regression, where there is no time-series cointegration; (ii) heterogeneous panel cointegration, where each individual has its own specific cointegration relation; (iii) homogeneous panel cointegration, where individuals have the same cointegration relation; and (iv) near-homogeneous panel cointegration, where individuals have slightly different cointegration relations determined by the value of a localizing parameter. Phillips and Moon (1999) investigated these four models and developed panel asymptotics for regression coefficients and tests using both sequential and joint limit arguments. In all cases considered the pooled estimator is consistent and has a normal limiting distribution. In fact, for the spurious panel regression, Phillips and Moon (1999) showed that under quite weak regularity conditions, the pooled least squares estimator of the slope coefficient β is $\sqrt{N}$-consistent for the long-run average relation parameter β and has a limiting normal distribution. Also, Moon and Phillips (1998) showed that a limiting cross-section regression with time-averaged data is also $\sqrt{N}$-consistent for β and has a limiting normal distribution. This is different from the pure time-series spurious regression where the limit of the OLS estimator of β is a nondegenerate random variate that is a functional of Brownian motions and is therefore not consistent for β. The idea in Phillips and Moon (1999) is that independent cross-section data in the panel adds information and this leads to a stronger overall signal than the pure time-series case. Pesaran and Smith (1995) studied limiting cross-section regressions with time-averaged data and established consistency with restrictive assumptions on the heterogeneous panel model. This differs from Phillips and Moon (1999) in that the former use an average of the cointegrating coefficients which is different from the long-run average regression coefficient. This requires the existence of cointegrating time-series relations, whereas the long-run average regression coefficient β is defined irrespective of the existence of individual cointegrating relations and relies only on the long-run average variance matrix of the panel. Phillips and Moon (1999) also showed that for the homogeneous and near-homogeneous cointegration cases, a consistent estimator of the long-run regression coefficient can be constructed which they call a pooled FM estimator. They showed that this estimator has faster convergence rate than the simple cross-section and time-series estimators. Pedroni (2000) and Kao and Chiang (2000) also investigated limit theories for various estimators of the homogeneous panel cointegration regression model. See also Phillips and Moon (2000) for a concise review. In fact, the latter paper also shows how to extend the above ideas to models with individual effects in the data generating process. For the panel spurious regression with individual specific deterministic trends, estimates of the trend coefficients are obtained in the first step and the detrended data is pooled and used in least squares regression to estimate β in the second step. Two different detrending procedures are used based on OLS and GLS regressions. OLS detrending leads to an asymptotically more efficient estimator of the long-run average coefficient β in pooled regression than GLS detrending. Phillips and Moon (2000) explain that "the residuals after time series GLS detrending have more cross section variation than they do after OLS detrending and this produces great variation in the limit distribution of the pooled regression estimator of the long run average coefficient".

Moon and Phillips (1999) investigated the asymptotic properties of the Gaussian MLE of the localizing parameter in local to unity dynamic panel regression models with deterministic and stochastic trends. Moon and Phillips found that for the homogeneous trend model, the Gaussian MLE of the common localizing parameter is $\sqrt{N}$-consistent, while for the heterogeneous trends model, it is inconsistent. The latter inconsistency is due to the presence of an infinite number of incidental parameters (as $N \to \infty$) for the individual trends. Unlike the fixed effects dynamic panel data model where this inconsistency due to the incidental parameter problem disappears as $T \to \infty$, the inconsistency of the localizing parameter in the Moon and Phillips model persists even when both N and T go to infinity. Moon and Phillips (2000) show that the local to unity parameter in a simple panel near-integrated regression model can be consistently estimated using pooled OLS. When deterministic trends are present, pooled panel estimators of the localizing parameter are asymptotically biased. Some techniques are developed to obtain consistent estimates of this localizing parameter but only in the region where it is negative. These methods are used to show how to perform efficient trend extraction for panel data. They are also used to deliver consistent estimates of distancing parameters in nonstationary panel models where the initial conditions are in the distant past. The joint asymptotics in the paper rely on $N/T \to 0$, so that the results are most relevant in panels where T is large relative to N.

Pesaran, Shin and Smith (1999) derived the asymptotics of a pooled mean group (PMG) estimator. The PMG estimation constrains the long-run coefficients to be identical, but allows the short-run and adjustment coefficients as the error variances to differ across the cross-sectional dimension. Binder, Hsiao and Pesaran (2000) considered estimation and inference in panel vector autoregressions (PVARS) with fixed effects when T is finite and N is large. A maximum likelihood estimator as well as unit root and cointegration tests are proposed based on a transformed likelihood function. This MLE is shown to be consistent and asymptotically normally distributed irrespective of the unit root and cointegrating properties of the PVAR model. The tests proposed are based on standard chi-square and normal distributed statistics. Binder, Hsiao and Pesaran also show that the conventional GMM estimators based on standard orthogonality conditions break down if the underlying time series contain unit roots. Monte Carlo evidence is provided which favors MLE over GMM in small samples.

Recently, Kauppi (2000) developed a new joint limit theory where the panel data may be cross-sectionally heterogeneous in a general way. This limit theory builds upon the concepts of joint convergence in probability and in distribution for double indexed processes by Phillips and Moon (1999) and develops new versions of the law of large numbers and the central limit theorem that apply in panels where the data may be cross-sectionally heterogeneous in a fairly general way. Kauppi demonstrates how this joint limit theory can be applied to derive asymptotics for a panel regression where the regressors are generated by a local to unit root with heterogeneous localizing coefficients across cross-sections. Kauppi discusses issues that arise in the estimation and inference of panel cointegrated regressions with near-integrated regressors. Kauppi shows that a bias corrected pooled OLS for a common cointegrating parameter has an asymptotic normal distribution centered on the true value irrespective of whether the regressor has near or exact unit root. However, if the regression model contains individual effects and/or deterministic trends, then Kauppi's bias corrected pooled OLS still produces asymptotic bias. Kauppi also shows that the panel FM estimator is subject to asymptotic bias regardless of how individual effects and/or deterministic trends are contained if the regressors are nearly rather than exactly integrated. This indicates that much care should be taken in interpreting empirical results achieved by the recent panel cointegration methods that assume exact unit roots when near unit roots are equally plausible.

Granger and Hyung (1999) consider the problem of estimating a dynamic panel regression model when the variables in the model are strongly correlated with individual-specific size factors. For a large N cross-country panel with small T, the size variable could be country-specific like its area or time-varying like population or total income. They show that if the size is not explicitly taken into account, one gets a spurious regression. In particular, they show that implementing unit root tests is likely to lead to the wrong decision. Moreover, if the size variable is slightly varying over time or its distribution has thick tails (such as a panel of countries including Luxembourg and Cyprus as well as China and India), postsample predictions are biased. A pooling model appears to fit well in-sample, but forecast poorly out-of-sample if the individual-specific size factor has a fat-tailed distribution. A panel model with individual-specific effects could be problematic if the panel series has a very short time dimension. Since individual constant terms are estimated poorly, the forecasts based on them are poor. These problems may be more serious if the individual-specific factor is not constant but time-varying.

Kao, Chiang and Chen (1999) apply the asymptotic theory of panel cointegration developed by Kao and Chiang (2000) to the Coe and Helpman (1995) international R&D spillover regression. Using a sample of 21 OECD countries and Israel, they re-examine the effects of domestic and foreign R&D capital stocks on total factor productivity of these countries. They find that OLS with bias correction, the fully modified (FM) and the dynamic OLS (DOLS) estimators produce different predictions about the impact of foreign R&D on total factor productivity (TFP), although all the estimators support the result that domestic R&D is related to TFP. Kao, Chiang and Chen's empirical results indicate that the estimated coefficients in the Coe and Helpman's regressions are subject to estimation bias. Given the superiority of the DOLS over FM as suggested by Kao and Chiang (2000), Kao, Chiang and Chen leaned towards rejecting the Coe and Helpman hypothesis that international R&D spillovers are trade related.

12.4 PANEL COINTEGRATION TESTS

12.4.1 Kao Tests

Kao (1999) presented two types of cointegration tests in panel data, the DF and ADF type tests. Consider the panel regression model

$$y_{it} = x_{it}'\beta + z_{it}'\gamma + e_{it} \tag{12.15}$$

where $x_{it} = x_{i,t-1} + \varepsilon_{it}$ and e_{it} is $I(1)$. The DF type tests can be calculated from the estimated residuals

$$\widehat{e}_{it} = \rho\widehat{e}_{i,t-1} + \nu_{it} \tag{12.16}$$

where $\widehat{e}_{it} = \widetilde{y}_{it} - \widetilde{x}_{it}'\widehat{\beta}$. In order to test the null hypothesis of no cointegration, the null can be written as H_0: $\rho = 1$. The OLS estimate of ρ and the t-statistic are given as

$$\widehat{\rho} = \frac{\sum_{i=1}^{N}\sum_{t=2}^{T}\widehat{e}_{it}\widehat{e}_{i,t-1}}{\sum_{i=1}^{N}\sum_{t=2}^{T}\widehat{e}_{it}^2}$$

and

$$t_\rho = \frac{(\widehat{\rho}-1)\sqrt{\sum_{i=1}^{N}\sum_{t=2}^{T}\widehat{e}_{i,t-1}^2}}{s_e} \tag{12.17}$$

where $s_e^2 = (1/NT)\sum_{i=1}^{N}\sum_{t=2}^{T}\left(\widehat{e}_{it} - \widehat{\rho}\widehat{e}_{i,t-1}\right)^2$. Kao proposed the following four DF type tests by assuming $z_{it} = \{\mu_i\}$:

$$\mathrm{DF}_\rho = \frac{\sqrt{N}T(\widehat{\rho}-1) + 3\sqrt{N}}{\sqrt{10.2}}$$

$$\mathrm{DF}_t = \sqrt{1.25}t_\rho + \sqrt{1.875N}$$

$$\mathrm{DF}_\rho^* = \frac{\sqrt{N}T(\widehat{\rho}-1) + \dfrac{3\sqrt{N}\widehat{\sigma}_\nu^2}{\widehat{\sigma}_{0\nu}^2}}{\sqrt{3 + \dfrac{36\widehat{\sigma}_\nu^4}{5\widehat{\sigma}_{0\nu}^4}}}$$

and

$$\mathrm{DF}_t^* = \frac{t_\rho + \dfrac{\sqrt{6N}\widehat{\sigma}_\nu}{2\widehat{\sigma}_{0\nu}}}{\sqrt{\dfrac{\widehat{\sigma}_{0\nu}^2}{2\widehat{\sigma}_\nu^2} + \dfrac{3\widehat{\sigma}_\nu^2}{10\widehat{\sigma}_{0\nu}^2}}}$$

where $\widehat{\sigma}_\nu^2 = \widehat{\sum}_u - \widehat{\sum}_{u\varepsilon}\widehat{\sum}_\varepsilon^{-1}$ and $\widehat{\sigma}_{0\nu}^2 = \widehat{\Omega}_u - \widehat{\Omega}_{u\varepsilon}\widehat{\Omega}_\varepsilon^{-1}$. While DF_ρ and DF_t are based on the strong exogeneity of the regressors and errors, DF_ρ^* and DF_t^* are for the cointegration with endogenous relationship between regressors and errors.

For the ADF test, we can run the following regression:

$$\widehat{e}_{it} = \rho\widehat{e}_{i,t-1} + \sum_{j=1}^{p} \vartheta_j \Delta\widehat{e}_{i,t-j} + \nu_{itp} \tag{12.18}$$

With the null hypothesis of no cointegration, the ADF test statistics can be constructed as

$$\mathrm{ADF} = \frac{t_{\mathrm{ADF}} + \dfrac{\sqrt{6N}\widehat{\sigma}_\nu}{2\widehat{\sigma}_{0\nu}}}{\sqrt{\dfrac{\widehat{\sigma}_{0\nu}^2}{2\widehat{\sigma}_\nu^2} + \dfrac{3\widehat{\sigma}_\nu^2}{10\widehat{\sigma}_{0\nu}^2}}} \tag{12.19}$$

where t_{ADF} is the t-statistic of ρ in (12.18). The asymptotic distributions of DF_ρ, DF_t, DF_ρ^*, DF_t^* and ADF converge to a standard normal distribution $N(0, 1)$ by sequential limit theory.

12.4.2 Residual-based LM Test

McCoskey and Kao (1998) derived a residual-based test for the null of cointegration rather than the null of no cointegration in panels. This test is an extension of the LM test and the locally best invariant (LBI) test for an MA unit root in the time-series literature. Under the null, the asymptotics no longer depend on the asymptotic properties of the estimating spurious regression, rather the asymptotics of the estimation of a cointegrated relationship are needed. For models which allow the cointegrating vector to change across the cross-sectional observations, the asymptotics depend merely on the time-series results as each cross-section is estimated independently. For models with common slopes, the estimation is done jointly and therefore the asymptotic theory is based on the joint estimation of a cointegrated relationship in panel data.

For the residual-based test of the null of cointegration, it is necessary to use an efficient estimation technique of cointegrated variables. In the time-series literature a variety of methods have been shown to be efficient asymptotically. These include the fully modified (FM) estimator of Phillips and Hansen (1990) and the dynamic least squares (DOLS) estimator as proposed by Saikkonen (1991) and Stock and Watson (1993). For panel data, Kao and Chiang (2000) showed that both the FM and DOLS methods can produce estimators which are asymptotically normally distributed with zero means.

The model presented allows for varying slopes and intercepts:

$$y_{it} = \alpha_i + x_{it}'\beta_i + e_{it} \tag{12.20}$$

$$x_{it} = x_{i,t-1} + \varepsilon_{it} \tag{12.21}$$

$$e_{it} = \gamma_{it} + u_{it} \tag{12.22}$$

and

$$\gamma_{it} = \gamma_{i,t-1} + \theta u_{it}$$

where u_{it} are $\mathrm{IID}(0, \sigma_u^2)$. The null hypothesis of cointegration is equivalent to $\theta = 0$.

The test statistic proposed by McCoskey and Kao (1998) is defined as follows:

$$\mathrm{LM} = \frac{\frac{1}{N}\sum_{i=1}^{N}\frac{1}{T^2}\sum_{t=1}^{T} S_{it}^2}{\widehat{\sigma}_e^2} \tag{12.23}$$

where S_{it} is a partial sum process of the residuals, $S_{it} = \sum_{j=1}^{t}\widehat{e}_{ij}$, and $\widehat{\sigma}_e^2$ is defined in McCoskey and Kao. The asymptotic result for the test is

$$\sqrt{N}(\mathrm{LM} - \mu_v) \Rightarrow N(0, \sigma_v^2) \tag{12.24}$$

The moments, μ_v and σ_v^2, can be found through Monte Carlo simulation. The limiting distribution of LM is then free of nuisance parameters and robust to heteroskedasticity.

Urban economists have long sought to explain the relationship between urbanization levels and output. McCoskey and Kao (1999) revisited this question and tested the long-run stability of a production function including urbanization using nonstationary panel data techniques. McCoskey and Kao applied the IPS test and LM in (12.23) and showed that a long-run relationship between urbanization, output per worker and capital per worker cannot be rejected for the sample of 30 developing countries or the sample of 22 developed countries over the period 1965–89. They do find, however, that the sign and magnitude of the impact of urbanization varies considerably across the countries. These results offer new insights and potential for dynamic urban models rather than the simple cross-section approach.

12.4.3 Pedroni Tests

Pedroni (2000) also proposed several tests for the null hypothesis of cointegration in a panel data model that allows for considerable heterogeneity. His tests can be classified into two categories. The first set is similar to the tests discussed above, and involves averaging test statistics for cointegration in the time series across cross-sections. For the second set, the averaging is done in pieces so that the limiting distributions are based on limits of piecewise numerator and denominator terms.

The first set of statistics includes a form of the average of the Phillips and Ouliaris (1990) statistic:

$$\tilde{Z}_\rho = \sum_{i=1}^{N}\frac{\sum_{t=1}^{T}(\hat{e}_{i,t-1}\Delta\hat{e}_{it} - \hat{\lambda}_i)}{\left(\sum_{t=1}^{T}\hat{e}_{i,t-1}^2\right)} \tag{12.25}$$

where $\hat{e}_{it}$ is estimated from (12.15) and $\hat{\lambda}_i = \frac{1}{2}\left(\widehat{\sigma}_i^2 - \widehat{s}_i^2\right)$, for which $\widehat{\sigma}_i^2$ and $\widehat{s}_i^2$ are individual long-run and contemporaneous variances of the residual $\hat{e}_{it}$. For his second set of statistics, Pedroni defines four panel variance ratio statistics.

Let $\hat{\Omega}_i$ be a consistent estimate of Ω_i, the long-run variance–covariance matrix. Define $\hat{L}_i$ to be the lower triangular Cholesky decomposition of $\hat{\Omega}_i$ such that in the scalar case $\hat{L}_{22i} = \hat{\sigma}_\varepsilon$ and $\hat{L}_{11i} = \hat{\sigma}_u^2 - \hat{\sigma}_{u\varepsilon}^2/\hat{\sigma}_\varepsilon^2$ is the long-run conditional variance. Here we consider only one of these statistics:

$$Z_{t_{\hat{\rho}_{NT}}} = \frac{\sum_{i=1}^{N}\sum_{t=2}^{T}\hat{L}_{11i}^{-2}(\hat{e}_{i,t-1}\Delta\hat{e}_{it} - \hat{\lambda}_i)}{\sqrt{\tilde{\sigma}_{NT}^2\left(\sum_{i=1}^{N}\sum_{t=2}^{T}\hat{L}_{11i}^{-2}\hat{e}_{i,t-1}^2\right)}} \tag{12.26}$$

where $\tilde{\sigma}_{NT} = (1/N)\sum_{i=1}^{N}\hat{\sigma}_i^2/\hat{L}_{11i}^2$.

It should be noted that Pedroni bases his test on the average of the numerator and denominator terms, respectively, rather than the average for the statistic as a whole. Using results on convergence of functionals of Brownian motion, Pedroni finds the following result:

$$Z_{t_{\hat{\rho}_{NT}}} + 1.73\sqrt{N} \Rightarrow N(0, 0.93)$$

Note that this distribution applies to the model including an intercept and not including a time trend. Asymptotic results for other model specifications can be found in Pedroni (2000). The intuition on these tests with varying slopes is not straightforward. The convergence in distribution is based on individual convergence of the numerator and denominator terms. What is the intuition of rejection of the null hypothesis? Using the average of the overall test statistic allows more ease in interpretation: rejection of the null hypothesis means that enough of the individual cross-sections have statistics "far away" from the means predicted by theory were they to be generated under the null.

Pedroni (1999) derived asymptotic distributions and critical values for several residual-based tests of the null of no cointegration in panels where there are multiple regressors. The model includes regressions with individual-specific fixed effects and time trends. Considerable heterogeneity is allowed across individual members of the panel with regards to the associated cointegrating vectors and the dynamics of the underlying error process. By comparing results from individual countries and the panel as a whole, Pedroni (2001) rejects the strong PPP hypothesis and finds that no degree of cross-sectional dependency would be sufficient to overturn the rejection of strong PPP.

12.4.4 Likelihood-based Cointegration Test

Larsson, Lyhagen and Löthgren (1998) presented a likelihood-based (LR) panel test of cointegrating rank in heterogeneous panel models based on the average of the individual rank trace statistics developed by Johansen (1995). The proposed LR-bar statistic is very similar to the IPS t-bar statistic in (12.7)–(12.10). In Monte Carlo simulation, Larsson et al. investigated the small sample properties of the standardized LR-bar statistic. They found that the proposed test requires a large time-series dimension. Even if the panel has a large cross-sectional dimension, the size of the test will be severely distorted.

Groen and Kleibergen (1999) proposed a likelihood-based framework for cointegrating analysis in panels of a fixed number of vector error correction models. Maximum likelihood estimators of the cointegrating vectors are constructed using iterated generalized method of moments (GMM) estimators. Using these estimators Groen and Kleibergen construct likelihood ratio statistics to test for a common cointegration rank across the individual vector error correction models, both with heterogeneous and homogeneous cointegrating vectors. Groen and Kleibergen (1999) applied this likelihood ratio test to a data set of exchange rates and appropriate monetary fundamentals. They found strong evidence for the validity of the monetary exchange rate model within a panel of vector correction models for three major European countries, whereas the results based on individual vector error correction models for each of these countries separately are less supportive.

12.4.5 Finite Sample Properties

McCoskey and Kao (1999) conducted Monte Carlo experiments to compare the size and power of different residual-based tests for cointegration in heterogeneous panel data: varying slopes and varying intercepts. Two of the tests are constructed under the null hypothesis of no cointegration. These tests are based on the average ADF test and Pedroni's pooled tests in (12.25)–(12.26). The third test is based on the null hypothesis of cointegration which is based on the McCoskey and Kao LM test in (12.23). Wu and Yin (1999) performed a similar comparison for panel tests in which they consider only tests for which the null hypothesis is that of no cointegration. Wu and Yin compared ADF statistics with maximum eigenvalue statistics in pooling information on means and p-values, respectively. They found that the average ADF performs better with respect to power and their maximum eigenvalue-based p-value performs better with regards to size.

The test of the null hypothesis was originally proposed in response to the low power of the tests of the null of no cointegration, especially in the time-series case. Further, in cases where economic theory predicted a long-run steady state relationship, it seemed that a test of the null of cointegration rather than the null of no cointegration would be appropriate. The results from the Monte Carlo study showed that the McCoskey and Kao LM test outperforms the other two tests.

Of the two reasons for the introduction of the test of the null hypothesis of cointegration, low power and attractiveness of the null, the introduction of the cross-section dimension of the panel solves one: all of the tests show decent power when used with panel data. For those applications where the null of cointegration is more logical than the null of no cointegration, McCoskey and Kao (1999), at a minimum, conclude that using the McCoskey and Kao LM test does not compromise the ability of the researcher in determining the underlying nature of the data.

Recently, Hall, Lazarova and Urga (1999) proposed a new approach based on principal components analysis to test for the number of common stochastic trends driving the nonstationary series in a panel data set. The test is consistent even if there is a mixture of $I(0)$ and $I(1)$ series in the sample. This makes it unnecessary to pretest the panel for unit root. It also has the advantage of solving the problem of dimensionality encountered in large panel data sets.

12.5 ESTIMATION AND INFERENCE IN PANEL COINTEGRATION MODELS

For panel cointegrated regression models, the asymptotic properties of the estimators of the regression coefficients and the associated statistical tests are different from those of the time-series cointegration regression models. Some of these differences have become apparent in recent works by Kao and Chiang (2000), Phillips and Moon (1999) and Pedroni (2000). The panel cointegration models are directed at studying questions that surround long-run economic relationships typically encountered in macroeconomic and financial data. Such a long-run relationship is often predicted by economic theory and it is then of central interest to estimate the regression coefficients and test whether they satisfy theoretical restrictions. Chen, McCoskey and Kao (1999) investigated the finite sample properties of the OLS estimator, the t-statistic, the bias-corrected OLS estimator and the bias-corrected t-statistic. They found that the bias-corrected OLS estimator does not improve over the OLS estimator in general. The results of Chen et al. suggested that alternatives, such as the fully modified (FM) estimator or dynamic OLS (DOLS) estimator may be more promising in cointegrated panel regressions. Phillips and Moon (1999) and Pedroni (2000) proposed an FM estimator, which can be seen as a generalization of Phillips and Hansen (1990). Recently, Kao and Chiang (2000) proposed an alternative approach based on a panel dynamic least squares (DOLS) estimator, which builds upon the work of Saikkonen (1991) and Stock and Watson (1993).

Consider the following panel regression:

$$y_{it} = x_{it}'\beta + z_{it}'\gamma + u_{it} \tag{12.27}$$

where $\{y_{it}\}$ are 1×1, β is a $k \times 1$ vector of the slope parameters, z_{it} is the deterministic component, and $\{u_{it}\}$ are the stationary disturbance terms. We assume that $\{x_{it}\}$ are $k \times 1$ integrated processes of order one for all i, where

$$x_{it} = x_{i,t-1} + \varepsilon_{it}$$

Under these specifications, (12.27) describes a system of cointegrated regressions, i.e. y_{it} is cointegrated with x_{it}. The OLS estimator of β is

$$\widehat{\beta}_{\text{OLS}} = \left[\sum_{i=1}^{N}\sum_{t=1}^{T}\widetilde{x}_{it}\widetilde{x}_{it}'\right]^{-1}\left[\sum_{i=1}^{N}\sum_{t=1}^{T}\widetilde{x}_{it}\widetilde{y}_{it}\right] \tag{12.28}$$

It is easy to show that

$$\frac{1}{N}\sum\nolimits_{i=1}^{N}\frac{1}{T^2}\sum\nolimits_{t=1}^{T}\widetilde{x}_{it}\widetilde{x}_{it}' \xrightarrow{p} \lim_{N\to\infty}\frac{1}{N}\sum\nolimits_{i=1}^{N}E\left[\zeta_{2i}\right] \tag{12.29}$$

and

$$\frac{1}{N}\sum_{i=1}^{N}\frac{1}{T}\sum_{t=1}^{T}\widetilde{x}_{it}\widetilde{u}_{it} \Rightarrow \lim_{N\to\infty}\frac{1}{N}\sum_{i=1}^{N}E\left[\zeta_{1i}\right] \tag{12.30}$$

using sequential limit theory, where

$$\begin{array}{lll} z_{it} & E\left[\zeta_{1i}\right] & E\left[\zeta_{2i}\right] \\ 0 & 0 & \frac{1}{2} \\ 1 & 0 & 0 \\ \mu_i & -\frac{1}{2}\Omega_{\varepsilon ui}+\Delta_{\varepsilon ui} & \frac{1}{6}\Omega_{\varepsilon i} \\ (\mu_i, t) & -\frac{1}{2}\Omega_{\varepsilon ui}+\Delta_{\varepsilon ui} & \frac{1}{15}\Omega_{\varepsilon i} \end{array} \tag{12.31}$$

and

$$\Omega_i = \left[\begin{array}{cc} \Omega_{ui} & \Omega_{u\varepsilon i} \\ \Omega_{\varepsilon ui} & \Omega_{\varepsilon i} \end{array}\right]$$

is the long-run covariance matrix of $\left(u_{it}, \varepsilon_{it}'\right)'$, also $\Delta_i = \left[\begin{array}{cc} \Delta_{ui} & \Delta_{u\varepsilon i} \\ \Delta_{\varepsilon ui} & \Delta_{\varepsilon i} \end{array}\right]$ is the one-sided long-run covariance. For example, when $z_{it} = \{\mu_i\}$, we get

$$\sqrt{N}T\left(\widehat{\beta}_{\mathrm{OLS}} - \beta\right) - \sqrt{N}\delta_{NT} \Rightarrow N\left(0, 6\Omega_{\varepsilon}^{-1}\left(\lim_{N\to\infty}\frac{1}{N}\sum_{i=1}^{N}\Omega_{u.\varepsilon i}\Omega_{\varepsilon i}\right)\Omega_{\varepsilon}^{-1}\right) \tag{12.32}$$

where $\Omega_{\varepsilon} = \lim_{N\to\infty}(1/N)\sum_{i=1}^{N}\Omega_{\varepsilon i}$ and

$$\delta_{NT} = \left[\frac{1}{N}\sum_{i=1}^{N}\frac{1}{T^2}\sum_{t=1}^{T}\left(x_{it}-\overline{x}_i\right)\left(x_{it}-\overline{x}_i\right)'\right]^{-1} \times\frac{1}{N}\left[\sum_{i=1}^{N}\Omega_{\varepsilon i}^{1/2}\left(\int\widetilde{W}_i \mathrm{d}W_i'\right)\Omega_{\varepsilon i}^{-1/2}\Omega_{\varepsilon ui}+\Delta_{\varepsilon ui}\right] \tag{12.33}$$

Kao and Chiang (2000) studied the limiting distributions for the FM and DOLS estimators in a cointegrated regression and showed they are asymptotically normal. Phillips and Moon (1999) and Pedroni (2000) also obtained similar results for the FM estimator. The reader is referred to the cited papers for further details. Kao and Chiang also investigated the finite sample properties of the OLS, FM and DOLS estimators. They found that (i) the OLS estimator has a non-negligible bias in finite samples, (ii) the FM estimator does not improve over the OLS estimator in general, and (iii) the DOLS estimator may be more promising than OLS or FM estimators in estimating the cointegrated panel regressions.

Choi (1999) studied the asymptotic properties of OLS, Within and GLS estimators for an error component model that involves both stationary and nonstationary regressors. Choi's simulation results indicated that the feasible GLS estimator is more efficient than the Within estimator. Choi (1999c) also studied instrumental variable estimation for an error component model with stationary and nearly nonstationary regressors.

12.6 FURTHER READING

Cermeño (1999) extends Andrews' (1993) median-unbiased estimation for autoregressive/unit root time series to panel data dynamic fixed effects models. This estimator is robust to heteroskedasticity and serial correlation in the individual dimension. However, this method is justified only for a purely autoregressive model. This estimator is used to evaluate conditional convergence among 48 US states, 13 OECD countries and two wider samples from the Penn World Tables with 57 and 100 countries. Support for conditional convergence is found only among US states and the 13 OECD countries.

Hecq, Palm and Urbain (2000) extend the concept of serial correlation common features analysis to nonstationary panel data models. This analysis is motivated both by the need to study and test for common structures and co-movements in panel data with autocorrelation present and by an increase in efficiency due to pooling. The authors propose sequential testing procedures and test their performance using a small-scale Monte Carlo. Concentrating upon the fixed effects model, they define homogeneous panel common feature models and give a series of steps to implement these tests. These tests are used to investigate the liquidity constraints model for 22 OECD and G7 countries. The presence of a panel common feature vector is rejected at the 5% nominal level.

Murray and Papell (2000) propose a panel unit root test in the presence of structural change. In particular, they propose a unit root test for nontrending data in the presence of a one-time change in the mean for a heterogeneous panel. The date of the break is endogenously determined. The resultant test allows for both serial and contemporaneous correlation, both of which are often found to be important in the panel unit roots context. Murray and Papell conduct two power experiments for panels of nontrending, stationary series with a one-time change in means and find that conventional panel unit root tests generally have very low power. Then they conduct the same experiment using methods that test for unit roots in the presence of structural change and find that the power of the test is much improved.

Yin and Wu (2000) propose stationarity tests for a heterogeneous panel data model. The authors consider the case of serially correlated errors in the level and trend stationary models. The proposed panel tests utilize the Kwaitkowski et al. (1992) test and the Leybourne and McCabe (1994) test from the time-series literature. Two different ways of pooling information from the independent tests are used. In particular, the group mean and the Fisher-type tests are used to develop the panel stationarity tests. Monte Carlo experiments are performed that reveal good small sample performance in terms of size and power.

NOTES

1. This chapter is based upon Baltagi and Kao (2000).
2. Chiang and Kao (2001) have recently put together a fairly comprehensive set of subroutines, NPT 1.2, for studying nonstationary panel data. NPT 1.2 can be downloaded from http://web.syr.edu/~cdkao.

3. Testing for cointegration in panel data by combining p-value tests is a straightforward extension of the testing procedures in this section. For cointegration tests, the relevant model is equation (12.15). We let G_{iT_i} be a test for the null of no cointegration and apply the same tests and asymptotic theory in this section.

PROBLEMS

12.1 *A simple linear trend model with error components*. This is based on problem 97.2.1 in *Econometric Theory* by Baltagi and Krämer (1997). Consider the following simple linear trend model:

$$y_{it} = \alpha + \beta t + u_{it} \quad i = 1, 2, \ldots, N;\; t = 1, 2, \ldots, T$$

where y_{it} denotes the gross domestic product of country i at time t. The disturbances follow the one-way error component model given by

$$u_{it} = \mu_i + \nu_{it}$$

where $\mu_i \sim \mathrm{IID}(0, \sigma_\mu^2)$ denote the random country (time-invariant) effects and $\nu_{it} \sim \mathrm{IID}(0, \sigma_\nu^2)$ denote the remainder effects. These error components are assumed to be independent of each other and among themselves. Our interest is focused on the estimates of the trend coefficient β, and the estimators to be considered are ordinary least squares (OLS), first difference (FD), the fixed effects (FE) estimator, assuming the μ_i's are fixed effects, and the generalized least squares estimator (GLS), knowing the true variance components, which is the best linear unbiased estimator in this case.

(a) Show that the OLS, GLS and FE estimators of β are identical and given by $\widehat{\beta}_{\mathrm{GLS}} = \widehat{\beta}_{\mathrm{OLS}} = \widetilde{\beta}_{\mathrm{FE}} = \sum_{i=1}^{N}\sum_{t=1}^{T} y_{it}(t-\bar{t})/N\sum_{t=1}^{T}(t-\bar{t})^2$ where $\bar{t} = \sum_{t=1}^{T} t/T$.

(b) Show that the variance of the OLS, GLS and FE estimators of β is given by $\mathrm{var}(\widehat{\beta}_{\mathrm{GLS}}) = \mathrm{var}(\widehat{\beta}_{\mathrm{OLS}}) = \mathrm{var}(\widetilde{\beta}_{\mathrm{FE}}) = 12\sigma_\nu^2/NT(T^2-1)$ and is therefore $O(N^{-1}T^{-3})$.

(c) Show that this simple linear trend model satisfies the necessary and sufficient condition for OLS to be equivalent to GLS.

(d) Show that the FD estimator of β is given by $\widehat{\beta}_{\mathrm{FD}} = \sum_{i=1}^{N}(y_{iT} - y_{i1})/N(T-1)$ with $\mathrm{var}(\widehat{\beta}_{\mathrm{FD}}) = 2\sigma_\nu^2/N(T-1)^2$ of $O(N^{-1}T^{-2})$.

(e) What do you conclude about the asymptotic relative efficiency of FD with respect to the other estimators of β as $T \to \infty$? Hint: See solution 97.2.1 in *Econometric Theory* by Song and Jung (1998). Also, use the fact that $\sum_{t=1}^{T} t^2 = T(T+1)(2T+1)/6$ and $\sum_{t=1}^{T} t = T(T+1)/2$.

12.2 Download the International R&D spillovers panel data set used by Kao, Chiang and Chen (1999) along with the GAUSS subroutines NPT 1.2 from http://web.syr.edu/~cdkao. Using this data set, replicate the following results:

(a) Perform the Harris and Tzavalis (1999) panel unit root tests on total factor productivity, domestic R&D and foreign R&D capital stocks.

Show that the null hypothesis of nonstationarity is not rejected for all three variables.

(b) Perform the Kao (1999) and Pedroni (2000) panel cointegration tests on the regression relating total factor productivity to domestic and foreign R&D stocks. Show that the null hypothesis of no cointegration is rejected.

(c) Estimate the cointegrating relationship using the Kao and Chiang (2000) procedure. Hint: This example is used to illustrate NPT 1.2, see Chiang and Kao (2001).

References

Aasness, J., E. Biorn and T. Skjerpen, 1993, Engle functions, panel data, and latent variables, *Econometrica* **61**, 1395–1422.

Abowd, J.M. and D. Card, 1989, On the covariance structure of earnings and hours changes, *Econometrica* **57**, 411–445.

Abrevaya, J., 1997, The equivalence of two estimators of the fixed-effects logit model, *Economics Letters* **55**, 41–43.

Abrevaya, J., 1999, Leapfrog estimation of a fixed-effects model with unknown transformation of the dependent variable, *Journal of Econometrics* **93**, 203–228.

Abrevaya, J., 2000, Rank estimation of a generalized fixed-effects regression model, *Journal of Econometrics* **95**, 1–23.

Ahn, S.C. and S. Low, 1996, A reformulation of the Hausman test for regression models with pooled cross-section time-series data, *Journal of Econometrics* **71**, 309–319.

Ahn, S.C. and P. Schmidt, 1995, Efficient estimation of models for dynamic panel data, *Journal of Econometrics* **68**, 5–27.

Ahn, S.C. and P. Schmidt, 1997, Efficient estimation of dynamic panel data models: Alternative assumptions and simplified estimation, *Journal of Econometrics* **76**, 309–321.

Ahn, S.C. and P. Schmidt, 1999a, Modified generalized instrumental variables estimation of panel data models with strictly exogenous instrumental variables, Chapter 7 in C. Hsiao, K. Lahiri, L.F. Lee and M.H. Pesaran, eds., *Analysis of Panels and Limited Dependent Variable Models* (Cambridge University Press, Cambridge), 171–198.

Ahn, S.C. and P. Schmidt, 1999b, Estimation of linear panel data models using GMM, Chapter 8 in L. Mátyás, ed., *Generalized Method of Moments Estimation* (Cambridge University Press, Cambridge), 211–247.

Aigner, D.J. and P. Balestra, 1988, Optimal experimental design for error component models, *Econometrica* **56**, 955–971.

Alessie, R., A. Kapteyn and B. Melenberg, 1989, The effects of liquidity constraints on consumption: Estimation from household panel data, *European Economic Review* **33**, 547–555.

Alonso-Borrego, C. and M. Arellano, 1999, Symmetrically normalized instrumental variable estimation using panel data, *Journal of Business and Economic Statistics* **17**, 36–49.

Altonji, J.G. and A. Siow, 1987, Testing the response of consumption to income changes with (noisy) panel data, *Quarterly Journal of Economics* **102**, 293–328.

Alvarez, J. and M. Arellano, 1997, The time series and cross-section asymptotics of dynamic panel data estimators, working paper (CEMFI, Madrid).

Amemiya, T., 1971, The estimation of the variances in a variance-components model, *International Economic Review* **12**, 1–13.

Amemiya, T. and T.E. MaCurdy, 1986, Instrumental-variable estimation of an error components model, *Econometrica* **54**, 869–881.

Andersen, T.G. and R.E. Sørensen, 1996, GMM estimation of a stochastic volatility model: A Monte Carlo study, *Journal of Business and Economic Statistics* **14**, 328–352.

Anderson, T.W. and C. Hsiao, 1981, Estimation of dynamic models with error components, *Journal of the American Statistical Association* **76**, 598–606.

Anderson, T.W. and C. Hsiao, 1982, Formulation and estimation of dynamic models using panel data, *Journal of Econometrics* **18**, 47–82.

Andrews, D.W.K., 1993, Exactly median-unbiased estimation of first order autoregressive/unit root models, *Econometrica* **61**, 139–165.

Andrews, D.W.K. and B. Lu, 2001, Consistent model and moment selection procedures for GMM estimation with application to dynamic panel data models, *Journal of Econometrics* **101**, 123–164.

Angrist, J.D. and A.B. Krueger, 1995, Split sample instrumental variable estimates of return to schooling, *Journal of Business and Economic Statistics* **13**, 225–235.

Angrist, J.D. and W.K. Newey, 1991, Over-identification tests in earnings functions with fixed effects, *Journal of Business and Economic Statistics* **9**, 317–323.

Anselin, L., 1988, *Spatial Econometrics: Methods and Models* (Kluwer Academic Publishers, Dordrecht).

Anselin, L., 2001, Spatial econometrics, Chapter 14 in B. Baltagi, ed., *A Companion to Theoretical Econometrics* (Blackwell Publishers, Massachusetts), 310–330.

Antweiler, W., 2001, Nested random effects estimation in unbalanced panel data, *Journal of Econometrics* **101**, 295–313.

Arellano, M., 1987, Computing robust standard errors for within-groups estimators, *Oxford Bulletin of Economics and Statistics* **49**, 431–434.

Arellano, M., 1989, A note on the Anderson–Hsiao estimator for panel data, *Economics Letters* **31**, 337–341.

Arellano, M., 1990, Some testing for autocorrelation in dynamic random effects models, *Review of Economic Studies* **57**, 127–134.

Arellano, M., 1993, On the testing of correlated effects with panel data, *Journal of Econometrics* **59**, 87–97.

Arellano, M. and S. Bond, 1991, Some tests of specification for panel data: Monte Carlo evidence and an application to employment equations, *Review of Economic Studies* **58**, 277–297.

Arellano, M. and O. Bover, 1995, Another look at the instrumental variables estimation of error-component models, *Journal of Econometrics* **68**, 29–51.

Arellano, M. and B. Honoré, 2000, Panel data models: Some recent developments, in J. Heckman and E. Leamer, eds., *Handbook of Econometrics* (North-Holland, Amsterdam), forthcoming.

Arellano, M., O. Bover and J.M. Labeaga, 1999, Autoregressive models with sample selectivity for panel data, Chapter 2 in C. Hsiao, K. Lahiri, L.F. Lee and H. Pesaran, eds., *Analysis of Panels and Limited Dependent Variable Models* (Cambridge University Press, Cambridge), 23–48.

Ashenfelter, O., 1978, Estimating the effect of training programs on earnings with longitudinal data, *Review of Economics and Statistics* **60**, 47–57.

Ashenfelter, O. and G. Solon, 1982, Longitudinal labor market data-sources, uses and limitations, in *What's Happening to American Labor Force and Productivity Measurements?* (Upjohn Institute for Employment Research), 109–126.

Avery, R.B., 1977, Error components and seemingly unrelated regressions, *Econometrica* **45**, 199–209.

Avery, R.B., L.P. Hansen and V.J. Hotz, 1983, Multiperiod probit models and orthogonality condition estimation, *International Economic Review* **24**, 21–35.

Bailar, B.A., 1975, The effects of rotation group bias on estimates from panel surveys, *Journal of the American Statistical Association* **70**, 23–30.

Bailar, B.A., 1989, Information needs, surveys, and measurement errors, in D. Kasprzyk, G.J. Duncan, G. Kalton and M.P. Singh, eds., *Panel Surveys* (John Wiley, New York), 1–24.

Baillie, R.T. and B.H. Baltagi, 1999, Prediction from the regression model with one-way error components, Chapter 10 in C. Hsiao, K. Lahiri, L.F. Lee and H. Pesaran, eds., *Analysis of Panels and Limited Dependent Variable Models* (Cambridge University Press, Cambridge), 255–267.

Balestra, P., 1973, Best quadratic unbiased estimators of the variance–covariance matrix in normal regression, *Journal of Econometrics* **2**, 17–28.

Balestra, P., 1980, A note on the exact transformation associated with the first-order moving average process, *Journal of Econometrics* **14**, 381–394.

Balestra, P. and M. Nerlove, 1966, Pooling cross-section and time-series data in the estimation of a dynamic model: The demand for natural gas, *Econometrica* **34**, 585–612.

Balestra, P. and J. Varadharajan-Krishnakumar, 1987, Full information estimations of a system of simultaneous equations with error components structure, *Econometric Theory* **3**, 223–246.

Baltagi, B.H., 1980, On seemingly unrelated regressions with error components, *Econometrica* **48**, 1547–1551.

Baltagi, B.H., 1981a, Pooling: An experimental study of alternative testing and estimation procedures in a two-way error components model, *Journal of Econometrics* **17**, 21–49.

Baltagi, B.H., 1981b, Simultaneous equations with error components, *Journal of Econometrics* **17**, 189–200.

Baltagi, B.H., 1984, A Monte Carlo study for pooling time-series of cross-section data in the simultaneous equations model, *International Economic Review* **25**, 603–624.

Baltagi, B.H., 1985, Pooling cross-sections with unequal time-series lengths, *Economics Letters* **18**, 133–136.

Baltagi, B.H., 1986, Pooling under misspecification: Some Monte Carlo evidence on the Kmenta and the error components techniques, *Econometric Theory* **2**, 429–440.

Baltagi, B.H., 1987, On estimating from a more general time-series cum cross-section data structure, *The American Economist* **31**, 69–71.

Baltagi, B.H., 1988a, Prediction with a two-way error component regression model, Problem 88.1.1, *Econometric Theory* **4**, 171.

Baltagi, B.H., 1988b, An alternative heteroscedastic error components model, Problem 88.2.2, *Econometric Theory* **4**, 349–350.

Baltagi, B.H., 1989a, The equivalence of the Boothe–MacKinnon and the Hausman specification tests in the context of panel data, Problem 89.3.3, *Econometric Theory* **5**, 454.

Baltagi, B.H., 1989b, Applications of a necessary and sufficient condition for OLS to be BLUE, *Statistics and Probability Letters* **8**, 457–461.

Baltagi, B.H., 1990, The error components regression model: Conditional relative efficiency comparisons, *Statistical Papers* **31**, 1–13.

Baltagi, B.H., 1993a, Nested effects, Problem 93.4.2, *Econometric Theory* **9**, 687–688.

Baltagi, B.H., 1993b, Useful matrix transformations for panel data analysis: A survey, *Statistical Papers* **34**, 281–301.

Baltagi, B.H., ed., 1995a, Panel data, *Journal of Econometrics* **68**, 1–268.

Baltagi, B.H., 1995b, *Econometric Analysis of Panel Data* (John Wiley, Chichester).

Baltagi, B.H., 1995c, Testing for correlated effects in panels, Problem 95.2.5, *Econometric Theory* **11**, 401–402.

Baltagi, B.H., 1995d, Testing for fixed effects in logit and probit models using an artificial regression, Problem 95.5.4, *Econometric Theory* **11**, 1179.

Baltagi, B.H., 1996a, Testing for random individual and time effects using a Gauss–Newton regression, *Economics Letters* **50**, 189–192.

Baltagi, B.H., 1996b, Heteroskedastic fixed effects models, Problem 96.5.1, *Econometric Theory* **12**, 867.

Baltagi, B.H., 1997a, Testing for linear and loglinear error component regression against Box–Cox alternatives, *Statistics and Probability Letters* **33**, 63–68.

Baltagi, B.H., 1997b, A joint test for functional form and random individual effects, Problem 97.1.3, *Econometric Theory* **13**, 307–308.

Baltagi, B.H., 1997c, Hausman's specification test as a Gauss–Newton regression, Problem 97.4.1, *Econometric Theory* **13**, 757.

Baltagi, B.H., 1998, Within two way is equivalent to two withins one way, Problem 98.5.2, *Econometric Theory* **14**, 687.

Baltagi, B.H., 1999a, Specification tests in panel data models using artificial regressions, *Annales D'Économie et de Statistique* **55–56**, 277–297.

Baltagi, B.H., 1999b, The relative efficiency of the between estimator with respect to the within estimator, Problem 99.4.3, *Econometric Theory* **15**, 630–631.

Baltagi, B.H. and U. Blien, 1998, The German wage curve: Evidence from the IAB employment sample, *Economics Letters* **61**, 135–142.

Baltagi, B.H. and Y.J. Chang, 1994, Incomplete panels: A comparative study of alternative estimators for the unbalanced one-way error component regression model, *Journal of Econometrics* **62**, 67–89.

Baltagi, B.H. and Y.J. Chang, 1996, Testing for random individual effects using recursive residuals, *Econometric Reviews* **15**, 331–338.

Baltagi, B.H. and Y.J. Chang, 2000, Simultaneous equations with incomplete panels, *Econometric Theory* **16**, 269–279.

Baltagi, B.H. and J.M. Griffin, 1983, Gasoline demand in the OECD: An application of pooling and testing procedures, *European Economic Review* **22**, 117–137.

Baltagi, B.H. and J.M. Griffin, 1984, Short and long run effects in pooled models, *International Economic Review* **25**, 631–645.

Baltagi, B.H. and J.M. Griffin, 1988a, A generalized error component model with heteroscedastic disturbances, *International Economic Review* **29**, 745–753.

Baltagi, B.H. and J.M. Griffin, 1988b, A general index of technical change, *Journal of Political Economy* **96**, 20–41.

Baltagi, B.H. and J.M. Griffin, 1995, A dynamic demand model for liquor: The case for pooling, *Review of Economics and Statistics* **77**, 545–553.

Baltagi, B.H. and J.M. Griffin, 1997, Pooled estimators vs. their heterogeneous counterparts in the context of dynamic demand for gasoline, *Journal of Econometrics* **77**, 303–327.

Baltagi, B.H. and J.M. Griffin, 2001, The econometrics of rational addiction: The case of cigarettes, *Journal of Business Economics and Statistics*, forthcoming.

Baltagi, B.H. and C. Kao, 2000, Nonstationary panels, cointegration in panels and dynamic panels: A survey, *Advances in Econometrics* **15**, 7–51.

Baltagi, B.H. and S. Khanti-Akom, 1990, On efficient estimation with panel data: An empirical comparison of instrumental variables estimators, *Journal of Applied Econometrics* **5**, 401–406.

Baltagi, B.H. and W. Krämer, 1994, Consistency, asymptotic unbiasedness and bounds on the bias of s^2 in the linear regression model with error component disturbances, *Statistical Papers* **35**, 323–328.

Baltagi, B.H. and W. Krämer, 1995, A mixed error component model, Problem 95.1.4, *Econometric Theory* **11**, 192–193.

Baltagi, B.H. and W. Krämer, 1997, A simple linear trend model with error components, Problem 97.2.1, *Econometric Theory* **13**, 463.

Baltagi, B.H. and D. Levin, 1986, Estimating dynamic demand for cigarettes using panel data: The effects of bootlegging, taxation, and advertising reconsidered, *Review of Economics and Statistics* **68**, 148–155.

Baltagi, B.H. and D. Levin, 1992, Cigarette taxation: Raising revenues and reducing consumption, *Structural Change and Economic Dynamics* **3**, 321–335.

Baltagi, B.H. and Q. Li, 1990a, A comparison of variance components estimators using balanced versus unbalanced data, Problem 90.2.3, *Econometric Theory* **6**, 283–285.

Baltagi, B.H. and Q. Li, 1990b, A Lagrange multiplier test for the error components model with incomplete panels, *Econometric Reviews* **9**, 103–107.

Baltagi, B.H. and Q. Li, 1991a, A transformation that will circumvent the problem of autocorrelation in an error component model, *Journal of Econometrics* **48**, 385–393.

Baltagi, B.H. and Q. Li, 1991b, A joint test for serial correlation and random individual effects, *Statistics and Probability Letters* **11**, 277–280.

Baltagi, B.H. and Q. Li, 1991c, Variance component estimation under misspecification, Problem 91.3.3, *Econometric Theory* **7**, 418–419.

Baltagi, B.H. and Q. Li, 1992a, Variance component estimation under misspecification, Solution 91.3.3, *Econometric Theory* **8**, 430–433.

Baltagi, B.H. and Q. Li, 1992b, A monotonic property for iterative GLS in the two-way random effects model, *Journal of Econometrics* **53**, 45–51.

Baltagi, B.H. and Q. Li, 1992c, Prediction in the one-way error component model with serial correlation, *Journal of Forecasting* **11**, 561–567.

Baltagi, B.H. and Q. Li, 1992d, A note on the estimation of simultaneous equations with error components, *Econometric Theory* **8**, 113–119.

Baltagi, B.H. and Q. Li, 1992e, An approximate transformation for the error component model with MA(q) disturbances, Problem 92.4.3, *Econometric Theory* **8**, 582–583.

Baltagi, B.H. and Q. Li, 1993, An approximate transformation for the error component model with MA(q) disturbances, Solution 92.4.3, *Econometric Theory* **9**, 692–694.

Baltagi, B.H. and Q. Li, 1994, Estimating error component models with general MA(q) disturbances, *Econometric Theory* **10**, 396–408.

Baltagi, B.H. and Q. Li, 1995, Testing AR(1) against MA(1) disturbances in an error component model, *Journal of Econometrics* **68**, 133–151.

Baltagi, B.H. and Q. Li, 1997, Monte Carlo results on pure and pretest estimators of an error component model with autocorrelated disturbances, *Annales D'Économie et de Statistique* **48**, 69–82.

Baltagi, B.H. and D. Li, 1999, Prediction in the spatially autocorrelated error component model, Problem 99.2.4, *Econometric Theory* **15**, 259.

Baltagi, B.H. and D. Li, 2001, Prediction in the panel data model with spatial correlation, in L. Anselin and R.J.G.M. Florax, eds., *New Advances in Spatial Econometrics* (Springer-Verlag), forthcoming.

Baltagi, B.H. and N. Pinnoi, 1995, Public capital stock and state productivity growth: Further evidence from an error components model, *Empirical Economics* **20**, 351–359.

Baltagi, B.H. and B. Raj, 1992, A survey of recent theoretical developments in the econometrics of panel data, *Empirical Economics* **17**, 85–109.

Baltagi, B.H. and P.X. Wu, 1999, Unequally spaced panel data regressions with AR(1) disturbances, *Econometric Theory* **15**, 814–823.

Baltagi, B.H., Y.J. Chang and Q. Li, 1992a, Monte Carlo evidence on panel data regressions with AR(1) disturbances and an arbitrary variance on the initial observations, *Journal of Econometrics* **52**, 371–380.

Baltagi, B.H., Y.J. Chang and Q. Li, 1992b, Monte Carlo results on several new and existing tests for the error component model, *Journal of Econometrics* **54**, 95–120.

Baltagi, B.H., Y.J. Chang and Q. Li, 1998, Testing for random individual and time effects using unbalanced panel data, *Advances in Econometrics* **13**, 1–20.

Baltagi, B.H., T.B. Fomby and R.C. Hill, eds., 2000, Nonstationary panels, panel cointegration, and dynamic panels, *Advances in Econometrics,* Vol. 15 (Elsevier Science, Amsterdam).

Baltagi, B.H., J.M. Griffin and D. Rich, 1995, Airline deregulation: The cost pieces of the puzzle, *International Economic Review* **36**, 245–258.

Baltagi, B.H., J.M. Griffin and W. Xiong, 2000, To pool or not to pool: Homogeneous versus heterogeneous estimators applied to cigarette demand, *Review of Economics and Statistics* **82**, 117–126.

Baltagi, B.H., J. Hidalgo and Q. Li, 1996, A non-parametric test for poolability using panel data, *Journal of Econometrics* **75**, 345–367.

Baltagi, B.H., S.H. Song and B.C. Jung, 1999, Simple LM tests for the unbalanced nested error component regression model, working paper (Department of Economics, Texas A&M University).

Baltagi, B.H., S.H. Song and B.C. Jung, 2000, A comparative study of alternative estimators for the unbalanced two-way error component regression model, working paper (Department of Economics, Texas A&M University).

Baltagi, B.H., S.H. Song and B.C. Jung, 2001, The unbalanced nested error component regression model, *Journal of Econometrics* **101**, 357–381.

Baltagi, B.H., S.H. Song and W. Koh, 1999, Testing panel data regression models with spatial error correlation, working paper (Department of Economics, Texas A&M University).

Banerjee, A., 1999, Panel data unit roots and cointegration: An overview, *Oxford Bulletin of Economics and Statistics* **61**, 607–629.

Battese, G.E. and T.J. Coelli, 1988, Prediction of firm level technical efficiencies with a generalized frontier production function and panel data, *Journal of Econometrics* **38**, 387–399.

Becker, G.S., M. Grossman and K.M. Murphy, 1994, An empirical analysis of cigarette addiction, *American Economic Review* **84**, 396–418.

Becketti, S., W. Gould, L. Lillard and F. Welch, 1988, The panel study of income dynamics after fourteen years: An evaluation, *Journal of Labor Economics* **6**, 472–492.

Beggs, J.J., 1986, Time series analysis in pooled cross-sections, *Econometric Theory* **2**, 331–349.

Beggs, J.J. and M. Nerlove, 1988, Biases in dynamic models with fixed effects, *Economics Letters* **26**, 29–31.

Behrman, J.R. and A.B. Deolalikar, 1990, The intrahousehold demand for nutrients in rural south India: Individual estimates, fixed effects and permanent income, *Journal of Human Resources* **25**, 665–696.

Beierlein, J.G., J.W. Dunn and J.C. McConnon, Jr., 1981, The demand for electricity and natural gas in the Northeastern United States, *Review of Economics and Statistics* **63**, 403–408.

Bell, K.P. and N.R. Bockstael, 2000, Applying the generalized-moments estimation approach to spatial problems involving microlevel data, *Review of Economics and Statistics* **82**, 72–82.

Bellmann, L., J. Breitung and J. Wagner, 1989, Bias correction and bootstrapping of error component models for panel data: Theory and applications, *Empirical Economics* **14**, 329–342.

Belsley, D.A., E. Kuh and R.E. Welsch, 1980, *Regression Diagnostics: Identifying Influential Data and Sources of Collinearity* (John Wiley, New York).

Ben-Porath, Y., 1973, Labor force participation rates and the supply of labor, *Journal of Political Economy* **81**, 697–704.

Bera, A.K., W. Sosa-Escudero and M. Yoon, 2001, Tests for the error component model in the presence of local misspecification, *Journal of Econometrics* **101**, 1–23.

Berg, M.D., Q. Li and A. Ullah, 2000, Instrumental variable estimation of semi-parametric dynamic panel data models: Monte Carlo results on several new and existing estimators, *Advances in Econometrics* **15**, 297–315.

Bernard, A. and C. Jones, 1996, Productivity across industries and countries: Time series theory and evidence, *Review of Economics and Statistics* **78**, 135–146.

Berndt, E.R., Z. Griliches and N. Rappaport, 1995, Econometric estimates of prices indexes for personal computers in the 1990's, *Journal of Econometrics* **68**, 243–268.

Berry, S., P. Gottschalk and D. Wissoker, 1988, An error components model of the impact of plant closing on earnings, *Review of Economics and Statistics* **70**, 701–707.

Bertschek, I. and M. Lechner, 1998, Convenient estimators for the panel probit model, *Journal of Econometrics* **87**, 329–371.

Berzeg, K., 1979, The error component model: Conditions for the existence of the maximum likelihood estimates, *Journal of Econometrics* **10**, 99–102.

Berzeg, K., 1982, Demand for motor gasoline, a generalized error components model, *Southern Economic Journal* **49**, 462–471.

Bhargava, A., 1991a, Estimating short and long run income elasticities of foods and nutrients for rural south India, *Journal of the Royal Statistical Society* **A154**, 157–174.

Bhargava, A., 1991b, Identification and panel data models with endogenous regressors, *Review of Economic Studies* **58**, 129–140.

Bhargava, A. and J.D. Sargan, 1983, Estimating dynamic random effects models from panel data covering short time periods, *Econometrica* **51**, 1635–1659.

Bhargava, A., L. Franzini and W. Narendranathan, 1982, Serial correlation and fixed effects model, *Review of Economic Studies* **49**, 533–549.

Binder, M., C. Hsiao and M.H. Pesaran, 2000, Estimation and inference in short panel vector autoregressions with unit roots and cointegration, working paper (Department of Economics, University of Maryland).

Biorn, E., 1981, Estimating economic relations from incomplete cross-section/time-series data, *Journal of Econometrics* **16**, 221–236.

Biorn, E., 1992, The bias of some estimators for panel data models with measurement errors, *Empirical Economics* **17**, 51–66.

Biorn, E., 1996, Panel data with measurement errors, Chapter 10 in L. Mátyás and P. Sevestre, eds., *The Econometrics of Panel Data: A Handbook of the Theory With Applications* (Kluwer Academic Publishers, Dordrecht), 236–279.

Biorn, E., 2000, Panel data with measurement errors: Instrumental variables and GMM procedures combining levels and differences, *Econometric Reviews* **19**, 391–424.

Biorn, E. and E.S. Jansen, 1983, Individual effects in a system of demand functions, *Scandinavian Journal of Economics* **85**, 461–483.

Biorn, E. and T.J. Klette, 1998, Panel data with errors-in-variables: Essential and redundant orthogonality conditions in GMM-estimation, *Economics Letters* **59**, 275–282.

Björklund, A., 1985, Unemployment and mental health: Some evidence from panel data, *The Journal of Human Resources* **20**, 469–483.

Björklund, A., 1989, Potentials and pitfalls of panel data: The case of job mobility, *European Economic Review* **33**, 537–546.

Blanchard, P., 1996, Software review, Chapter 33 in L. Mátyás and P. Sevestre, eds., *The Econometrics of Panel Data: A Handbook of the Theory With Applications* (Kluwer Academic Publishers, Dordrecht), 879–913.

Blanchard, P. and L. Mátyás, 1996, Robustness of tests for error components models to non-normality, *Economics Letters* **51**, 161–167.

Blundell, R., 1988, Consumer behaviour: Theory and empirical evidence — A survey, *The Economic Journal* **98**, 16–65.

Blundell, R. and S. Bond, 1998, Initial conditions and moment restrictions in dynamic panel data models, *Journal of Econometrics* **87**, 115–143.

Blundell, R. and S. Bond, 2000, GMM estimation with persistent panel data: An application to production functions, *Econometric Reviews* **19**, 321–340.

Blundell, R. and C. Meghir, 1990, Panel data and life-cycle models, in J. Hartog, G. Ridder and J. Theeuwes, eds., *Panel Data and Labor Market Studies* (North-Holland, Amsterdam), 231–252.

Blundell, R. and R.S. Smith, 1991, Conditions initiales et estimation efficace dans les modèles dynamiques sur données de panel, *Annales D'Économie et de Statistique* **20–21**, 109–123.

Blundell, R., S. Bond and F. Windmeijer, 2000, Estimation in dynamic panel data models: Improving on the performance of the standard GMM estimator, *Advances in Econometrics* **15**, 53–91.

Blundell, R., C. Meghir and P. Neves, 1993, Labor supply and intertemporal substitution, *Journal of Econometrics* **59**, 137–160.

Blundell, R., S. Bond, M. Devereux and F. Schiantarelli, 1992, Investment and Tobin's q: Evidence from company panel data, *Journal of Econometrics* **51**, 233–257.

Boehmer, E. and W.L. Megginson, 1990, Determinants of secondary market prices for developing country syndicated loans, *The Journal of Finance* **45**, 1517–1540.

Borus, M.E., 1982, An inventory of longitudinal data sets of interest to economists, *Review of Public Data Use* **10**, 113–126.

Boumahdi, R. and A. Thomas, 1991, Testing for unit roots using panel data, *Economics Letters* **37**, 77–79.

Bound, J., D.A. Jaeger and R.M. Baker, 1995, Problems with instrumental variables estimation when the correlation between the instruments and the endogenous explanatory variables is weak, *Journal of the American Statistical Association* **90**, 443–450.

Bound, L., C. Brown, G.J. Duncan and W.L. Rodgers, 1990, Measurement error in cross-sectional and longitudinal labor market surveys: Validation study evidence, in J. Hartog, G. Ridder and T. Theeuwes, eds., *Panel Data and Labor Market Studies* (North-Holland, Amsterdam), 1–19.

Bover, O. and M. Arellano, 1997, Estimating dynamic limited variable models from panel data, *Investigaciones Economicas* **21**, 141–165.

Bowden, R.J. and D.A. Turkington, 1984, *Instrumental Variables* (Cambridge University Press, Cambridge).

Breitung, J., 2000, The local power of some unit root tests for panel data, *Advances in Econometrics* **15**, 161–177.

Breitung, J. and M. Lechner, 1999, Alternative GMM methods for nonlinear panel data models, Chapter 9 in L. Mátyás, ed., *Generalized Method of Moments Estimation* (Cambridge University Press, Cambridge), 248–274.

Breitung, J. and W. Meyer, 1994, Testing for unit roots in panel data: Are wages on different bargaining levels cointegrated?, *Applied Economics* **26**, 353–361.

Bresson, G., F. Kramarz and P. Sevestre, 1991, Heterogeneous labour and the dynamics of aggregate labour demand: Some estimations using panel data, *Empirical Economics* **17**, 153–168.

Breusch, T.S., 1987, Maximum likelihood estimation of random effects models, *Journal of Econometrics* **36**, 383–389.

Breusch, T.S. and L.G. Godfrey, 1981, A review of recent work on testing for autocorrelation in dynamic simultaneous models, in D.A. Currie, R. Nobay and D. Peel, eds., *Macroeconomic Analysis, Essays in Macroeconomics and Economics* (Croom Helm, London), 63–100.

Breusch, T.S. and A.R. Pagan, 1979, A simple test for heteroskedasticity and random coefficient variation, *Econometrica* **47**, 1287–1294.

Breusch, T.S. and A.R. Pagan, 1980, The Lagrange multiplier test and its applications to model specification in econometrics, *Review of Economic Studies* **47**, 239–253.

Breusch, T.S., G.E. Mizon and P. Schmidt, 1989, Efficient estimation using panel data, *Econometrica* **57**, 695–700.

Brown, J.N. and A. Light, 1992, Interpreting panel data on job tenure, *Journal of Labor Economics* **10**, 219–257

Brown, P., A.W. Kleidon and T.A. Marsh, 1983, New evidence on the nature of size-related anomalies in stock prices, *Journal of Financial Economics* **12**, 33–56.

Brown, R.L., J. Durbin and J.M. Evans, 1975, Techniques for testing the constancy of regression relationships over time, *Journal of the Royal Statistical Society* **37**, 149–192.

Browning, M., A. Deaton and M. Irish, 1985, A profitable approach to labor supply and commodity demands over the life cycle, *Econometrica* **53**, 503–543.

Burke, S.P., L.G. Godfrey and A.R. Termayne, 1990, Testing AR(1) against MA(1) disturbances in the linear regression model: An alternative procedure, *Review of Economic Studies* **57**, 135–145.

Butler, J.S. and R. Moffitt, 1982, A computationally efficient quadrature procedure for the one factor multinominal probit model, *Econometrica* **50**, 761–764.

Cameron, C. and P. Trivedi, 1998, *The Analysis of Count Data* (Cambridge University Press, New York).

Campbell, J.R. and B.E. Honoré, 1993, Median unbiasedness of estimators of panel data censored regression models, *Econometric Theory* **9**, 499–503.

Canzoneri, M.B., R.E. Cumby and B. Diba, 1999, Relative labor productivity and the real exchange rate in the long run: Evidence for a panel of OECD countries, *Journal of International Economics* **47**, 245–266.

Cardellichio, P.A., 1990, Estimation of production behavior using pooled microdata, *Review of Economics and Statistics* **72**, 11–18.

Carpenter, R.E., S.M. Fazzari and B.C. Petersen, 1998, Financing constraints and inventory investment: A comparative study with high-frequency panel data, *Review of Economics and Statistics* **80**, 513–519.

Carraro, C., F. Peracchi and G. Weber, eds., 1993, The econometrics of panels and pseudo panels, *Journal of Econometrics* **59**, 1–211.

Case, A.C., 1991, Spatial patterns in household demand, *Econometrica* **59**, 953–965.

Cashel-Cordo, P. and S.G. Craig, 1990, The public sector impact of international resource transfers, *Journal of Development Economics* **32**, 17–42.

Cecchetti, S., 1986, The frequency of price adjustment: A study of the newsstand prices of magazines, *Journal of Econometrics* **31**, 255–274.

Cermeño, R., 1999, Median-unbiased estimation in fixed-effects dynamic panels, *Annales D'Économie et de Statistique* **55–56**, 351–368.

Chamberlain, G., 1980, Analysis of covariance with qualitative data, *Review of Economic Studies* **47**, 225–238.

Chamberlain, G., 1982, Multivariate regression models for panel data, *Journal of Econometrics* **18**, 5–46.

Chamberlain, G., 1984, Panel data, Chapter 22 in Z. Griliches and M. Intrilligator, eds., *Handbook of Econometrics* (North-Holland, Amsterdam), 1247–1318.

Chamberlain, G., 1985, Heterogeneity, omitted variable bias and duration dependence, Chapter 1 in J.J. Heckman and B. Singer, eds., *Longitudinal Analysis of Labor Market Data* (Cambridge University Press, Cambridge), 3–38.

Chamberlain, G., 1993, Feedback in panel data models, working paper (Department of Economics, Harvard University).

Chamberlain, G. and Z. Griliches, 1975, Unobservables with a variance-components structure: Ability, schooling and the economic success of brothers, *International Economic Review* **16**, 422–449.

Chamberlain, G. and K. Hirano, 1999, Predictive distributions based on longitudinal earnings data, *Annales D'Économie et de Statistique* **55–56**, 211–242.

Chang, H.S., 1979, A study of industry location from pooled time-series and cross-section data: The case of cotton textile mills, *Quarterly Review of Economics and Business* **19**, 75–88.

Chang, H. and C. Lee, 1977, Using pooled time-series and cross-section data to test the firm and time effects in financial analyses, *Journal of Financial and Quantitative Analysis* **12**, 457–471.

Charlier, E., B. Melenberg and A. van Soest, 1995, A smoothed maximum score estimator for the binary choice panel data model with an application to labour force participation, *Statistica Neerlandica* **49**, 324–342.

Charlier, E., B. Melenberg and A. van Soest, 2001, An analysis of housing expenditure using semiparametric models and panel data, *Journal of Econometrics* **101**, 71–107.

Chen, B., S. McCoskey and C. Kao, 1999, Estimation and inference of a cointegrated regression in panel data: A Monte Carlo study, *American Journal of Mathematical and Management Sciences* **19**, 75–114.

Chesher, A., 1984, Testing for neglected heterogeneity, *Econometrica* **52**, 865–872.

Chiang, M.H. and C. Kao, 2001, Nonstationary panel time series using NPT 1.2 — A user guide (Center for Policy Research, Syracuse University).

Chib, S., 1996, Inference in panel data models via Gibbs sampling, Chapter 24 in L. Mátyás and P. Sevestre, eds., *The Econometrics of Panel Data: A Handbook of the Theory With Applications* (Kluwer Academic Publishers, Dordrecht), 639–651.

Choi, I., 1999a, Unit root tests for panel data, working paper (Department of Economics, Kookmin University, Korea).

Choi, I., 1999b, Asymptotic analysis of a nonstationary error component model, working paper (Department of Economics, Kookmin University, Korea).

Choi, I., 1999c, Instrumental variables estimation of a nearly nonstationary error component model, working paper (Department of Economics, Kookmin University, Korea).

Choi, I., 2000, Instrumental variables estimation of a nearly nonstationary, heterogeneous error component model, working paper (Department of Economics, Kookmin University, Korea).

Chow, G.C., 1960, Tests of equality between sets of coefficients in two linear regressions, *Econometrica* **28**, 591–605.

Chowdhury, G., 1991, A comparison of covariance estimators for complete and incomplete panel data models, *Oxford Bulletin of Economics and Statistics* **53**, 88–93.

Chowdhury, G. and S. Nickell, 1985, Hourly earnings in the United States: Another look at unionization, schooling, sickness, and unemployment using PSID data, *Journal of Labor Economics* **3**, 38–69.

Coakley, J. and A.M. Fuertes, 1997, New panel unit root tests of PPP, *Economics Letters* **57**, 17–22.

Coakely, J., F. Kulasi and R. Smith, 1996, Current account solvency and the Feldstein–Horioka puzzle, *Economic Journal* **106**, 620–627.

Coe, D. and E. Helpman, 1995, International R&D spillovers, *European Economic Review* **39**, 859–887.

Collado, M.D., 1997, Estimating dynamic models from time series of independent cross-sections, *Journal of Econometrics* **82**, 37–62.

Conley, T.G., 1999, GMM estimation with cross sectional dependence, *Journal of Econometrics* **92**, 1–45.

Contoyannis, P. and N. Rice, 2000, The impact of health on wages: Evidence from the British Household Panel Survey, *Empirical Economics,* forthcoming.

Conway, K.S. and T.J. Kniesner, 1992, How fragile are male labor supply function estimates, *Empirical Economics* **17**, 170–182.

Corbeil, R.R. and S.R. Searle, 1976a, A comparison of variance component estimators, *Biometrics* **32**, 779–791.

Corbeil, R.R. and S.R. Searle, 1976b, Restricted maximum likelihood (REML), estimation of variance components in the mixed model, *Technometrics* **18**, 31–38.

Cornwell, C. and P. Rupert, 1988, Efficient estimation with panel data: An empirical comparison of instrumental variables estimators, *Journal of Applied Econometrics* **3**, 149–155.

Cornwell, C. and P. Rupert, 1997, Unobservable individual effects, marriage, and then the earnings of young men, *Economic Inquiry* **35**, 285–294.

Cornwell, C. and P. Schmidt, 1992, Models for which the mle and the conditional mle coincide, *Empirical Economics* **17**, 67–75.

Cornwell, C. and W.N. Trumbull, 1994, Estimating the economic model of crime with panel data, *Review of Economics and Statistics* **76**, 360–366.

Cornwell, C., P. Schmidt and R.C. Sickles, 1990, Production frontiers with cross-sectional and time-series variation in efficiency levels, *Journal of Econometrics* **46**, 185–200.

Cornwell, C., P. Schmidt and D. Wyhowski, 1992, Simultaneous equations and panel data, *Journal of Econometrics* **51**, 151–181.

Crépon, B. and J. Mairesse, 1996, The Chamberlain approach, Chapter 14 in L. Mátyás and P. Sevestre, eds., *The Econometrics of Panel Data: A Handbook of the Theory With Applications* (Kluwer Academic Publishers, Dordrecht), 323–390.

Crépon, B., F. Kramarz and A. Trognon, 1997, Parameters of interest, nuisance parameters and orthogonality conditions: An application to autoregressive error components models, *Journal of Econometrics* **82**, 135–156.

Culver, S.E. and D.H. Papell, 1997, Is there a unit root in the inflation rate? Evidence from sequential break and panel data model, *Journal of Applied Econometrics* **35**, 155–160.

Das, K., 1979, Asymptotic optimality of restricted maximum likelihood estimates for the mixed model, *Calcutta Statistical Association Bulletin* **28**, 125–142.

Davidson, R. and J.G. MacKinnon, 1993, *Estimation and Inference in Econometrics* (Oxford University Press, New York).

Davis, P., 2001, Estimating multi-way error components models with unbalanced data structures using instrumental variables, *Journal of Econometrics*, forthcoming.

Deaton, A., 1985, Panel data from time series of cross-sections, *Journal of Econometrics* **30**, 109–126.

Deschamps, P., 1991, On the estimated variances of regression coefficients in misspecified error components models, *Econometric Theory* **7**, 369–384.

DeStavola, B.L., 1986, Sampling designs for short panel data, *Econometrica* **54**, 415–424.

Dielman, T.E., 1989, *Pooled Cross-sectional and Time Series Data Analysis* (Marcel Dekker, New York).

Dionne, G., R. Gagne′ and C. Vanasse, 1998, Inferring technological parameters from incomplete panel data, *Journal of Econometrics* **87**, 303–327.

Dormont, B., 1989, *Introduction à l'économetrie des données de panel: Théorie et application a des échantillons d'entreprises* (Editions du CNRS, Paris).

Driscoll, J.C. and A.C. Kraay, 1998, Consistent covariance matrix estimation with spatially dependent panel data, *Review of Economics and Statistics* **80**, 549–560.

Duncan, G.J. and D.H. Hill, 1985, An investigation of the extent and consequences of measurement error in labor economic survey data, *Journal of Labor Economics* **3**, 508–532.

Duncan, G.J. and B. Holmlund, 1983, Was Adam Smith right after all? Another test for the theory of compensating wage differentials, *Journal of Labor Economics* **1**, 366–379.

England, P., G. Farkas, B.S. Kilbourne and T. Dou, 1988, Explaining occupational sex segregation and wages: Findings from a model with fixed effects, *American Sociological Review* **53**, 544–558.

Entorf, H., 1997, Random walks with drifts: Nonsense regression and spurious fixed-effect estimation, *Journal of Econometrics* **80**, 287–296.

Evans, M.A. and M.L. King, 1985, Critical value approximations for tests of linear regression disturbances, *Australian Journal of Statistics* **27**, 68–83.

Evans, P. and G. Karras, 1996, Convergence revisited, *Journal of Monetary Economics* **37**, 249–265.

Fiebig, D., R. Bartels and W. Krämer, 1996, The Frisch–Waugh theorem and generalized least squares, *Econometric Reviews* **15**, 431–443.

Fisher, F.M., 1970, Tests of equality between sets of coefficients in two linear regressions: An expository note, *Econometrica* **38**, 361–366.

Fleissig, A.R. and J. Strauss, 1997, Unit root tests on real wage panel data for the G7, *Economics Letters* **56**, 149–155.

Frankel, J.A. and A.K. Rose, 1996, A panel project on purchasing power parity: Mean reversion within and between countries, *Journal of International Economics* **40**, 209–224.

Freeman, R.B., 1984, Longitudinal analyses of the effects of trade unions, *Journal of Labor Economics* **2**, 1–26.

Frees, E.W., 1995, Assessing cross-sectional correlation in panel data, *Journal of Econometrics* **69**, 393–414.

Frees, E.W., V.R. Young and Y. Luo, 1999, A longitudinal data analysis interpretation of credibility models, *Insurance: Mathematics and Economics* **24**, 229–247.

Fuller, W.A. and G.E. Battese, 1973, Transformations for estimation of linear models with nested error structure, *Journal of the American Statistical Association* **68**, 626–632.

Fuller, W.A. and G.E. Battese, 1974, Estimation of linear models with cross-error structure, *Journal of Econometrics* **2**, 67–78.

Galbraith, J.W. and V. Zinde-Walsh, 1995, Transforming the error-component model for estimation with general ARMA disturbances, *Journal of Econometrics* **66**, 349–355.

Gardner, R., 1998, Unobservable individual effects in unbalanced panel data, *Economics Letters* **58**, 39–42.

Gerdtham, U.G. and M. Löthgren, 2000, On stationarity and cointegration of international health expenditure and GDP, *Journal of Health Economics* **19**, 461–475.

Ghosh, S.K., 1976, Estimating from a more general time-series cum cross-section data structure, *The American Economist* **20**, 15–21.

Girma, S., 2000, A quasi-differencing approach to dynamic modelling from a time series of independent cross-sections, *Journal of Econometrics* **98**, 365–383

Goldberger, A.S., 1962, Best linear unbiased prediction in the generalized linear regression model, *Journal of the American Statistical Association* **57**, 369–375.

Gourieroux, C. and A. Monfort, 1993, Simulation-based inference: A survey with special reference to panel data models, *Journal of Econometrics* **59**, 5–33.

Gourieroux, C., A. Holly and A. Monfort, 1982, Likelihood ratio test, Wald test, and Kuhn–Tucker test in linear models with inequality constraints on the regression parameters, *Econometrica* **50**, 63–80.

Granger, C.W.J. and N. Hyung, 1999, Spurious stochastics in a short time-series panel data, *Annales D'Économie et de Statistique* **55–56**, 299–315.

Graybill, F.A., 1961, *An Introduction to Linear Statistical Models* (McGraw-Hill, New York).

Greene, W.H., 2000, *Econometric Analysis* (Prentice Hall, New Jersey).

Griffin, J.M., 1982, The welfare implications of externalities and price elasticities for telecommunications pricing, *Review of Economics and Statistics* **64**, 59–66.

Griffiths, W.E. and J.R. Anderson, 1982, Using time-series of cross-section data to estimate a production function with positive and negative marginal risks, *Journal of the American Statistical Association* **77**, 529–536.

Griliches, Z. and J.A. Hausman, 1986, Errors in variables in panel data, *Journal of Econometrics* **31**, 93–118.

Griliches, Z. and J. Mairesse, 1984, Productivity and R&D at the firm level, in Z. Griliches, ed., *R&D, Patents and Productivity* (University of Chicago Press, Chicago), 339–374.

Griliches, Z. and J. Mairesse, 1998, Production functions: The search for identification, in S. Strom, ed., *Essays in Honour of Ragnar Frisch*, Econometric Society Monograph Series (Cambridge University Press, Cambridge).

Groen, J.J.J., 2000, The monetary exchange rate model as a long-run phenomenon, *Journal of International Economics* **52**, 299–319.

Groen, J.J.J. and F. Kleibergen, 1999, Likelihood-based cointegration analysis in panels of vector error correction models, discussion paper 99–055/4 (Tinbergen Institute, The Netherlands).

Grunfeld, Y., 1958, The determinants of corporate investment, unpublished Ph.D. dissertation (University of Chicago, Chicago).

Guilkey, D.K. and J.L. Murphy, 1993, Estimation and testing in the random effects probit model, *Journal of Econometrics* **59**, 301–317.

Gurmu, S., 1996, Testing for fixed effects in logit and probit models using an artificial regression, Solution 95.5.4, *Econometric Theory* **12**, 872–874.

Gurmu, S., 2000, The relative efficiency of the between-estimator with respect to the within-estimator, Solution 99.4.3, *Econometric Theory* **16**, 454–456.

Haavelmo, T., 1944, The probability approach in econometrics, *Supplement to Econometrica* **12**, 1–118.

Hadri, K., 1999, Testing the null hypothesis of stationarity against the alternative of a unit root in panel data with serially correlated errors, manuscript (Department of Economics and Accounting, University of Liverpool).

Häggström, E., 2000, Properties of Honda's test for random individual effects in non-linear regressions, *Statistical Papers,* forthcoming.

Hahn, J., 1997, Efficient estimation of panel data models with sequential moment restrictions, *Journal of Econometrics* **79**, 1–21.

Hahn, J., 1999, How informative is the initial condition in the dynamic panel model with fixed effects? *Journal of Econometrics* **93**, 309–326.

Hajivassiliou, V.A., 1987, The external debt repayments problems of LDC's: An econometric model based on panel data, *Journal of Econometrics* **36**, 205–230.

Hajivassiliou, V.A., 1994, Estimation by simulation of the external debt repayment problems, *Journal of Applied Econometrics* **9**, 109–132.

Hajivassiliou, V.A. and P.A. Ruud, 1994, Classical estimation methods for LDV models using simulation, Chapter 40 in R.F. Engle and D.L. McFadden, eds., *Handbook of Econometrics* (North-Holland, Amsterdam), 2383–2441.

Hall, S., S. Lazarova and G. Urga, 1999, A principal components analysis of common stochastic trends in heterogeneous panel data: Some Monte Carlo evidence, *Oxford Bulletin of Economics and Statistics* **61**, 749–767.

Hamerle, A., 1990, On a simple test for neglected heterogeneity in panel studies, *Biometrics* **46**, 193–199.

Hamermesh, D.S., 1989, Why do individual-effects models perform so poorly? The case of academic salaries, *Southern Economic Journal* **56**, 39–45.

Han, A.K. and D. Park, 1989, Testing for structural change in panel data: Application to a study of U.S. foreign trade in manufacturing goods, *Review of Economics and Statistics* **71**, 135–142.

Hansen, B.E., 1999, Threshold effects in non-dynamic panels: Estimation, testing and inference, *Journal of Econometrics* **93**, 345–368.

Hansen, L.P., 1982, Large sample properties of generalized method of moments estimators, *Econometrica* **50**, 1029–1054.

Haque, N.U., K. Lahiri and P. Montiel, 1993, Estimation of a macroeconomic model with rational expectations and capital controls for developing countries, *Journal of Development Economics* **42**, 337–356.

Harris, R.D.F. and E. Tzavalis, 1999, Inference for unit roots in dynamic panels where the time dimension is fixed, *Journal of Econometrics* **91**, 201–226.

Harrison, D. and D.L. Rubinfeld, 1978, Hedonic housing prices and the demand for clean air, *Journal of Environmental Economics and Management* **5**, 81–102.

Hartley, H.O. and J.N.K. Rao, 1967, Maximum likelihood estimation for the mixed analysis of variance model, *Biometrika* **54**, 93–108.

Hartog, J., G. Ridder and J. Theeuwes, eds., 1990, *Panel Data and Labor Market Studies* (North-Holland, Amsterdam).

Harville, D.A., 1969, Quadratic unbiased estimation of variance component for the one way classification, *Biometrika* **56**, 313–326.

Harville, D.A., 1977, Maximum likelihood approaches to variance component estimation and to related problems, *Journal of the American Statistical Association* **72**, 320–340.

Hausman, J.A., 1975, An instrumental variable approach to full information estimators for linear and certain nonlinear econometric models, *Econometrica* **43**, 727–738.

Hausman, J.A., 1978, Specification tests in econometrics, *Econometrica* **46**, 1251–1271.

Hausman, J.A. and W.E. Taylor, 1981, Panel data and unobservable individual effects, *Econometrica* **49**, 1377–1398.
Hausman, J.A. and D. Wise, 1979, Attrition bias in experimental and panel data: The Gary income maintenance experiment, *Econometrica* **47**, 455–473.
Hausman, J.A., B.H. Hall and Z. Griliches, 1984, Econometric models for count data with an application to the patents–R&D relationship, *Econometrica* **52**, 909–938.
Hayashi, F. and T. Inoue, 1991, The relation between firm growth and q with multiple capital goods: Theory and evidence from Japanese panel data, *Econometrica* **59**, 731–753.
Heckman, J.J., 1979, Sample selection bias as a specification error, *Econometrica* **47**, 153–161.
Heckman, J.J., 1981a, Statistical models for discrete panel data, in C.F. Manski and D. McFadden, eds., *Structural Analysis of Discrete Data with Econometric Applications* (MIT Press, Cambridge), 114–178.
Heckman, J.J., 1981b, The incidental parameters problem and the problem of initial conditions in estimating a discrete time–discrete data stochastic process, in C.F. Manski and D. McFadden, eds., *Structural Analysis of Discrete Data with Econometric Applications* (MIT Press, Cambridge), 179–195.
Heckman, J.J., 1981c, Heterogeneity and state dependence, in S. Rosen, ed., *Studies in Labor Markets* (Chicago University Press, Chicago), 91–139.
Heckman, J.J. and G.J. Borjas, 1980, Does unemployment cause future unemployment? Definitions, questions and answers from a continuous time model of heterogeneity and state dependence, *Economica* **47**, 247–283.
Heckman, J.J. and T.E. MaCurdy, 1980, A life-cycle model of female labor supply, *Review of Economic Studies* **47**, 47–74.
Heckman, J.J. and B. Singer, 1985, *Longitudinal Analysis of Labor Market Data* (Cambridge University Press, Cambridge).
Heckman, J.J. and R. Willis, 1975, Estimation of a stochastic model of reproduction: An econometric approach, in N. Terleckyi, ed., *Household Production and Consumption* (National Bureau of Economic Research, New York), 99–138.
Heckman, J.J. and R. Willis, 1977, A beta-logistic model for the analysis of sequential labor force participation by married women, *Journal of Political Economy* **85**, 27–58.
Hecq, A., F.C. Palm and J.P. Urbain, 2000, Testing for common cyclical features in non-stationary panel data models, *Advances in Econometrics* **15**, 131–160.
Hemmerle, W.J. and H.O. Hartley, 1973, Computing maximum likelihood estimates for the mixed A.O.V. model using the W-transformation, *Technometrics* **15**, 819–831.
Henderson, C.R., 1953, Estimation of variance components, *Biometrics* **9**, 226–252.
Herriot, R.A. and E.F. Spiers, 1975, Measuring the impact of income statistics of reporting differences between the current population survey and administrative sources, *Proceedings of the Social Statistics Section* (American Statistical Association), 147–158.
Hillier, G.H., 1990, On the normalization of structural equations: Properties of direction estimators, *Econometrica* **58**, 1181–1194.
Hoch, L., 1962, Estimation of production function parameters combining time-series and cross-section data, *Econometrica* **30**, 34–53.
Hocking, R.R., 1985, *The Analysis of Linear Models* (Brooks/Cole Company, Monterey, CA).
Hocking, R.R. and M.H. Kutner, 1975, Some analytical and numerical comparisons of estimators for the mixed A.O.V. model, *Biometrics* **31**, 19–28.
Holly, A., 1982, A remark on Hausman's specification test, *Econometrica* **50**, 749–759.
Holly, A. and L. Gardiol, 2000, A score test for individual heteroscedasticity in a one-way error components model, Chapter 10 in J. Krishnakumar and E. Ronchetti, eds., *Panel Data Econometrics: Future Directions* (North-Holland, Amsterdam), 199–211.
Holtz-Eakin, D., 1988, Testing for individual effects in autoregressive models, *Journal of Econometrics* **39**, 297–307.

Holtz-Eakin, D., 1994, Public-sector capital and the productivity puzzle, *Review of Economics and Statistics* **76**, 12–21.

Holtz-Eakin, D., W. Newey and H.S. Rosen, 1988, Estimating vector autoregressions with panel data, *Econometrica* **56**, 1371–1395.

Holtz-Eakin, D., W. Newey and H.S. Rosen, 1989, The revenues–expenditures nexus: Evidence from local government data, *International Economic Review* **30**, 415–429.

Honda, Y., 1985, Testing the error components model with non-normal disturbances, *Review of Economic Studies* **52**, 681–690.

Honda, Y., 1991, A standardized test for the error components model with the two-way layout, *Economics Letters* **37**, 125–128.

Honoré, B.E., 1992, Trimmed LAD and least squares estimation of truncated and censored regression models with fixed effects, *Econometrica* **60**, 533–565.

Honoré, B.E., 1993, Orthogonality conditions for Tobit models with fixed effects and lagged dependent variables, *Journal of Econometrics* **59**, 35–61.

Honoré, B.E. and E. Kyriazidou, 2000a, Estimation of Tobit-type models with individual specific effects, *Econometric Reviews* **19**, 341–366.

Honoré, B.E. and E. Kyriazidou, 2000b, Panel data discrete choice models with lagged dependent variables, *Econometrica* **68**, 839–874.

Honoré, B.E. and A. Lewbel, 2000, Semiparametric binary choice panel data models without strictly exogenous regressors, working paper (Boston College, Massachusetts).

Horowitz, J.L. and C.F. Manski, 1998, Censoring of outcomes and regressors due to survey nonresponse: Identification and estimation using weights and imputations, *Journal of Econometrics* **84**, 37–58.

Horowitz, J.L. and M. Markatou, 1996, Semiparametric estimation of regression models for panel data, *Review of Economic Studies* **63**, 145–168.

Houthakker, H.S., 1965, New evidence on demand elasticities, *Econometrica* **33**, 277–288.

Houthakker, H.S., P.K. Verleger and D. Sheehan, 1974, Dynamic demand for gasoline and residential electricity, *American Journal of Agricultural Economics* **56**, 412–418.

Howrey, E.P. and H.R. Varian, 1984, Estimating the distributional impact of time-of-day pricing of electricity, *Journal of Econometrics* **26**, 65–82.

Hsiao, C., 1985, Benefits and limitations of panel data, *Econometric Reviews* **4**, 121–174.

Hsiao, C., 1986, *Analysis of Panel Data* (Cambridge University Press, Cambridge).

Hsiao, C., 1991, Identification and estimation of dichotomous latent variables models using panel data, *Review of Economic Studies* **58**, 717–731.

Hsiao, C., 1996, Logit and probit models, Chapter 16 in L. Mátyás and P. Sevestre, eds., *The Econometrics of Panel Data: A Handbook of the Theory With Applications* (Kluwer Academic Publishers, Dordrecht), 410–428.

Hsiao, C., 2001, Panel data models, Chapter 16 in B.H. Baltagi, ed., *A Companion to Theoretical Econometrics* (Blackwell Publishers, Massachusetts), 349–365.

Hsiao, C. and B. Sun, 2000, To pool or not to pool panel data, Chapter 9 in J. Krishnakumar and E. Ronchetti, eds., *Panel Data Econometrics: Future Directions* (North-Holland, Amsterdam), 181–198.

Hsiao, C. and A.K. Tahmiscioglu, 1997, A panel analysis of liquidity constraints and firm investment, *Journal of the American Statistical Association* **92**, 455–465.

Hsiao, C., T. Appelbe and C.R. Dineen, 1993, A general framework for panel data models with an application to Canadian customer-dialed long distance telephone service, *Journal of Econometrics* **59**, 63–86.

Hsiao, C., M.H. Pesaran and A.K. Tahmiscioglu, 1999, Bayes estimation of short run coefficients in dynamic panel data models, Chapter 11 in C. Hsiao, K. Lahiri, L.F. Lee and M.H. Pesaran, eds., *Analysis of Panels and Limited Dependent Variable Models* (Cambridge University Press, Cambridge), 268–296.

Hsiao, C., K. Lahiri, L.F. Lee and M.H. Pesaran, eds., 1999, *Analysis of Panels and Limited Dependent Variable Models* (Cambridge University Press, Cambridge).

Hujer, R. and H. Schneider, 1989, The analysis of labor market mobility using panel data, *European Economic Review* **33**, 530–536.

Im, K.S., M.H. Pesaran and Y. Shin, 1997, Testing for unit roots in heterogeneous panels, manuscript (Department of Applied Economics, University of Cambridge).

Im, K.S., S.C. Ahn, P. Schmidt and J.M. Wooldridge, 1999, Efficient estimation of panel data models with strictly exogenous explanatory variables, *Journal of Econometrics* **93**, 177–201.

Imbens, G., 1997, One-step estimators for over-identified generalized method of moments models, *Review of Economic Studies* **64**, 359–383.

Islam, N., 1995, Growth empirics: A panel data approach, *Quarterly Journal of Economics* **110**, 1127–1170.

Jennrich, R.I. and P.F. Sampson, 1976, Newton–Raphson and related algorithms for maximum likelihood variance component estimation, *Technometrics* **18**, 11–17.

Jimenez-Martin, S., 1998, On the testing of heterogeneity effects in dynamic unbalanced panel data models, *Economics Letters* **58**, 157–163.

Johansen, S., 1995, *Likelihood-Based Inference in Cointegrated Vector Autoregressive Models* (Oxford University Press, Oxford).

Johnson, J.A. and E.H. Oksanen, 1977, Estimation of demand for alcoholic beverages in Canada from pooled time series and cross sections, *Review of Economics and Statistics* **59**, 113–118.

Johnson, S.C. and K. Lahiri, 1992, A panel data analysis of productive efficiency in freestanding health clinics, *Empirical Economics* **17**, 141–151.

Jorion, P. and R. Sweeney, 1996, Mean reversion in real exchange rates: Evidence and implications for forecasting, *Journal of International Money and Finance* **15**, 535–550.

Judge, G.G., W.E. Griffiths, R.C. Hill, H. Lutkepohl and T.C. Lee, 1985, *The Theory and Practice of Econometrics* (John Wiley, New York).

Judson, R.A. and A.L. Owen, 1999, Estimating dynamic panel data models: A guide for macroeconomists, *Economics Letters* **65**, 9–15.

Kalton, G., D. Kasprzyk and D. McMillen, 1989, Nonsampling errors in panel surveys, in D. Kasprzyk, G.J. Duncan, G. Kalton and M.P. Singh, eds., *Panel Surveys* (John Wiley, New York), 249–270.

Kang, S., 1985, A note on the equivalence of specification tests in the two-factor multivariate variance components model, *Journal of Econometrics* **28**, 193–203.

Kao, C., 1999, Spurious regression and residual-based tests for cointegration in panel data, *Journal of Econometrics* **90**, 1–44.

Kao, C. and M.H. Chiang, 2000, On the estimation and inference of a cointegrated regression in panel data, *Advances in Econometrics* **15**, 179–222.

Kao, C. and J.F. Schnell, 1987a, Errors in variables in panel data with binary dependent variable, *Economics Letters* **24**, 45–49.

Kao, C. and J.F. Schnell, 1987b, Errors in variables in a random effects probit model for panel data, *Economics Letters* **24**, 339–342.

Kao, C., M.H. Chiang and B. Chen, 1999, International R&D spillovers: An application of estimation and inference in panel cointegration, *Oxford Bulletin of Economics and Statistics* **61**, 691–709.

Karlsson, S. and M. Löthgren, 2000, On the power and interpretation of panel unit root tests, *Economics Letters* **66**, 249–255.

Karlsson, S. and J. Skoglund, 2000, Maximum-likelihood based inference in the two-way random effects model with serially correlated time effects, paper presented at the Ninth International Conference on Panel Data, Geneva, Switzerland.

Kasprzyk, D., G.J. Duncan, G. Kalton and M.P. Singh, 1989, *Panel Surveys* (John Wiley, New York).

Kauppi, H., 2000, Panel data limit theory and asymptotic analysis of a panel regression with near integrated regressors, *Advances in Econometrics* **15**, 239–274.

Keane, M., 1993, Simulation estimation for panel data models with limited dependent variables, in G.S. Maddala, C.R. Rao and H.D. Vinod, eds., *Handbook of Statistics* (North-Holland, Amsterdam).

Keane, M., 1994, A computationally practical simulation estimator for panel data, *Econometrica* **62**, 95–116.

Keane, M.P. and D.E. Runkle, 1992, On the estimation of panel-data models with serial correlation when instruments are not strictly exogenous, *Journal of Business and Economic Statistics* **10**, 1–9.

Keane, M.P., R. Moffitt and D.E. Runkle, 1988, Real wages over the business cycle: Estimating the impact of heterogeneity with micro data, *Journal of Political Economy* **96**, 1232–1266.

Kelejian, H.H. and I. Prucha, 1999, A generalized moments estimator for the autoregressive parameter in a spatial model, *International Economic Review* **40**, 509–533.

Kiefer, N.M., 1980, Estimation of fixed effects models for time series of cross sections with arbitrary intertemporal covariance, *Journal of Econometrics* **14**, 195–202.

Kiefer, N.M., 1988, Economic duration data and hazard functions, *Journal of Economic Literature* **26**, 646–679.

Kim, B.S. and G.S. Maddala, 1992, Estimation and specification analysis of models of dividend behavior based on censored panel data, *Empirical Economics* **17**, 111–124.

Kinal, T. and K. Lahiri, 1990, A computational algorithm for multiple equation models with panel data, *Economics Letters* **34**, 143–146.

Kinal, T. and K. Lahiri, 1993, A simplified algorithm for estimation of simultaneous equations error components models with an application to a model of developing country foreign trade, *Journal of Applied Econometrics* **8**, 81–92.

King, M.L., 1983, Testing for autoregressive against moving average errors in the linear regression model, *Journal of Econometrics* **21**, 35–51.

King, M.L. and M. McAleer, 1987, Further results on testing AR(1) against MA(1) disturbances in the linear regression model, *Review of Economic Studies* **54**, 649–663.

King, M.L. and P.X. Wu, 1997, Locally optimal one-sided tests for multiparameter hypotheses, *Econometric Reviews* **16**, 131–156.

Kiviet, J.F., 1995, On bias, inconsistency and efficiency of some estimators in dynamic panel data models, *Journal of Econometrics* **68**, 53–78.

Kiviet, J.F., 1999, Expectations of expansions for estimators in a dynamic panel data model: Some results for weakly exogenous regressors, Chapter 8 in C. Hsiao, K. Lahiri, L.F. Lee and M.H. Pesaran, eds., *Analysis of Panels and Limited Dependent Variable Models* (Cambridge University Press, Cambridge), 199–225.

Kiviet, J.F. and W. Krämer, 1992, Bias of s^2 in the linear regression model with correlated errors, *Empirical Economics* **16**, 375–377.

Kleiber, C., 1997, Heteroskedastic fixed effects models, Solution 96.5.1, *Econometric Theory* **13**, 891–893.

Klevmarken, N.A., 1989, Panel studies: What can we learn from them? Introduction, *European Economic Review* **33**, 523–529.

Kmenta, J., 1986, *Elements of Econometrics* (MacMillan, New York).

Kniesner, T. and Q. Li, 2001, Semiparametric panel data models with heterogeneous dynamic adjustment: Theoretical consideration and an application to labor supply, *Empirical Economics*, forthcoming.

Koning, R.H., 1989, Prediction with a two-way error component regression model, Solution 88.1.1, *Econometric Theory* **5**, 175.

Koning, R.H., 1990, The equivalence of the Boothe–MacKinnon and the Hausman specification tests in the context of panel data, Solution 89.3.3, *Econometric Theory* **6**, 409.

Koning, R.H., 1991, A comparison of variance components estimators using balanced versus unbalanced data, Solution 90.2.3, *Econometric Theory* **6**, 425–427.

Koop, G. and M.F.J. Steel, 2001, Bayesian analysis of stochastic frontier models, Chapter 24 in B.H. Baltagi, ed., *A Companion to Theoretical Econometrics* (Blackwell Publishers, Massachusetts), 520–537.

Krishnakumar, J., 1988, *Estimation of Simultaneous Equation Models with Error Components Structure* (Springer-Verlag, Berlin).

Krishnakumar, J. and E. Ronchetti, 2000, *Panel Data Econometrics: Future Directions* (North-Holland, Amsterdam).

Kuh, E., 1959, The validity of cross-sectionally estimated behavior equations in time series applications, *Econometrica* **27**, 197–214.

Kumbhakar, S.C., 1991, Estimation and technical inefficiency in panel data models with firm- and time-specific effects, *Economics Letters* **36**, 43–48.

Kumbhakar, S.C., 1992, Efficiency estimation using rotating panel data models, *Economics Letters* **38**, 169–174.

Kwiatkowski, D., P.C.B. Phillips, P. Schmidt and Y. Shin, 1992, Testing the null hypothesis of stationarity against the alternative of a unit root, *Journal of Econometrics* **54**, 91–115.

Kyriazidou, E., 1997, Estimation of a panel data sample selection model, *Econometrica* **65**, 1335–1364.

Labeaga, J.M., 1999, A double-hurdle rational addiction model with heterogeneity: Estimating the demand for tobacco, *Journal of Econometrics* **93**, 49–72.

Laisney, F., M. Lechner and W. Pohlmeier, 1992, Innovation activity and firm heterogeneity: Empirical evidence from West Germany, *Structural Change and Economic Dynamics* **3**, 301–320.

LaMotte, L.R., 1973a, On non-negative quadratic unbiased estimation of variance components, *Journal of the American Statistical Association* **68**, 728–730.

LaMotte, L.R., 1973b, Quadratic estimation of variance components, *Biometrics* **29**, 311–330.

Lancaster, T., 1991, *The Econometric Analysis of Transition Data* (Cambridge University Press, New York).

Lancaster, T., 2000, The incidental parameter problem since 1948, *Journal of Econometrics* **95**, 391–413.

Larson, A.C. and J.S. Watters, 1993, A convenient test of functional form for pooled econometric models, *Empirical Economics* **18**, 271–280.

Larsson, R., J. Lyhagen and M. Löthgren, 1998, Likelihood-based cointegration tests in heterogeneous panels, working paper (Economics and Finance, No. 250, Stockholm School of Economics).

Lechner, M., 1995, Some specification tests for probit models estimated on panel data, *Journal of Business and Economic Statistics* **13**, 475–488.

Lechner, M. and J. Breitung, 1996, Some GMM estimation methods and specification tests for nonlinear models, Chapter 22 in L. Mátyás and P. Sevestre, eds., *The Econometrics of Panel Data: A Handbook of the Theory With Applications* (Kluwer Academic Publishers, Dordrecht), 583–611.

Lee, K., M.H. Pesaran and R. Smith, 1997, Growth and convergence in a multi-country empirical stochastic Solow model, *Journal of Applied Econometrics* **12**, 357–392.

Lee, L.F., 1979, Estimation of autocorrelated error components model with panel data, working paper (Department of Economics, University of Minnesota).

Lee, L.F., 1981, Efficient estimation of dynamic error components models with panel data, in O.D. Anderson and M.R. Perryman, eds., *Time-Series Analysis* (North-Holland, Amsterdam), 267–285.

Lee, L.F., 1987, Non-parametric testing of discrete panel data models, *Journal of Econometrics* **34**, 147–177.

Lee, L.F. and W.E. Griffiths, 1979, The prior likelihood and best linear unbiased prediction in stochastic coefficient linear models, working paper (Department of Economics, University of Minnesota).

Lee, M.J., 1999, A root-N-consistent semiparametric estimator for related effect binary response panel data, *Econometrica* **67**, 427–434.

Lee, M.J., 2001, First-difference estimator for panel censored-selection models, *Economics Letters* **70**, 43–49.

Levin, A. and C.F. Lin, 1992, Unit root test in panel data: Asymptotic and finite sample properties, discussion paper #92–93 (University of California at San Diego).

Levin, A. and C.F. Lin, 1993, Unit root tests in panel data: New results, discussion paper #93–56 (University of California at San Diego).

Leybourne, S.J. and B.P.M. McCabe, 1994, A consistent test for a unit root, *Journal of Business and Economic Statistics* **12**, 157–166.

Li, D., 1998, A joint test for functional form and random individual effects, Solution 97.1.3, *Econometric Theory* **14**, 154–156.

Li, D., 1999, Within two way is equivalent to two withins one-way, Solution 98.5.2, *Econometric Theory* **15**, 781–783.

Li, Q. and C. Hsiao, 1998, Testing serial correlation in semiparametric panel data models, *Journal of Econometrics* **87**, 207–237.

Li, Q. and T. Stengos, 1992, A Hausman specification test based on root N consistent semiparametric estimators, *Economics Letters* **40**, 141–146.

Li, Q. and T. Stengos, 1994, Adaptive estimation in the panel data error component model with heteroskedasticity of unknown form, *International Economic Review* **35**, 981–1000.

Li, Q. and T. Stengos, 1995, A semi-parametric non-nested test in a dynamic panel data model, *Economics Letters* **49**, 1–6.

Li, Q. and T. Stengos, 1996, Semiparametric estimation of partially linear panel data models, *Journal of Econometrics* **71**, 389–397.

Li, Q. and A. Ullah, 1998, Estimating partially linear models with one-way error components, *Econometric Reviews* **17**, 145–166.

Lichtenberg, F.R., 1988, Estimation of the internal adjustment costs model using longitudinal establishment data, *Review of Economics and Statistics* **70**, 421–430.

Lillard, L.A. and Y. Weiss, 1979, Components of variation in panel earnings data: American scientists 1960–1970, *Econometrica* **47**, 437–454.

Lillard, L.A. and R.J. Willis, 1978, Dynamic aspects of earning mobility, *Econometrica* **46**, 985–1012.

Little, R.J.A., 1988, Missing-data adjustments in large surveys, *Journal of Business and Economic Statistics* **6**, 287–297.

Lothian, J.R., 1996, Multi-country evidence on the behavior of purchasing power parity under the current float, *Journal of International Money and Finance* **16**, 19–35.

MaCurdy, T.A., 1982, The use of time series processes to model the error structure of earnings in a longitudinal data analysis, *Journal of Econometrics* **18**, 83–114.

MacDonald, R., 1996, Panel unit root tests and real exchange rates, *Economics Letters* **50**, 7–11.

Maddala, G.S., 1971, The use of variance components models in pooling cross section and time series data, *Econometrica* **39**, 341–358.

Maddala, G.S., 1977, *Econometrics* (McGraw-Hill, New York).

Maddala, G.S., 1983, *Limited Dependent and Qualitative Variables in Econometrics* (Cambridge University Press, Cambridge).

Maddala, G.S., 1987a, Recent developments in the econometrics of panel data analysis, *Transportation Research* **21**, 303–326.

Maddala, G.S., 1987b, Limited dependent variable models using panel data, *The Journal of Human Resources* **22**, 307–338.

Maddala, G.S., 1991, To pool or not to pool: That is the question, *Journal of Quantitative Economics* **7**, 255–264.

Maddala, G.S., ed., 1993, *The Econometrics of Panel Data*, Vols I and II (Edward Elgar Publishing, Cheltenham).

Maddala, G.S., 1999, On the use of panel data methods with cross country data, *Annales D'Économie et de Statistique* **55–56**, 429–448.

Maddala, G.S. and W. Hu, 1996, The pooling problem, Chapter 13 in L. Mátyás and P. Sevestre, eds., *The Econometrics of Panel Data: A Handbook of the Theory With Applications* (Kluwer Academic Publishers, Dordrecht), 307–322.

Maddala, G.S. and T.D. Mount, 1973, A comparative study of alternative estimators for variance components models used in econometric applications, *Journal of the American Statistical Association* **68**, 324–328.

Maddala, G.S. and S. Wu, 1999, A comparative study of unit root tests with panel data and a new simple test, *Oxford Bulletin of Economics and Statistics* **61**, 631–652.

Maddala, G.S., V.K. Srivastava and H. Li, 1994, Shrinkage estimators for the estimation of short-run and long-run parameters from panel data models, working paper (Ohio State University, Ohio).

Maddala, G.S., S. Wu and P.C. Liu, 2000, Do panel data rescue purchasing power parity (PPP) theory?, Chapter 2 in J. Krishnakumar and E. Ronchetti, eds., *Panel Data Econometrics: Future Directions* (North-Holland, Amsterdam), 35–51.

Maddala, G.S., R.P. Trost, H. Li and F. Joutz, 1997, Estimation of short-run and long-run elasticities of energy demand from panel data using shrinkage estimators, *Journal of Business and Economic Statistics* **15**, 90–100.

Magnus, J.R., 1982, Multivariate error components analysis of linear and nonlinear regression models by maximum likelihood, *Journal of Econometrics* **19**, 239–285.

Magnus, J.R. and A.D. Woodland, 1988, On the maximum likelihood estimation of multivariate regression models containing serially correlated error components, *International Economic Review* **29**, 707–725.

Mairesse, J., 1990, Time-series and cross-sectional estimates on panel data: Why are they different and why should they be equal?, in J. Hartog, G. Ridder and J. Theeuwes, eds., *Panel Data and Labor Market Studies* (North-Holland, Amsterdam), 81–95.

Manski, C.F., 1987, Semiparametric analysis of random effects linear models from binary panel data, *Econometrica* **55**, 357–362.

Mátyás, L., ed., 1992, Modeling panel data, *Structural Change and Economic Dynamics* **3**, 291–384.

Mátyás, L. and L. Lovrics, 1990, Small sample properties of simultaneous error components models, *Economics Letters* **32**, 25–34.

Mátyás, L. and L. Lovrics, 1991, Missing observations and panel data: A Monte Carlo analysis, *Economics Letters* **37**, 39–44.

Mátyás, L. and P. Sevestre, eds., 1996, *The Econometrics of Panel Data: A Handbook of the Theory With Applications* (Kluwer Academic Publishers, Dordrecht).

Mazodier, P., ed., 1978, The econometrics of panel data, *Annales de l'INSEE* **30–31**.

Mazodier, P. and A. Trognon, 1978, Heteroskedasticity and stratification in error components models, *Annales de l'INSEE* **30–31**, 451–482.

McCoskey, S. and C. Kao, 1998, A residual-based test of the null of cointegration in panel data, *Econometric Reviews* **17**, 57–84.

McCoskey, S. and C. Kao, 1999, Testing the stability of a production function with urbanization as a shift factor: An application of non-stationary panel data techniques, *Oxford Bulletin of Economics and Statistics* **61**, 671–690.

McCoskey, S. and T. Selden, 1998, Health care expenditures and GDP: Panel data unit root test results, *Journal of Health Economics* **17**, 369–376.

McElroy, M.B., 1977, Weaker MSE criteria and tests for linear restrictions in regression models with non-spherical disturbances, *Journal of Econometrics* **6**, 389–394.

McFadden, D.J., 1984, Qualitative response models, Chapter 24 in Z. Griliches and M. Intrilligator, eds., *Handbook of Econometrics* (North-Holland, Amsterdam), 1396–1457.

McFadden, D.J., 1989, A method of simulated moments for estimation of discrete response models without numerical integration, *Econometrica* **57**, 995–1026.

McKenzie, D.J., 2000a, Estimation of homogeneous stationary and non-stationary pseudo-panels, working paper (Department of Economics, Yale University).

McKenzie, D.J., 2000b, Estimation of unequally-spaced dynamic panels and pseudo-panels, working paper (Department of Economics, Yale University).

Meghir, C. and F. Windmeijer, 1999, Moment conditions for dynamic panel data models with multiplicative individual effects in the conditional variance, *Annales D'Économie et de Statistique* **55–56**, 317–330.

Mendelsohn, R., D. Hellerstein, M. Huguenin, R. Unsworth and R. Brazee, 1992, Measuring hazardous waste damages with panel models, *Journal of Environmental Economics and Management* **22**, 259–271.

Metcalf, G.E., 1996, Specification testing in panel data with instrumental variables, *Journal of Econometrics* **71**, 291–307.

Moffitt, R., 1993, Identification and estimation of dynamic models with a time series of repeated cross-sections, *Journal of Econometrics* **59**, 99–123.

Montmarquette, C. and S. Mahseredjian, 1989, Does school matter for educational achievement? A two-way nested-error components analysis, *Journal of Applied Econometrics* **4**; 181–193.

Moon, H.R. and P.C.B. Phillips, 1998, A reinterpretation of the Feldstein–Horioka regressions from a nonstationary panel viewpoint, working paper (Department of Economics, Yale University).

Moon, H.R. and P.C.B. Phillips, 1999, Maximum likelihood estimation in panels with incidental trends, *Oxford Bulletin of Economics and Statistics* **61**, 711–747.

Moon, H.R. and P.C.B. Phillips, 2000, Estimation of autoregressive roots near unity using panel data, *Econometric Theory* **16**, 927–997.

Moulton, B.R., 1986, Random group effects and the precision of regression estimates, *Journal of Econometrics* **32**, 385–397.

Moulton, B.R., 1987, Diagnostics for group effects in regression analysis, *Journal of Business and Economic Statistics* **5**, 275–282.

Moulton, B.R. and W.C. Randolph, 1989, Alternative tests of the error components model, *Econometrica* **57**, 685–693.

Mundlak, Y., 1961, Empirical production function free of management bias, *Journal of Farm Economics* **43**, 44–56.

Mundlak, Y., 1978, On the pooling of time series and cross-section data, *Econometrica* **46**, 69–85.

Munnell, A., 1990, Why has productivity growth declined? Productivity and public investment, *New England Economic Review,* 3–22.

Murray, C.J. and D.H. Papell, 2000, Testing for unit roots in panels in the presence of structural change with an application to OECD unemployment, *Advances in Econometrics* **15**, 223–238.

Nelson, C. and R. Startz, 1990, The distribution of the instrumental variables estimator and its t-ratio when the instrument is a poor one, *Journal of Business* **63**, S125–S140.

Nerlove, M., 1971a, Further evidence on the estimation of dynamic economic relations from a time-series of cross-sections, *Econometrica* **39**, 359–382.

Nerlove, M., 1971b, A note on error components models, *Econometrica* **39**, 383–396.

Nerlove, M., 2000a, Growth rate convergence, fact or artifact? An essay on panel data econometrics, Chapter 1 in J. Krishnakumar and E. Ronchetti, eds., *Panel Data Econometrics: Future Directions* (North-Holland, Amsterdam), 3–33.

Nerlove, M., 2000b, An essay on the history of panel data econometrics, paper presented at the Ninth International Conference on Panel Data, Geneva, Switzerland.

Nerlove, M. and P. Balestra, 1996, Formulation and estimation of econometric models for panel data, Chapter 1 in L. Mátyás and P. Sevestre, eds., *The Econometrics of Panel Data: A Handbook of the Theory With Applications* (Kluwer Academic Publishers, Dordrecht), 3–22.

Neyman, J. and E.L. Scott, 1948, Consistent estimation from partially consistent observations, *Econometrica* **16**, 1–32.

Nguyen, T.H. and C. Bernier, 1988, Beta and q in a simultaneous framework with pooled data, *Review of Economics and Statistics* **70**, 520–523.

Nickell, S., 1981, Biases in dynamic models with fixed effects, *Econometrica* **49**, 1417–1426.

Nijman, Th.E. and M. Verbeek, 1990, Estimation of time dependent parameters in linear models using cross section panels or both, *Journal of Econometrics* **46**, 333–346.

Nijman, Th.E. and M. Verbeek, 1992a, Nonresponse in panel data: The impact on estimates of a life cycle consumption function, *Journal of Applied Econometrics* **7**, 243–257.

Nijman, Th.E. and M. Verbeek, 1992b, The optimal choice of controls and pre-experimental observations, *Journal of Econometrics* **51**, 183–189.

Nijman, Th.E., M. Verbeek and A. van Soest, 1991, The optimal design of rotating panels in a simple analysis of variance model, *Journal of Econometrics* **49**, 373–399.

O'Connell, P.G.J., 1998, The overvaluation of purchasing power parity, *Journal of International Economics* **44**, 1–19.

Oh, K.Y., 1996, Purchasing power parity and unit roots tests using panel data, *Journal of International Money and Finance* **15**, 405–418.

Orme, C., 1993, A comment on 'a simple test for neglected heterogeneity in panel studies', *Biometrics* **49**, 665–667.

Owusu-Gyapong, A., 1986, Alternative estimating techniques for panel data on strike activity, *Review of Economics and Statistics* **68**, 526–531.

Pakes, A. and Z. Griliches, 1984, Estimating distributed lags in short panels with an application to the specification of depreciation patterns and capital stock constructs, *Review of Economic Studies* **51**, 243–262.

Pakes, A. and D. Pollard, 1989, Simulation and the asymptotics of optimization estimators, *Econometrica* **57**, 1027–1058.

Palda, K.S. and L.M. Blair, 1970, A moving cross-section analysis of demand for toothpaste, *Journal of Marketing Research* **7**, 439–449.

Papell, D., 1997, Searching for stationarity: Purchasing power parity under the current float, *Journal of International Economics* **43**, 313–332.

Patterson, H.D. and R. Thompson, 1971, Recovery of inter-block information when block sizes are unequal, *Biometrika* **58**, 545–554.

Pedroni, P., 1999, Critical values for cointegration tests in heterogeneous panels with multiple regressors, *Oxford Bulletin of Economics and Statistics* **61**, 653–678.

Pedroni, P., 2000, Fully modified OLS for heterogeneous cointegrated panels, *Advances in Econometrics* **15**, 93–130.

Pedroni, P., 2001, Purchasing power parity tests in cointegrated panels, *Review of Economics and Statistics*, forthcoming.

Peracchi, F., 2001, The European Community Household Panel: A review, *Empirical Economics*, forthcoming.

Peracchi, F. and F. Welch, 1995, How representative are matched cross-sections? Evidence from the current population survey, *Journal of Econometrics* **68**, 153–179.

Pesaran, M.H. and R. Smith, 1995, Estimating long-run relationships from dynamic heterogenous panels, *Journal of Econometrics* **68**, 79–113.

Pesaran, M.H. and Z. Zhao, 1999, Bias reduction in estimating long-run relationships from dynamic heterogeneous panels, Chapter 12 in C. Hsiao, K. Lahiri, L.F. Lee and M.H. Persaran, eds., *Analysis of Panels and Limited Dependent Variable Models* (Cambridge University Press, Cambridge), 297–322.

Pesaran, M.H., Y. Shin and R. Smith, 1999, Pooled mean group estimation of dynamic heterogeneous panels, *Journal of the American Statistical Association* **94**, 621–634.

Pesaran, M.H., R. Smith and K.S. Im, 1996, Dynamic linear models for heterogenous panels, Chapter 8 in L. Mátyás and P. Sevestre, eds., *The Econometrics of Panel Data:*

A Handbook of the Theory With Applications (Kluwer Academic Publishers, Dordrecht), 145–195.

Phillips, P.C.B. and B.E. Hansen, 1990, Statistical inference in instrumental variables regression with $I(1)$ processes, *Review of Economic Studies* **57**, 99–125.

Phillips, P.C.B. and H. Moon, 1999, Linear regression limit theory for nonstationary panel data, *Econometrica* **67**, 1057–1111.

Phillips, P.C.B. and H. Moon, 2000, Nonstationary panel data analysis: An overview of some recent developments, *Econometric Reviews* **19**, 263–286.

Phillips, P.C.B. and S. Ouliaris, 1990, Asymptotic properties of residual based tests for cointegration, *Econometrica* **58**, 165–193.

Pirotte, A., 1999, Convergence of the static estimation toward long run effects of dynamic panel data models, *Economics Letters* **53**, 151–158.

Pitt, M. and L.F. Lee, 1981, The measurement and sources of technical inefficiency in Indonesian weaving industry, *Journal of Development Economics* **9**, 43–64.

Pliskin, L., 1991, The covariance transformation and the instrumental variables estimator of the fixed effects model, *Oxford Bulletin of Economics and Statistics* **53**, 95–98.

Prucha, I.R., 1984, On the asymptotic efficiency of feasible Aitken estimators for seemingly unrelated regression models with error components, *Econometrica* **52**, 203–207.

Prucha, I.R., 1985, Maximum likelihood and instrumental variable estimation in simultaneous equation systems with error components, *International Economic Review* **26**, 491–506.

Quah, D., 1994, Exploiting cross section variation for unit root inference in dynamic data, *Economics Letters* **44**, 9–19.

Quah, D., 1996, Empirics for economic growth and convergence, *European Economic Review* **40**, 1353–1375.

Raj, B. and B. Baltagi, eds., 1992, *Panel Data Analysis* (Physica-Verlag, Heidelberg).

Randolph, W.C., 1988, A transformation for heteroscedastic error components regression models, *Economics Letters* **27**, 349–354.

Rao, C.R., 1970, Estimation of heteroscedastic variances in linear models, *Journal of the American Statistical Association* **65**, 161–172.

Rao, C.R., 1971a, Estimation of variance and covariance components — MINQUE theory, *Journal of Multivariate Analysis* **1**, 257–275.

Rao, C.R., 1971b, Minimum variance quadratic unbiased estimation of variance components, *Journal of Multivariate Analysis* **1**, 445–456.

Rao, C.R., 1972, Estimation variance and covariance components in linear models, *Journal of the American Statistical Association* **67**, 112–115.

Revankar, N.S., 1979, Error component models with serial correlated time effects, *Journal of the Indian Statistical Association* **17**, 137–160

Revankar, N.S., 1992, Exact equivalence of instrumental variable estimators in an error component structural system, *Empirical Economics* **17**, 77–84.

Ridder, G., 1990, Attrition in multi-wave panel data, in J. Hartog, G. Ridder and J. Theeuwes, eds., *Panel Data and Labor Market Studies* (North-Holland, Amsterdam), 45–67.

Ridder, G., 1992, An empirical evaluation of some models for non-random attrition in panel data, *Structural Change and Economic Dynamics* **3**, 337–355.

Ridder, G. and T.J. Wansbeek, 1990, Dynamic models for panel data, in R. van der Ploeg, ed., *Advanced Lectures in Quantitative Economics* (Academic Press, New York), 557–582.

Robertson, D. and J. Symons, 1992, Some strange properties of panel data estimators, *Journal of Applied Econometrics* **7**, 175–189.

Robins, P.K. and R.W. West, 1986, Sample attrition and labor supply response in experimental panel data: A study of alternative correction procedures, *Journal of Business and Economic Statistics* **4**, 329–338.

Roy, S.N., 1957, *Some Aspects of Multivariate Analysis* (John Wiley, New York).

Saikkonen, P., 1991, Asymptotically efficient estimation of cointegrating regressions, *Econometric Theory* **58**, 1–21.

Sala-i-Martin, X., 1996, The classical approach to convergence analysis, *Economic Journal* **106**, 1019–1036.

Sarantis, N. and C. Stewart, 1999, Is the consumption–income ratio stationary? Evidence from panel unit root tests, *Economics Letters* **64**, 309–314.

Sargan, J.D., 1958, The estimation of economic relationships using instrumental variables, *Econometrica* **26**, 393–415.

Schmidt, P., 1983, A note on a fixed effect model with arbitrary interpersonal covariance, *Journal of Econometrics* **22**, 391–393.

Schmidt, P. and R.C. Sickles, 1984, Production frontiers and panel data, *Journal of Business and Economic Statistics* **2**, 367–374.

Schmidt, P., S.C. Ahn and D. Wyhowski, 1992, Comment, *Journal of Business and Economic Statistics* **10**, 10–14.

Searle, S.R., 1971, *Linear Models* (John Wiley, New York).

Searle, S.R., 1987, *Linear Models for Unbalanced Data* (John Wiley, New York).

Searle, S.R. and H.V. Henderson, 1979, Dispersion matrices for variance components models, *Journal of the American Statistical Association* **74**, 465–470.

Sevestre, P., 1999, 1977–1997: Changes and continuities in panel data econometrics, *Annales D'Économie et de Statistique* **55–56**, 15–25.

Sevestre, P. and A. Trognon, 1983, Propriétés de grand échantillons d'une classe d'estimateurs des models autorégressifs á erreurs composées, *Annales de l'INSEE* **50**, 25–48.

Sevestre, P. and A. Trognon, 1985, A note on autoregressive error component models, *Journal of Econometrics* **28**, 231–245.

Shim, J.K., 1982, Pooling cross section and time series data in the estimation of regional demand and supply functions, *Journal of Urban Economics* **11**, 229–241.

Sickles, R.C., 1985, A nonlinear multivariate error components analysis of technology and specific factor productivity growth with an application to U.S. airlines, *Journal of Econometrics* **27**, 61–78.

Sickles, R.C. and P. Taubman, 1986, A multivariate error components analysis of the health and retirement study of the elderly, *Econometrica* **54**, 1339–1356.

Silver, J.L., 1982, Generalized estimation of error components models with a serially correlated temporal effect, *International Economic Review* **23**, 463–478.

Smith, R.P., 2000, Estimation and inference with non-stationary panel time-series data, working paper (Department of Economics, Birkbeck College, London).

Solon, G.S., 1986, Effects of rotation group bias on estimation of unemployment, *Journal of Business and Economic Statistics* **4**, 105–109.

Solon, G.S., 1989, The value of panel data in economic research, in D. Kasprzyk, G.J. Duncan, G. Kalton and M.P. Singh, eds., *Panel Surveys* (John Wiley, New York), 486–496.

Song, S.H. and B.C. Jung, 1998, A simple linear trend model with error components, Solution 97.2.1, *Econometric Theory* **14**, 286–289.

Song, S.H. and B.C. Jung, 2000, Prediction in the spatially autocorrelated error component model, Solution 99.2.4, *Econometric Theory* **16**, 149–150.

Staiger, D. and J.H. Stock, 1997, Instrumental variables regression with weak instruments, *Econometrica* **65**, 557–586.

Stimson, J.A., 1985, Regression in space and time: A statistical essay, *American Journal of Political Science* **29**, 914–947.

Stock, J. and M. Watson, 1993, A simple estimator of cointegrating vectors in higher order integrated systems, *Econometrica* **61**, 783–820.

Suits, D., 1984, Dummy variables: Mechanics vs. interpretation, *Review of Economics and Statistics* **66**, 177–180.

Swallow, W.H. and L.F. Monahan, 1984, Monte Carlo comparison of ANOVA, MIVQUE, REML, and ML estimators of variance components, *Technometrics* **26**, 47–57.

Swamy, P.A.V.B., 1971, *Statistical Inference in Random Coefficient Regression Models* (Springer-Verlag, New York).

Swamy, P.A.V.B. and S.S. Arora, 1972, The exact finite sample properties of the estimators of coefficients in the error components regression models, *Econometrica* **40**, 261–275.

Swamy, P.A.V.B. and G.S. Tavlas, 2001, Random coefficient models, Chapter 19 in B.H. Baltagi, ed., *A Companion to Theoretical Econometrics* (Blackwell Publishers, Massachusetts), 410–428.

Taub, A.J., 1979, Prediction in the context of the variance-components model, *Journal of Econometrics* **10**, 103–108.

Tauchen, G., 1986, Statistical properties of generalized method of moments estimators of structural parameters obtained from financial market data, *Journal of Business and Economic Statistics* **4**, 397–416.

Taylor, W.E., 1980, Small sample considerations in estimation from panel data, *Journal of Econometrics* **13**, 203–223.

Toro-Vizcarrondo, C. and T.D. Wallace, 1968, A test of the mean square error criterion for restrictions in linear regression, *Journal of the American Statistical Association* **63**, 558–572.

Townsend, E.C. and S.R. Searle, 1971, Best quadratic unbiased estimation of variance components from unbalanced data in the one-way classification, *Biometrics* **27**, 643–657.

Toyoda, T., 1974, Use of the Chow test under heteroscedasticity, *Econometrica* **42**, 601–608.

Trognon, A., 1978, Miscellaneous asymptotic properties of ordinary least squares and maximum likelihood estimators in dynamic error components models, *Annales de l'INSEE* **30–31**, 632–657.

Ullah, A. and N. Roy, 1998, Nonparametric and semiparametric econometrics of panel data, Chapter 17 in A. Ullah and D.E.A. Giles, eds., *Handbook on Applied Economic Statistics* (Marcel Dekker, New York), 579–604.

Valliant, R., 1991, Variance estimation for price indexes from a two-stage sample with rotating panels, *Journal of Business and Economic Statistics* **9**, 409–422.

van den Doel, I.T. and J.F. Kiviet, 1994, Asymptotic consequences of neglected dynamics in individual effects models, *Statistica Neerlandica* **48**, 71–85.

van der Gaag, J., B.M.S. van Praag, F.F.H. Rutten and W. van de Ven, 1977, Aggregated dynamic demand equations for specialistic-outpatient medical care (estimated from a time-series of cross-sections), *Empirical Economics* **2**, 213–223.

Vella, F. and M. Verbeek, 1998, Whose wages do unions raise? A dynamic model of unionism and wage determination for young men, *Journal of Applied Econometrics* **13**, 163–168.

Vella, F. and M. Verbeek, 1999, Two-step estimation of panel data models with censored endogenous variables and selection bias, *Journal of Econometrics* **90**, 239–263.

Verbeek, M., 1990, On the estimation of a fixed effects model with selectivity bias, *Economics Letters* **34**, 267–270.

Verbeek, M., 1996, Pseudo panel data, Chapter 11 in L. Mátyás and P. Sevestre, eds., *The Econometrics of Panel Data: A Handbook of the Theory With Applications* (Kluwer Academic Publishers, Dordrecht), 280–292.

Verbeek, M. and Th.E. Nijman, 1992a, Testing for selectivity bias in panel data models, *International Economic Review* **33**, 681–703.

Verbeek, M. and Th.E. Nijman, 1992b, Can cohort data be treated as genuine panel data?, *Empirical Economics* **17**, 9–23.

Verbeek, M. and Th.E. Nijman, 1993, Minimum MSE estimation of a regression model with fixed effects and a series of cross-sections, *Journal of Econometrics* **59**, 125–136.

Verbeek, M. and Th.E. Nijman, 1996, Incomplete panels and selection bias, Chapter 18 in L. Mátyás and P. Sevestre, eds., *The Econometrics of Panel Data: A Handbook of the Theory With Applications* (Kluwer Academic Publishers, Dordrecht), 449–490.

Verbeek, M. and F. Vella, 2000, Estimating dynamic models from repeated cross-sections, working paper (K.U. Leuven, Belgium).

Verbon, H.A.A., 1980, Testing for heteroscedasticity in a model of seemingly unrelated regression equations with variance components (SUREVC), *Economics Letters* **5**, 149–153.

Wagner, G.G., R.V. Burkhauser and F. Behringer, 1993, The English public use file of the German socio-economic panel, *The Journal of Human Resources* **28**, 429–433.

Wallace, T.D., 1972, Weaker criteria and tests for linear restrictions in regression, *Econometrica* **40**, 689–698.

Wallace, T.D. and A. Hussain, 1969, The use of error components models in combining cross-section and time-series data, *Econometrica* **37**, 55–72.

Wan, G.H., W.E. Griffiths and J.R. Anderson, 1992, Using panel data to estimate risk effects in seemingly unrelated production functions, *Empirical Economics* **17**, 35–49.

Wansbeek, T.J., 1989, An alternative heteroscedastic error components model, Solution 88.1.1, *Econometric Theory* **5**, 326.

Wansbeek, T.J., 1992, Transformations for panel data when the disturbances are autocorrelated, *Structural Change and Economic Dynamics* **3**, 375–384.

Wansbeek, T.J. and P. Bekker, 1996, On IV, GMM and ML in a dynamic panel data model, *Economics Letters* **51**, 145–152.

Wansbeek, T.J. and A. Kapteyn, 1978, The separation of individual variation and systematic change in the analysis of panel data, *Annales de l'INSEE* **30–31**, 659–680.

Wansbeek, T.J. and A. Kapteyn, 1982a, A class of decompositions of the variance–covariance matrix of a generalized error components model, *Econometrica* **50**, 713–724.

Wansbeek, T.J. and A. Kapteyn, 1982b, A simple way to obtain the spectral decomposition of variance components models for balanced data, *Communications in Statistics* **A11**, 2105–2112.

Wansbeek, T.J. and A. Kapteyn, 1983, A note on spectral decomposition and maximum likelihood estimation of ANOVA models with balanced data, *Statistics and Probability Letters* **1**, 213–215.

Wansbeek, T.J. and A. Kapteyn, 1989, Estimation of the error components model with incomplete panels, *Journal of Econometrics* **41**, 341–361.

Wansbeek, T.J. and A. Kapteyn, 1992, Simple estimators for dynamic panel data models with errors in variables, Chapter 13 in R. Bewley and T. Van Hoa, eds., *Contributions to Consumer Demand and Econometrics: Essays in Honor of Henri Theil* (St. Martin's Press, New York), 238–251.

Wansbeek, T.J. and T. Knapp, 1999, Estimating a dynamic panel data model with heterogeneous trends, *Annales D'Économie et de Statistique* **55–56**, 331–349.

Wansbeek, T.J. and R.H. Koning, 1989, Measurement error and panel data, *Statistica Neerlandica* **45**, 85–92.

Weiss, M., 1985, A multivariate analysis of loss reserving estimates in property-liability insurers, *The Journal of Risk and Insurance* **52**, 199–221.

White, H., 1980, A heteroskedasticity-consistent covariance matrix estimator and a direct test for heteroskedasticity, *Econometrica* **48**, 817–838.

White, H., 1984, *Asymptotic Theory for Econometricians* (Academic Press, New York).

White, H., 1986, Instrumental variables analogs of generalized least squares estimators, in R.S. Mariano, ed., *Advances in Statistical Analysis and Statistical Computing*, Vol. 1 (JAI Press, New York), 173–277.

Winkelmann, R., 2000, *Econometric Analysis of Count Data* (Springer-Verlag, Berlin).

Winkelmann, L. and R. Winkelmann, 1998, Why are the unemployed so unhappy? Evidence from panel data, *Economica* **65**, 1–15.

Wolpin, K.I., 1980, A time series–cross section analysis of international variation in crime and punishment, *Review of Economics and Statistics* **62**, 417–421.

Wooldridge, J.M., 1995, Selection corrections for panel data models under conditional mean independence assumptions, *Journal of Econometrics* **68**, 115–132.

Wooldridge, J.M., 1997, Multiplicative panel data models without the strict exogeneity assumption, *Econometric Theory* **13**, 667–678.

Wooldridge, J.M., 1999, Distribution-free estimation of some nonlinear panel data models, *Journal of Econometrics* **90**, 77–97.

Wooldridge, J.M., 2000, A framework for estimating dynamic, unobserved effects panel data models with possible feedback to future explanatory variables, *Economics Letters* **68**, 245–250.

Wu, J.L., 2000, Mean reversion of the current account: Evidence from the panel data unit-root test, *Economics Letters* **66**, 215–222.

Wu, S. and Y. Yin, 1999, Tests for cointegration in heterogeneous panel: A Monte Carlo study, working paper (Department of Economics, State University of New York at Buffalo).

Wu, Y., 1996, Are real exchange rates nonstationary? Evidence from a panel data set, *Journal of Money, Credit and Banking* **28**, 54–63.

Wyhowski, D.J., 1994, Estimation of a panel data model in the presence of correlation between regressors and a two-way error component, *Econometric Theory* **10**, 130–139.

Xiong, W., 1995, Nested effects, Solution 93.4.2, *Econometric Theory* **11**, 658–659.

Xiong, W., 1996a, A mixed-error component model, Solution 95.1.4, *Econometric Theory* **12**, 401–402.

Xiong, W., 1996b, Testing for correlated effects in panels, Solution 95.2.5, *Econometric Theory* **12**, 405–406.

Yin, Y. and S. Wu, 2000, Stationarity tests in heterogeneous panels, *Advances in Econometrics* **15**, 275–296.

Zabel, J., 1992, Estimating fixed and random effects models with selectivity, *Economics Letters* **40**, 269–272.

Zellner, A., 1962, An efficient method of estimating seemingly unrelated regression and tests for aggregation bias, *Journal of the American Statistical Association* **57**, 348–368.

Ziemer, R.F. and M.E. Wetzstein, 1983, A Stein-rule method for pooling data, *Economics Letters* **11**, 137–143.

Ziliak, J.P., 1997, Efficient estimation with panel data when instruments are predetermined: An empirical comparison of moment-condition estimators, *Journal of Business and Economic Statistics* **15**, 419–431.

Index